Echoes of Exile

WAR, MEMORY, AND CULTURE

Series published in cooperation with

THE CENTER FOR THE STUDY OF
WAR & MEMORY
at the UNIVERSITY OF SOUTH ALABAMA

Echoes of Exile

A Family's Odyssey through the Holocaust and Cold War

DANIELA SPENSER

THE UNIVERSITY OF ALABAMA PRESS
Tuscaloosa

The University of Alabama Press
Tuscaloosa, Alabama 35487-0380
uapress.ua.edu

Typeface: Alegreya

Cover image: (*Top*) Ruth and Kurt´s wedding in Prague in 1946, courtesy of Daniela Spenser; (*bottom*) Alfie Samba (AdobeStock_335331324.jpeg)

Cover design: Sandy Turner Jr.

Cataloging-in-Publication data is available from the Library of Congress.
ISBN: 978-0-8173-2239-7 (cloth)
ISBN: 978-0-8173-6211-9 (paper)
E-ISBN: 978-0-8173-9566-7

For all who knew Ruth, and for those who did not, I want to bring her to life.

To remember Kurt, Anna and Vilém.

For Vladimír, the love of Ruth's life.

For Daniel, always; for Milena and Matías, my hopes.

Contents

Illustrations

Figures

Maps

Preface

> "Everything that needs to be said has already been said. But since no one was listening, everything must be said again."
>
> —André Gide, *Le traité du Narcisse*

Ruth, my mother, died on August 28, 2013, in Prague, a few days before reaching her eighty-eighth birthday. Her former colleague Zuzana Slobodová wrote an obituary that portrayed her extraordinary life. The London *Guardian* published the tribute, which I circulated among friends and fellow historians. A notable author remarked that the article contained all the elements for a biography.[1]

The idea intrigued and moved me.

Born Ruth Charlotte Ornsteinová in September 1925, my mother became Grollová after her first marriage, to Kurt Groll, and Tosková when she married Vladimír Tosek. I was Ruth's only child. Kurt was my father. Vladimír had his own children. As I set out to research this book, the original idea to write a biography of one person became transfigured into the history of a family of assimilated Jews in Czechoslovakia, whose lives spread across Europe and beyond in ways about which I had been mostly ignorant. While dismantling my mother's apartment in London and another in Prague, I found two unassuming suitcases filled with crumpled letters and curling photographs, as well as yellowing, crumbling newspapers and dog-eared journals.

Ruth, Kurt, Vladimír, and their respective parents had lived through the maelstrom of twentieth-century world history, but living with them under the same roof one would not know it. It was not until the 1990s that my mother gave several interviews about her upbringing in Czechoslovakia, her school years and military service in England, and snippets from her life in Prague after the World War II before emigrating for the second time in 1968. She never provided details. My father did not breathe a word to me about his escape from Czechoslovakia to Palestine in 1939, his imprisonment in Greece after a botched skirmish waged by the British Commonwealth army against the German troops on the Peloponnesian peninsula in 1941, and the several years he spent in German labor camps in Upper Silesia before being marched west in 1945. The blue tattoo on my grandmother's left forearm spoke for her because she never did; her ordeal in three concentration camps was the most painful to reconstruct. I had to research and recover her story from the historical ruins and memory of other survivors. In the process of my inquiries, I discovered my grandfather's extraordinary historical foresight: he had always anticipated and avoided the worst disasters. Vladimír did not reveal much about his past to his children while he lived in Czechoslovakia. It might have been painful or embarrassing, or both. It was not until he and his children lived apart and could no longer meet legally that during a clandestine rendezvous in Hungary in the summer of 1986 he told them his family story—though he omitted important matters concerning himself from the description.

The story begins around the time of the Austro-Hungarian Empire's collapse and ends after the fall of the Berlin Wall, "that spontaneous, joyful epitome of people power."[2] Parts I and II explore the protagonists' experiences of emigration as they escaped or failed to escape Nazism and the Holocaust and examine how they survived wartime and exile before returning home. Part III begins with life in communist Czechoslovakia during the hard-hitting Stalinist era when my mother's life was made especially difficult because of her association with men high up in the party and the state hierarchy who were falsely accused of treason, persecuted, and (some of them) hanged. For his part, Vladimír was an uncritical champion of the regime during the fifties and early sixties. However, as a leading journalist on Czechoslovak television, with a powerful intellect, he managed to navigate through the labyrinthine system and resorted to collaboration to survive and succeed as a publicist. When the promising Prague Spring of 1968 (which aimed to democratize the asphyxiating regime) broke out, Vladimír engaged in it with audacity. The peaceful striving for democracy ended in catastrophe, however, on both the national and personal level.

The military invasion of Czechoslovakia by the Soviet-led Warsaw Pact armies in August 1968 forced Ruth and Vladimír to flee to what for both was their second exile. Their life abroad, detailed in part IV, did not acquire a real significance until they joined others of their cohort in helping to build cultural and intellectual bridges to the Czechoslovakia that they had left behind. The book ends (part V) with the fall of the Berlin Wall and the liberation of the country from the suffocating communist regime. The political exiles that left in 1968 were eager to return. Contrary to the expectations that Ruth, her friends, and Vladimír—had he lived—held that they would return home to establish a more democratic socialist regime, they were disillusioned. Upon their homecoming, they found that the political and social vision that they had defended vigorously for over twenty years had become obsolete and unwelcome.

An impressive body of literature, documentaries, and movies—academic, biographical, autobiographical and fictional—has been produced on every subject dealt with in this book. I have written here as a daughter and a granddaughter, as a participant in several of the historical episodes, and primarily as a historian. In the process, I wiped away streams of tears. I mined documents in public archives of several countries and rummaged through personal chests. I read a vast amount of secondary literature, novels, memoirs, testimonies, letters; examined photos; and conducted numerous interviews with the aim of writing a narrative that captures the contingencies, uncertainties, sensibilities, chaos, and dilemmas in which the book's characters had to make often life-threatening choices, and in which they were often tossed about without being able to set their course and destination.

I could not write a full-scale biography or draw a full-blown characterization of any one of them. I lived with them for only a limited period of time, and far too many documents had been destroyed by the totalitarian regimes that did not want to leave traces of their crimes; some archives had been plundered or burned, others are still inaccessible. And then there were the silences. . . .

Much of my mother's personal memorabilia had been lost during her periodic dislocations; the ones she mourned most were parts of her military uniform. The state took my father's personal belongings because there was no one to claim them when he died in Prague in 1975. Vladimír's possessions fit into one of the trunks found after he passed away in London in 1987. What I was left with were fragments, as well as my memory and that of others to illuminate personal details, knowing that those memories were selective and by no means a substitute for history.[3]

There have been many reasons for writing this book. I wanted to draw the experiences of the characters on the large canvas of history as a contribution to making sense of Europe's twentieth century, described variably as "savage," "forgotten," "arrogant," "dark," or as the "age of extremes." To do so, I have woven and spun personal, historical, mundane, and momentous threads to create what I believe is a distinctive fabric. I hope that my book speaks to the world of today, bearing testimony of the past to be used as an orientation map to understand the present in anticipation of the future.

To remember is a duty that the younger generations owe to their ancestors, particularly when our predecessors faced unspeakable horrors, were broken and humiliated, or especially when they could not or did not want to speak for themselves. In this book, I have tried to answer questions I never asked when I could have, due to my woeful lack of curiosity. Ruth had several opportunities to tell her story, which she did with gusto; none of the other characters who populate this book had that chance. By recovering their neglected stories, I have sought to bring them back to life for the reader. Last but not least, I have wanted my Mexican son and grandchildren to meet them so that they too will know where they have come from.

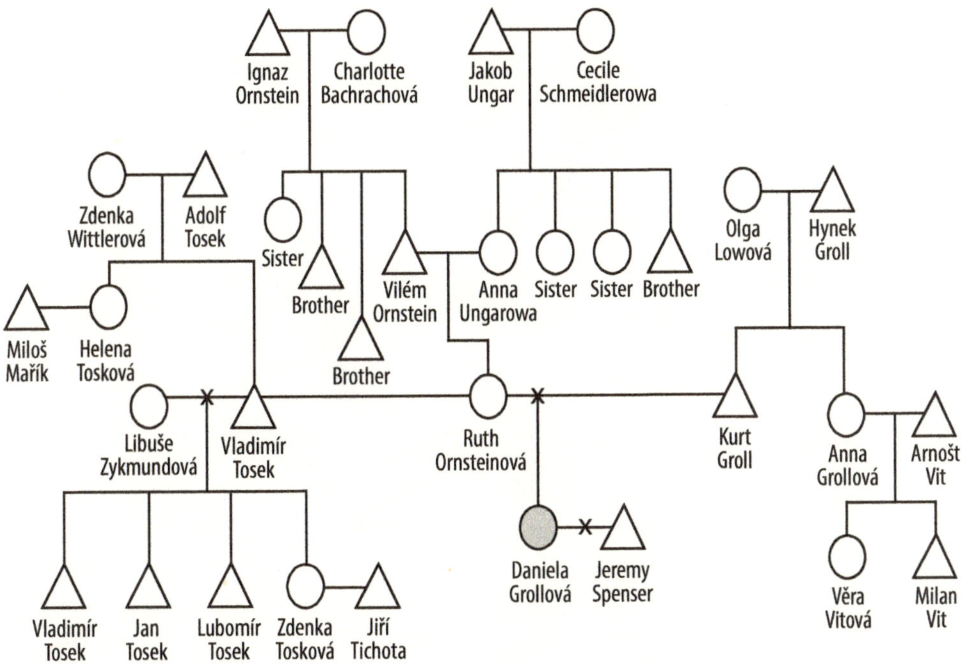

FIGURE 1. Family tree

Acknowledgments

This book could not have been written if it were not for the unlimited academic freedom accorded by the Centro de Investigaciones y Estudios Superiores en Antropología Social (CIESAS). For over forty years CIESAS has allowed me to teach, research, write, and travel as I wish and plan, guided by my conscience, convictions, intellectual needs, and curiosity. The research and elaboration of the book received generous financing from the Sistema Nacional de Investigadores, overseen by the National Council for Research, Science, Humanities, and Innovation (CONAHCYT). The CONAHCYT's program to provide researchers with assistants was fundamental to the book's success. I want to acknowledge the assistance of Raúl Téllez, Valeria Tapia, Norma Sofia Rivera, and Nicolás Rodríguez, all indispensable during the project's research and completion.

This book, like any book, is a collective enterprise. Dozens of individuals contributed to its making with their testimonies, ideas, comments, research material, and suggestions for readings. I hope that technology will not push archivists and librarians out of business; no artificial intelligence can replace human intelligence and emotions. I would like to acknowledge the assistance of individuals in the National Archives of Great Britain and the British Library, in the Wiener Library and the Imperial War Museum in London; in the US Holocaust Museum, the National Archive, and the Library of Congress in Washington, DC; the National Archive, the Military National Archive and the archive of the Ministry of the Interior in Prague; the archives of the Czechoslovak radio and television; and in the archive at Yad Vashem in Jerusalem and the Jabotinsky Institute in Tel Aviv. The Shoah Foundation, founded by Steven Spielberg, was fundamental in recovering testimonies on which parts of this book are based.

The writer and biographer Michael Scammell is the book's godfather. After he read the *Guardian* obituary for my mother written by her colleague and friend Zuzana Slobodová, he detected a kernel of a biography. This book ended being somewhat different from a strict biography, but I owe him the inspiring suggestion. Two friends stand out for their generosity, accompanying me all along during the book's elaboration: Dan La Botz went over each chapter, giving me feedback on its content and helping with the editing of the text; the nitpicker Jiří Boreš read every word in every chapter, making scrupulous criticisms. My late cousin Věra Vítová shared family documents, photographs, and her memories.

Friends and colleagues read parts of the manuscript or listened to my monothematic spins, adding ideas, commenting with criticisms, aiding with research, or providing material I had no idea existed: Alberto Aziz, Petr Balajka, Milada Bazant, Kamila Bendová, Hana Bortlová, Martin Bouda, Laura Brade, Kateřina Březinová, Petr Brod, Jana Burešová, John Burstein, Kateřina Čapková, Milan Drápala, Margarita Estrada, Gabriela Frías, Alejandro González, Marie Hakansson, Roman Janas, Karel Kovanda, Jan Láníček, Judith Lifshitz, Petr Orság, Vilém Prečan, Daniel Růžička, Radek Schovánek, Karel Sieber, Jiřina Šiklová, Jiřina Šmejkalová, Petruška Šustrová, Tomáš Tichák, Prokop Tomek, Oldřich Tůma, and Michal Zourek.

The Czech historian Jiří Suk read the entire text at the precise moment when I needed the encouragement that the book had a meaning for readers without borders. Anna Koffer, Věra Neubauer, Eva Turner, and Líba Taylor commented on chapter drafts fresh from the burner or listened on Zoom to just-written paragraphs. My colleague Rachel Sieder improved substantially one chapter while the painter Lida Penkova was an invaluable listener to our shared history, always challenging me with the right questions. I am grateful to Blanca Mendoza and José Francisco Valdés, space scientists, for reading the manuscript from the perspective of their universe. Vladimír Tosek's children were ever so helpful introducing me to his world: Honza, Lubek, and Zdenka and Vladimír's son-in-law, Jiří Tichota. Brígida von Mentz kindly translated several letters from the German and was always an inspiring interlocutor. Daniel Waterman, the editor in chief of the University of Alabama Press, deserves a special mention for his patience while the manuscript was being reviewed by three anonymous readers whose criticisms helped to improve the text. To all, my unmitigated gratitude!

Echoes of Exile

Part I

1

The Seeds of Catastrophe

My grandparents Anna Ungarowa and Vilém Ornstein came from the opposite sides of the Austro-Hungarian Empire, a conglomerate of nations, religions, and languages aspiring to free themselves from the central seat of power in Vienna. World War I put an end to the empire and paved the way for the creation of multinational states. Poland in the east and Czechoslovakia in the west were two of the nation-states resulting from the new territorial and political arrangements.

Their countries were worlds apart geographically, but when Anna and Vilém met they had many things in common. Jews in both countries lived cheek by jowl with their neighbors—Czechs, Slovaks, Ukrainians, Hungarians, Germans, Ruthenians, Lithuanians, Russians—more on an equal footing with this variegated population in Czechoslovakia than in Poland. Generally, the Jews from the east, the Ostjuden streaming to the blossoming Czechoslovakia in search of better life opportunities (especially from the poor shtetls), were received with prejudices and scorn by the more prosperous Czech and German population.

Anna, called Anka by her family and friends, was a beautiful woman in her early twenties when she met Vilém, who happened to be on a business trip in Poland to sell wood. In May 1924 they tied the knot. By marrying Anna, Willi (as he was better known) rose above the prejudices against the Polish Jews, defied traditions, and showed scorn for the flourishing German nationalism in democratic Czechoslovakia as much as for Jewish nationalism or Zionism.

Anna

Anna was born in 1901 in Silesian Bielsko, a small town situated southwest from Kraków of the Austrian Galicia. By the time she married and became pregnant in 1925, her family lived in Przemyśl, a town located east of Kraków, where in September she gave birth to her daughter Ruth. From then on, Przemyśl was Anna's family residence, to which Ruth would return to visit her grandparents, aunts and uncle, and when in danger to seek refuge. Ruth never learned to speak Polish or Yiddish (which her grandparents spoke), so her mother tongue was her father's German.

Nestled in the foothills of the Carpathian Mountains on the Ukrainian border, Przemyśl was a town of over fifty thousand inhabitants and an important railway junction, with few motor cars about. Goods and people were driven by horse wagons on the cobbled streets. The river San meandered through the town's vicinities. Przemyśl was a mosaic of nationalities and religions living side by side in peace despite occasional skirmishes. Poles were the majority, followed closely by Jews. The orthodox were awaiting the Messiah in the east part of the town while the reformist Jews on the west side leaned toward Zionism and socialism. Next in terms of population were the Ukrainians of different religious hues—Eastern Orthodox, Catholics, Protestants—and of various political persuasions. The real estate and businesses lay mainly in Jewish hands, yet Jews had limited access to civil service in a country in which they were classified as second-class citizens. And yet, Przemyśl Jews—belonging to a town ruled by the Austro-Hungarian Empire—seemed to have been several rungs up in social and political standing than Jews confined to the Russian imperial order.[1]

Anka attended German schools in Bielsko before moving to Przemyśl with her parents (Jakob Ungar and Cecilie Schmeidlerowa), one brother, and two sisters. The street where her parents lived, Ulica Dworskiego, was described as a nice neighborhood by one of its inhabitants, whose father was a well-heeled business partner of a sewing machine factory: "We had no running water or a flush toilet or even a gas stove. For water we had a barrel standing in the kitchen, and each day a big man would bring two buckets at a time to fill it up." The apartments' floors were covered with creaking rough hard boards, polished in the living room. The kitchen had a large tile stove with an oven, heated with wood, keeping the apartment warm in winter when temperatures dropped to freezing or below. Such affluent families typically had maids and governesses. A maid would fire the stove in the morning to make breakfast. Since there was no running water in the apartments, people went to the public bathhouse with steam and a pool to partake in the mikvah, the ritual bath that took place on Fridays before Shabbat candle-lighting. If the family had the luxury of a bathtub in the apartment, water still had to be carried and heated on a wood stove. The toilet was in the hallway; when in the winter the septic tank froze, pots were used instead. "We were well off," summed up one dweller. His sister described their lifestyle in that mixed neighborhood of gentiles and Jews, officials, and professional people—living at a fair distance from the orthodox Jews' section of the city on the other side of the riverbank—as "upper class."[2]

In this neighborhood some apartment buildings had courtyards with access to a water well for washing clothes, as well as poles and clotheslines where tenants dried their laundry. Children played in the yard and sun-starved residents gathered there to chat and catch rays of sun. For those who attended Saturday services, synagogues were within walking distance. Speaking German was considered a sign of learning and culture. German democracy was so admired that the enlightened Jews wished that they could send their children to Berlin or Vienna to be educated.[3]

Anka belonged to this milieu before she met Vilém. Both were part of the assimilated Jewish middle class, had attended German schools, and communicated in the language they shared. Marrying at the age of twenty-three, Anna was past her prime time in the traditional view. The fact that she married a man of her choice, not one arranged by a matchmaker or her parents, said a great deal about her, her husband, and their parents' modern outlook on life.

Vilém

Vilém was born in 1896 in the provincial town of Trnovany northwest of Prague in the region known as the Sudetenland, bordering the German state of Saxony. This entire German-speaking province, endowed with lush forests and lined by rivers, was ceded to Czechoslovakia from the broken Austro-Hungarian empire after World War I. The son of Ignaz Ornstein and Charlotte Bachrachová, Vilém grew up in the small and provincial Trnovany, but it was the neighboring Teplice-Šanov, a boom city with a health resort, which had the modern character that attracted people from near and far. Renowned for its springs, which were believed to cure many ailments, it had grown to some thirty thousand inhabitants. In the late nineteenth century, it expanded into a regional industrial metropolis despite the opposition put up by the spa commission, which feared industrialization would disrupt or destroy the lucrative health spas and shatter the town's tranquility. This opposition had a positive effect, leading to the regulation of the booming industry to protect the spas.[4]

The blossoming German town attracted an entrepreneurial and working-class population. Czechs, Jews, and Poles brought with them their ethnic, national, and political diversity but also engendered tensions. Czech and German became the official languages to the displeasure of the

German majority, which opposed even the creation of Czech schools. True, Teplice's anti-Semitism was mitigated by the long-time coexistence with the Jews, their adherence to the German nationality, and by the fact that the rich Jews were accepted into the local upper class. Teplice Germans' other adversaries were the politically active social democrats, whether they were Czech or German or Jewish.[5]

When World War I erupted in the summer of 1914, Vilém was eighteen years old. A year later he was conscripted into the Austro-Hungarian imperial army, witnessing the collapse of the old regime and the birth of Czechoslovakia from its ruins. In the war's aftermath, he was well prepared to embark on a comfortable, if not lucrative, life as a salesman, provided the country's economy kept on prospering. Vilém had completed German elementary school, four years of gymnasium, and four years of German commerce academy—which was a remarkable level of training.[6]

After Czechoslovakia was created in 1918, a faction of the Sudeten Germans rejected the new republic because of its liberal, democratic principles and Slavic identity. They were inclined to join the German Reich next door or remain faithful to the nonexistent empire. Willi was averse to any notion of ethnonational "people's community," which the losers in the war wanted to establish in the Sudetenland. He was also uninterested in the Zionist movement, even though Teplice was a stronghold of Czechoslovak Zionism.[7] The German-speaking Vilém adhered consciously and with his heart to the Czech social-democratic minority.

After the war, Willi worked as a salesman for private firms dedicated to the management of forests and the lumber industry. The job took him around the country and abroad. In 1923 he turned up in Przemyśl, met Anka, and married her in 1924. After Ruth was born, they left Poland and settled in Teplice, close to his parents and extended family. There, Ruth began her primary education in a German Jewish school.[8]

Teplice during the 1920s was a lively and prosperous city with a cosmopolitan ambience and an exciting artistic scene comprising the opera, art exhibitions, choirs, and Czech, German, and American films in the cinemas. One could enjoy the Czech Philharmonic Orchestra, the National Theater, and other Prague theaters' performances in Czech and German; a renowned baritone soloist took the stage one night and a celebrated violinist on another.[9] But the world economic crisis at the end of the decade altered the town's lively rhythm and dimmed Vilém's bright prospects.

What pained Vilém, in addition to the economic decline of a town that prided itself on prosperous industries, were the manifestations of the right-wing nationalists who confronted the Czech and German social

FIGURE 2. Ruth with her mother during the 1930s

democrats and communists in bloody clashes on the streets. The mild-mannered Vilém, then in his thirties, balding and with a clean round face radiating warmth, decided to move to Prague with his happy-go-lucky six-year-old daughter Ruth and Anka, his beautiful and elegant wife.[10]

Prague

With no property or savings to their name, the Ornsteins settled in the capital around 1933. Willi's economic situation, his decision to leave the trouble-riven Sudetenland as early as he did, his adhesion to the Czech nationality rather than to the Jewish or German during the 1930 census, and the fact that Anka had adopted Czechoslovak citizenship instead of remaining Polish all proved to be blessings in the long run. Instead of adhering to the status of a minority in the tension-ridden multinational state, they opted for assimilation into the Czech majority and acquire the rights of full-fledged citizens. Both Willi and Anka spoke Czech with an accent that would have made them strangers in any city in the country, but the cosmopolitan civilized and congenial Prague had the capacity to embrace many quirks. Ruth, for her part, switched to Czech from German seamlessly.[11]

Even with Vilém in and out of jobs as a traveling salesman during the 1930s, the family was not penniless. Anka had greater economic and social aspirations than Vilém could give her; she tread on Persian rugs, served food on silver plate, and might have worn or aspired to wear a diamond ring. She also paid a nanny to look after Ruth while she attended to her hobbies like playing bridge several times a week. Grandmother Charlotte came from Teplice to live with them in Prague for a while to help with the expenses.[12]

In addition to the economic tribulations, Vilém was acutely aware of the advancing menace around him. Adolf Hitler had espoused a pan-German nationalism, viciously anti-Slavic and anti-Semitic; he viewed politics as a "racial" struggle in which German minorities abroad were the Reich's "racial comrades" in need of its protection. The surge of German nationalism in the Sudetenland and the growing influence of the National Socialist German Workers' Party from across the border must have been alarming. The Nazi Party came to power through participation in Germany's democratic process and had established itself as the largest single party in the Reichstag. Its "racial" platform was gradually accompanied by anti-Jewish violence. Germany had become a fascist state. Thousands of German refugees began to stream to Czechoslovakia, mostly to Prague. Yet many Jews continued to be confident that "it can't happen here."[13] Vilém cast his lot with the Czech social democrats and socialists in national and municipal elections against the right-wing parties; however, he also refused to support the Zionists who were active in the Jewish Party.[14] With all that was transpiring, he was on edge.

In Prague, the Ornsteins moved from one rented apartment to another. When she spoke of it later, Ruth's voice was steady as if the moves had no effect on her life. She went to Czech schools, had friends from many backgrounds, and used to travel with her mother to visit grandparents in Przemyśl. Ruth was not brought up within the Jewish faith and was exposed to only some traditions. The family attended services in the temple on high holidays and anti-Semitism had no effect on her life.[15] Not until 1939.

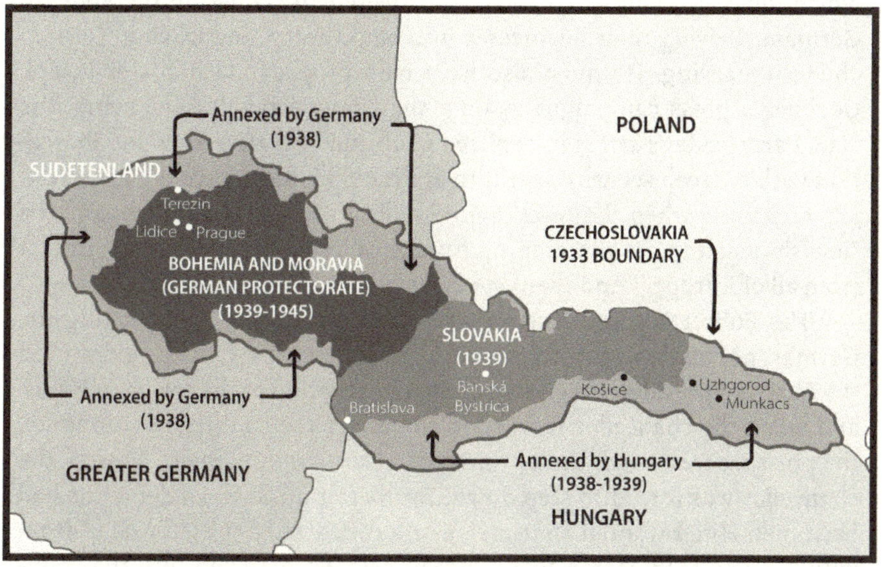

Map 1. Partition of Czechoslovakia in 1938–39

The Mutilated Country

Hitler's vision of a powerful Germany fed the desire of the Sudeten nationalists to recapture the imagined lost past. Under the leadership of Konrad Henlein, a gymnastics instructor, they formed a party that was fascist in all but name and scored an important electoral triumph in 1935. Henlein declared loyalty to the Nazi ideals, demanded political autonomy for the Sudeten Germans, and annexation to the German Reich. He claimed that his concern was the protection of the rights of the Sudeten Germans from the "chauvinistic Prague government." The economic crisis added reasons to demand separation from Czechoslovakia. It was true that the

Czechoslovak government's nationality policy, such as the employment of only Czechs in the government service and favoring Czechs over Germans in granting contracts, led to resentment among some Germans. But the whipped-up frenzy over a negotiable issue, which could have been solved by respect for all groups and civic equality, as the optimistic president Edvard Beneš told the Sudeten inhabitants, was fundamentally a pretext to provoke an international crisis, leading to the mutilation of Czechoslovakia and its eventual subjugation as part of Hitler's relentless march toward the conquest of all of Europe.[16]

Like millions of others, Willi listened to Hitler's ranting on the radio, which included claims that the Czechs were exterminating the Sudeten Germans, driving their businesses into bankruptcy, and leaving German children starving. He must also have read propaganda minister Joseph Goebbels's press campaigns against the "Prague rabble," following one Nazi Party leader's arrest in Teplice in autumn 1937 after a violent altercation with a Czech security agent. In addition, he must have felt it personally menacing when the Nazi regime radicalized its strategy to solve the "Jewish question" by threatening to remove Jews from Germany, in fact from all of Europe.[17] And then one catastrophe followed another.

The Führer accused Austria and Czechoslovakia of persecuting the German population that he promised to protect. First, Hitler pressured the Austrian president to give freedom of operation to the Austrian Nazis, and when the chancellor refused to surrender the country's sovereignty, the pressure increased. Under threat of a German invasion of Austria, the chancellor was forced to step down. Even after all German demands had been met, Hitler wanted an invasion and concocted a "plea for help" from within Austria. In March 1938 German soldiers marched into the country. The Anschluss, the merging of Austria and the German Reich, took place amid cheering crowds on the streets and rejoicing among the Sudeten Germans in the neighboring Czechoslovakia, whose self-confidence it reinforced. A witness reported a pro-Nazi rally—a "nightmare of flags, swastikas," posters of Hitler, and ear-splitting "heils" in the town hall—presumably in Teplice. The government mobilized several hundred thousand soldiers in response, for the time being to defuse the crisis.[18]

The government feared that Czechoslovakia could be next. Hitler's instruction to Henlein was to make demands for justice for the Sudeten population that would be "unacceptable to the government." The Sudeten leader did just that. Every concession the government was willing to make to the Sudeten Germans in order to safeguard the integrity and sovereignty of the country was dismissed on its face. Hitler wanted a fight.[19]

To avoid war, British prime minister Neville Chamberlain sought to appease the warmongering Hitler, believing that the Führer's rise to power was a logical consequence of legitimate German grievances resulting from the country's harsh treatment by the victors after World War I. Furthermore, the prime minister believed that Nazism was a useful bulwark against communism and Bolshevik Russia. Together with the French, the British agreed that the Czechoslovaks should give up all areas where the population was more than 50 percent German. Subsequently, the country split between those who advocated acquiescing to the German demands and those determined to fight them. The announcement in early September 1938 of imminent mobilization came like a bolt out of the blue, but people were ready to defend their country. Sirens blaring, some people digging shelters while others tried on gas masks, days and nights of feverish activity: the eruption of war seemed imminent. All reservists under the age of forty were to report for duty.[20] That order missed Willi by a hair's breadth. Ruth had just turned thirteen and must have gone to school as usual, schoolbag on her back and a gas mask at her side.

Weeks later, on September 30, Hitler, Chamberlain, French president Édouard Daladier, and Italian leader Benito Mussolini imposed on Czechoslovakia the Munich agreement, with no Czech politician invited to the Bavarian capital; "sitting in a semicircle of armchairs around a large fireplace in the city's palatial new Nazi Party headquarters, [they] essentially dismembered Czechoslovakia." The European statesmen did not go to Munich to fight but to beg for peace, capitulating to Hitler.[21]

The Munich Agreement stipulated the transfer of the Sudetenland from Czechoslovakia to the German Reich on the understanding that this was to be Hitler's last territorial demand. German troops crossed into northern Bohemia on October 1, 1938. The Czechoslovak army vacated the region and the Wehrmacht, took over the executive power in the occupied territory. The annexation of the Sudetenland was a happy day for Hitler's followers, whom they hailed as a savior. On losing the Sudetenland, Czechoslovakia was deprived of large swaths of its territory, population, national income, strategic minerals, industries, and its defensible borders. President Beneš abdicated on October 5, a few days after the Munich verdict. After he recovered from a mental and physical collapse, he left Czechoslovakia for England on October 22. "Undoing Munich" never left the president's mind; in the meantime, the country was living in suspense.[22]

From a distance, Willi witnessed the violence inflicted on the Sudetenland's Jewish population, on those opposed to the annexation to Germany, and on people identified as enemies of the Reich. Social democrats, communists, Czechs, and Jews who had not fled filled detention camps in the Sudetenland and the concentration camps in Germany. If Czechoslovakia "wished to show loyalty to Germany," Hitler commanded, it should drive every Jew out of the country, following Germany's example, making the region Jew-free. Subsequently, personal attacks on Jewish actors, musicians, and writers became the vogue, and not only in the Sudetenland. Even in such a venerable institution as the National Theater, Jews were attacked by other members of the theater.[23]

It did not take long for Hitler to incorporate the rest of the country into the Reich. The pretext was that the Czechoslovak government did not take the right measures against the Jews and a simmering conflict between the Czech and the Slovak government, which under German pressure was asserting its autonomy. Monsignor Jozef Tiso, the archbishop of Bratislava and the Slovak version of Pétain, stood before the choice of either declaring Slovakia's independence and allegiance to Germany or being swallowed by Hungary. The American ambassador in Paris noted that "the present situation in Slovakia has been created deliberately by the Germans because of the refusal of the Czech government and people to hand over control of their country to Germany."[24] On March 10, 1939, unbeknown to the world, Hitler let his underlings know, "We go in on Wednesday March 15 and smash the whole misbegotten Czechoslovakian construct."[25]

Active resistance was out of the question and the new fainthearted president, Emil Hácha, signed the decree tying the Czechoslovak people's destiny to that of the Greater German Reich. Czechoslovakia became the Protectorate of the Bohemian and Moravian lands, and its citizens became Reich citizens. The SS (extralegal paramilitary protection squads) and the Gestapo (the German political police), many of them from the Sudetenland, became conspicuous in most Czech towns assisting the governing German authorities. By occupying the Czech territories, Hitler broke the Munich Agreement, sending the message that he would not abide by any international treaty.[26]

Had Willi lost his job if he still had one before the occupation? Was Ruth prevented from going to school because Jewish pupils had been barred from continuing in public institutions?[27] When exactly did Vilém conceive the plan to leave Czechoslovakia? His new passport was issued in March 1938, extended in March 1939; he picked it up on March 30. Ruth at thirteen had no serious understanding of any of the previous months' events until she became aware that her father was getting ready to leave Prague.

2

A Journey into the Unknown

By leaving occupied Czechoslovakia in April 1939, Ruth's father saved their lives. Daring to risk an uncertain future, he spared himself and his daughter the ignominy of being singled out as *Untermenschen* (subhuman), as the Nazis referred to the Jews, avoided the possibility of persecution, and eluded captivity or death. Ruth's mother did not go with them. Family lore had it that she remained behind because she wanted to hide whatever possessions they had and planned to follow them as soon as she could. It came out only later in conversations with Ruth that her mother had stayed behind because she had a lover; nothing has come to light about him. The price Anka paid for her decision was colossal.

The Refugee Crisis

Jewish and antifascist refugees had been streaming into Czechoslovakia since Hitler's rise to power in 1933; they arrived in a country that did not welcome them. Periodic waves of persecution in Germany, in Austria after the Anschluss, and in the Sudetenland after its annexation to the Reich impelled throngs to cross the border into Czechoslovakia, robbed of their possessions and bank deposits. Expelling Jews from the Sudetenland was inhumane and "contrary to the intentions of the Munich Agreement," which guaranteed the protection of their property rights. The German government, wrote the British ambassador to Germany Sir Nevile Meyrick Henderson, should be urged "to refrain from such expulsions," which amounted to Jews being dumped into Czechoslovakia, where feelings against them were rising.[1] But such admonitions, expressed by the same government that had signed the Munich Agreement, fell on deaf ears.

After the whole of Czechoslovakia had been brought under the Nazi rule as the Protectorate of Bohemia and Moravia and the Slovak fascist state had come into being in March 1939, many of those refugees began to look for ways to get out. Neither the Jews, nor individuals who belonged to democratic political parties, nor the Czechoslovak government leaders being pushed out of office were safe. Several humanitarian organizations had been on hand to assist them. This network included American Unitarians, British socialists, and Prague Jewish workers responding to changes in circumstances as war seemed to be approaching. In Britain, sympathy for the refugees after the annexation of the Sudetenland, especially given the role that Britain played in the dismemberment of Czechoslovakia, prompted the public and some prominent figures who felt the weight of British responsibility to bring assistance to the powerless population. Public fundraising, money donated thanks to liberal newspapers' appeals and to the Trades Union Congress, together with the London Lord Mayor's Fund, comprised a reasonable sum with which the British Committee for Refugees from Czechoslovakia, founded in October 1938, could maneuver. These organizations considered it paramount that British visas be granted to the refugees in danger.[2]

The Flight

Vilém Ornstein might not have been on the Gestapo's arrest list of prominent Jews or political activists, but as a Jew and a social democrat, though not active in any party, he was firm about wanting to leave Czechoslovakia. Ruth remembered her father's determination to emigrate and his assertion that "I am taking the child with me." Keeping the family together as so many did, which prevented them from leaving in time, was not Willi's concern when Anka decided to stay behind.[3]

Vilém could have attempted to send Ruth on the Kindertransport, the children's transports that with British help took more than six hundred Czechoslovak children to England over several months before the war broke out. But he chose to undertake the responsibility for her safe emigration himself. Ruth's father did not have the money or possessions to buy his way out, which was one way to persuade the Nazi authorities to grant exit permits in exchange for Jewish property. Some countries had immigration quotas; some closed their borders to refugees while others sold visas, which Vilém could not afford. Jewish refugees were not welcome in Latin American countries and the visas that consuls made available were a black-market commodity.[4] Vilém attempted to emigrate to Palestine but failed. Another solution had to be found.

As Vilém was looking for routes to get out, the Ornsteins experienced the Nazi anti-Jewish policies, such as the signs hoisted on buildings forbidding Jews to enter restaurants or news of synagogues around the country burned down, which local populations were desperately salvaging from the flames.[5] Worse was to come. Ruth might have been confused, her mother was perhaps distraught.

Vilém was in a hurry. He received his passport two weeks after the occupation. After a brief period when the German authorities refused to issue visas, emigration was legal again with a Gestapo permit. Even with a permit, securing a visa was a problem. The British legation in Prague was overwhelmed by applicants, while the foreign relief organizations were busy helping people, often assisting entire families in immediate danger or trying to decide who seemed to be in greater distress than others. For people for whom nothing could be done, the recommendation was to go to Poland illegally. The selfless and daring Englishwoman Doreen Warriner, who chose to lead one of the relief organizations—the British Committee for Refugees from Czechoslovakia—was crisscrossing the occupied territories to spirit refugees to safety instead of pursuing her academic career as an economist. When she reached dead ends, she distributed money and her card to be presented by its holder to the consulate in the Polish town of Katowice where one could apply for a British visa. Her maneuverings on behalf of the refugees led to her expulsion from Prague on April 23, 1939, to avoid the arrest planned by the Gestapo.[6]

Vilém chose the Polish route. One night in April 1939 he and Ruth boarded the train at the Wilson station in Prague. The farewell from Anka may not have been heartrending: "You go, and I will come later" was how Ruth remembered it. It was unlikely that anyone would have seen them off at the railway station. For Ruth at the age of thirteen the trip seemed an adventure while the separation from her mother was expected to be temporary.[7] Little did she know that this separation would leave an indelible mark on the adult she became.

The organizational details of the escape, fraught with danger and risk of arrest, are lost to history. With a backpack each, father and daughter took the train from Prague to Moravská Ostrava in the eastern part of the country. Vilém paid for the tickets. Their luggage was light; Ruth tucked two dresses into her bundle. They traveled on a night train that both the refugees and the Gestapo knew was leaving at eleven o'clock. On arrival, they were to contact a trustworthy local guide to get them across the frontier. It was known that the Polish government used the border patrol and spies to spot and return immigrants to avoid incurring German wrath. In addition to swarms of Jews and political refugees, dozens of young men were crossing the border determined to form an army to liberate Czechoslovakia from Nazism. Miners led them through abandoned shafts, railwaymen smuggled them on trains. Those caught were imprisoned or returned to where they came from.[8]

Having arrived early in the morning to an unknown city occupied by the Wehrmacht, father and daughter waded through the snow to the Palace Hotel where they met their guide, whose services had been most likely arranged beforehand. Whoever he was, the guide hid them until nightfall when another one took them on a trek of several miles across the snow-covered border to a Polish village, hid them in a barn, and vanished. The fear of being discovered by the Polish police was fearsome. To Vilém's relief a good Samaritan appeared with a lorry the following night, hid them underneath a heap of hay, and drove to Katowice. From there they managed to reach Kraków.[9] All in all, it is remarkable that Vilém managed to leave Czechoslovakia with Ruth as early as April 1939, a month after the German occupation and four months before war broke out.

After their arrival in Kraków, Ruth was delighted to be taken to Przemyśl to stay with her beloved grandparents, aunts, and uncle, while her father was seeing about the next leg of the journey. The British Committee for Refugees from Czechoslovakia kept them afloat, in tandem with the Quakers and the local Jewish community.

Each refugee registered at the British consulate in Katowice or an office in Kraków where the Czechoslovak consulate also had its seat and gave them a helping hand. While waiting for British visas, the refugees socialized and schemed. Even after registering, a refugee was guaranteed neither a visa nor travel arrangements, though being registered helped those with no Polish visas and protected them from the police on the lookout for illegals. Thus, refugees who could show a document that they were on the list of the organization and had the possibility of transportation out of the country would generally avoid harassment. If for some reason they were locked up, they were usually released upon the request of the British. The Polish police were eager to see that the emigrants leave Poland fast. Even the committee's workers were not exempt from surveillance by the Gestapo on the Czechoslovak side of the border, "who kn[e]w all about what is going on in Katowice and Kraków."[10]

Getting the refugees to Britain was a monumental task and a race against time. The visas were granted by the Home Office in England, but they could take weeks or months to arrive and when they did it was up to the committee to decide who should get them. Visas were refused to people who seemed politically untrustworthy in the eyes of the refugee organizers, who were accused of preferring to give visas to political refugees and to the communists from among them. Highest on the list were people who with the committee's help had arrived in Poland before the occupation of Czechoslovakia; then came the political refugees. Jews were last and were to "be selected on the basis of their suitability for emigration," meaning their assimilation into the host society (though the phrase was never specified in order to avoid charges of anti-Semitism). Pregnant women whose husbands were already in England received special consideration. There were the rare occasions when desperate refugees fell into the smugglers' trap, paying large sums of money and jewelry in exchange for the promise to get them to Great Britain. Sometimes someone who was on the list and had been waiting for a long time could not be found or the person was too ill to travel; in other cases the refugees had lost patience and taken off east, to the Soviet Union. Furthermore, trains from the south to the Baltic seaport of Gdynia where ships set sail for Britain were not always reliable, nor was the telephone service dependable for speedy communication between the organizers in the south and their coworkers at the port. The state of the shipping line was another problem, for not all ships had acceptable accommodations for the refugees. Also, tensions abounded because the refugees were split into political and linguistic groups—communists, social democrats, Sudetenland Germans, Austrians, Czech Jews—all vying to get ahead of others to obtain the invaluable visa, which some believed they deserved more than others.[11]

Ruth was sheltered in Przemyśl until the first or second week of May, when the name Ornstein appeared on the transport list ready to sail for Britain. Many refugees had to wait for weeks for their visas, so Vilém was fortunate that theirs arrived no more than three weeks after they had crossed the Polish border. Furthermore, the humanitarian organization gave preference to the political refugees over Jews. Aunt Pola brought Ruth to Kraków by train. That was the last time they saw each other. In no time Vilém and Ruth took a train north to Gdynia, where they boarded a ship for Sweden. Ruth saw the sea for the first time. It was a difficult journey; the sea was rough, and the children on board were sick. In Malmö they took a train across Sweden and another ship to cross the North Sea to Britain, disembarking after long hours on board in Tilbury, on the east coast.[12]

The Landing

After the British committee had taken care of thousands of refugees' safe arrivals to Britain, it had the moral obligation, even with scarce resources, to see to it that their well-being continued. The committee was faced with the long-standing ambivalent attitude of the British government and public toward Jewish immigration, defined largely by Britain's national and imperialist interests. The society was imbued with a strain of anti-Semitism, expressed in jokes, stereotypes, disparagement, and accusations that Jews were conspiring to take power through international finance and communism. The Jewish aspiration to create a state in British-mandated Palestine, creating turmoil in the Arab-dominated region and threatening commerce to the Far East, was also a factor in public perception of the Jews. None of these circumstances precluded Jews from being prominent figures in the cabinet. The fact was that British anti-Semitism, or the fear that the door to Jewish refugees might be opened too wide, was more social and snobbish than racial and extremist like it was within Nazism. However, given the British appeasement of Hitler, the government had no authority to criticize the Nazi regime's treatment of the Jews. Believing also that Jews were incapable of adapting to local mores, the government preferred that they emigrate to other countries, except Palestine, where the British controlled their influx in order not to upset the demographic and political balance between the Jews and the Arab population in a conflict-ridden region. The government had to choose between its commitments to the world of Jewry and its promises to the world of Islam, for the British empire was to a considerable extent Muslim.[13]

This was the prevailing political ambience when father and daughter arrived in England. They stayed together in a modest hostel for refugees near London. A fortnight later, Vilém left the accommodation provided by the British committee while Ruth was placed in a foster home. Living suddenly with strangers could be a happy or calamitous experience, depending on the character of the benefactors as well as on the child's capacity to adapt to a foreign environment without understanding its language and mores. Ruth used to say that she liked the family Glenwright from Meopham, a village near Gravesend in Kent in southeast England. It was a family of teachers still on holidays; Ruth did not mention any children. She stayed with them for two months until the British committee opened a hostel for refugee children from Czechoslovakia in Broadstairs, a coastal town in Kent. By the time Ruth left the Glenwright family, she had mastered some English. It was to her advantage that she was raised in an assimilated Jewish family so that neither religion nor dietary laws played any role in her settling in Britain, where few foster homes could accommodate the Jewish faith and kosher food.[14]

Between leaving the home of the Glenwrights and starting Ramsgate County school for girls in Broadstairs, Ruth spent a fortnight or so in a summer camp. It was in the hostel and the camp that Ruth struck up her first friendships with adolescent girls and boys her age who shared her background and life trajectory as German- and Czech-speaking Jews from Czechoslovakia: Miriam, Kony, Hedy, Max, Bobby, Mela, and others. One of the wardens of the hostel was Evžen, better known as Janči Loebl, a twenty-two-year-old Slovak communist who Ruth came to trust and remember all her life.[15]

When the British committee interviewed the forty-three-year-old Vilém a few days after his arrival in England, he explained that his wife was still in Prague; that following the German invasion he left Czechoslovakia because he was Jewish; that he entered Poland illegally; and that he touched the British shore on May 18. He had neither means nor relatives in England. His trade was timber, and his plan was to emigrate to Canada. Having Czech and not German citizenship, Vilém was spared the internment that so many of his Sudetenland fellow citizens had to undergo while their background was being investigated for possible, though unlikely, Nazi affiliations. He was aware that he could not take any employment in the United Kingdom, but there did not seem to be pressure exerted on him to leave. To the contrary, Vilém was given the committee's courtesy of dental treatment in a hospital.[16]

Did he really plan to emigrate to Canada, or was this a pro forma statement? One wonders because in June the committee staff noted that he needed an English partner to be able to set up a business and raised the possibility of arranging for his wife's coming to England. Did Vilém plan to become an entrepreneur? He mentioned an acquaintance in Wales who could help him out and a possible business partner in Canada's timber trade. However, with the British government's absorption of the committee and the establishment of the Czech Refugee Trust Fund in July 1939 to assist emigration and settlement of Czechoslovak refugees, the government changed its original intention to send them to other countries to now providing them with conditions to settle down in Britain. There was some intimation that Vilém was to be sent to the countryside until his wife's arrival. "The Trust has no reason to doubt his reliability," a committee social worker noted in March 1940.[17]

Edmond Castle

It was in late August 1939 that Germany took the world by surprise by signing the nonaggression pact with the Soviet Union, understood to be Germany's Bolshevik adversary. And a few days later, on September 1, 1939, Hitler invaded Poland. In doing so, Germany violated all previous agreements, and Hitler lost the trust unduly accorded to him by the British peace-seekers, the same ones who had caved to his demand to annex the Sudetenland to the Third Reich. Britain declared war on Germany.[18]

It was a Sunday when Germany attacked Poland. In England, places of entertainment were ordered to be closed, churches to remain open; schools were suspended for a week and people were to keep off the streets. To make cities safe, protective barrage balloons went up against the expected war airplanes, but the German air force, the Luftwaffe, attacked British shipping, not the British Isles. A German U-boat sank a British passenger liner, with British and American lives lost. A few weeks later, the battleship *Royal Oak* went down. The Royal Air Force did not retaliate. Ruth had just turned fourteen years old.

What was known as the phony war, the lull before the storm, as the expectation of German invasion was referred to, dragged from September 1939 until May 1940. The winter was cold, transport made difficult by snowdrifts. The British would be remembered as calm, good-spirited and disciplined even when the phone, telegraph, and electric lights were cut off. As bombardments were expected and it was thought that poison gas would spread, masks were issued to the population to always carry with them. Volunteers dug trenches, built air-raid shelters, and prepared sandbags to protect buildings; a blackout was imposed, motorcar headlights had to be reduced to a feeble slit, windows were covered with black curtains or cardboards, streetlights were switched off, and train lights were dimmed to a glow, giving the cities an eerie quality.[19]

With the expectation of a German attack, the trust evacuated children housed along the eastern shoreline, first to different hostels further southwest, near Brighton, where they then began school. But being on the eastern or the southern coast boiled down to the same thing: both were insecure should air raids take place. So by April 1940 the trust was obliged to close the hostels situated near the seaboard and look for alternatives elsewhere. In a matter of few weeks, Ruth had been separated from her mother, from her father, from her foster family, if that mattered, and was moved again. Chance had it that the owners of the reconstructed Edmond Castle, near the village Hayton in what was then Cumberland County close to the Anglo-Scottish border, were willing to rent their majestic nineteenth-century country house to the trust. Sometime in the spring of 1940, the children and adolescents were evacuated north.[20] Ruth, the teenage Czech-Jewish refugee, now lived with dozens of other youngsters in an environment that did not resemble anything she had known until then.

In Ruth's memory of the two and half years she spent in Edmond Castle, what stood out was the appalling cold inside its unheated rooms and the Brampton school that she loved so much. The castle's environs had much to offer. It was surrounded by a grand, lush garden, studded with trees, beyond which extended valleys, plains, and woods that allowed carefree exploration and excursions on foot or bicycles. Like all hostels organized by the trust, Edmond Castle had a British warden and an elected refugee "mother" or "father," responsible for the running of the establishment. Hedwig Huenigen, "Mutter Huenigen," the mother of Ruth's new friend Hedy, became that mother to all the children.[21]

Most of the youngsters in the castle had similar harrowing stories to tell of losses and family's separations, of risky escapes, of fear and uncertainty that accompanied their journey to England. With a staff of likeminded men and women, Hedwig Huenigen took care of some forty children and teenagers between the ages of five and sixteen, most of them Jewish. She was kind and firm. Some children bore their condition with fortitude, others suffered from homesickness and depression after being separated from their parents. Huenigen took care of their souls and clothes.[22] Ruth found the environment congenial, safe, and a substitute for a family.

Life in the castle was austere, following a strict order. All had to partake in the domestic duties: peel potatoes, wash the dishes, fetch firewood, feed the chickens. They had to look after themselves and make sure to complete their homework even by candlelight when electricity was switched off. The adolescents were put in charge of the smaller children. Ruth at fourteen had an eight-year-old Czech girl under her wing. The sleeping quarters were not only cold (with no heating installations) but overcrowded, with not much space for privacy. The English cuisine, which some found to be bland, was also limited by tight rations. Periodically medical inspectors saw to it that the children were vaccinated, measured, weighed, and (if Ruth's experience was like that of other children in other hostels at that time), the regular diet was supplemented with disgusting halibut or cod liver oil. For lack of sun, the children might have received additional doses of vitamin D.[23]

There was time for play, for learning and performing Czech and Slovak folk dances, for poetry readings, and for singing by the campfire. Ruth learned to play the accordion and joined the castle orchestra. The children and adolescents were indoctrinated with patriotic pep talks by their elders, encouraged in showing solidarity with each other, and imbued with a sense of responsibility toward the country that had given them refuge and was now on war footing. It was an atmosphere propitious for making friends and establishing furtive relationships. A memory book that survived among Ruth's meager wartime possessions, scribbled in Czech and German, echoes those patriotic rumblings, the conviction that victory would be achieved, that Germany would be defeated, and that she would return home. One teenager quoted Tomáš Garrigue Masaryk, the emblematic president of free and democratic Czechoslovakia during the 1920s and 1930s: "Better to perish fighting then living in slavery." Another oft repeated motto was "don't forget your mother tongue, because one's motherland is irreplaceable."[24]

FIGURE 3. Edmond Castle during World War II. Ruth is the girl with glasses.

Most children and adolescents in Edmond Castle were from Prague Jewish families, while some others were from the German Sudetenland, Bohemia, Slovakia, Germany, or Austria. Many spoke not just one but several languages: they spoke Czech, Slovak, and German, even Hungarian, and all also had English education at school. Some did not know any Czech; others did not know any German; most, like Ruth, were bilingual. The entries in the memory book reflect both the complexity and uniqueness of the refugees' national and cultural life in Edmond Castle. Janči Loebl and his Austrian wife, Friederike ("Fritzi" for short), joined the castle's staff sometime in 1941—though not for long. He had to be constantly on the move because the British intelligence was on his heels, due to his role as a central figure in the Czechoslovak Communist Party who spent time lecturing British audiences about the superiority of the Soviet Union as a political, social, and economic system. During the time that he spent at the castle, he added the communist outlook and Soviet literature to the ideological and cultural curriculum.[25]

The dominant identity that the elders instilled in the youngsters was Czechoslovak, social democratic, or communist. True, Great Britain gave them refuge, but they were focused on winning the war alongside the other Allies—not on serving and saving the British Empire and pledging loyalty to the King. Though Jewish suffering throughout Europe was known, and the boarders who were mostly Jews with family members still in Czechoslovakia were subject to persecution, Jewish traditions and consciousness did not seem to be cultivated in Edmond Castle. Zionism was out of the question, since it would have competed with Czechoslovak nationalism or with the idea of building communism after the war.[26]

Ruth celebrated both her fifteenth birthday in September 1940 and her sixteenth in 1941 at Edmond Castle. Those were her saddest days. No one could substitute for her father: "I saw very little of him, very little." He might have visited her on one occasion or another but no more. She did not have money to go to London and it was inadvisable to travel by train after the enemy bombing started in earnest in the summer of 1940 and continued through the following months. Her refuge was school and homework. She could make and retain friends, so much so that she kept their letters till the end of her life. In one interview conducted in 1996, Ruth presented an image of herself as a studious teenager, reading books, listening to classical music, and missing her family terribly. In a photo of a row of adolescent girls, she stood out as one of the tallest, her head covered with thick black wavy hair reaching to her shoulders, her eyes screened behind eyeglasses; the dresses she wore were handouts and did not reflect her taste in clothes. In fact, Ruth never set much store on elegance. Whether on a bicycle or among friends, she looked serious, even though she recalled the years spent in Edmond Castle as joyful.[27]

Despite the air war on England and the German tanks rolling into one country after another on the European continent with all the attendant destruction and suffering, and with England expecting an imminent invasion, the boarders in Edmond Castle celebrated Christmas 1940 in peace. The castle was ensconced in a rural, inland area, surrounded by meadows, fields, and woodlands; Carlisle, the nearest town, was never a target for Germans bombs since it had no industry and was not an important city. Ruth never mentioned air-raid sirens or having to scramble for shelters. There were sporadic air-raid warnings in Carlisle but no enemy bombers flying over their heads. Even here cars had to have their beams shielded to safeguard the area from possible enemy detection, but if a raid and an explosion took place, it was because a pilot had lost his way and target.

The End of Safe Haven

While in the north, Ruth knew very little about her father. Vilém had registered for war service in May 1940, lived through the thick and thin of the Battle of Britain during the summer and autumn of 1940, and witnessed the subsequent nightly Luftwaffe bombing of London, which damaged civil and historic buildings and killed civilians. After Britain had eased restrictions on the refugees' employment, recognizing their usefulness as a labor force in the war effort, Vilém was allowed to seek a job and was supported by the trust fund until he found one. He briefly corresponded with Anka (who remained in the German protectorate) through an address in the United States. The last communication Ruth recalled from this period was a letter saying, "I am going to my parents but won't live at home."[28] For years this enigmatic message made no sense until the revelation about Jews being deported to concentration camps in the east. No written word from Anka survived the war.

Vilém wanted to be useful but was not fit for the war effort. A medical examination showed that bad eyesight and mild arteriosclerosis made him ineligible for active military service. Ruth recalled that his job was clearing rubble after bombings, which could not have been light work for a man of forty-four years old with an ailing heart. At one time he was registered as an employee of a manufacturing firm in central London, recommended for the job due to his qualifications as a speaker of Czech, German, Polish, and English, his education, and managerial capabilities.[29]

Sometime during 1942 the organization looking after the welfare of the refugees ceased renting Edmond Castle. The stately manor's "family" was forced to disperse. Young men who had reached military age joined the army, with the desire to win the war and return home. The Czechoslovak government-in-exile was eager to assure that the growing generation did not lose its sense of belonging to the motherland, language, and customs and was not lost to emigration: it would be needed for the imagined postwar rebuilding of democratic Czechoslovakia. With that purpose in mind the government-in-exile relocated the younger children to a hostel and a school in Wales, removing obstacles to establishing elementary and secondary schools such as the lack of qualified teachers and textbooks in the Czech language (these had to be typed and duplicated). The Czech army helped.[30]

Ruth was sorry to leave Edmond Castle and part with her friends. She remained in Carlisle for several more months in order to finish school, renting a room with the money from the trust fund, supplemented perhaps by money from her father. One afternoon she and her friends went to the movie theater. Afterward they sneaked into the abandoned Edmond Castle through a broken window. They strolled from one empty room to another. Each chamber brought back joyful memories and some nostalgia. Ruth's eyes welled with tears.[31] Whether she perceived it or not, one era in her life was ending, while an unknown chapter lay ahead.

Through going to an English school, Ruth had adopted English ways and learned to speak the language to perfection, without becoming quite English. She adopted the rules of fair play and was outgoing and emotionally unrestrained. Not yet of age, she matured into an independent young woman pining for friendships, love, and family. Ruth received good education and care from her foster parents. She graduated from Brampton County school in June 1942 successfully with straight As, at the top of her class of twenty-five students. The school headmaster, Mr. Wood, who also taught science, had commended her academic accomplishments already in 1941 and lavished praise on Ruth at the end of her final year as a student who was "both orderly and accurate," demonstrated "quite mature" reasoning, and possessed "a most inquiring turn of mind." First among equals, she was a "most progressive pupil with great potentialities" who should "prove worthy of special opportunities." Mister Wood augured Ruth's bright future "in her own country"; he encouraged her to go on to university studies.[32]

But by 1942 Ruth knew a great deal about the devastation caused by the war, the pain inflicted on Jews in the invaded territories, Czechoslovakia's sufferings at the hands of the occupiers, the obliteration of entire villages and their inhabitants as a reprisal for resistance to German rule, men being murdered, and women, men and children deported to concentration camps. She had lost contact with her mother and her Polish family. Thus, instead of going to the university, Ruth, who was almost seventeen years old, decided to play her part in fighting the Nazis and fascism to end the war on behalf of her motherland. Times were grave, meriting solemn words and requiring courageous deeds: "I can't study, I have to fight."[33]

3

Joining the Battlefield

"VITAL TO THE OFFENSIVE": these words glared in block letters and bold designs from posters affixed to the walls in public spaces. "Thousands of women needed now" appealed recruiting centers and employment exchanges, as they sought personnel to enroll into the army, navy, and air force. "No British woman will stand aside" called the War Ministry; thousands of British girls who had just left school and women who had been working at a job responded. Nothing could match the sense of duty, patriotism, and exhilaration that joining the war effort meant, even if it was on the home front far from the battle line.[1] Refugee women from countries occupied by Germany responded as well, believing that by joining the war effort in Britain they were helping the liberation of their own country from Nazism.

The Czechoslovak-British Friendship Club

Ruth reached London sometime in the middle of 1942 burning with desire to join the army. Her age did not allow it, so she had to wait a few more months. Coming from the quietude of the north she found the city on a war's footing, characterized by Allied troops milling about on the streets and the sound of the sirens. While the government imposed a blackout, in the evenings the cinemas and theaters played to enthusiastic audiences of soldiers and civilians. Security was tightened. After heavy German bombing during 1940 and 1941, many buildings were leveled to the ground, but Londoners faced adversities in good spirit.

Brimming with energy, Ruth looked for a job and a place to live. In no time, she immersed herself in the cultural and political milieu of London, where Czechoslovak artists in exile enjoyed freedom for literary, musical, theatrical, and journalistic expressions that were stifled in the occupied homeland. She was enthralled by the friendship and patriotism of the Czechoslovak-British club, where she found a secretarial job. Ruth was put in charge of typing letters, collecting members' contributions, and running errands. She was happy to be nearer to her father, who was stationed at an army unit not far from London.[2]

The friendship club had opened in September 1941 under the auspices of the Czechoslovak government-in-exile and was strongly influenced by the communists. The Sudeten Germans exiled to London from Czechoslovakia were divided: some, who felt loyalty to their political brethren, joined the club while others were drawn by their national identity to German-speaking organizations. Numerous Czechoslovak parties vied to influence the hearts and minds of the British public on whose behalf Chamberlain had signed the Munich Agreement in 1938. They also sought to influence the politically and ideologically varied exile community with an eye to returning to the homeland and building a country based ostensibly on democratic principles even when they did not agree on its meaning: communists, social democrats, national socialists, and Sudeten Germans had different visions for the future.[3]

The club was managed jointly by a representative of the government-in-exile and by Janči Loebl and his wife, whom Ruth had known from her school years. Hedwig Hoenigen, "Mutti" from Edmond Castle, was the club's catering manager. Located in western London, the club attracted visitors through its restaurant, which served favorite Czech dishes. The other attraction was the opportunity for military men and women to drop in when on leave. The club became a meeting place where one could drink coffee, read the newspapers, discuss world and personal issues, and make plans. Soon after the club's foundation in London, branches were set up in major cities around Britain. They were administered by fervent communists who did not hide their radical pro-Soviet leanings, to the displeasure of the host country.[4]

The respected independent member of the British parliament Eleanor Rathbone stood fast by the Czechoslovak refugees. But when war began, she was concerned that by toeing Stalin's line during the Hitler-Stalin pact of nonaggression, which lasted from 1939 to 1941, the communists propagated the then-Soviet view that the British war effort was imperialist and should be stopped. Thus, Rathbone viewed the Czechoslovak refugees' running the clubs as engaging in sabotage, "doing their best to help our defeat by weakening the springs of our effort."[5] For the same reason, the clubs were not above the suspicion of the British intelligence and the London Metropolitan Police.

It was public knowledge that when Germany attacked the Soviet Union in June 1941, the communists—who had supported the German-Soviet pact of neutrality lock, stock, and barrel in 1939 and who refused to support the war effort once war broke out and to collaborate with the Czechoslovak government-in-exile in assisting the British war effort—reversed their position on Soviet orders, which stipulated that "in connection with the agreement between the USSR and Czechoslovakia, a directive has been issued to Czechoslovak comrades in America and England calling for collaboration with the Beneš government and participation in Czechoslovak military operations."[6]

The British intelligence service was aware of the conflicts among the communists related to the controversial pact between the Soviet Union and Germany, which some rejected as anachronistic. It knew of the cold-shouldering experienced by party members who had not supported the pact and refused to abide by the party discipline. It was conscious of the difficulties the pact posed to attaining the necessary wartime unity among the Communist Party members, the government-in-exile, and the numerous factions of the diaspora. Wanting to know more about the communists' aims, the British intelligence service infiltrated their ranks, in particular through frequenting the friendship club: "Our agent appears to have become very friendly with Loebl's assistant and will probably be taking her out to dinner shortly. On the whole, therefore, I think we shall be able to get a fairly useful information about the Club in the future."[7] Throughout the war years, British intelligence intercepted communications exchanged among the communists and inspected their bank accounts to see where their income came from. Agents shadowed them around the country, as communist ideologues lectured the British public on the need to open a second front to engage the German land forces on the European continent and spoke on the achievements of the Soviet Union or Czechoslovak suffering during the Nazi occupation. Only thanks to the ongoing war effort and Great Britain's protection of the Czechoslovak government-in-exile that the suspicion of antagonistic interests and past resentments did not erupt into an open international clash.

As Ruth had been raised in the communist and patriotic environment by her mentors at Edmond Castle, the political disputations taking place in the club and the lectures she attended strengthened her left-leaning worldview. She lived with a roommate or alone (unusual for Ruth in contrast to having lived with her family, but indicative of the changing times and her independent mind), followed the news on the radio, and absorbed the conversations about events in the club where she worked until late at night.

Uncertainty and instability reigned in the lives of individuals and at the front. The refugees fervently desired an end to the war and to emigration. Impatient and naive, echoing the communists' rigmarole, Ruth dismissed the British military accomplishments: "The campaign in Libya is not so glorious for the English. Well, they let all the imperial forces to fight while they polish their buttons and boots." She relished the fact that the Russians were inflicting a heavy beating on Hitler and lamented the sufferings and losses they received in return. The launching of the second front on the continental Europe by the Anglo-American alliance was the only scenario that could change the situation. It was this mood that led Ruth to end many letters to her friends with salutations such as "Heil Stalin," "Rot Front," or "Down with Capitalism."[8]

No matter where the refugees stood politically or which ideological faction they belonged to, all anxiously watched the war unfolding. They followed the changing balance of military power on the battlefield, the tally of German losses and gains on the eastern front and in North Africa, hoping for the opening of the second front in Europe to ease the German onslaught against the Soviet Union. But in the summer of 1942, Winston Churchill was categorical: "Our best chance of winning the war is with the big bombers," not by confronting the Germans in an open field. In 1943 the cabinet's Joint Intelligence Committee still hoped for German internal collapse did not rule out the Soviet Union's downfall due to the Nazi offensive on that front. For the time being, the invasion of the continent was deemed premature.[9]

The WAAF

By the spring of 1943 Ruth, at seventeen-and-a-half years old, was eligible to join the army. The war conditions allowed women as young as Ruth to make personal choices; hers was to enlist in May at one of the recruiting stations to serve in the Women's Auxiliary Air Force (WAAF). In doing so, she was responding to the appeal by the War Office calling on women to join the armed units in order to free men for the front. Ruth never explained why she joined the air force and not the army, which also had women's auxiliary units. Would she have joined the Czechoslovak army or air force if it had women's branches the way the British did? It was true, as the recruiting posters advertised, that serving in the WAAF meant being with the men who fly. The Royal Air Force, the most elite branch of the British military, enjoyed a fascination that the other unit lacked, and so by association did the WAAF.[10]

Once Ruth signed up for service, the first order of business was a medical examination. Ruth's record stated that her eyesight was below the average, otherwise she was healthy and ready for physical training at RAF's center at Innsworth, a village situated a couple hundred miles northwest from London. Once she arrived at the training site, the next steps were teaming up with other recent recruits, finding her room in the barracks, and receiving a uniform together with other garments. And then the military drills began.[11]

Women who were interviewed after the war fondly recalled the blue-and-gray uniforms they received on their arrival to the airfield. These were as smart as the pilots' uniforms, although the cap did not quite match the rest of the outfit in elegance. The buttoning followed the men's style. The recruits were allotted other items of clothes "from the skin out:" skirts, shirts, tunics, vests, bras and knickers ("twilights and blackouts," as they called them), beige lisle stockings, shoes, a black tie, a cap with a brass badge, and blue-and-white striped pajamas, which made some feel like prisoners. The distribution and selection of the clothes could take several hours. Putting items on and taking them off in search of the right size and shape, one recruit remembered, could be hilarious.[12]

The women were quartered in bitterly cold barracks, twenty or more in each room. Their bedding consisted of a mattress, blankets, a pillow, sheets, and a pillowcase. The beds were hard, the blankets scratchy. The initial drill included instruction on how to tie a tie and how to polish the brass buttons on the uniforms and the black shoes, "which incidentally we had to put on then and there, steep them and our stockinged feet in warm water, and go to our dinner with them wet, so that by the morning, they fitted our feet!" Food was served in a mess hall, where hundreds of people ate at the same time, all talking at once. It was so loud that it was difficult to hold a conversation. The cooking staff was also in uniform "but with hideous white overalls and haircatchers (for hygienic reasons)."[13] The aroma of the mess quickly became familiar, for it was the same at every post and in every army hut. The army hut and the uniform had to be kept in impeccable order. Everything was inspected. Things had to be folded and placed in the correct position before the drill on the parade ground. Initially, no one complained.

The military drill consisted of the women being divided by height into squads, with a sergeant in charge teaching them how to march, how to walk without swinging their arms in the same direction as their legs, and how to salute their superiors. The hopeless ones, who had to be taught even to distinguish right from left, had their own squad. "Why are there so many drills?" "Why are so many people always telling us what to do?" some of the new recruits asked themselves. But one had to adjust to the fact that these were armed forces and one had to follow orders, like it or not, shine or rain, literally. Some of the young women dropped out and went home, others found the preparation for the war effort exciting. There was little spare time, because so much of it was spent polishing shoes, buttons, and badges until one felt that she had reached a state of perfection.[14]

One can imagine that Ruth went through a similar experience and ruminations as her companions. After having acquired elementary military discipline, including an acquaintance with the ins and outs of weapons, women were assigned noncombatant roles even if some believed that they had the same capabilities and valor to engage in combat on the battlefield as men. Overall, women were assigned jobs in industrial production, agriculture, or services in support of the war effort. Ruth remembered with a chuckle that after one month's training, she could choose between being a cook or being an electrician. She chose the latter. Assigned to an experienced aircraft electrician, she trekked behind him with his tool case, passing him the maintenance instruments as required. It was a vital job but unappealing. Ruth aspired to more.[15]

"Y" Service

Ruth joined the WAAF after the Germans had been defeated at Stalingrad in February 1943 and had been driven out of Africa and Sicily. Indeed, the German defeats turned the tide of the war in favor of the Allies. The Royal Air Force was on the offensive, with air raids targeting German industrial districts. In March it was Berlin, then Essen Krupp factories, followed by the destruction of much of Hamburg, the Reich's second-largest city.

Ruth was eager to play her part in these events. During one of her free days in London, parading her blue WAAF uniform with the "flashes" of Czechoslovakia proudly displayed on her shoulders, she wandered into a café. There she met a woman her age in a similar uniform; they chatted in the washroom. Did Ruth speak German? She did. It was her mother tongue. "I can't tell you what we do," reacted her new acquaintance, but in that case Ruth should report to her superior telling him just that.[16] From there events accelerated quickly.

Ruth was interviewed by a selection board at the WAAF directorate in London. She underwent a series of tests and was recruited for what was known in the cryptic language of the British intelligence as "Y" service. The initial was derived from the two words, wireless interception, "wi" or "Y." It stood for the interception of wireless messages enciphered by the German Enigma machine and transmitted by the German air force, navy, or the army. British mathematicians, chess players, and cryptanalysts had broken the code in 1940.[17]

In the case of the Luftwaffe, the secret messages were used to communicate between the ground controllers and the flight pilots, and between the high command and divisions and corps levels of the navy and air force. As the "Y" service was highly sensitive, initially only English or Irish women, daughters or nieces of diplomats and journalists, were recruited to it. They knew German from when they lived with their parents in German speaking countries. As the war progressed, native German speakers who knew regional accents and slang were required irrespective of their background and hierarchy in this class-conscious society. Thus Ruth's superiors were English women, while her immediate peers were refugee women like herself from the occupied countries: Norway, Austria, Denmark, Greece, the Netherlands, Belgium, Poland, and Czechoslovakia. The foreign women had to be screened for security. Ruth was cleared.[18]

The RAF's "Y" activities were developed at stations dotted around the country and abroad, operated mainly by women endowed with an excellent hearing and calm disposition. Their job was intercepting and recording German fighter pilots' movements and conversations among themselves and with their ground controllers, as well as radio messages transmitted from German airfields. One had to be capable of working under pressure, have the patience to sit for hours waiting for an enemy station to make noise, twiddle with the radio knobs until a discernable message was heard, and remain alert even if meals and sleep patterns might be disrupted. The women were trained in Morse code and in wireless procedures to scan the airwaves for enemy traffic. It was imperative to provide speedy translations of scribbled notes into an intelligible language on a lined pad in longhand and fast communication to the RAF pilots grounded nearby. The listening stations adjoining air force bases allowed the RAF to engage the enemy fast and prevent their penetration into the British airspace, blocking some bombing operations. Deciphering the messages also served to gather information about the enemy's defenses, provided technical information for planning purposes, explained the operation of radio countermeasures, and gave information on enemy navigational aids. The relatively new technology of radio detection and ranging, or radar, allowed the recognition of aircrafts at distances of hundreds of miles, making it possible to discern friends from foes, the British Spitfires and Hurricanes from the German Messerschmitts and Junkers. Radar made it possible to get British planes in the air soon enough to intercept and engage enemy aircraft and shoot them down. It was a battle of wits. The ideal outcome was to capture the enemy pilots alive for interrogation, even rescuing them from the sea. The WAAF listeners' proximity to the field of action made them feel that their contribution to the war effort was not empty rhetoric and that what they did mattered.[19]

By joining the interception service, Ruth was promoted instantly to the rank of sergeant, and her pay was raised. She was sent to one listening station and moved periodically from one to another—Hawkinge, Canterbury, West Kingsdown—all located in Kent County in southeast England where the RAF had a major base that guarded the approaches to London.[20] It was territory familiar to Ruth because she had lived briefly after her arrival in England four years before. Then, she was thirteen years old; now she was eighteen and adapting fast to her new circumstances.

Each listening station was fitted so that technically it could carry out the interception of the Luftwaffe messages and conversations from as close a range as possible. Ruth's job description was a linguist, not trained in deciphering the enemy codes, which was the domain of the Government Code and Cypher School. However, women like her developed a sense for nuances in the language in which the German pilots communicated among themselves and with their ground controllers who guided their course, altitude, and orientation. With the linguists' help, the changing codes could be cracked because the German pattern of coding (such as girls' names or the names of birds) was not difficult to break. When a Luftwaffe pilot was captured and his plane recovered, it was a boon. He and the material found in the crashed aircraft such as diaries, letters, official and personal documents, were thoroughly examined and often provided vital intelligence of operational value about novel technology used aboard the planes, the Luftwaffe system of communications, and the mindset of the enemy. Some prisoners of war were persuaded to become collaborators with the British. Such intelligence was essential to the success in the war.[21]

With headphones clamped to their ears as they twiddled the dials on their sets day and night in six-hour shifts, the WAAF operatives logged every word, number, and message heard on the airwaves. "Berta, berta fünf," Ruth would later recall as one of the messages she jotted down and passed on to the officers standing on a platform in a big room, maps in front of them, and recording, interpreting, and taking action to intercept German bombers intending to attack targets in Britain. When the relayed message allowed a pilot to shoot down an enemy plane, a hooray resounded in the listening station.

On occasion, two or three women listening to the same frequency overheard several German men talking together. As they translated the messages into longhand, they might not have agreed on their meaning. They could not lose precious time debating the correct interpretation: only one rendition had to be passed to the squadron leader. One of them recalled, "We often got writer's cramp as we had to use some sort of shorthand in order to get everything we heard down on paper as quickly as possible, and if a pencil needed sharpening or would not write for some reason or another there was panic until we found another one. After 10 minutes of this scribbling, we had about 20 minutes to write it legibly and send off."[22]

After Ruth moved to the listening station, she could not maintain contacts with her friends in London; nor is it likely that she remained in touch with her father during this time. For over two years, she could not disclose where she lived and what she did. Ruth, like the other women working for "Y," may have had to sign the Official Secrets Act forbidding her from speaking about her wartime activities for thirty years. Despite all, she made new friendships in this otherwise hermetic world and with them created a family-like environment. There were not many opportunities to spend the money that the women received for their work, except on cigarettes, sweets, and makeup. It was there that Ruth started to smoke, becoming a chain-smoker for the rest of her life.

The Air Ministry was conscious of its duty and role as a guardian of its female recruits and its staff members did a great deal of thinking and writing about how best to take care of the WAAFs. The ministry encouraged sports: for example, bicycles became popular as a means for WAAF operatives to explore the local area. There was the occasional movie, concert, or drama performed by the same air force crews. At Christmas there were parties and charitable visits to children in hospitals. For relaxation there was a common room with a radio, a ping-pong table, and sometimes dancing. The women always had to appear in uniforms, which some thought put them at a disadvantage in relation to civilian women in printed frocks and high-heeled shoes. At the dancing parties, women usually outnumbered men. None of that bothered Ruth, who was proud of her uniform, which she wore as a WAAF for two and half years. She kept some of its elements at home in Prague for many years; it reminded her of some of the finest hours in her life.[23]

The WAAF women found it entertaining to eavesdrop on German pilots' private cockpit conversations during night shifts when there were few enemy pilots about. The listeners were privy to talk about girlfriends, what the pilots intended to do when their shift was over, a town they planned to visit. When bad weather prevented flying on both sides, the operatives tuned to the German U-boats off the east coast of Britain to eavesdrop on conversations about the marines' last meal ashore, which, one listener recalled, "made our mouths water; stories of their last hours spent with their women made our hair curl!" Such liberties were quickly snuffed out by the women's superiors.[24]

Being a linguist at an "Y" station was exhilarating as well as stressful. Earphones were part of the daily gear; some listeners developed ear problems. Nocturnal shifts were grueling. When off work, the WAAFs had to catch up on their sleep during the day. The mandated shift length was six hours, but if it happened to end when listening to a coded message was in progress, the work could not be interrupted and so the women might work overtime. After an exhausting stint, the operatives rested in a billet housing fifteen of them or more, where each had her own bed and a small side table. The wooden huts or brick barracks were usually cold, fuel being rationed. Bathrooms and toilets were located at a distance, with rats and mice running around. The washing and showering rooms were communal, and bath water was restricted. Men's and women's quarters were separate, and their segregation was enforced.[25]

In October 1943 the listeners were taught a new technique, dubbed "ghost voices," to intercept enemy conversations. The linguists tuned into the Luftwaffe frequencies and passed themselves off as the German flight command. Using high-power transmitters to reach far into enemy territory, specially selected men and women interfered with the Luftwaffe communications, giving the German pilots instructions to go to a certain altitude or transmitting false weather warnings to make them land. The pilots did what the supposed ground stations told them to do. Accents, nuances, cadences and local intonations in German were essential for the deception to work. Fake coordinates and false targets disoriented the pilots over the British Channel, fooling them into thinking that the land beneath them was Belgium and not Sussex. The feigned orders frequently made it possible for the British pilots to shoot down their adversaries. When the Luftwaffe flight command became wise to the trick, it issued new codes to their pilots and ground controllers, which had to be cracked all over again.[26]

Ruth served as one of the ghost voices. When relating her experience, she beamed. Sitting next to the British navigator who maneuvered to silence the German ground controller, using the German codes, Ruth instructed the Luftwaffe pilot to fly at such and such an altitude and to follow a particular course, so that the British flight pilot could get him. "The German planes flew to where I told them," she recalled.[27] One interviewer amazed by the story paused to ask Ruth, "Wait, so you navigated them against the British planes?" "Yes," Ruth replied. She navigated the German pilots so that the British could meet them and shoot them down. When interviewed during the 1970s, she recalled one such event:

> One particular day I was doing this and I was given a plane, incidentally the German girls on the other side, they would of course react to this because they would hear this and they would hear that there was another so called enemy voice on the same frequency and they would say, this is *eine Feindstimme, eine Feindstimme,* this is an enemy voice, an enemy voice don't listen to it don't listen to it, we again would say *wir sind die echte Stimme,* we are the real voice, listen to us so much so that in the end their pilot was completely confused and didn't know who was who but on that one occasion there was one Junker 88 flying over the channel, and I was given the exact course and height to lead him over the Isle of Wight, which I did and the captain said you know *fliegen Sie Honey achtzehn, caruso sechsundzwanzig,* things like that, and suddenly I lost touch with him, and that was that, and a couple of hours later I was told that the RAF station over the Isle of Wight got him down.[28]

Ruth repeated this larger-than-life story many times. She wanted to stress that her contribution to the war effort was real, that the dancing, the cinemas, and the boyfriends she missed were irrelevant in comparison to this vital work.

The War's End

The war was exhausting, debilitating, and the German military machine was gradually breaking. The combined might of the British and American forces, in tandem with the armies of the other western Allies, outweighed Germany in material resources even as the final outcome was still months away. Churchill's objective was not to kill every German but to bring the war to a victorious conclusion "at a cost tolerable to the British people." His second objective was to avoid the liquidation of the British Empire; the third, which was not evident at the time, was to ensure that the German threat to Britain was not replaced by the Soviet threat.[29]

The prime minister's latter concern was justified. The communists were emboldened by the "ten great victories" inflicted against the enemy in "ten crushing blows," as Stalin presented the evident Soviet military successes. For its part, the Czechoslovak government-in-exile considered the Soviet Union and its western allies' overpowering Germany as auguring peaceful coexistence after the war. President Beneš believed that Czechoslovakia had to line up behind the three dominant powers—Great Britain, the United States, and the Soviet Union—to guarantee its own independence and sovereignty to prevent another Munich. While the idea that the Soviet Union could become the determining force in postwar central

Europe was unacceptable to the Poles, Beneš welcomed such a scenario as a barrier against Germany. Furthermore, Beneš shared Stalin's long-standing interpretation of the war against Hitler as a pan-Slavic struggle against the traditional German enemy, given that the Slav states were predominantly the main victims of Nazi aggression. Indeed, in 1943 Stalin began to move in the direction of creating a political and diplomatic alliance with and among those states; significantly, his regime's propaganda stressed the necessity of Slavic unity.[30]

When President Beneš traveled to Moscow in December 1943 to sign the Soviet-Czechoslovak treaty of friendship, mutual aid, and postwar cooperation to offset the danger posed by Germany, not all of his allies agreed with his position. That much he did know. What he did not know was the degree to which the communists in London and Moscow were engaged together in implementing the postwar political course designed in the Soviet capital. He did not realize the extent to which they intended to block his intentions and to distort the meaning of the pact of collaboration with the Soviet Union, which promised to defend every inch of Czechoslovak sovereignty. He was aware that the Communist Party was a force to reckon with in postwar Czechoslovakia but had no idea of its intentions to wrest power from the president and his democratic ilk, with Soviet help.[31]

Before Beneš arrived in Moscow, the Czechoslovak communist leaders exiled in the Soviet capital had consulted with the Bulgarian Georgi Dimitrov, head of the recently dissolved Communist International or Comintern, through which Stalin had controlled communist parties in other countries. Dimitrov was Stalin's close and loyal subordinate, acting on his behalf during the negotiations with the Czechoslovaks. Dimitrov received Klement Gottwald, the leading Czechoslovak communist in Soviet exile and intermediary between the communists in England, Beneš, and the Soviets. He recorded, "To hear him talk, Beneš is quite radical. Acknowledges that the Com(munist) party of Czechoslovakia is the strongest party and ought to assume a leadership role in the future government." For their part, the communists were confident that Beneš was conveniently playing into their hands, but Dimitrov persuaded them otherwise: "To bear in mind that Beneš's sole aim is to tie their hands, to ensure that they will not have freedom of action during the destruction of Germany, and if he can, even to discredit them."[32] Anticipating Stalin's postwar regional arrangements, Dimitrov counseled the Czechoslovak communists to take advantage of the government-in-exile's favorable disposition toward them but to refuse collaboration with and participation in the current administration, with the intent of forcing the government to court them.

Even as these negotiations were going on, the end of the conflict was in sight. At the new year's dawn, the air war raged over Berlin. Germany was losing the occupied eastern territories and was anxious to retain the few allies it still had. Overall, one can only speculate about how much aggression the secret listeners had prevented by gathering timely information about the German planes and by helping stop the Luftwaffe pilots from penetrating British airspace. During the months of 1944, German raids decreased, finally ending in May of that year. Yet, unbeknown to the British, Germany was working on a new weapon of retaliation while the Allies were preparing to land in France.[33] Both events were etched in Ruth's wartime memories.

On June 6, 1944, the Allied troops landed at Normandy in northern France. Once they succeeded in breaching the German lines, penetrating the French interior in mid-July and liberating the Netherlands and Belgium from German occupation in the fall, the listeners heard less and less of the Luftwaffe commands from the English side of the Channel. Finally, they stopped hearing them altogether. The "Y" service activities had to be redrawn. However, the reorganization was complicated by the recent ominous German invention of the "flying bombs," the V-1, *Vergeltung* ("retaliation"). Their destructive nature stayed with Ruth for the rest of her life. Known also as doodlebugs for the buzzing noise they made, these bombs began to rain down on London and on other big cities in mid-June with the aim of causing devastating material damage and demoralizing the public. These pilotless planes, with their characteristic noise, became deadly when the noise stopped. The "buzz bombs" fell to the ground destroying anything and everything near their target, ending many lives and leaving craters twenty to thirty meters in diameter. The V-1 rockets were followed by the supersonic V-2 ballistic missiles with even more destructive effects; these bombs could not be heard until they exploded. Still, while they caused much material destruction, only about 20 percent reached the greater London area.[34]

The rockets were aimed at cities but were anxiously observed from the listening stations in Kent, which happened to lie in the "bomb alley." Because they flew at a low altitude, radar could not detect them, and so RAF could not stop them. But at the time of their launching, Germany was already short of manpower and the rockets were produced by a workforce that included malnourished prisoners of war and forced laborers; their destructive power ultimately made no strategic difference, in part because their manufacture was expensive and slow. By the end of the year, most German bases for the launching of the missiles had been captured.[35]

Paris had been liberated in August 1944, Belgium in September. Germany's loss of the Netherlands meant that interception stations in the south and east coasts of England could no longer intercept any planes, so the Air Ministry decided to move the operation to the continent. First, suitable and safe accommodation had to be found for the WAAF personnel; then, the receiving and recording equipment had to be moved to a suitable building and made operational. Ruth was relocated to recently liberated Brussels. She was given a hotel room, which must have been a luxury after sharing communal barracks. Most likely, this happened at the beginning of 1945. The new job required that she interrogate German prisoners of war, most of them Luftwaffe pilots shot down or U-boat crews rescued from the sea.[36]

When she later recalled sitting in front of the German military staff, interpreting their answers to a British Air Ministry intelligence officer's questions, Ruth did not remember the content of those exchanges: rather, she remembered her feelings as she faced the prisoners. By then, she knew of the war horrors inflicted on Jews and on the population in occupied territories. She recalled how she had to contain herself not to express the disgust that the conversations provoked in her: "One had a strange feeling. According to the Geneva convention every war prisoner was obliged to state his name, service number, and where he served. That was all. Of course, the English wanted to know much more. How many people there were, what was happening, what was their recruitment, that was what we interpreted. But it was a strange feeling because I was telling myself, good gracious these Germans are creeps, and I must treat them decently? For the English this was very important, to treat them decently, not rudely. I wanted to tell them all kinds of things. But I could not, I had to be decent."[37] The British interrogators wanted details: the type of war equipment the Germans used, their battle and service reminiscences, the economic conditions on the German home front, their politics, their religion, their personal matters, the names of military and Gestapo service personnel with whom they had come into contact. Even though some information was gleaned about the treatment of the Jews, the interrogations were geared chiefly toward finding out about crimes inflicted on Allied military personnel and atrocities against the civilian populations across the German-occupied areas.[38]

Intelligence was also garnered through bugging conversations among the prisoners. From such unguarded chats the British intelligence officers learned that the Germans were aware of their slaughtering Russians and Jews, of their brutal treatment; they also heard individuals admitting to having committed war crimes. The prisoners shared that even when they might have disapproved of such atrocities, they did not interfere or protest, fearing to endanger their positions. The intelligence reports noted a general lack of sense of personal responsibility: the Germans claimed that they simply obeyed orders. Few expressed any remorse. The information informed the advancing Allied forces about the mentality of the defeated Germans; after the war, it enabled them to pursue, indict, and try suspected war criminals.[39]

Only with time did Ruth become fully cognizant of her small (albeit important) role in lifting the lid on the German intentions and their secret air plans to destroy Britain, and of her part in contributing to saving lives and shortening the war. Like some other women, Ruth treasured the years spent as a "Y" listener as the most exciting of her life. While on the job, she acquired many skills. She perfected her command of languages and developed the knack for speedy and accurate interpretation as well as the craft of simultaneous translation; she learned that teamwork was indispensable and led to camaraderie among people working together for a common purpose. The long shifts as a listener turned her into an untiring worker capable of performing under pressure but also made her into an inveterate chain-smoker. Her sergeant's cap and epaulettes, which she kept in a drawer at home, reminded her of those times. She remained an intense personality, feeling as if she were living in urgency all the time. Life in exile and in war taught Ruth to be self-reliant. Work became central to her emotional and economic well-being. She became a practical person, not a philosopher. Wearing the same uniform as air force men, working alongside them without thinking about the issue of emancipation, Ruth always considered herself as an equal to men. In sum, maturing as a teenage refugee and then participating in the war effort steeled Ruth to deal with the existential trials that lay ahead.

In May 1945 Germany capitulated. The London monuments that had survived the German bombs were floodlighted. Delirious crowds thronged in front of Buckingham Palace. King George VI declared the end of the war. Winston Churchill stepped onto the balcony and solemnly announced, "Advance Britannia! Long live the cause of freedom! God save the King!"[40] Lancaster bombers flew overhead dropping red and green flares. But on victory day Ruth was not with her WAAF companions to celebrate. Instead, she was on a journey to look for her mother.

Part II

4

Life in Hell

All things considered, Anna was lucky that she entered the gates of hell a physically strong woman of forty, that she stayed in Terezín ghetto for as long as she did, and that she spent only a few weeks in the Auschwitz extermination camp, escaping death when she was loaded onto a slow-moving train to an unknown destination. After a few weeks of forced labor in ravaged Hamburg, Anna ended her torturous journey in Bergen-Belsen, where, at the end of the war, the Nazis dumped those prisoners who had not been either murdered or worn down by hardships and illnesses. The camp was liberated by the British army in April 1945. She survived.

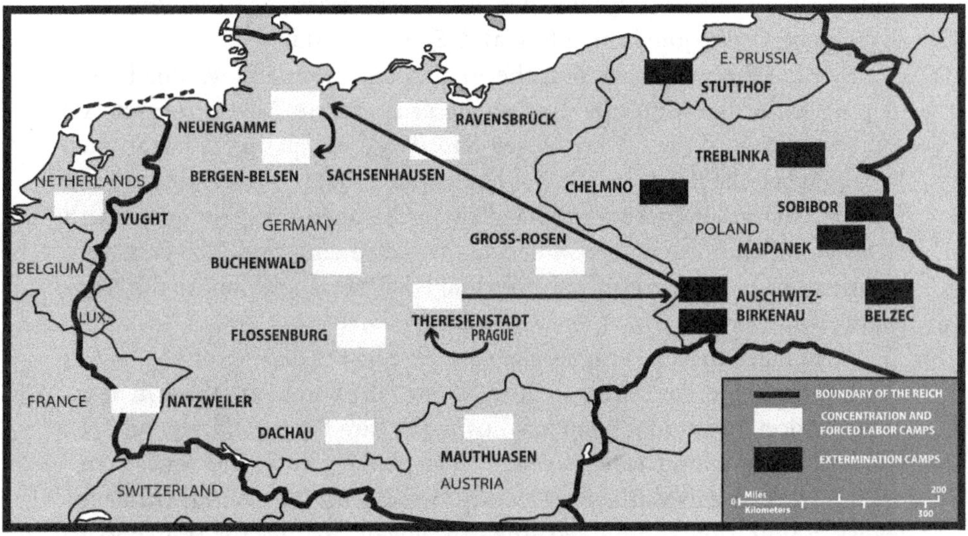

Map 2. Itinerary of Anna's journey from Prague to Bergen-Belsen, 1941–1945

The Departure

After Willi and Ruth left Prague in April 1939, Anka might have been looking for acquaintances willing to keep her possessions until normalcy returned. But moving about Prague was not easy. As early as May the protectorate government began to implement the ignominious anti-Jewish legislation. The order "Jews not allowed to enter" was posted in public places. This included parks, swimming pools, and public transport. Jews had to give up radio sets and dispose of their jewelry; anti-Jewish regulations included the cancellation of bank transactions and a ban on the transfer of property abroad (which had been possible just a few weeks earlier). Jews were allowed to shop only at particular shops and at particular times. Certain streets were off limits, and Jews could not transport household goods or go out at night. In July Jews were removed from public life altogether, as they could not hold jobs, appear in courts of law, belong to public organizations, participate in politics, perform before audiences, or teach in schools except Jewish schools. Finally, all Jews had to hand their businesses over to non-Jews.[1]

Anka had neither a job to lose nor a business to abandon. She corresponded with her family until September 1939, when Germany and the Soviet Union invaded Poland. The occupiers agreed that the dividing line would run along the River San in Przemyśl, the town where her parents lived—communicating across it was now impossible. Before communications between Anka and Willi ended as well, she managed to let him know that she wanted to join him in England. She never did.

By the time war broke out, the British relief workers who had been helping with migration matters left the protectorate. The European exit routes, used until then, were closed and illegal escapes were hazardous. By 1941, when the Reich authorities determined that Jews were not to leave Europe but rather to be ghettoized or imprisoned, roughly one fourth of Bohemia and Moravia Jews had managed to emigrate. The rest were trapped and at the mercy of the eventual Nazi "final solution" to the "Jewish problem."[2]

Anka failed to leave Prague; she may have had to depend on the Jewish community's care, consisting in the distribution of money to those in need, organization communal kitchens, hospitals, care for the elderly, schools, children's homes, and a labor exchange, all paid for by limited Jewish contributions. This existential uncertainty lasted until the Central Office for Jewish Emigration summoned Anka in November 1941 for transport to Terezín. By then the German authorities had added Sara to her name and the humiliating six-pointed badge, the Star of David, to her chest. It was a way to distinguish Jews from Aryans and to isolate them from friendly Czech neighbors; adding insult to injury, the Jewish community office was in charge of dispatching the transport slips.[3]

In Bondage

In northwestern Bohemia, Terezín had been transformed from a garrison for the Czechoslovak army to a civilian town and prison until the German authorities designated it a Jewish ghetto in 1941. Life in the town of over three thousand inhabitants, surrounded by homesteads, went on without much disruption until 1942, even while one of its parts was acquiring a sinister guise. Anka was selected for the first transport, GH 345, a week after the ghetto was set up in November. Her deportation followed on the heels of a construction team of several hundred able-bodied men sent to Terezín to prepare the basic living conditions for the delivery of Jews from the protectorate.

She arrived together with one thousand women, children, and men, disgorged at the closest railway station after a three-hour train trip from Prague. Bohušovice, the name of the place, was three kilometers (a little under two miles) from Terezín. From the railway end stop the hazed travelers slogged for several hours to reach the ghetto with heavy luggage. They were allowed to take fifty kilograms with them (about 110 pounds). Their carefully packed clothes, life mementos, and homemade pastries had to be given up on arrival under the gaze and command of the SS and the Czech gendarmerie; that is to say, their goods were stolen.[4]

On crossing the ghetto's ramparts into what was formerly a garrison of brick walls built in the eighteenth century to a star-shaped ground plan, the Jews became prisoners. The barrack assigned to them that cold November day was far from adequate: people had to sleep on the floor, there was no heating, sanitary, or medical facilities. Seeing the desolation, women set out to fill the bare spaces, basements, and attics, decorating the walls to make them resemble homes; men made beds, procured straw mattresses, hammered nails into the walls to hang the meager clothing, built latrines, and set aside rooms as sickbays. Over time, communal kitchens were set up to provide bare amounts of food and drink (including black water that resembled coffee). In an improvised kitchen in the first barrack and later in the barracks that were added to hold the ghetto's increasing population, women cooked meals to complement the unappetizing and insufficient potato and turnip soups and the undrinkable coffee for which one had to stand in long lines in any weather. Additional provisions of food were acquired by stealing, barter, on the black market, and—when the Czech gendarmes looked the other way—smuggling vegetables from the fields outside the ghetto, where Jewish women cultivated vegetables to feed the Germans. Through ingenuity and imagination, potatoes and potato peels could be transformed into cakes and birthday presents. But fresh protein and vitamins were unavailable; hunger was a fact of daily life, as were the bedbugs, fleas, lice, and dirt that added to the prisoners' misery.[5]

As 1941 rolled into 1942, more prisoners arrived—men, women, and children—not only from the protectorate but from Germany and Austria, from the Netherlands and Denmark. The ghetto sprawled, more barracks and houses had to be made available for the new arrivals and the local civil population had to be evacuated. Terezín became a so-called Jewish city, the Nazi alibi to divert the outside world's attention from the ghetto's penal conditions, diseases, malnutrition, and the occasional suicide. Then, thousands of its residents began to be moved to undisclosed destinations in the east.

The Germans let the ghetto be run by the Jewish elders, who required that the prisoners work, men chiefly in construction, women in cleaning, cooking, and agriculture. Terezín was run like a labor camp. The Jewish elders periodically drew the lists of people to be deported. The understanding was that as long as the Germans needed Jewish labor to contribute to their war economy, they would let Jews live in the ghetto. But work was important in other ways: it gave meaning and structure to the otherwise abnormal and humiliating existence of performing slave labor for the enemy while constantly facing death.

Work was the means to survival. Some jobs and positions meant better chances of privileged access to food, to better accommodation, and most importantly to the exemption from deportations. By design or luck, Anka worked in the ghetto as a nurse. Because doctors and nurses were indispensable, the Germans were more lenient toward them, and the Jewish elders could justify striking them from the transport lists. Conditions in the ghetto hospital were congenial due to the Germans' fear that epidemic diseases such as jaundice, typhoid, scarlet fever, pneumonia, or measles might spread to the rest of the population. But their spread was unavoidable in such an overcrowded and insanitary environment, in which medical attention did not reach everyone.[6]

One tool for survival in such a hostile environment was adaptation. This was easier for some than for others. Women were generally better equipped to make friends than men. A family was a vital support but fear of or actual separations due to deportations or premature death were causes of distress. Anka was alone, which might have been a blessing; she had neither her husband nor her daughter to lose. She was responsible just for herself and had the energy and time to care for others. The ability to communicate in this conglomeration of people from different countries speaking several languages was another asset. Anka had the advantage of being able to move seamlessly from one language to another, overcoming linguistic barriers. Well-versed in Czech, Polish, and German, the *Lager-spräche*, she spoke the languages of the majority as well as the language of the privileged few in power.[7]

Terezín inmates eagerly watched the progress of the war. As radio receivers were illegal and their owners persecuted, the prisoners obtained news from German sources. *Der Neue Tag* was the German newspaper in the protectorate. It was posted on billboards every day, acquainting the prisoners with the German version of events. After the German defeat at Stalingrad in February 1943 and the British and American triumphs in Sicily, the Germans stopped informing the ghetto's population of news from the front. But illegal radios and gossip from the Czech police and the Terezín grapevine filled the void. By 1943 the prisoners understood that the tide of war was turning against Germany and that conflict's end was in sight.[8]

By 1944, Anka was an old hand in Terezín. She had witnessed many instances of preparations for transports, seen people she knew register, pack and panic, gather at the assembling place or to hide, observed the heart wrenching goodbyes and despairs at family members' separations, and experienced the final departures and the emptiness after friends and acquaintances left.[9]

The Jewish elder in Terezín, Jakob Edelstein, the head of the Jewish Council (*Judenrat*), wrote in October 1942 a carefully worded letter to a friend in Geneva in which he intimated the harsh conditions in the ghetto. Gerhart Riegner, a delegate of the World Jewish Congress, received a copy of the letter and gave it to Karl Burckhardt, the chairman of the International Red Cross. By then, Hitler's order to destroy all the Jews was known. Since Burckhardt considered that protesting the treatment of the Jews was useless, he requested the German foreign office in Berlin to allow a visit by a Red Cross delegation to the Terezín ghetto and camps in Poland. This request proved to be a turning point for Terezín in general and for Anka specifically.[10]

Succumbing to the pressure from the Red Cross and the Danish government after the arrival of Danish Jews to Terezín, the German authorities sought to disguise the ghetto's harsh reality by refurbishing the town, humanizing its appearance. Part and parcel of the beautification of the ghetto was the deportation of the excess population, whose presence resulted in overcrowded dwellings, malnourishment, and all the symptoms of life lived in a prison. Commencing in December 1943, Terezín houses were painted and shops set up—their windows full of goods that had been stolen from the Jews on their arrival to the ghetto. There was a café where musicians who had not been deported yet played their repertoire; banks were opened and fake money circulated, grass was sown, a playground built, a cinema, a dancing hall, and a school arranged—all to counterfeit German civility.[11]

So that Terezín did not appear overcrowded and to make the hoax credible, in May 1944 several thousand ghetto inmates were moved east to where the Germans had been carrying out genocide of the Jews, unknown to the world, to the prisoners, or to the Red Cross. The ghetto commandant, Karl Rahm, rallied the selected men, women, and children for deportation to the courtyard of one of the barracks. "He stopped some of the deportees, questioned them about their work, and exempted them if their answers pleased him. Most of those he granted this favor were strong, healthy young men or handsome girls." Family members and friends watched this "gamble with human lives." Each transport waited for departure until it was complete. In the morning the prisoners selected for deportation marched to a waiting freight train. With the quota fulfilled, the doors shut, and the train left. Seven thousand five hundred and three souls left that May 1944. Anka was one of them.[12] The delegation visited Terezín and was duped as expected.

Oświęcim

The grueling journey from Terezín and the arrival at Auschwitz (as the Polish town Oświęcim was known in German), the scenes of shrieking SS men with hunting whips in hand, guns in their belts, and polished high boots, and furious frightening dogs unleashed on the prisoners have been described, evoked by witnesses, painted, and examined to the fullest. The transport that left Terezín on May 18 was not different from previous and subsequent transports: people crammed in a train like cattle; one pail with water at one end, and a waste pail to serve as a toilet at the other, humiliating and inadequate; fetid stench, thirst, and the travelers' groaning and howling.

Anka, packed in one of the cattle cars, traveled along the Bohemian border through what was then no longer Poland, reaching the gates of no return for millions the following night. The sign reading "Oświęcim," which stood side by side with the one announcing "Auschwitz," must have been familiar. Before the Germans turned it into a hell pit in 1942, it was a small Jewish town like any other she had passed by while growing up. To those who were close to the barred openings or cracked boards of the wagon, the smoke in the distance might have appeared like a factory, confirming that the prisoners were going to a work camp. The arrival dispelled any such illusion.

Prisoners from the Eb transport 467 were not shaved on arrival.[13] But like everybody else, they were dispossessed of anything of real or symbolic value. The rumor had it that the dwelling to which they were assigned was to be visited by the Red Cross delegation. In anticipation of such an inspection, the Germans had established a family camp in the summer of 1943 to give some semblance of normality. The delegation never arrived. Since there was no more need for the family camp, it was dismantled in the summer of 1944.[14] It is hard to imagine that the Red Cross visit could have taken place with smoke belching from the chimneys day and night and the stench betraying the camp's purpose to extinguish, not preserve life.

Anka must have heard Polish being spoken all around and become aware of Polish capos and female prisoners holding the upper hand—and the tattoo pen with which one of them scarred her left forearm. If Anka's fellow prisoner was tattooed with the letter A followed by the number 4116, hers could not have been much different.[15] The tattooing was done with a primitive tool that looked like a penholder with a thick needle at the end. The better the tattooist's handwriting, the more neatly tattooed the number. The operation was slightly painful and rapid, done as if on a conveyor belt. One's number was like a voucher to get bread and soup.[16]

The selection that followed was degrading. Women had to promenade naked in front of Nazis—men who held the power to decide whether the prisoners would live or die. Then came the bath. The newcomers may have been whispered to by the experienced prisoners that the faucets would shower either water or gas on them. Having emerged out of the bath alive, the inmates were hurried to their quarters in the family camp. Togetherness—the human contact, sleeping on the same bunk with someone one could trust—were fundamental for a person's relative well-being.[17]

But this humanness was constantly diminished by the brutalizing orders, bullying, mud, standing for hours at roll counts, and the incessant hunger and thirst. "Those roll calls! 'Alles zum Appell!' Jesus Christ, no, no," recalled one Czech survivor.[18] According to one commandant of the Treblinka extermination camp, the ruthlessness imposed— the whips, the shouting, the stripping naked of the new arrivals, forcing them to run—was devised for the benefit of the guards, to make them believe that the victims were not human beings and to prevent them from identifying with the prisoners.[19]

One had to learn quickly how to get ahead in Auschwitz. The Germans hated the Poles and were suspicious of any understanding between the German and the Polish prisoners. In turn, the Polish capos in the women's camp, who had been imprisoned as "antisocial" elements and aspired to move up the hierarchy, sought to ingratiate themselves with the Germans by subjecting the prisoners to harsh treatment. While Czech and German were the languages that dominated in Terezín, Polish and German were the languages of Auschwitz. "Knowing German meant life," wrote Primo Levi from his experience. Not understanding the orders meant that one could receive a punishment without knowing why. So, it might have been vital that Anka had mastered both. She understood Yiddish, another language spoken in the camp, which allowed her to broaden human contacts beyond the boundaries set by national origin.[20]

Being sent to a gas chamber was always a possibility, but Anka was assigned the task of distributing food. To gain such an advantageous position, one had to plot and struggle. The job consisted of carrying heavy wooden soup barrels hanging on thick wood or iron poles, laid across several women's shoulders. The casks contained bitter liquid with rotten potatoes, which was initially hot but could be cold by the time it reached the prisoners' blocks. The privilege lay in the fact that after the barrels were emptied, the women could dive into the containers to scrape whatever was stuck to the sides and the bottom. The distribution of food could be also hazardous, for it could happen that female prisoners would attack the transport of food pails while they were carried from the kitchen to the barracks. Bowls in which food was served were a valuable commodity, and people had to keep a constant eye on their own bowls to prevent them from being stolen. Without the containers, the prisoners were forced to eat the soup with their hands, and when too hot, the soup could not be scooped.[21]

Average life expectancy in Auschwitz was six months. People who had arrived in December 1943 were likely to be exterminated by June 1944. Thus, those who arrived in May 1944, like Anka, were optimistic. It was not their turn yet. Rumors circulated that Jews capable of work were to be sent to places where the Germans needed labor. People between fifteen and forty would be chosen. Older and younger groups would be excluded and exterminated.[22]

Anka became camp-wise, learning that one's age was a matter of life and death. It was then that she knocked two years off her age. In 1944 she was forty-three years old, a strong woman whose beauty might have been diminished by malnourishment and brutal living conditions, but good looking, nevertheless. It was a blessing that it was summertime, that cold was not another hardship oppressing the prisoners. On selection, Anka made it to a labor camp.

As Anka recalled later, one day in August 1944 (or it could have been July) she was loaded into a cattle car of a train with several hundred other inmates and moved westward toward Germany. It was escorted by army soldiers instead of the feared SS. Leaving Auschwitz was a miracle.[23]

Clearing Rubble

In devastating air raids in the summer of 1943, the American and British bombers destroyed most of Hamburg, demolishing its industrial districts. Then the RAF bombed Berlin to smithereens, destroying houses, killing people, raining explosives down on the government quarter, burning one building after another. Firestorms prevented people from leaving the air raid shelters, where many suffocated. To the Germans' disbelief Cologne and Munich followed.[24]

The military situation became dramatic. More and more men from the civilian sector were deployed on the front line, though never in sufficient numbers. Measures to draft labor into the Wehrmacht led to temporary lack of manpower in the armaments industry, which could not employ large numbers of unskilled workers. Some government officials recommended the employment of women, which other functionaries vehemently rejected. As the Nazis needed working hands, both non-Jewish and Jewish prisoners from the concentration camps in the east had to substitute the men drafted to the front line, even in the arms industry.[25]

Jews were still meant to be exterminated but the selections carried out in the camps served the purpose of saving the useful ones for work, despite the possibility, as one Nazi leader feared, "that every new work camp and every new group of a thousand of Jews selected to work would survive and be liberated."[26] At the same time, the annihilation of Jews continued due to the appalling living conditions in the labor camps, starvation, or bombing.

Anka and her cohort reached Hamburg after a few days of travel. The ruined city had several concentration labor camps attached to the port. The prisoners were moved from one to another, according to the needs in construction or in clearing rubble after bombing. The weather was getting colder and the clothes and shoes the prisoners wore were far from adequate. Being housed in silos, guarded by elderly Wehrmacht soldiers, was an improvement over the previous tyranny. The main enemies were hard labor and hunger, but above all the Allies' bombing attacks, from which there was no escape. The prisoners had no safe shelters, and it could happen that if they worked close to an armament factory targeted by the Allies for bombing, the danger was all the greater. Prisoners and their guards, huddled in shelters, could die together during an air raid.[27]

In a terrible irony, in faraway England Ruth served in the air force, which in the final throes of war was demolishing Hamburg and its vicinities, razing houses to the ground, and sacrificing human lives—the civilian population as well as German soldiers, the guards, and Jewish prisoners—while her mother was clearing the rubble caused by the sustained aerial bombardment and in danger of being an air raid casualty.

Survivor testimonies attest unanimously to the expressions of solidarity and compassion manifested by French and Italian prisoners of war and occasionally by German citizens, who were living in a dilapidated city but sometimes had access to food, water, and the basic necessities of life. The prisoners of war shared their meager food rations and sometimes their love with the Jewish women who were starved of both. Anka recalled finding morsels of bread hidden under a stone that a German left for her to discover at an opportune moment.[28]

In the company of other former Auschwitz inmates, mainly Czech women, Anka's work consisted in removing rubble after houses had been bombed and streets strewn with bricks and shrapnel, in filling holes caused by the air raids, repairing damaged pipelines, and digging trenches with shovels. The soup they received was one degree better than the previous hogwash, but far from filling. If the soup contained a whole potato, a piece of fish or meat, the women received it with gratitude, even if the meat was that of a horse. Yet hunger drove them to scavenge garbage piles in bombed middle-class neighborhoods and to collect cigarette butts, which they rolled in whatever paper they could find to swap later for a piece of bread if they did not smoke themselves. Stealing became another survival skill. Nevertheless, the prisoners' endurance was eroding.[29]

The next camp in which Anka had to face the prospect of annihilation, whether through hard labor, bombing, hunger, or brutal treatment, was in Hamburg-Tiefstack. But in March 1945 the camp suffered a heavy air raid, leveling to the ground anything that had still been standing. The Tiefstack prisoners were put on trains and moved to the next station. It was early April 1945. The train moved by fits and starts until it reached its destination: Bergen-Belsen. "The ghoulish sight that greeted them topped anything they had seen to date."[30]

Deliverance

Sometime in the middle of April 1945 Ruth was on leave in London. As usual, she went to the Czechoslovak-British Friendship Club, which had become the cultural and social oasis for the refugees and the military on a break. A telephone rang, A woman asked for Mr. Ornstein, who was not there. Ruth came to the phone, and the woman on the other end of the line said that her husband (a soldier in an American military unit) knew Ruth's father, and the husband had overheard that there was a sizeable group of Czech women in the recently liberated concentration camp Bergen-Belsen; perhaps Ruth's mother was one of them?

Ruth had thought that her mother was dead. As previously described, in Anka's last, mysterious letter to Ruth's father, Anka wrote that she was going to be with her parents but would not live in their house. The message did not make sense at the time. It was written most likely from Terezín before Anka was deported to Auschwitz in May 1944 and delivered to the family through the Red Cross. By 1945 enough was known about the extermination camps in Poland for Ruth and her father to conclude that Anka had been murdered. But in April 1945 she decided to find out for herself. She went back to her WAAF unit and was given all the facilities to travel within twenty-four hours to a place few knew anything about.[31]

In her WAAF uniform, Ruth flew first to Brussels. The local RAF office arranged her flight to Celle, which was close to the concentration camp and where the British army had set up its military headquarters after arriving at a truce with the Wehrmacht. On Ruth's arrival to surroundings devastated by repeated Allied bombing, the local field rabbi arranged for an automobile to take her to the camp. The trees along the way bore the announcements *Achtung typhusgefahr*—Danger typhus—and white flags with black skull-and-crossbones. The English driver soon excused himself, let Ruth off, and drove away. With a military khaki sack on her shoulder, Ruth, not yet twenty years old, walked toward one of the barbed-wired gates of Bergen-Belsen.[32] From circumstantial evidence, it seems that Ruth reached the camp in early May, three weeks after British and the Canadian military personnel had first entered the decaying compound. She was spared the worst.

When on April 15 the army officers approached the camp, they were numbed by what unfurled before their eyes: thousands of prisoners, dead and alive, lying about in filth or naked, in pools of urine and excrement, bodies tangled and heaped outside or in reeking huts, creeping and crawling skeletons covered in parched skin, emaciated faces, shaven heads, sunken eyes, some hanging on the barbed wire, sitting, or standing listlessly. There was no food, water, or electricity. Rotten turnips lay scattered in the cookhouses. Through a megaphone, one British officer let the internees know "that food and water were on their way, the German rule in the camp was over and that we were doing everything in our power to relieve their misery."[33]

Restoring electricity, bringing in food and administering it, reconnecting the water pipelines, and burying the dead were the army's priorities. Urgent medical attention was provided initially by the Royal Army Medical team, though not in sufficient numbers and capability. Due to lack of hygiene and water, the camp was infested with lice and typhus raged throughout. Inmates kept on dying. German and Hungarian soldiers—men and women who had not fled the camp—were put to work burying the dead in mass graves and washing the inmates from weeks of neglect for which they bore the responsibility.[34]

Inmates with sparks of life in them were stunned by the sudden change in the color of the soldiers' uniforms. Their disbelief was interspersed with gratitude. Those who felt strong enough ventured to survey the camp and approached the gate; some stormed a locked warehouse, taking in haste anything that could be of use. Much of the provision they found was rotten. As food was brought to the camp and prepared, the fittest inmates raided the kitchens at mealtimes, people begging and endeavoring to steal food and take it to the huts. Under the circumstances, devouring any kind food could be fatal. Discipline was necessary. People who had survived could take a turn for the worse and die in the arms of friends and family with whom they had undergone the dreadful journey from the beginning.[35]

An all-male team of British medical students arrived at the end of April. They were billeted in a barrack, one mile distant from the camp, previously occupied by the camp guards. "We were shown our barracks and told that tea would be ready in the Officers Mess at 5 o'clock." The tea was sumptuous: "white bread, margarine and jam and we were waited on by the Hungarian Army waiters."[36] Each doctor was assigned to a hut to administer food with extreme care because the inmates' empty and starving stomachs could not hold anything but a dietetic nourishment. Some people were beyond medical help. SS barracks outside the camp were turned into hospitals while German nurses among others were tasked with disinfecting and washing the patients. Wrapped in clean blankets, they were moved to the makeshift hospital. The job was overwhelming. As more and more inmates left the camp, the huts were gradually burned down with the Nazi flags and Hitler's portraits, while the Union Jack went up. As the former inmates were provided with decent clean clothes and surrounded by compassion, people's dignity began to be restored. Women returned to womanhood as their breasts grew back and they menstruated again. Many put their skills to work as soon as they recovered some strength; a Romanian tailor and a Czech hairstylist sold their talents "for the price of 15 cigarettes and much talk."[37]

Ruth arrived at the entrance gate of the camp where the administration block was located. By then, the heaps of the dead bodies that had piled up had been interred. Ruth approached the British soldier on duty. Could he inform her whether a woman by the name Anna Ornstein might be there? The soldier threw up his arms in despair. Thousands of nameless inmates had been dying every day; he would not know; a person might be listed one hour and dead the next because of the widespread typhus.

A young woman in a fairly good physical condition standing nearby the gate overheard the conversation. She was slightly older than Ruth and must have known English. Was Ruth looking for Anna Ornstein, Anka, the wife of Willi from Prague who lived at an address she named? Ruth was flabbergasted. The young woman's name was Markéta Druckerová, or Marieta. Twenty-six years old or so, she was Czech and knew many details about Anka's life. They had been together since Terezín. Anka had became her substitute mother, they had looked after each other. Yes, Anka was in the camp.[38]

Marieta led Ruth to a hut shared by other women. Ruth was in shock at the prospect of seeing her mother alive. Marieta asked her to wait outside while she went in to prepare Anka, who had been weakened by typhus, for the news. She feared that Anka's surprise at seeing her daughter might kill her. Marieta entered the dwelling. Ruth overheard her conversation with someone whose hoarse voice she did not identify as her mother's. Marieta invented a story about a group of nurses that had arrived from England and suggested that perhaps Ruth could be among them. Anka did not see why her daughter could be a nurse and why should she be in Bergen-Belsen? The conversation went back and forth; Ruth lost her composure and barged into the hut.

Ruth did not recognize her mother, but Anka recognized her daughter and fainted. A Belgian medical woman doctor was on hand and brought her back to consciousness with an injection. Anka weighed some forty odd kilograms (around eighty-eight pounds), her hair had turned white; she had no teeth and was emaciated to the bone. At forty-four years old, she looked haggard. In Terezín Anka had worked as a nurse, which postponed her deportation; in Oświęcim she distributed soup, which allowed her extra helpings; in Hamburg she cleared ruins with her bare hands while bombs rained all around without hitting her; and in Bergen-Belsen she collapsed from exhaustion, malnutrition, and typhus.

Ruth and her mother had not seen each other for six years; the last time, Ruth had been a thirteen-year-old girl. In interviews, Ruth reproduced the first conversations between the two as something like this: "Where's father?" "In London." Did Ruth have a photo of him? Ruth did. Anka looked at the photo and exclaimed, astonished, "Good heavens, he aged." Ruth smiled in amazement: evidently, Anka had not seen herself in a mirror. Did Ruth have any civilian clothes? Ruth did. She had a brown twinset in her soldier's sack. Anka put it on, it flapped around her thin body, but never mind; did Ruth have lipstick?[39]

The news that Ruth had found her mother was a sensation. The British officers also thought it a miracle and invited Ruth and Anka for an afternoon tea. Nothing to worry about, they would offer her only suitable food in the officers' canteen—neither the white bread that Anka craved so much, nor smoked meat. Tea was served. Anka was beside herself at seeing the variety of food and the color of the fruit. She spied some spring onions on a nearby table, which were not on offer. Anka confessed to Ruth later that the onions were so beautiful that she could not resist taking them. Ruth was embarrassed.[40]

It was May, the weather was warm. Ruth and her mother strolled under the tree canopies and talked. Anka told her about the soup she carried on the wooden poles, about the strange smell in Oświęcim, about the transports that kept on arriving and the people who kept on disappearing in the gas chambers, about holding on to the hope that she would be spared. As she talked, her eyes were glued to the ground. Whenever she spotted a cigarette butt, she picked it up. Ruth offered Anka whole cigarettes (as a soldier, she had plenty). But used to scavenging, Anka thought it was a waste to leave such nice butts lying on the ground.[41]

Ruth accompanied her mother during the initial convalescence in a hospital outside the camp until it became clear that Anka needed thorough rehabilitation. Count Folke Bernadotte, a former businessman and army officer who headed the Swedish Red Cross, organized a rescue mission of some seven thousand former prisoners of Bergen-Belsen. Before returning to England to cheers by Vilém and friends and to her unit, Ruth saw to it that her mother would be taken to Sweden. In a better physical condition than others who had to be carried on stretchers, in July 1945 Anka left Bergen-Belsen by train for the port of Lübeck and by ship to a Swedish sanatorium. She did not have time to correct her date of birth and traveled to Sweden officially two years younger than she was.

Medical care, good food, clean bed, a soap, a hairbrush, and kindness restored Anka's health.[42]

Both the British army and Ruth helped to deliver her mother from the nightmare brought about by Anka's mistaken calculations made in 1939, when nobody had any idea what was in store for the Jews in general and for her personally. Anka survived because of her ingenuity, friends' support and affection (Marieta's especially), and ability to adapt to the severe, humiliating, and pitiless conditions. How she faced the threat of extermination, we don't know. It was a blessing that Anka went through the rings of hell on her own and that the suffering of other family members did not add to hers. The occupations she was assigned in the camps were serendipitous. And when Anka was at her lowest point, Ruth appeared, restoring her mother's dignity and womanhood. Unlike millions of displaced people who had no idea where to go after the war, what place to call home, Anka did. Ruth's presence helped to tie together the broken ends of her life, and Willi's photograph validated that there was life after hell.

5

Sailing to Palestine

Kurt Groll was Ruth's first husband and my father. His background and wartime experience were similar to those of the family into which he married after the war: the Jewish experience of painful emigration, separation from parents and sister, and wartime tribulations. He grew up during the waning years of the Austro-Hungarian Empire in Valašské Meziříčí, a small town in southern Moravia sitting at the foot of a mountain range with two rivers meandering down its side. Kurt began to learn the alphabet around the time that World War I began. His father, Hynek, in peacetime a clerk for a glassmaking firm, was drafted into the army during his late thirties. The family—Kurt's mother, Olga, and Anna, a younger sister—lived frugally on a soldier's pay. When the war ended, Hynek returned home from the front with broken health, resuming his old job. Though he had served in the Austro-Hungarian imperial army, his loyalty to the newly created sovereign state of Czechoslovakia was unwavering. On every May Day, Hynek put a red carnation into his jacket buttonhole to make a statement of allegiance to its social-democratic ideals.

Kurt attended primary and secondary schools in his hometown. He spoke Czech and German, acquired a smattering of English, and developed love for books and music. Spinoza's humanistic philosophy and Goethe's *Faust* were his favorite readings; he played tunes from Beethoven's symphonies on a mouth harmonica and whistled melodies from Antonín Dvořák's operas with his sister. The town's enlightened populace cherished good education for men and women, economic prosperity, and parliamentary liberalism. Its Jewish population comprised a negligible 4 percent amid the Catholic majority. Being Jewish was a fact of life; Kurt was not brought up either to deny it or to cultivate it. The family paid membership dues to the local Jewish community and attended the synagogue services on high holidays. Certainly, anti-Semitism existed in Valašské Meziříčí. The most shocking manifestation took place in 1899 when

FIGURE 4. Kurt with his sister, Anna, in Valašské Meziříčí during the 1920s.

its synagogue was vandalized. But even as anti-Semitism intensified in Czechoslovakia during the 1930s, echoing German anti-Jewish propaganda, Valašské Meziříčí lay on the outskirts of these developments. If poverty and anti-Semitism were the main ingredients fostering Zionism, Kurt had not suffered either of them.[1]

A man of great intelligence, Kurt was a pleasure-seeker who had neither the discipline nor the interest to pursue a formal career. He studied law but not enough time to graduate. Around 1931 he moved from the provincial Valašské Meziříčí to the cosmopolitan Prague. Apart from music, work was his lifelong passion, negotiating with clients, selling, and buying anything that made profit. His business occasionally took him out of the capital city, though never abroad. Kurt was a short, thin man, with round glasses correcting his nearsightedness; his gray-blue eyes were set in a cleanly shaved oval face and with prematurely receding brown hairline. In normal times he never left home without carrying a briefcase. When in March 1939 the Germans occupied Czechoslovakia, Kurt was a thirty-year-old bachelor.

Departure

Kurt did not apply for a passport until May 1939. Once he obtained it, he sought an exit permit and a visa to emigrate. Where to, we do not know. Leaving the protectorate was a cumbersome process even though between 1939 and 1941 the Nazis preferred to "solve" the "Jewish question" by emigration—and if that did not proceed fast enough, by expulsion. He must have planned his departure in detail; in anticipation of leaving the protectorate and before the Germans prevented the transfer of property and money abroad, the business savvy Kurt sent whatever possessions and savings he had to a storage facility and a bank in Italian Trieste. However, the outbreak of the war in September found him trapped in the protectorate.

What kept Kurt in mutilated Czechoslovakia for so long? After the Munich Agreement and the German annexation of the Sudetenland at the end of 1938, Jews were subjected to hysterical anti-Semitic propaganda coming from Germany and adopted by the Czech and Slovak fascists. In these circumstances, and especially after the entire country was incorporated into the Reich, Jews who had the means, connections, and courage sought to leave their homeland. Owing to the Nazi "racial" laws, Kurt may have lost his job as a clerk in the insurance company in which he was employed. Did he postpone his departure because of his mother, his ailing father who had to retire prematurely from his job and would die in 1941, and his younger sister? He may have lacked the necessary documents and the money to pay the taxes and fees that the German authorities demanded before granting the exit permit, or he may have been unable to procure a visa to a country of his choice. He must have known that the Nazis wanted to make the lives of the Jews as unbearable as possible so that they would have no choice but to leave while at the same time creating unsurmountable obstacles for their departure.[2]

By the summer of 1939, emigrating to Palestine was an option, whether legally or illegally. But that choice was enmeshed in a maelstrom of personal, national, and internationaldecisions and calculations. To make Europe free of Jews, the Reich authorities facilitated Jewish emigration to Palestine but demanded a high price for it. In addition to the bureaucratic rigmarole imposed on the applicants, Jews seeking to leave were required to forsake their property and money. Young people could take off more easily than the elderly, who hesitated to leave the lives they had always known. As a result, families were separated. Worse, by 1941 the borders of the occupied territories were sealed.

The British, who had governed Palestine since the breakup of the Ottoman Empire during World War I, oversaw immigration to the territory, issuing certificates to control the Jewish entry for economic and political reasons. Starting in January 1939, they began limiting the growth of the Jewish population to appease the local Arabs who opposed it. War was in the air and the British sought to placate the Arab populace, which had rioted before and could do so again, as locals feared becoming a minority and believed their existence was endangered by the influx of Jews and their demand for more land. Furthermore, they feared that the Arabs both in Palestine and the neighboring Arab states might refuse to support and assist the British in wartime. Prime Minister Neville Chamberlain wrote in April 1939 that from a strategic viewpoint, it was preferable to offend the Jews rather than the Arabs.[3]

The Arab-Jewish conflict had a long history. As World War I drew to a close in 1917, the British government promised the Jewish community in Palestine that it would endorse the creation of a Jewish homeland without jeopardizing the civil and religious rights of the existing non-Jewish communities. The Palestinian Arab population comprised 91 percent of the roughly seven hundred thousand people living in the territory, while the Jews were a growing minority by way of immigration, hoping to overcome their marginality. The Arabs had consistently rejected the project of a Jewish homeland as an independent state. The animosity between the two groups grew, with the Jews acquiring some of the best agricultural land in Palestine and with it an economic preponderance. Between 1936 and

1939, the Palestine Arabs revolted against the British Mandate's policies favorable to the Jews, attacking Jewish life and property, which prompted the British to train Jewish military units and to authorize the creation of a Jewish defense force. All parties involved sought different political and religious solutions, involving issues such as the access to holy places and the protection of Jewish and other minorities' rights in Palestine. Contradictory promises had been made and various proposals were hatched. Partition of Palestine into two parts was one, the creation of two separate states was another, but neither the Arabs nor the Jews could agree on the terms. Another plan was the creation of a single state for Jews and Arabs, but the looming war put an end to further negotiations and led to more restrictions on legal immigration.[4]

One branch of the Jewish nationalists, the radical Zionists, considered control and suspension of immigration to be a betrayal of the British promise to create Jewish homeland in the land of their ancestors. As such, the Zionists ignored the law that regulated immigration and set out to organize unauthorized transports to Palestine. In response, the British subtracted from the quota of legal entry an indeterminate number of entry certificates to make up for the illegal entrants. In addition, failing to appreciate the extent to which German policies drove Jews to Palestine, Britain determined that no German Jews could emigrate to British territories, alleging that they were enemy aliens and that the Nazis were planting spies among the refugees. By 1939, the excluded category comprised all Jews from the territories occupied by the Reich, including Czechoslovakia.[5]

For its part, the Yishuv (the Jewish community in Palestine) and the Jewish Agency that governed it expected the arriving Jews to strengthen its numbers in anticipation of creating the Jewish homeland, realizing the ancient dream that one day the destroyed Jewish Temple would be rebuilt. Initially at least, the Jewish Agency opposed the illegal immigration promoted by the Zionists for fear that it might upset the balancing act between the Palestinian Arabs, the British, and the Yishuv's project to create a Jewish state. It took some time before the agency came to appreciate the danger that the German aggression posed for the European Jews. The war and the news from the refugees recounting Jews' suffering in concentration camps changed the Yishuv's position toward the illegal immigration, accepting it as the means to combat both immigration restrictions and British policy even as the community hoped this would not to endanger its safe standing in Palestine.[6]

Zionists of different ideological hues were the prime organizers of the "aliyah" (literally "ascent," in reference to the immigration to the Holy

Land), and when that was curtailed, of clandestine voyages, or aliyah bet, to rescue the Jews from the territories occupied by Germany. They refused to abide by the British immigration regulations because of their conviction that Palestine belonged to the Jews. In that they agreed with the Jewish community. The Zionists had no patience either for British imposed quotas or for the cautious Yishuv leadership's opposition to their endeavor.[7]

Topping the series of contradictions was Germany's favorable attitude toward emigration to Palestine, not only as a way of expelling the Jews from Europe but also as a means of provoking both Jewish and Arab animosity toward His Majesty's government. As such, Germany supported the organizers of the illegal voyages until 1941.[8] Finally, there were the European Jews, urgently seeking to escape from the Nazi onslaught on their countries, who became beneficiaries as much as scapegoats of these political machinations, which they often did not know about or understand.

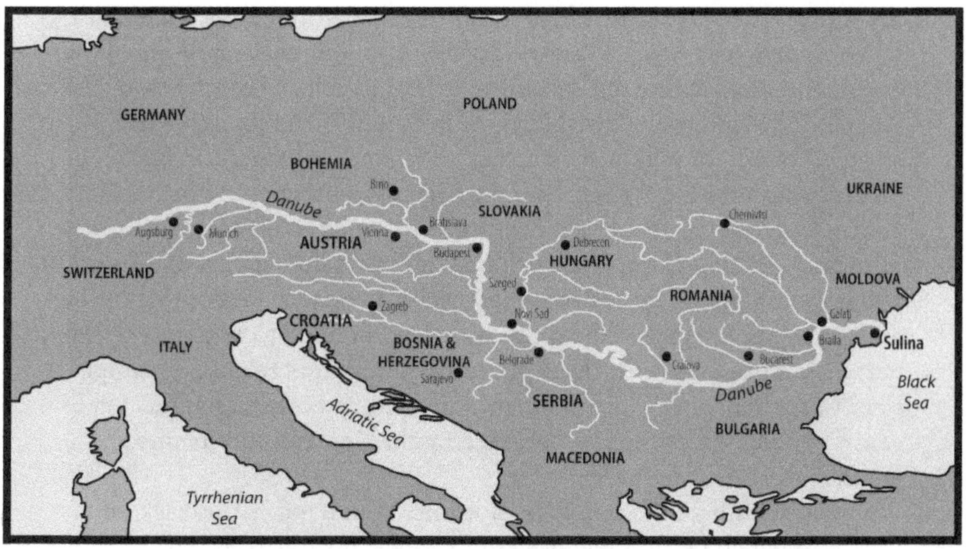

MAP 3. The flow of the Danube River from Germany toward Romania and its delta at the Black Sea

The Danube Route

This was the environment in which the Zionist organizers of the clandestine journeys to Palestine operated in 1939 to get as many Czech, Slovak, Austrian, German, and Hungarian Jews as possible out of the Nazi reach. After the British Parliament had approved the establishment of a trust fund for the Czechoslovak refugees, a portion of which was destined for the emigration to Palestine, leaving the protectorate was contingent on the Gestapo's exit permits and the British immigration certificates. Preference was given to wealthy Jews who could bring money to invest in Palestine. The Zionists already settled in the British Mandate favored Jews who were willing to live under the harsh conditions in a territory reputed primitive by European settlers' standards. In Prague the most energetic and committed organizers were the Zionists, while the smugglers of the human cargoes found an opportunity to make money. To get the job done, all had to collaborate with the German authorities to procure the exit permits. The Jewish religious community in Prague was ordered to coordinate the emigration.[9]

Kurt was not a Zionist—he was not politically active at all—but being a Jew qualified him to enlist into a transport out of the protectorate to Palestine. His avowed goal for emigration was to join an army to fight the war on the side of the Allies. He registered with the Jewish emigration authority in Prague's Palestine office, the body that represented the emigrating Jews before the Zentralstelle für Jüdische Auswanderung (the German head office for Jewish emigration), which had the last word. His effort to emigrate took place against enormous bureaucratic odds. The process was humiliating because of the harsh treatment to which the applicants were subjected, being compelled to commit themselves to never returning, leaving all property behind, collecting documents of all sorts, and standing in line for hours at the Gestapo headquarters for them to be authenticated. The Palestine office was then on hand to arrange the exit permits and to help with the organizational matters relative to emigration. Compliance with the German bureaucracy cost the hapless applicants a good sum of money, pocketed by the Gestapo and its unscrupulous helpers.[10]

Finally, with all the necessary documents in hand, a rucksack on his back into which he fit a few pieces of clothes, his toiletries, possibly the harmonica that was his lifelong companion, and a blanket, and wearing high boots as the voyage organizers prescribed, Kurt gathered with several hundred men like him at the main railway station in Prague at an appointed time and day in late October 1939. After being thoroughly inspected, they boarded a train that took them to Bratislava, the capital of the fascist Slovak state, where Jews were not welcome. Accommodated in a warehouse that to one of the refugees looked like a prison because they were not allowed to come and go at will, eight hundred bodies to the count, they waited for several weeks before undertaking the next leg of the journey. Though they were well-fed and not mistreated, the uncertainty of what was to come next was unnerving.[11]

War had broken out. The only option for travel to Palestine was the Danube River, an international waterway with no passport controls and no visas required. The mighty river gathered mountain waters in the German Black Forest, then flowed through several countries before draining into the Black Sea in Romania. Invisible borders separated Germany from Austria, Czechoslovakia from Hungary, Yugoslavia from Romania.

One day, with no prior warning, the refugees were led to the river port in Bratislava and put on the *Spyroula*, a holiday boat with a German crew and a swastika flag flying on its mast. It was a relief that the boat floated down the stream from Bratislava and not up to Vienna. The refugees left the Slovak capital in early November. They sailed past Budapest, then Belgrade, finally reaching the Iron Gate, a gorge on the Danube River that divided the Carpathian and the Balkan Mountains, forming part of the invisible boundary between Serbia and Romania. The boat had a capacity for two hundred and fifty passengers but eight hundred were squeezed on board. The line for the toilet was so long that many relieved themselves into the Danube instead. The boat glided down the river, stopping at different ports along the way where the passengers begged for food and the local Jews obliged, while Austrian, Hungarian, and Romanian refugees pleaded to join those on board. By the time they reached the Danube delta, several hundred more crammed the boat. It reached the Romanian port of Sulina on November 22, just as the fall was turning into winter.[12]

Sulina was a small settlement, surrounded by marshes and swamps and covered in groves of willow trees. The nearest railway station was forty miles up the river, so supplies for the population had to be transported from the station on horse-drawn carts and on sledges in winter. When the *Spyroula* reached the port, another boat, the *Saturnus*, had already docked there. Between the two, over one thousand women, men, and children converged around the river outlet, way beyond what the local conditions could bear. The expectation was that they would soon be on a seaworthy ship for the final crossing to Palestine.[13]

The two untiring organizers of the voyages to Palestine in the fall of 1939 were Eri Jabotinsky and Wilhelm Perl. Eri, born in 1910, was the son of the world-renowned Zionist Vladimir Jabotinsky, known for his 1938 quote "eliminate the diaspora or the diaspora will eliminate you," and of Ania Gelperin. Born in 1880 to a Russian Jewish family in Odesa, Vladimir lived variably in Palestine, Rome, Paris, and London, separated from his wife and son for long stretches at a time. Jabotinsky was a staunch defender of the Jewish homeland in Palestine, knowing full well that the British opposed it. He passed along to his son his Zionist convictions, including the belief that one should disregard borders and anything else that kept Jews from Eretz Israel. This also made him stand by his determination to remain stateless until he could become the citizen of a Jewish state when one was created. What the British called illegal, Eri and the radical Zionists called free immigration. Despite having lived in Palestine with his parents on and off, Eri did not become a Palestinian citizen until the summer of 1939. This status helped him to travel freely as he worked to get as many Jews there as possible, scouring Europe to raise money and awareness of the Jewish plight.[14] Eri was successful most of the time, even at the cost of personal safety.

Perl was born in Prague in 1906; he became a lawyer in Vienna with a degree in international business but put his profession on hold. He joined the Zionist movement and became an active antifascist, close to Vladimir Jabotinsky. To achieve an independent Jewish state became the goal of his life. If he needed to team up with Greek smugglers or with private travel agencies that had sprung up to traffic Jews so that they could leave for Palestine, so be it. One of the shady figures who participated in this endeavor was Robert Mandler, a businessman originally from Austria, who aided Perl and Eri Jabotinsky in the emigration of Jews from Prague but failed to save his own life. After he had collaborated with the Gestapo in getting the Jews out of the protectorate, helping himself to some of the proceeds from the payments they were forced to make to receive exit permits, he was deported to Terezín and murdered in Auschwitz.[15]

Full of energy and with a sense of humor, Eri achieved remarkable success in his organizing efforts. In the fall of 1939, he resided in Bucharest, Romania's capital, which had the advantage of sitting midway between where the Jews were and where they were going. From there, he was able to oversee the deals with shipping companies to secure riverboats as well as the sea ships. Jabotinsky and Perl worked together to get the Jews out of Prague, Vienna, Berlin and Budapest to the Romanian port and from there to Palestine, although at times the collaboration was overwhelmed by personal squabbles and jealousies. The endeavor could also be a financial risk: because of the possibility of fraud by unscrupulous shipowners or middlemen, money that had been laboriously raised could be lost overnight.[16]

At the end of November, the temperature in Sulina fell drastically, but the ship to take the refugees from Romania to their anticipated destiny had not arrived. The leadership of the venture deliberately withheld from the refugees the misfortunes that befell the organizers. The Danube froze and life on the barges without heating was trying. The able-bodied men broke the ice to access water. To alleviate the problem, the organizers of the scheme hired the riverboat *Stefanu*, which was not fit for travel but had heating. Women and children were transferred there. A third boat, the *Grien*, arrived from Hungary at the end of December, adding another five hundred or so human beings to those already in Sulina.[17]

The riverboats were not suitable for seafaring; meanwhile, wartime imposed restrictions on the use of seaworthy ships. Only vessels retired from service because of age or poor conditions were available to the Zionists, but these required repairs and refitting for use as passenger ships. Prices to hire them soared. The aliyah activists were at the mercy of shipping agents, owners, fair or not, and had to bear the costs of delays or failure when a ship was damaged or did not appear as agreed. At the behest of the British, the Balkan governments pressured shipping companies not to cooperate with the activists so as to prevent the passage of Jewish refugees to Palestine. In addition, shipping agents, captains, and crews became hard to hire as they were alerted to the British seizing ships off the Palestine coast, arresting crews and confiscating ships. Shipowners had to weigh the advantage between the greater profit from trafficking Jews or the safety of engaging in less lucrative legitimate trade. To counteract the strict controls on shipping, the organizers of the voyages to Palestine approached neutral countries to allow them to register ships as their vessels and fly their flags. Competition among the organizers—trying to accomplish the same goal for the same people—caused further delays and led prices to soar.[18]

The year 1939 rolled into 1940. According to Eri Jabotinsky's plan, on arrival to Sulina a ship would take the riverboats' passengers on board and set sail. Instead, his lieutenants were busy taking care of the day-to-day survival of between fifteen hundred and two thousand women, men, and children on three boats, while he was searching for additional funds to pay for the hire of the SS *Sakarya* for which he had already made a deposit. In fact, the ship had arrived off the coast of Sulina on December 10, but the owners refused to leave until Eri and his associates met an increased price.

The cold was affecting the refugees' health. Some people suffered frostbites; Kurt, like most men of his age, endured the icy weather with fortitude. Dysentery broke out but because it was winter, the passengers were at least spared malaria. By some arrangement, the *Sakarya*'s owners allowed close to eight hundred women and children to board the vessel. Being a coal carrying ship, it was not fit to transport human beings. First, inches of thick coal dust had to be removed, and sleeping galleries, kitchens, stairs, lavatories, and larders had to be built to render it fit for the refugees.[19]

High-level British functionaries were aware that Jews in flight from the German occupation of their homelands were marooned in Sulina. The case attracted publicity in England through the vigorous protest made by Vladimir Jabotinsky in London, who pleaded with the Foreign Office to lift "the Palestine ban." Life on the boats in Sulina was an agony and dangerous in view of the expected German invasion of the Balkans, he argued. Jabotinsky pleaded with members of the House of Commons that under the circumstances, there was no right or wrong: "only the argument of humanity has the right to be heard." The Foreign Office rejected the plea from this "stormy petrel in politics." It replied, "It is understood that these unfortunate people were induced to embark upon their present journey by unscrupulous tourist agents who concealed from them the fact that persons not having immigration permit are prohibited from entering Palestine." The Zionists were offended by the Foreign Office's reply, since they thought of themselves as saving lives.[20]

The British government knew full well the details of the Jewish refugees stranded in Sulina, but thrust the responsibility on the Romanian government and the European Danube Commission (including a German delegate from whom not much collaboration could be expected). They did not mention the limited issuance of certificates for Jews to reach Palestine in safety and relative comfort. British functionaries recommended to the Romanian government that it prevent unfit ships planning to undertake dangerous clandestine voyages from anchoring in their ports, knowing very well that so many interests were involved that it was difficult to stop the combination of humanitarian aid carried out by the Zionists and the business of carrying Jews to Palestine by the smugglers. Ultimately, it placed the responsibility on the Germans for their persecution of Jews, a well as on the organizers of the illegal immigration traffic.[21]

The government of Great Britain knew that the solution to the Jewish immigration lay in its control, as limits on it had been set in the white paper published by the Colonial Office in May 1939. The policy allowed gradual legal immigration, limited to ten thousand people a year for five years, and restricted land sales to Jews. Then between October 1939 and March 1940, the British government suspended immigration altogether due to the illegal entry of Jews to Palestine, making the situation even worse. After war broke out in September, the Zionists responded to the imposed controls by organizing clandestine voyages to Palestine with an ever-greater zeal.[22]

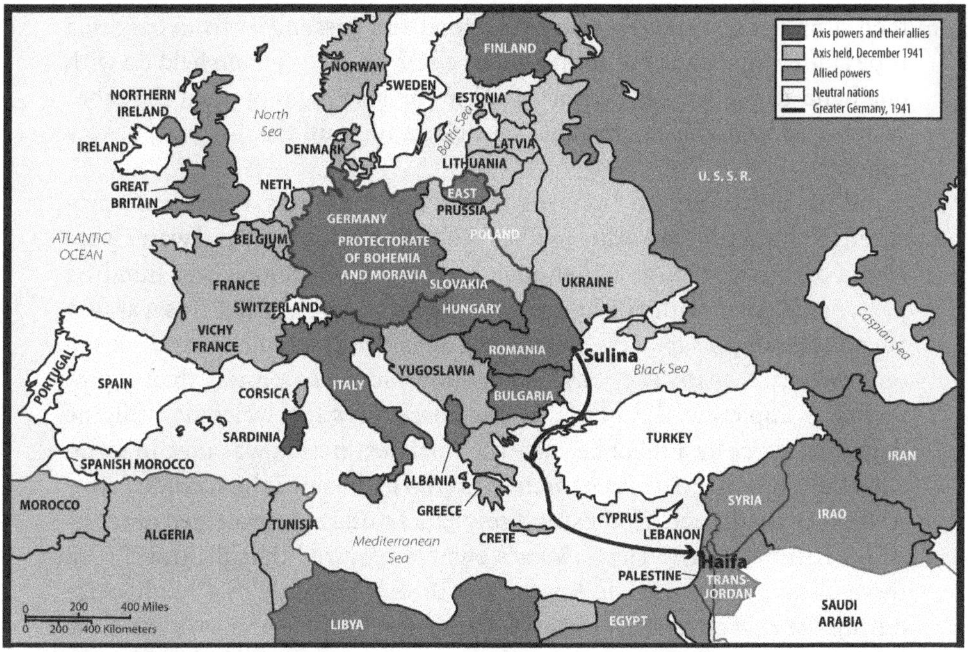

Map 4. Kurt's journey from the port of Sulina to Haifa in Palestine, 1940

The SS *Sakarya*

The Turkish-registered coal carrying vessel that Eri Jabotinsky and Willi Perl had hired belonged to the brothers Avni and Kemal Oglu, both in their twenties, assisted by a crew of about fifteen who were not the most competent sailors. On arrival in Sulina, the Turks did not expect so many passengers ready to board the ship and raised the price. That meant that more paying passengers had to be added to meet the cost. To find the money, Perl traveled to Vienna and Budapest and brought an additional boatload of more than five hundred Austrian and Hungarian Jews. Furthermore, when the Turks learned of the mission's purpose, they were reluctant to carry out the agreement. They feared that the British would confiscate the vessel engaged in illegal traffic and imprison the crew, as had happened to other shipowners before.[23]

The *Sakarya*, with its captain, the Turkish owners, and twenty-three-year-old Leyla (either a cousin or girlfriend who acted as their interpreter) onboard, anchored in the open sea about a mile distant from the Danube's delta. The ship could be reached only by a boat and only if weather allowed. It could happen that when braving the waves was too dangerous, the passengers accommodated on the ship to escape the cold were left with no food supplies. It was a feat to hoist up food and passengers from barges: a rope ladder was made out for people to climb on. Young men held on with one hand to the rope ladder attached to the ship, as they used the other to help children, the elderly, and the sick clamber up the dangling rickety rungs.[24]

With additional aid from the Jewish organizations, funds were procured to pay in full for *Sakarya*'s hire. Wood and some food and water were stored on board, though not enough for a cargo of twenty-three hundred passengers (even without the precariousness of the supplies, this was way beyond the ship's capacity). Finally, the *Sakarya* raised anchor and set sail on February 1, 1940. The Turks, appearing more like pirates than a professional ship crew, did not make the passengers feel welcome; still, the departure came as a relief because the final destination was now in sight. Kurt was on board. The Romanian Jews who had helped the stranded river passengers with food, clothes, and some fuel came too, smuggled onto the ship when necessary. The *Sakarya*'s owners required that Eri travel with them to take the responsibility for any British reprisals that might arise during the voyage. To Eri's chagrin, because of space, some Jews had to be left behind on Sulina's pier, stone-faced and fearing for their lives.[25]

The *Sakarya* sailed under the Panamanian flag. Eri had secured a so-called collective visa for most passengers, to show in case of an inspection in the open sea that the *Sakarya* was sailing to Latin America. Consuls issued such visas on the understanding that the ship would not enter their country. Some of the refugees possessed Paraguayan visas obtained from the consul in Prague, permitting them to visit that landlocked country. As the Palestine government was sure to bar the passengers from landing, would a Paraguayan visa permit them to land in Paraguay, enquired the Foreign Office of its diplomat in Asunción?[26] It knew the answer to the question it posed, because it knew of the scheme that had animated the procurement of the visas.

The journey was hard on most passengers. Despite the previous cleaning of the soot, the ship's walls were still covered with a coat of coal dust, there was no lighting and not enough berths; bunks served as the sleeping quarters. Still, when people got seasick, doctors were on hand to comfort them. For the young the trip was an adventure, a temporary affair before Germany would be defeated and they could return to liberated Czechoslovakia or to the other subjugated countries. For the Zionists it was a journey toward settling in a new homeland. In the face of adversity, the voyage organizers tapped into the abundance of talent on board. There were Viennese musicians, poets, and cabaret actors, all of them called upon to perform for their fellow passengers. The Zionist leaders themselves entertained the refugees with Hebrew songs, lyrics of love, of battle and freedom, and all joined intoning "Hatikvah," the song of hope (which became Israel's national anthem). Couples who tied the knot during the voyage brought a measure of happiness to other travelers.

The activists had to be firm and tactful in quashing the occasional grumblings because of long lines for everything and not enough of anything. People had to rotate to help with providing services for all. Water was drawn from the sea. Feeding the entire population on board—morning, noon and night—was a feat. The organizers even managed a kosher kitchen. When one man died, a Jewish burial was improvised. The body was put into a sugar bag, enveloped in a straw mat, and attached to a plank to make it appear as a coffin; with bricks tied as a weight, the body was lowered into the sea by two cords, not thrown overboard. A rabbi was on hand to offer a Kaddish, the prayer for the dead.[27]

The *Sakarya* alternately braved the stormy seas or sailed in alluring calm, traveling a little more than 1,450 kilometers (about 900 miles) in thirteen days. Occasionally, people had to move from one side of the ship to the other to balance its weight so that the overcrowded vessel would not capsize. The voyage took the passengers from the cold of Romania to Turkish warmth and greenery; it was a solace to observe the mesquite and minarets as they appeared on the shoreline. Mishaps happened. Once a boiler had to be repaired, then the ship had to stop at the port of Zonguldak to buy coal because there had not been enough of it in Romania. Local Jewish communities sent food to the refugees, who appreciated oranges the most. On February 10, the *Sakarya* passed by the Turkish island of Tenedos. After the ship emerged from the strait of Bosporus and Dardanelles in the Aegean Sea, it was approached by what turned out to be a warship of the British Royal Navy. Armed marines boarded the *Sakarya*, handed chocolate to the children, and ordered the captain to steer the ship toward the Palestinian port of Haifa, where they were heading anyway. While this turn of events was a reason of unprecedented joy for the passengers, who celebrated it with music and thunderous cheers for Great Britain and Eretz Israel, the British saw things differently. They were intercepting an illegal cargo, which they had known all along was on its way to Palestine.[28]

The British and the Palestinian authorities had been following the *Sakarya*'s trajectory closely, thanks to Vladimir Jabotinsky's letters of protest to the authorities in London, which guaranteed the ship's safe arrival. The British in the Colonial Office and the high commissioner in Jerusalem knew that the vessel was not a contraband ship and that it had no enemy agents on board; however, both the Contraband Control Service and the Emergency Power Regulations, could be invoked as a pretext to examine the ship outside the territorial waters of Palestine. No matter what, the high commissioner intended to prevent the refugees from landing in Haifa.[29]

Correspondence zoomed back and forth between the authorities in London and in Jerusalem about what to do with the *Sakarya*'s passengers ever since the ship commenced its voyage. Should they confiscate the ship? Imprison the crew? Prevent the passengers from landing? The high commissioner was adamant that the passage of the refugees was politically motivated, while the Colonial Office in London was more conciliatory. The commissioner's position was that clandestine immigration into Palestine had been taking place for a long time, and that it had been perfected to the point that now it was "similar to the slave trade or rum running."[30] To adjudicate the matter would not resolve the problem because the Palestine judiciary system was lenient toward the Jewish immigrants. The high commissioner wanted to take the matter from the hands of the courts and deal with it himself, but the Colonial Office objected.

The refugees did not know what lay in store for them, but even if they did, the prospect of internment on their arrival would not have deterred them from risking a dangerous journey after everything they had been subjected to and the certainty of a far greater suffering in their countries of origin. The clandestine immigration of Jews from war-torn Europe and away from persecution was a conundrum for which the British found no satisfactory solution.[31]

Atlit

Seeing Haifa from a distance on February 13, 1940, Eri Jabotinsky was ecstatic: "The rising sun lent a special reddish colour to the whole landscape. The [Mount] Carmel was like some giant sleeping on the sea shore. The city of Haifa, climbing up from the harbour and clinging to the mountain's flank, was enveloped in the riot of colour of its gardens, its buildings, and its roofs."[32] Eri, who felt that he was back home, was the first to disembark. The British police, who were waiting for him, accused him of illegally transporting Jews and took him away.

The *Sakarya*'s passengers, Kurt among them, had thronged the deck in expectation. Women and children, the sick, and the elderly were allowed to land while the men were kept on board until March 8 even at the cost of separating families. Every day the police brought pita bread, sour milk, and fruit to feed them. Even medical attention was available. The men were kept on board because there was not enough space in the detention camps to which they were to be taken; it also ostensibly allowed the British to examine their background to show the Arab population that officials were taking the limitation on Jewish immigration seriously. Finally, in the middle of March the *Sakarya*'s male passengers were divided into two groups and sent to the detention camps, either to Atlit twenty kilometers (about 12.5 miles) south of Haifa, where the women and children had been transferred on arrival to Haifa, or to Sarafand further south, reserved just for men. It was a disheartening disappointment for the *Sakarya*'s Jews to arrive in what for some was the Holy Land and for all an escape from the German persecution only to be treated like aliens, deprived of freedom when they felt they had not committed any crime.[33]

The *Sakarya*'s Turkish captain and the owners produced a contract that never mentioned Palestine as the final point of disembarkation, which meant that they could not be put in jail and the ship could not be confiscated. Their interception in international waters was a contravention of international law, the owners argued in Haifa district court, since the ship was prevented from sailing to its alleged destination, whether in Panama or Paraguay. The courts sided with the refugees, "invariably moved by the sad plight of the immigrants, and every technicality is stretched in their favour," as the high commissioner complained. He sought to circumvent the court's leniency by removing the power from the courts and vesting it in the executive, but this scheme was rejected by the Foreign Office in London.[34] The *Sakarya* and its crew were free. Eri remained jailed.

The detention of the *Sakarya*'s passengers had nothing or little to do with the fear of German spies on board; rather, it was meant to serve as a cautionary tale for the organizers of any future illegal ships to Palestine. Allowing the refugees to land and releasing the crew was "a bull point in Zionist propaganda."[35] Did the British ever catch a spy on a clandestine ship? "If I were a German, I would not lay much belief in the services of a Jewish spy," Eri commented wryly.[36]

All things considered, it was a senseless detention, useless except for perhaps mollifying the Arab population. If one of its goals was to deter the organization of further clandestine ships, it backfired. The war was on and so was the subjection of Jews to tyranny in the Reich and in the countries it had occupied. The detained men and women wanted to live a normal life or be useful; some wanted to build the Jewish homeland, others to fight the enemy on the side of the Allies.[37] Instead, they were idle for five months.

Kurt was interned in Atlit with other *Sakarya* passengers, men and women in separate sections. The camp comprised sixty huts with dormitories, kitchens, dining halls, a hospital bay, and sanitary facilities, accommodating some two thousand detainees. It was located between the Mediterranean Sea and the road leading north to Haifa and south to Tel Aviv. An alley of tall slim palm trees led to the compound, surrounded by a low fence of barbed wire and a menacing high fence, with watchtowers standing at each corner. The refugees lived in wooden barracks, thirty to sixty men in each; the doors were bolted every day at 6 p.m. The barracks were divided into parts, sleeping quarters on one side and the washrooms on the other. Medical service was provided. Nuisances included scorpions, while infectious diseases were an ever-present risk. During the day, the inmates could do anything they liked, except leaving the camp. Mostly they were bored. One distraction was cleaning the barracks, another hunting for lice. The food was inadequate and of poor quality, upsetting many stomachs. Black coffee, bread, and halva (a sweet made out of sugar, almonds, and honey) comprised the staple diet. The detainees lacked toothpaste, soap, shaving cream, and razors, as well as cigarettes and books to read. The weather was pleasant except for when the wind blew sand from the desert and the temperature rose to 50 degrees centigrade (122 degrees Fahrenheit). The refugees were policed by the British, Palestinian Jews, and Arabs. Escaping was impossible as well as undesirable: Where would one go?[38]

Initially, the British overseers treated the refugees as criminals or with a condescension that the inmates resented. To protest the contemptuous treatment and the inadequate food, the Zionists organized a hunger strike shortly after their arrival. To prevent scabbing by those who disagreed with the protest, the ringleaders occupied the kitchen and the larders. Conditions improved. With time, enterprising inmates opened a café, then another, even a restaurant and a kosher kitchen. Conflicts arose between one group of Zionists and another, between the Czech- and the German-speaking Jews. Those who were eager to join the war effort were at loggerheads with men who did not want to fight but sought to settle down. German was resented as a language of communication but for many it was the only one they knew. English was the language to learn in addition to Hebrew and Arabic.[39]

While Kurt remained in Atlit, the *Sakarya* continued to make diplomatic noise. Vladimir Jabotinsky and his wife (him in Washington, her in London) kept on protesting their son's imprisonment, demanded that he be freed, and insisted that his Palestine citizenship should not be revoked as the authorities threatened to do. Eri's "crime," wrote his mother to the secretary of state for the Colonies, was to have saved over two thousand lives from the Nazis' ill-treatment. At this time, Vladimir was in the United States to raise a Jewish division of the British Army to fight for the Allies, an effort that the British War Office was not interested in supporting. Jabotinsky carried no weight in England or the United States. His plea on behalf of his son was ignored.

British intelligence had been intercepting letters written in Russian between husband and wife, and in translation learned about Eri's reaffirmation of his conviction that the *Sakarya*'s voyage was legal and that his prison conditions were not so bad. In his public letters, Jabotinsky argued that holding a young man in prison during these trying times was unjustified. To deprive a Jew of his Palestinian citizenship, Eri's father contended, was to make him liable to German persecution; Eri might be a troublesome politician, but he was not a criminal. To no avail. To free him, the British authorities responded, would encourage other organizers of illegal crossings, would aggravate the Arab population, and acquiesce to the German government's encouragement of the Jewish emigration to Palestine. As the flurry of dispatches were being exchanged, news arrived on August 4 that Vladimir Jabotinsky had died. It was now politically expedient to release Eri, who two days later left the same jail that his father had occupied in Acre in 1920, close to the Lebanese border.[40]

Whether the *Sakarya* passengers' liberation from Atlit was related to Eri's or occurred to make room for those who arrived on the next ship is unclear, but the inmates were released on August 12,1940. The discharge of well over a thousand individuals from the camp was done in an orderly manner at daybreak. Buses were waiting at the gate. After breakfast, the men, women, and children were taken to a place of their choice: to Haifa, Jerusalem, or Tel Aviv.

Some hurried to the wall of the destroyed Temple to thank the Almighty for the good fortune of having survived the tribulations, some went to look for a job or hoped to set up a business, others dispersed to become settlers in kibbutzim, dedicated to agriculture. It was a handicap to know only German, and few knew any Hebrew. Numerous men with no previous military experience volunteered to receive training at the British military camp in Gedera, eager to join the war effort under the command of the Czechoslovak Military Mission for the Near East.[41]

Kurt took a bus to Haifa. Like the rest of the Jewish refugees who arrived on clandestine ships, he lacked any legal protection and could not have had much money. Unlike some, he did not seek security by applying for Palestinian citizenship. On being discharged from the detention camp, he very likely received an identity card. In Haifa, Kurt enlisted into the British army. Fighting the enemy was the obvious choice for many of the released immigrants.[42]

6

A Prisoner of War

Kurt escaped the German persecution in Czechoslovakia through a daring journey to Palestine. The British authorities detained him, alleging that the Germans may have planted spies among the Jews with whom he was fleeing from the Nazis. At the same time, they sought to show the Arab population their resolve to contain the flow of Jewish immigrants. Cleared and freed from the detention camp five months later, Kurt joined the British army. He was captured in Greece during a failed evacuation of the British forces, becoming a Jewish prisoner of war in a German camp. There, he was protected from extermination not only by international law but also by his British comrades in arms, who claimed him as their Jew. Kurt never divulged the total of his wartime experience.

Into the Army

After the war, the Czechoslovak Ministry of Defense inquired why Kurt had joined the British army and not units of his native country fighting the Germans. He replied in writing that the former rejected his application to join it. In fact, like most Jews who emigrated to Palestine, Kurt was entangled in an external situation over which he had no control and chose what seemed to him to be the best, perhaps the only, option.[1]

The Czechoslovak Military Mission for the Near East was created in July 1940, a month before Kurt was released from Atlit. The mission was subordinate to the British High Command, but it wanted to stake out its territory in the region, even knowing it would be a modest one. Its desired goal was the liberation of Czechoslovakia by strengthening the Allied coalition. To become a respectable force and grow into a battalion, the Czechoslovak mission needed seasoned personnel, officers, and soldiers. Some had already been stationed in Palestine, others arrived after the fall of France in June 1940. The Czechoslovak consulate in Jerusalem, representing the exiled government in London, was the initial conduit for recruiting military personnel for the mission. The detention camps were full of enthusiastic patriots who on their release were eager to join the war effort. While still in the camp, they met with the consulate's envoys, who gave them pep talks about their obligations to the motherland and in a veiled threat intimated that enlistment in the Czechoslovak army was obligatory.[2]

But the consulate had to compete for the minds and hearts of the detainees with the Zionist organization Hitachdut Olej Czechoslovakia. Set up before the war, now with about eight hundred members, it was composed of German- and Czech-speaking Jews, some of them former members of parliament from the prewar Jewish Party. Its mission was to support the newly arrived immigrants. Hitachdut was vehemently opposed to their joining the Czechoslovak army as mandated by the consulate in Jerusalem. Its position was that every Jewish refugee was bound to their new country, not to the liberation of Czechoslovakia. Like the Jewish Agency, they hoped to enlist the immigrants into the projected Jewish legion to fight first on the side of the Allies and then after the war for the Palestinian homeland.[3]

The refugees in Atlit were split, since not all of them were Zionists. Furthermore, some wanted to join the war effort while others wanted to set up a business or become kibbutz settlers. Kurt, who was not a Zionist, knew all along that he wanted to fight for the Allies' cause. What united all of the camp's inmates was the need for legal protection. But those who chose joining the Czechoslovak army were threatened with being excluded from the Jewish organizations such as the trade union Histadrut and would not be able to count on assistance from Hitachdut. On the other hand, rumor had it that those who preferred to adhere to the Jewish community in Palestine would be declared deserters, unable to return to Czechoslovakia after the war. Some camp inmates may also have been influenced in their decision-making by other calculations, such as hope of being released soon or securing protection if they took this or that side.[4] But overall, the refugees' choice was between their loyalty to the Yishuv, the Jews in Israel, and to the creation of the Jewish homeland or loyalty to Czechoslovakia and the Allies' cause.

The Czechoslovak consul and the military leaders were aware that the British High Command and the commissioner were reluctant to allow too many Jews into the mission in the making. They knew that the British feared the Arabs' animosity toward the Jewish presence in the military units as much as they were conscious of anti-Semitism within the rank and file of the Czechoslovak military. But the Jewish volunteers, who desired to join the army before they were liberated from the camps, represented the manpower with which the consul Josef Kadlec hoped to strengthen the Czechoslovak Military Mission. To no avail: the high commissioner warned that the Jews incorporated into the mission should not be "detrimental" to the unit, meaning the mission needed to the balance between Jews and non-Jews; to the consul's chagrin, the commissioner was emphatic that the Jews released from detention should not be used to strengthen the mission. Thus, hundreds of Jewish volunteers had to be turned down. As it happened, the mission in the end included 40 percent of Jewish soldiers and officers, comprising a battalion of over four hundred men ready for battle.[5]

The British proposed to include Jews barred from joining the Czechoslovak forces in unskilled nonfighting units, the Pioneer Corps, irrespective of their political convictions. The Pioneer Corps was designed for people who did not fit easily into any single ethnic or national group and who the British did not trust because they came from the enemy territory. Thus, thousands of German, Czech, Hungarian, and Austrian nationals joined the Pioneer Corps if they wanted to assist the Allied war effort to liberate their home countries from the Nazi terror.

Kurt was released from Atlit on August 12 and registered with the Pioneer Corps in Haifa the following day. He must have made up his mind while still in detention, thus choosing a third way. There is no evidence that he applied to the Czechoslovak consulate to join the military mission. Kurt's reasons for choosing the path he did are unknown.

This peculiar British institution did not require military training. Its emblem was a crossed pick and shovel and its motto "work conquers all." Being a working unit of unskilled labor, the Pioneer Corps had been put to work on engineering and construction projects and repairs. The recruits had to have sufficient knowledge of English, and meet certain physical criteria of height, weight, and chest circumference. Eighty percent of the corps consisted of illegal immigrants to British territories. Kurt, like the rest, may have been taught some military tactics, lessons in day battles and night encounters, offensive actions, ambushes, retreats, pursuits, firing strategies, elements of artillery, tanks and aircraft, basic field intelligence, patrolling, cooperation, medical duties, values and norms of team spirit, the principle of never abandoning the wounded, and doing the utmost to avoid being taken a prisoner.[6] So, knowledgeable about some military affairs, equipped with ankle-high boots, a cap, a helmet, a jacket, and a service number with the prefix PAL for Palestinian, sometime in the fall of 1940 private Groll was ready to depart for the front.

The Kalamata Debacle

Kurt was part of a mission to Greece in what the commanders in chief concluded years later had been a "military gamble" by the British forces, inadequately equipped and inferior in terms of controlling air space.[7] Greece was a minor theater of war in which Britain engaged for political gains, sacrificing military considerations. It was a neutral country that wanted to remain so, but the threat of German intervention motivated the British government to send a small air force contingent and army units in November 1940 to forestall German aggression. Indeed, at the end of the year, Hitler had drawn up plans for an invasion. The British increased the delivery of arms to Greece in the middle of January of the following year and in March 1941 the first British convoy sailed from Alexandria, landing at the port of Piraeus. Kurt might have been part of that expedition. The Greeks received the British with jubilation. But on April 6, the German army invaded Greece on the grounds that it had violated its neutrality and allowed the British army to enter the country. An uneven war ensued.[8]

Not only was the strength of the armies imbalanced, but the British ground forces faced rugged mountainous terrain, making it difficult to move ahead. The roads were poor; a few narrow paths climbing over the hills were suitable for ox wagons but not fit for motor vehicles. Thus, the Greek troops covered the hilly country, the British the main roads. The climate in March and April was severe, snow and rain made the roads treacherous. Still, one soldier lapsed into lyricism when observing the surroundings despite the difficulties he faced: "Even in an army convoy one cannot help noticing the beautiful countryside. The winding roads, and mountain tracks melting into the distance. The roads, no matter how beautiful, were not designed to carry heavy army traffic and it was not long before one of the lorries fell over the side down into the valley below."[9]

The Germans outmaneuvered the joint British and Greek forces, who lost the will to fight. Their leaders capitulated. The British Middle East Joint Planning Staff decided to evacuate the country on April 17. Some of the British Expeditionary Forces managed to evacuate to Egypt; some troops, short of ammunition and supplies, escaped to the hills. The German air force bombarded the port of Piraeus to prevent further evacuation of the British army. The British general in charge issued the command not to surrender but to make for the Peloponnese peninsula to evacuate the troops from its beaches, while securing a safe passage for the panic-stricken royal government and the king's family to Crete.[10]

The British and the Commonwealth soldiers set out on a march toward the Peloponnese peninsula, expecting to be rescued by the Royal

Navy from its shores, which turned out shortly to mark the line between safety and imprisonment or death. In the town of Kalamata, in the western corner of the peninsula, the soldiers clashed with the better-armed German units, protected by Luftwaffe. To avoid being taken prisoners, soldiers hid in the thickets of olive trees and orange groves, awaiting the appearance of the rescue ships on moonlit nights.

The Royal Navy ships arrived. Between April 28 and 29, 1941, dates that Kurt could not have forgotten but never spoke about, the Germans attacked the very quay from which the boats were evacuating the soldiers. With no adequate arms or air cover by the Royal Air Force, with wounded soldiers to look after, it was impossible to defend the dock against the German artillery fire and to continue attempting to board the ships anchored at a distance from the beach. The brigadier in charge called his army to surrender. The awaiting ships were informed that an enemy Italian fleet was approaching. The rumor proved false, but the ships left, abandoning thousands of soldiers at the mercy of the Germans, condemning them to captivity.[11]

Kurt was one of the seven thousand British, Commonwealth, and Palestinian soldiers stranded on the beach. One of the marooned soldiers later recalled, "What a contrast to our triumphant entry into Athens in troop laden lorries that streamed from the old cargo ship docked at the port of Piraeus that had ferried us from Alexandria a few months previously! Then the smiling, cheering populace, waving flags and shawls, blowing kisses, wept tears of joy at the sight of khaki uniforms."[12]

Captivity

Initially, the Germans held the captives on the outskirts of Kalamata, then in barracks at Corinth and Salonica. The prisoners suffered from inadequate food, poor sanitation, overcrowding, and maladies from drinking dirty water. The Greek Red Cross and the generosity of the local people alleviated some of their hardships. Peddlers approached the compounds in which the prisoners were held to sell them figs and loaves of bread. By the international law, the Germans were obligated to treat the prisoners of war decently. But in the Greek barracks, the German captors did not feel bound by any legal constraints. Considering the Jews—especially the Jews from Germany and the occupied countries—as rebels, guilty of treason against the fatherland, they treated their powerless victims with contempt.[13]

From the temporary camps in Greece, the Germans transported the prisoners to permanent camps in Germany, Austria, and elsewhere in the enlarged Reich. One of the captives wrote in his memoir that on leaving "the old Turkish barracks in Salonica we lined up, faint with hunger, a few possessions under our arms, then counted and pushed into some sort of column to begin our march through the streets of Salonica—past the curious Greek people who lined the pavements, silently watching our ignominious departure." Black-shawled women shed tears, men with caps pulled down "over their dark fear-filled eyes hung sheepishly in the background." Compassionate women handed the prisoners pieces of bread.[14]

The captives were taken to a railway station or loaded on trucks, despite their movement burdening the means of transport at the time of Hitler's invasion of the Soviet Union, which had commenced a few weeks earlier. Sometime in the summer of 1941, Kurt and his comrades in arms were loaded onto sealed trains to prevent their escape and were transported through Yugoslavia to Germany or Austria. The Jews among them were segregated from the other prisoners but did not have to wear the yellow star. Hunger and thirst were constant during the journey; toilets were unavailable and it was an ordeal to relieve oneself in a corner of a moving carriage into a container that then had to be thrown out of the moving train. The smells and the ignominy stayed with the prisoners for a long time.[15]

Kurt's next stop was the German POW camp in Wolfsberg, located south of the town of Görlitz in Lower Silesia, in what today is the Polish town of Zgorzelec. The Czechoslovak border was a stone's throw away. It was in Wolfsberg that Kurt was put back on the map as a prisoner of war, a status that carried the restoration of some human rights. Unlike the concentration camps prisoners, who were nameless throughout their incarceration, Kurt and the other POWs became numbers with a name, a place of origin, and a year of birth. Looking straight into the camera, Kurt was photographed with his glasses on, holding a slate with both hands bearing the number 4902 in bold letters. Fingerprinted, Kurt was registered as a Palestinian 11976, as a Jew, and an *E* for *Engländer* as one belonging to the British army. Though the Nazis usually added "Israel" to Jewish men's names to distinguish them from the rest of the population, this did not happen to Kurt. He put down a friend's address in Haifa as a person to contact, not his family in Valašské Meziříčí, very likely to protect them.[16]

East of Wolsberg, in Upper Silesia, lay the largest of all the prisoner of war camps and Kurt's final stop. To reach Lamsdorf (Łambinowice in Polish) on foot, the prisoners marched on a winding road through flat farmland before entering a pine and chestnut forest, behind which extended the fenced camp, hidden from the public eye. On entering the camp, they encountered a brick guardhouse on one side; on the other side, across the

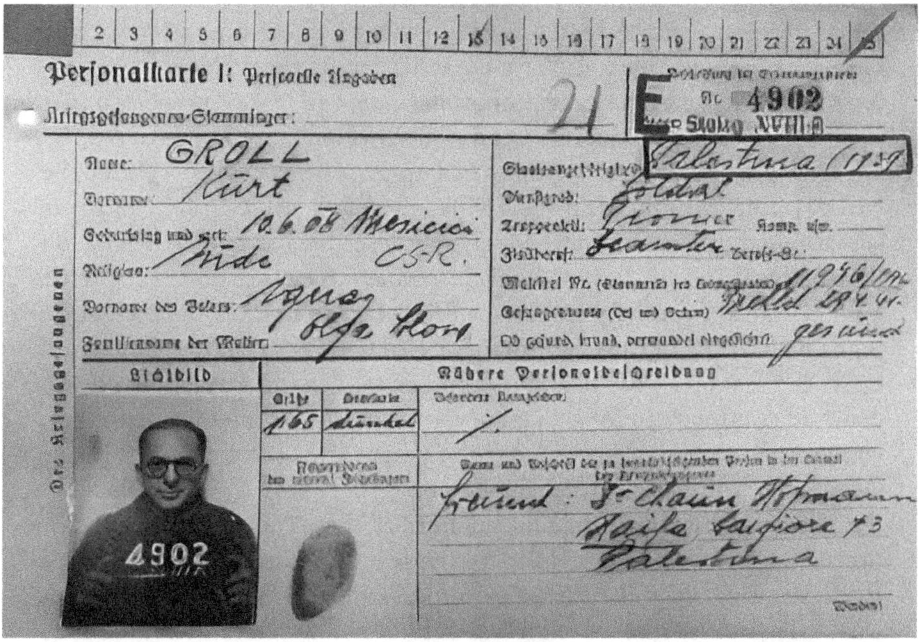

FIGURE 5. Kurt's registration as a prisoner of war in Wolsberg, 1941.

path leading to the compound, stood a stone eagle atop a swastika. Further down the lane were the camp offices and a punishment block where prisoners were held in solitary confinement. Watchtowers equipped with machine guns, rifles, searchlights, and sentries with binoculars high above stood at each corner of the camp. Like all camps, Stalag VIII B (as it was designated) was surrounded by outer and inner wire fencing, nailed to wooden stakes. For anyone who wanted to escape, a warning line around the outer perimeter of barbed wire made it perilous. Touching or crossing it, one was liable to be shot without notice. This was particularly dangerous for prisoners depressed from being locked up who wandered to the prohibited zone, only to be shot dead.[17]

The prisoners were crowded in old barracks dating from before the Great War or in new brick buildings, each with bare furnishings; there were no glass windows, only shutters that were bolted at night from the outside. A bucket for urine stood in one corner of the room when the barrack was locked. Planks fastened together served as beds in three tiers. The men slept on mattresses filled with straw, their coats and worn blankets serving as covers. The top bed was the best; one could hide there, and it was more difficult to steal one's secrets, a prisoner remembered. "The bunk was not just a bed, it was a combination of a wardrobe, store cupboard, hiding place, and most important a retreat. It was on the bed that one read letters, cried, dreamed and wondered and hoped."[18]

One prisoner described the desolation of being locked behind the barbed wires, with no control over his life as follows: "Captivity in life is something that very few could adequately describe. You have to feel it. You have to live it and you have to know just what it means to appreciate what a mental strain captivity is. We experienced through our incarceration many physical handicaps, but none were so hard as to bear as the mental ones. The monotony of life and its apparent endlessness practically drove you mad. You yearned for a change; you yearned for something different; you yearned for female company; you yearned for the company of your loved ones; and you yearned for home."[19] There was water for cooking but not enough for bathing and washing clothes. The unsanitary conditions and close quarters bred lice "in the seams of our trousers and battle blouses and laid eggs like strings of miniature pearls on our pubic hairs." It was so degrading "that we felt it was our job to contaminate the guards as well." To do so, the prisoners collected the lice and managed to throw them at the guards' clothing. The secret weapon worked. The guards were horrified, burned their bedding, and had the entire camp deloused. It restored the prisoners' spirit.[20]

Meals were distributed in badly heated rooms. To keep warmer, the prisoners had to steal coal to feed the stoves in their rooms: "The method was to tie our trousers at the bottom and fill them with coal and march back to the barn as best we could." They shared loaves of bread, to eat with a bowl of slop masquerading as a soup sometimes with something solid in it. "No matter what the food was like we always carefully carried it back to our bed space there to crouch over to eat it and eat it before someone else cast their greedy eyes on it."[21]

The Germans were unprepared to find Jewish captives among the British and Commonwealth soldiers and to deal with the obligation to treat them according to the Geneva convention for prisoners of war, preserving their lives and dignity and even preserving their burial customs. From the registration cards, the camp commandants knew who among the prisoners was a Jew and who was not. They wanted to mark the Jews with a distinctive badge, but the British would have none of it. If outbursts against the Jews occurred, they were usually the result of personal animosities and not orders from above. Anti-Semitic manifestations by the British soldiers were rare; friendships prevailed. In 1941 there were about 1,160 Palestine

Jewish prisoners in Stalag VIII B. Kurt shared his incarceration with some of the fellow soldiers caught during the Kalamata misadventure and with men captured in France, Northern Africa, Crete, and the territories the Germans had occupied.[22]

As prisoners of war, the inmates were entitled to the Red Cross relief packages and to parcels from home, which reduced the brutality of the imprisonment and the malnourishment they had to endure. On the rare reflection Kurt made about his life in prison later to his wife, he recalled with glee that as they were part of the British cohort, the Germans could not withhold the Red Cross parcels from the Jews. He relished chocolate the most. However, the Germans did what they could to bully the Jews, reducing their food rations or withholding parcels under the pretense of looking for forbidden material or stealing some of their contents out of jealousy that the prisoners received what the Germans lacked.[23]

The prisoners arrived at the camp in tattered clothes and worn out shoes. The Geneva convention related to the treatment of prisoners of war, signed in 1929 by Germany and forty-six other nations, stipulated that the signatory countries had to supply them with adequate food, clothes, and shoes. But the Lamsdorf authorities provided the prisoners with the bare necessities: uniforms and overcoats captured from the soldiers of Europe's defeated armies, often bloodstained and with bullet holes, and wooden clogs instead of shoes. The Germans must have had stores of good uniforms, because in December 1941 the prisoners were photographed, Kurt among them: thirteen soldiers clad in smart uniforms, with solid boots on, some sitting with hands comfortably laying on their laps, others standing with hands behind their backs in front of beech trees, their silhouettes reflected in the puddles after a recent rain. The photograph was taken for the prisoners to send home, accompanied by a Christmas greeting card, showing that they were alive and treated well. The image of well-being was also choreographed for the benefit of the Red Cross's delegation, which happened to be performing an inspection of the camp and would do so regularly thereafter.[24]

The prisoners of war were entitled to corresponding with their families but were not allowed to disclose their whereabout and living conditions: "Any word about starving, ill treatment or complaints would cause the blacking out of the words or card destroyed."[25] Kurt corresponded with his mother and sister in Valašské Meziříčí until 1942, when he lost contact with them. He did not find out until 1945, after the war ended, that they had been imprisoned in the Terezín ghetto. He may have known of his father's death, which occurred the previous year.

The prisoners broke the monotony of life in the camp by organizing sport events and musical performances. Thanks to parcels from home and from the Red Cross, they received books and organized a "barbed-wire university" to while away hours, days, and months. They put together a string band and a swing band with an accordion, a banjo, a guitar, and a harmonica (which could have been Kurt's); they constructed props for theater performances and playing cards out of the cardboard in which they had received their parcels. Even the Germans were entertained.[26]

Most Englishmen in the camp did not understand German. Kurt did, but there was the danger of appearing to pander to the Germans if one spoke the language, so he may have refrained from using it, though not from listening and understanding what was being said around him. Kurt was cautious and decided to sit out the war in the camp. But not all prisoners accepted their condition passively; many made the dangerous attempt to escape; if caught, they were likely to be shot. Hence, the choice to escape was for the bravest—for those who found the tedium and hardships of the confinement intolerable.[27]

Laboring for the Enemy

Stalag VIII B consisted of the main compound and dozens of labor attachments in satellite camps. Among other things, the Geneva convention laid down regulations for labor by prisoners of war. The Wehrmacht honored the convention provided the prisoners worked diligently in the Arbeitskommandos—working groups—to which they were assigned. The Germans considered that doing so was a concession, not an obligation. Germany needed labor as its swelled armed force sucked manpower from factories, mines, construction sites, transport enterprises, and farms. That labor was available in concentration, forced labor, and prisoner of war camps, to which Germany considered it was entitled as a source of energy to feed its war economy.

Labor in dangerous environments, in the production of weapons or ammunition, or in services related to fighting units was forbidden. Hours of work were supposed to be equal to those of civilians; meanwhile, the prisoners were entitled to adequate food and accommodations. Delegations from the International Committee of the Red Cross were authorized to visit the camps and the labor detachments to ensure that the prisoners' living and working conditions conformed to the basic standards. If the Germans moderated their behavior, it was for fear of Allied retaliation against their own prisoners.[28]

Out of resentment of having to work for their enemy, prisoners sabotaged the workday when they could; when they could not, they worked resigned to the possibility of better food rations. They regarded it as their duty to deliver shoddy work and undermine Germany's economy and morale, hoping that in doing so they could help the Allies' effort to win the war. Confrontations between the prisoners and the guards who oversaw them at work were frequent. The foremen did not distinguish between men who did not work because of resistance, weakness, or illness. Even when the Jewish prisoners of war worked halfheartedly or were too feeble or sick, the Geneva convention protected them from being deported to Auschwitz, which lay only a few hours further to the east. Kurt and his fellow prisoners were aware of their privileged position, using the Geneva convention stipulations to fend off the strict German regime.[29]

Consequently, Jewish prisoners of war in the British and American armed forces were the best-protected Jews in the Third Reich. They could mount (albeit minimal) resistance to improve their living and working conditions. Its success depended on dynamics of the war, on the solidarity of fellow prisoners, and the disposition of the commandants and the prison guards.[30] Confidence in each other, bonds created among the prisoners, warmth and affection must have alleviated some of their pain and conditions of inhumanity to which they were subjected. Kurt recalled occasional human contact and English prisoners' solidarity with Jews.

The British prisoners of war, Jews and non-Jews, worked at a close distance to forced labor camps in sites attached to Stalag VIII B. From a relatively privileged position as prisoners of war, legally protected from German brutality, they witnessed the hapless prisoners who worked in mines and in agriculture on behalf of the German state or for private companies that profited from their cheap labor. They were shocked by the differences in their well-being. The desolate-looking laboring groups on their way to work and back that the Stalag war prisoners encountered awoke their compassion. Even though they could not exchange information, they could, Kurt later remarked, help them with food and cigarettes, giving some to their guards to look the other way.[31]

Upper Silesia was a vital industrial belt, abounding in coal and salt mines, stone quarries, munition and paper factories, fields, lumber mills, and foundries. The prisoners were assigned from the main camp to the attached labor camps for weeks or months to work for private contractors, exploiting the rich raw materials and making use of the manufacturing infrastructure. In early 1942, in freezing winter, Kurt was part of a labor group sent to work in Niklasdorf (Mikulovice in Czech), one of the detachment camps located southwest of Lamsdorf. His group was assigned to the granite and marble factory owned by Franz Liemert, a German industrialist engaged in extracting the stone from the local quarry. It was hard work. One prisoner described the dawn of another working day: "We trudged to work without food or drink, head down backs bent, gazing at the heels of the man in front."[32]

Drilling in the quarry with explosives was done twice a day. One had to shelter from the flying shrapnel after the blast. It took several men to haul the large blocks of stone weighing several tons when the stone failed to fall into the pit. The blocks then had to be cut into different sizes and transported to the masonry sheds. The workers had to be careful constantly not to hurt their hands; there was no medical service and when an injury occurred, the prisoners had to treat themselves as best they could. One prisoner remembered working in the quarry with seasoned German miners, mostly elderly country folk whose families had worked there for generations. Their conversations swirled around Germany's, Britain's, and America's military successes and losses, each side extolling the triumphs and minimizing the fatalities of the other side in a region that had not yet suffered war's ravages.[33]

Kurt and his buddy Abraham Maeroff were among those who worked in the quarry halfheartedly. As Liemert complained to the main camp administration, they did so when the foreman stood nearby and sat down when he left. Liemert's frustration stemmed not only from the fact that these Jewish prisoners of war did not deliver the number of hours of work expected from them, but also from the fact that he could not enforce discipline. Even after he jailed other recalcitrants from the work group for several days, on their release they still refused to work. Claiming that the food was inadequate for the hard physical labor they exerted, the prisoners cited the Geneva convention. Here were prisoners of war who could not be made to comply with a regular workload, unlike German workers who would be infringing the law if they refused to abide by the workday rules. Liemert demanded their removal from his firm and a heavy punishment, never mentioning the lack of acceptable food that was at the heart of the dispute.[34] It was beyond the German industrialist's understanding that an international law could protect prisoners of war, Jews included.

The Germans feared the civilian population's cooperation with the prisoners of war in aiding them to escape, and tried to prevent any contact between them. The prisoners' interaction with the civilian population was invigorating. For Kurt, working side by side with Czech laborers was an opportunity to try to reestablish contact with his mother and sister after it had been lost in 1942. Valašské Meziříčí was a two-hour drive away from Mikulovice. When Kurt's acquaintances went home on holidays, he entrusted those who lived in southern Moravia to help him find out what happened to his sister and mother, who ceased to answer his letters. On their return, they brought good homemade pastries and reports about the progress of the war, but no news about Kurt's family.[35]

In 1944 planes began to fly over the prisoners' heads and the sound of guns was heard in the distance. "Something big was happening. How did we fit into it?" was one prisoner's question but surely on everybody's mind. It was winter, and sporting games were at a standstill. Only the Canadians made a skating rink out of the parade grounds, displaying their extraordinary skill. Food was in short supply. According to the Germans, the Allies' bombs prevented the Red Cross from delivering food parcels. Rumor had it that the Russians were advancing toward the camp and that the prisoners were to be moved to Germany. "But how? Again, rumors started to circulate, the strongest being that we were to march."[36]

Christmas 1944 was the last Kurt had to endure in the Lamsdorf camp. The cold was excruciating, several inches of snow covered the ground. Good news came from the camp's grapevine, which passed along radio reports that the Allies were scoring military successes, that Germany was losing the war, and that the Soviet army was pushing westward. The inmates had some supplies from the Red Cross parcels and home- distilled alcohol smuggled into the camp by the Poles from the adjoining villages. The possibility of evacuation was in the air; the prisoners were getting ready for the occasion, making packages with powdered cocoa, milk, tea, and chocolate bars and mending torn uniforms, socks, gloves, and balaclavas.Those who were fortunate to own them repaired boots in anticipation.[37]

7

A Return to the Mother Country

The war was over, and Kurt was waiting for repatriation from Palestine. In November 1945 he wrote home: "My imprisonment ended with a march of five hundred miles from Upper Silesia to Kassel from 22 January to 10 March. The Americans reached us on 30 March and on 9 April I flew to England." In two short sentences, Kurt compressed a harrowing trudge in the bitter winter cold from the prisoner of war camp in the eastern corner of the Reich to a concentration camp in the heart of Germany. "My own adventures are not so interesting, there is time for them." That time never came.[1]

Why did my father convey only snippets of his wartime experience? Did he conceive it as years of wasted youth and talent? Was he unable or unwilling to recall and share the humiliations, the wounds inflicted, the sufferings he and others underwent? Did he feel shame for falling into captivity with no war accomplishments to be proud of or guilt for having survived the hardships of war and imprisonment while others perished? He may have found that captivity was impossible to describe or wanted to draw a line under that life and get on with what he considered to be a normal existence without remorse, bitterness, or vengeance. Or, perhaps, my father did not want to burden me with memories of such difficult times.

On the March

On January 22, 1945, Kurt and his companions were summoned from the barracks to the parade grounds, counted once again, and formed into columns in preparation for evacuation. The Germans' attack on the Soviet Union had failed spectacularly; they were now aware of the Red Army's closing in from the east. The prisoners of war welcomed the Soviet advance. They had been anticipating the flight from the camp but did not know when it would occur, while their guards had only a vague idea about the evacuation routes, the forms of transport, the accommodation to be found along the way, the food supply, and their destination.[2]

To prepare for the journey, unsure of their future, the prisoners made sledges with planks torn off the bunks on which they had been sleeping, loading them with their modest possessions. The German guards, knowing that the Reich was disintegrating, had been instructed to endure to the end, to destroy any evidence of what had transpired in the camps, and to detonate the industrial installations before the Red Army overran them.[3] Once on their way toward Germany, the guards could be brutal or kind. For some it was a march to freedom; for others, a death march. The journey on foot through the snow and slush, thick fog, hunger, and cold, the dirty, ragged, sick, or wounded prisoners traveling ten to forty kilometers (about six to twenty-five miles) a day for several months, has been described in numerous testimonies. Here is one:

> It is my privilege and it is my pain to share this story here today
> It started not so long ago, in a land not far away
> The country's now called Poland, 'twas in nineteen forty-five
> When my father joined the Long, cold March to Freedom.
> . . . . .
> It was January of forty-five that Hitler's orders came
> For weeks on end they trudged their way over European plain
> No special clothes, no rations, half conscious and half-starved
> They shivered their way as they made their bid for freedom.
> . . . .
> Though thousands had set out upon, that long, cold road through hell
> Only twelve of father's group remained their story for to tell
> Of how they'd trudged through blinding snow with frostbite on their feet
> And with courage stepped that harsh, Long March to Freedom.[4]

Columns of prisoners marched simultaneously from different camps east to west along the borders of occupied Czechoslovakia or through its territory: POWs, survivors from the concentration camps, and inmates of the forced labor camps. The convoys crossed each others' paths but only the POWs occasionally received Red Cross parcels during the march. They rested in factories, churches, or in barns carpeted with straw or on bare floors, huddled to keep each other warm in below zero temperatures; some prisoners suffered from frostbite. There was nowhere to wash or shave. Sometimes, in barns with nothing to eat, prisoners would throw themselves on the straw to winnow grain from the chaff.[5]

After the prisoners had been counted in the morning to make sure that none of them had escaped during the night, whether with something warm in the stomach or not, the march continued. Endurance was essential; some despaired, others kept on hoping there would be an end to this suffering. It was encouraging to hear airplanes and the thunder of guns close or at a distance, but it was frightening when columns of prisoners, taken for the enemy on the move, were bombed.[6]

The guards directed some convoys north toward Hannover, some to the middle of Germany, some south toward Bavaria. Along the way, they came across advancing Allied troops and Wehrmacht soldiers in retreat, fallen trees blocking the roads, bombed buildings, frozen corpses lying on blood-stained snow, holes in their heads. The prisoners passed through barren plains and through villages where the guards tried to prevent their contact with the civil population to avoid possible assistance with flight. Even if a prisoner had the urge to escape, as many did, he would not know which way to go; and then there were the German informants who could call the police, the army, or the SS.[7]

Some villagers were hostile toward the marching prisoners, others were friendly. Some threw stones at them; one villager removed the pump shaft from a water well to prevent them from drinking while others shared hot soup, bread, coffee, or a cooked potato. "To moisten our lips we ate snow," one recalled. Theft was always the last resort to get food. Because of the unsanitary conditions and insufficient diet, prisoners died along the way from exhaustion as well as from pneumonia, diphtheria, pellagra, and other diseases.[8]

Kurt marched in the column of prisoners who took the road to the middle part of Germany. He and his companions arrived in Kassel on March 10, finding most of the city flattened by bombs. The US Army reached the town and the barracks or a storehouse in which the prisoners were billeted at the end of the month.

Liberation

What did Kurt feel when the American soldiers, "chewing gum and showering cigarettes on all," opened the gate of the prisoners' enclosure, declaring them free to walk about without a gun hovering behind, with food made available and water to shower? The cold weather had abated, the sun protruded through the clouds and the trees were dressed in green buds. The Red Cross distributed parcels without hindrance, enough even for the German guards and officers to help themselves.[9]

The British, Commonwealth, and Palestinian soldiers, disheveled after the march, flew to England with their meager belongings. Upon landing, they received new uniforms and boots. The English who did not need any medical treatment were free to go home. Kurt, who arrived in England on April 9, was sent by train to the military camp at Newcastle-Lyme, where he would wait for instructions to be demobilized.

The news of Germany's capitulation on May 8 and the declaration of peace reached Kurt in the camp's Keele Hall. There he learned that his demobilization could take place only in Palestine where he had been recruited into the army. It was unnerving to be still in England after Czechoslovakia was liberated from the German occupation in May. Kurt yearned to return home. A rumor reached him that the repatriation to Czechoslovakia from Palestine had been cancelled, but the rumor proved false.[10]

Kurt arrived in Palestine in July 1945, sporting still his Pioneer Corps uniform. The Zionist blue-and-white banners fluttered alongside the Union Jack in public spaces. And yet the Jewish community did not share the jubilation at the Allied coalition's victory and Germany's unconditional surrender. This triumph was overshadowed by the Jewish community's disappointment at not being able to secure the immigration of the concentration camps' survivors. After the horrors that had transpired in Europe became gradually known and thousands of Jews with no family and home to go to were housed in temporary camps for displaced people, Palestine was the only hope for many. But the 1939 white paper (one objective of which was to secure the Arab support for Britain's strategic and economic interests in the region) was still in place, and there was no international pressure strong enough to mitigate its effects. One other consideration of the British military in 1945 was to ensure that the Arab world did not gravitate toward the Russians.[11]

During the war there was calm in Palestine because everyone was engaged in the military effort, the Arabs and the Jews having come to a temporary truce. But in the last year of the war, radical Jewish political groups rebelled against the British Mandate's authority, targeting Arabs and British alike and weakening the Jewish Agency's policy of restraint. They stole arms, kidnapped British officers, damaged oil pipelines, and destroyed roads and bridges to protest the blockade on immigration. The Jews demanded certificates for immigration regardless of the quotas set by the white paper. They were still a minority in Palestine (which had over a million and half inhabitants) while thousands of Jews were waiting in camps, scattered in liberated Europe, ready to emigrate and settle down. The Arab League, formed in March 1945 in defense of the Arab Palestinians, was opposed to Jewish immigration and to the transfer of Arab land to Zionist hands. Tensions were smoldering. Relations between the mandate government and the Jews soured.

Palestine was in danger of setting aflame the entire Middle East if the Jewish and the Arab population were not consulted on the future of the land. The region was vital to the British imperial communication system, as control needed to be preserved over the Suez Canal, the Haifa port, and the oil pipeline from Iraq. Furthermore, "Palestine [was] a staging place on the air route to India and the Far East, and the starting point of the desert road to Baghdad."[12] But imperial interests notwithstanding, thousands of Jews were leaving the camps in Germany and Austria and heading for the Italian ports in the hope of reaching the coast of Palestine on overcrowded clandestine ships. When intercepted by the Royal Navy, the ships were sent back to Europe.[13]

Kurt was impervious to the turmoil taking place around him. He must have been aware of the plight of hundreds of thousands of Jews stranded in displacement camps around Europe, waiting eagerly to board ships to Palestine, arriving on unauthorized ships like himself a few years before, but now all he wanted was to get on a ship to leave. Their plight and the fight for the Jewish homeland were not his business. But first he had to be demobilized.

Kurt registered at the Czechoslovak repatriation mission for the Middle East in Jerusalem and at the consulate. Most applicants were Jews who paid no attention to the Jewish Agency's effort to keep them in Palestine with an eye to building the Jewish homeland. Kurt contacted his acquaintance Dr. Chaim Hoffmann in Haifa. Through Hoffmann, an honorary consul, Kurt learned that his mother and sister had survived the war. The man who brought the happy news was Dr. Hanuš Rebenwurtzel, a lawyer who before the war had taught Jewish religion to secondary school pupils in Vsetín, a stone's throw away from Valašské Meziříčí. He knew many people and people knew him; he may have known Kurt's family. Rebenwurtzel was also a refugee in Palestine, but he was a holder of the precious immigration certificate that allowed him legal existence. Sensitive to the Jewish soldiers' need for spiritual comfort and to the fact that there were not enough leaders to provide it, Rebenwurtzel learned the craft from a Czech rabbi and became one in his own right. He accompanied the Czechoslovak army throughout the war and looked after his flock when it ended.[14]

In September, Kurt received from reb Rebenwurtzel the best gift he could have wished for on the occasion of the Jewish New Year: the thrilling news that his sister and mother were healthy and back in Valašské Meziříčí.

As soon as he obtained the information, he hurried from Tel Aviv to Haifa, a couple of hours away by bus along the Mediterranean coast. Kurt was eager to deliver a letter for Rebenwurtzel—who was one of the few individuals who could travel freely—to take with him to Czechoslovakia.

Kurt wanted to know everything about what had happened to his mother and sister during the war and what their plans were. At war's end, when sorrow touched almost every family, while most Jews mourned their dead Kurt counted the living. Letters and news came in fast succession. Rebenwurtzel saw Kurt's sister, she looked well and was well dressed. Kurt's mother had hurt her hand and was unable to sign her name, let alone write a letter; but that would improve.[15] A lively correspondence ensued; the fate of the family during the war was gradually becoming clear.

Kurt's mother, Olga, born in 1879, and his sister, Anna, four years his junior, were summoned together with other Jews from Valašské Meziříčí to a transport bound for Terezín in September 1942. His father, Hynek, had died a year before. Mother and daughter had the fortune of spending the war together in the ghetto and not being selected for a transport east. Anna's good German kept her in good stead with her boss, who removed their names from the deportation list whenever they appeared there because Anna was allegedly indispensable to the war effort. While in their letters to Kurt they recounted the details of how they had spent the three years in Terezín and how they were saved from transports that would have led to their certain death, that history is much more complex and much of it irretrievably lost. After the war, liked most survivors of the Holocaust, they talked sparingly about their experience.

Olga and Anna remained in the camp until June 1945. One may surmise that in the last months of the war they witnessed the arrival of survivors from Auschwitz and Buchenwald as the Red Army and the Allies closed in on the German military and the Germans evacuated the remaining population from the concentration camps. They must have seen cattle trucks disgorging hundreds of survivors from the camps, which shook the ghetto's population: foul-smelling poor souls with shaven heads, skin and bone, and shabby clothes. Some of the prisoners arrived in Terezín for the second time, having spent time there before being transported to an extermination camp. Numerous prisoners who did not die during the trip to the ghetto died in the subsequent days and weeks. The former concentration camps inmates had been affected not only physically but also by the experience of living between life and death, to the point of having lost the capacity to communicate and coexist with others. They brought typhus, which spread fast through Terezín. First the Red Cross took over the management of the health system, then a Czech medical team did so; when the Soviet army arrived, it brought another medical crew. Repatriation from Terezín was hampered by chaos, characterized by trucks speeding away with escaping Germans, a lack of transport to move the inmates out of the camp, and the persisting fear that the typhus epidemic had not been eradicated fully. Returning home had to wait until it was certain that the journey would not jeopardize anybody's barely recovered well-being.[16]

When Anna and Olga arrived in their hometown after an absence of three years, they had to get accustomed to their new reality. For the time being, they had no place to live. There were thousands like them, counting the dead and sorting out their future. One was Arnošt Weinstein, a thirty-seven-year-old widower. Arnošt had a harrowing experience to relate. Born like Kurt in 1908 in a provincial Moravian town, he was transported to Terezín in December 1941. His wife, Hana, joined him a few months later and together they were deported during the last transport to Auschwitz in October 1944. Hana, pregnant with their child, did not survive. Arnošt did but from Auschwitz he was sent to the concentration camp of Dachau. His older brothers perished: Alfred in Auschwitz and Otto on the way out of Dachau in what for him was a death march.

When Terezín was liberated, the heartbroken Arnošt traveled there to look for his sister Lydia. Lydia had been deported to the ghetto with her husband and a little son on the same transport as Olga and Anna in the summer of 1942. The two families had known each other: they were guests at each other's weddings. Arnošt found Lydia but not her husband, who perished in Auschwitz; their son had died in Terezín from tuberculosis. Seeing the health catastrophe, Arnošt stayed to help the medical team, separating the sick from the healthy inmates. In the ghetto he must have stumbled on his acquaintance from before the war, the thirty-three-year-old Anna. A few weeks later, Anna let Kurt know that she was engaged to Arnošt, soon to be married.[17]

Kurt would not be able to attend Anna's and Arnošt's wedding, he regretfully wrote; there was still no date for his demobilization. Focused on practical matters, Kurt wanted to make sure that his mother, Anna, and Arnošt had the necessary clothes for the coming winter. He had no way of knowing that while he was imprisoned, the Czech police in Prague under the German tutelage had stripped him of his protectorate citizenship rights, including his right to property.[18] But even though Kurt had emigrated in 1939 after the complete Nazi takeover and after war broke out, he had stored his possessions in Italy before the catastrophe. Currently, he had no idea of their state. He also shared the experience of life in Tel

Aviv, a few steps from the sea where he used to go swimming, but he joked that the waves were too big and "the water too salty." He visited the Dead Sea but felt it had been created for lazy people: "There I lay on the surface and smoked a cigarette." In the final paragraph of this letter, Kurt referred to his incarceration in relatively close proximity to Oświęcim, "so I knew what went on there." Then he mentioned the seven-hundred-kilometer-long march to Germany.[19] His letters were unsentimental; life had to go on.

Kurt's sense of postwar bliss was untarnished by his memories: "There are few so happy people like me here who receive such good news." He exchanged letters with his mother and sister frequently, in which they would enclose each other's portraits. Kurt admitted to his loss of hair, in exchange receiving their photos as well as news about the wedding preparations. The one shadow marring his happiness was the lack of a date for his repatriation, among other reasons because he did not have a passport. Even if he had one, there was no transport available. Recently a group of officers managed to travel to Czechoslovakia by train but the trip through destroyed Europe took twenty-four days. On the positive side, Kurt was glad that his mother and sister were provided with a furnished apartment—a triumph. And between one happy note and another, Kurt inserted snippets about his life in captivity.[20]

By the time another letter arrived, Anna and Arnošt had been married. Shortly before the wedding, Arnošt applied for a change of his last name, from Weinstein to the Czech Vít. Fearing recurrence of anti-Semitism, he felt doing so would allow him to integrate better into the postwar society. The newlyweds had moved to a furnished apartment in Prague, which Arnošt received as a concentration camp victim. The clothes of someone named Mr. Hase, presumably the German previous tenant, were still hanging in the closets. Ironically, the rental contract for the apartment stipulated that the clothes were to be handled with care.[21]

On October 25, 1945, Kurt was demobilized. Although he had to travel to Jerusalem often to arrange his papers, he never mentioned the historic city in his correspondence, only the essentials of his daily life. He wrote that on demobilization he received civilian suits, one from the British monarch (popularly known in British culture as a "demob suit," issued to British military men after World War II), shoes, enough shirts and underwear, and no bedding. Since he had no relatives in Palestine, he was granted fifty-six days of paid holiday and a hotel room free of charge until he could find a job. There was still no prospect for repatriation. Army officers had priority.[22]

Kurt sought a job in an insurance company, but business transactions were so insignificant in Palestine at the time that he did not find one. Tel Aviv was expensive, so he thought of moving to Givat Chaim in the center of the country, one of the oldest kibbutzes in Palestine, founded in 1933 by the pioneering Zionists. It is difficult to imagine Kurt living the austere life of a kibbutznik and performing the tasks that the recently incorporated *chaverim* had to undertake, such as washing plates, pots, and pans or driving a pickax into the soil. All he wanted was to reunite with his family. "Ančo, you want to see me married," Kurt wrote once to his sister. "As far as I am concerned, at the beginning, I prefer to live with mami rather than with some strange woman. But on principle, nowadays I don't have objections to a marriage anymore as I used to have before."[23]

Life in Palestine continued to be turbulent. The British imposed a curfew after Jewish anti-British squads scorched several public buildings, including the post office, which might have explained why Kurt, "a victim of political passions" as he put it, was not receiving any letters. Kurt must have known better but did not inform his family about local events, perhaps out of precaution given the British censorship regulations. He mentioned the political trouble only as it precluded business from getting off the ground. Kurt thought of different trade deals that came to naught because naval transport was disrupted worldwide and also hampered because ships were not allowed to anchor in Palestinian ports out of fear that they might be carrying more immigrants. Letters took a long time to arrive, many got lost, so we don't know whether Kurt did go to the kibbutz. His main preoccupation was that his family at home should have enough warm clothes and fuel for the coming winter: "Mámo, I have worried about you for the last 5 years as much as you worried about me before. Be well and don't get cold. Kiss you. Your Kurt."[24]

In November the consulate in Jerusalem promised him a new passport. Repatriation was slowly underway. While waiting, Kurt made small packages to send, hoping that they would not be stolen on their way in a world starved of consumer goods. The consulate was being helpful in securing textiles from England for family members at home, but with a delay of ten to eleven months, which did not make sense to Kurt who hoped to be back in Czechoslovakia long before that. Did they have enough fuel in Prague? He hoped to be home by the spring of 1946.

Kurt's patience was wearing thin, he was bored, there was no work. He briefly got a dog but got rid of it because, he said in jest, all the dog wanted was to eat; then he thought of buying a cheap camera but abandoned that idea as well. He thought of importing Czech cut glass, but the deficient transport facilities also thwarted this business venture. The British had allowed trade with Czechoslovakia, but the goods had to go through England to let the middlemen earn something from the deals, which made the business transactions untenable. He was lonely. In Prague, Anča and Arnošt were expecting a baby. "It's possible that I shall leave at the end of May," he wrote to them. Kurt, then thirty-eight, let his sister and brother-in-law know where he kept his savings and bonds, in case something should happen to him before he was able to reach Prague.[25]

May came and Kurt changed his mind again. Instead of buying a ticket with his money and leaving on an impulse, he decided to wait it out. There was one advantage of being in Palestine: he did not have to be afraid of being a Jew, could say what he wanted, and criticize anyone he disliked. Kurt knew that the rigmarole in Palestine was more complicated than that, but he had no desire to get involved in local politics or even in its rich cultural life. His patience paid off and some business ventures were materializing, but his mind was fixed on the day he would get on a ship and leave. If the need arose, he would finish the business deal that he had entered into—exporting hops from Czechoslovakia to Palestine, where breweries had the capacity to supply beer to the British army in the whole of the Middle East—from home.[26] Thinking ahead, Kurt hoped that he could return to his old job in the insurance company Legie. But his liberation was not final until he held a ship ticket in his hand.

Sailing from Palestine

The repatriation was a protracted process. The first step was to obtain the right documents: a passport and a certificate that the applicant was a Czechoslovak citizen and had served in the army. Czechoslovak citizens who fought in the British army were required to provide evidence acceptable to the repatriation mission in Jerusalem. But Kurt did not have a document certifying he served in the Pioneer Corps of the British army. The history is murky, but most likely he applied while in Atlit, personally and not in writing. Hence, it took additional time before he secured a passport.

From the evidence available, Kurt never registered at the Czechoslovak consulate on his release from Atlit in 1940 and did not apply to join the Czechoslovak army. However, on his return to Czechoslovakia he claimed that the army did not accept him because of the quota dictating the number of Jews who could be accepted into the Czechoslovak army. One can surmise that he chose to enlist into the British army in Atlit due to the disputes among the Zionist groups as well as with their antagonists. Decisions made in 1940 responded to circumstances that no longer existed in

1945. Refugees who had applied for a Palestinian passport on their arrival, whether to legalize their status or because they wanted to belong to the Jewish homeland, were now ineligible for a Czechoslovak passport. Some tried to renege on their previous decision.[27]

When discussing the repatriation issues, the Czechoslovak military authorities and the consulate in Jerusalem never mentioned the reasons why Jews had emigrated to Palestine, the decimation of the Jewish population in Europe, or the horrors of the concentration camps during the war; they displayed no concern for the Jews who had taken the decision to avoid the catastrophe, the depth of which only now began to be known in full. When all legality was abolished after the German occupation, when travel from Czechoslovakia was forbidden and staying put meant endangering one's life, people made decisions to save their lives irrespective of legalities.

All in all, about three thousand people registered for repatriation at the general consulate in Jerusalem. Most were Jews. Occasional terrorists acts in Palestine triggered fear that Zionist organizations might thwart their repatriation. Individuals reported receiving threatening letters to dissuade them from leaving, because if they did so the country would lose valuable members of its population.[28] So in 1945 one nationalism continued to compete against another: both those espousing Zionism and Czechoslovak patriots were defending national and state interests, both nations needing every man and woman to help in its reconstruction after the war (or in the case of Palestine, to build a state that did not yet exist).

Demobilized soldiers from the Czechoslovak army had precedence to be repatriated over men who had served in the British army. Repatriation was hampered by the lack of transport facilities—trains, cars, and ships—at a time when the movement of people was overwhelming. The organization of the repatriation had to be orderly. All soldiers were required to leave with some money, which was provided by the repatriation mission, to take care of their accommodation and food expenses during the journey. Its distribution depended on the recipient's army rank. One was allowed to pack only personal objects. Books, letters, and diaries were subject to wartime censorship, which applied to all personal correspondence.[29] That regulation must have affected all the letters that Kurt received from his family in Czechoslovakia.

Wartime restrictions were still in place. There was a limit not only on how much money a person could carry but also on the currencies: one could possess only the currency of a country from which one traveled and to which one had the intention to arrive. Having a radio was prohibited.

Before setting out on the journey, the traveler had to register big pieces of luggage and store them in a compartment to which one had no access during the trip. Before leaving Palestine, passengers underwent a medical exam to make sure that they were vaccinated and did not carry any infectious diseases. Once equipped and prepared for travel, groups assembled with a leader in charge of their well-being and security, all with written documents in several copies according to strict regulations. The whole trajectory from Palestine to Czechoslovakia was said to be monitored by the Ministry of Defense.[30]

In July 1946, with all the documents required for leaving Palestine in hand, Kurt secured a berth on a ship. He packed his belongings and stored his trunk, prepared according to the prescribed weight. The group he was assigned to sailed from Haifa to Marseille. From the French port he made his way to Paris, where he boarded a train for Prague. The whistle sounded all aboard. The train pulled out of the station. It must have been depressing to ride through German towns and see chimneys sticking out into the sky, scorched and hollow buildings, and charred trees. Kurt struck up a conversation with a fellow passenger in the compartment, who like himself was going to Prague. Her name was Ruth Ornsteinová.

Part III

8

The Deadly Fifties

Ruth's parents, Anka and Willi, reunited in Czechoslovakia in 1945, but not for long. Willi's heart trouble cut his life short. Ruth and Kurt tried life together on their return to the country that both had been forced to leave in 1939, but not for long. When in 1948 the political regime changed radically to a system that looked alarmingly like the tyranny from which they had escaped, they decided to emigrate again. The attempt failed, as did their marriage. Ruth's life in Czechoslovakia during the 1950s turned into a series of tribulations that she faced with skills she had acquired during the war and by haphazardly adapting to the circumstances. Anka and Kurt lived their lives burdened by the memories of their past, which they kept to themselves.

Map 5. Czechoslovakia following the end of World War II

Homecoming

In March 1945 Willi applied for repatriation at the department of the Czechoslovak Ministry of Social Welfare in London. He did not know whether Anka was dead or alive. To the question of where he was to live on his return, he answered, "I don't know." It was not until Ruth had discovered her mother in Bergen-Belsen that Willi found out that his wife was alive. He put down on the questionnaire that he had a twenty-year-old daughter serving in the Women's Auxiliary Air Force who also wanted to be repatriated. So, with or without Anka, he and Ruth were to return to Czechoslovakia, where they thought they belonged.

Willi was the first to leave London for Prague, a city that was bombed only at the end of the war by disoriented American bombers, even as most Prague citizens were demoralized by the ferocity of the German rule. The end of the war and liberation in May restored hope despite the postwar chaos. Willi arrived in July. The journey took him several days through devastated German cities, the train passing through destroyed stations, but the damage he saw could hardly generate compassion from a man whose own family had suffered so much. On arrival, his most urgent tasks were to find a place to live and to secure a job. His application to the local government was fast-tracked because of his service in the army. Like most people, Willi may have visited acquaintances and friends, taking stock of the living and the dead. He may have been too shy to look for the clothes, jewels, and furniture that Anka had entrusted to acquaintances before being deported to Terezín. Some survivors found that the people in whose care they had left their property were pleased to see them and happily returned the linens or carpets entrusted to them, while others discovered that their possessions had long since been sold by their "caretakers," who argued that life during the war was difficult and they needed that money to survive.[1]

Willi was lucky. A refugee returning with nothing to his name, entitled to ration cards to obtain scarce food, he was in no position to be demanding. Yet, there were places and people to turn for aid. The Ministry of Social Welfare's repatriation office, the Council of the Jewish Religious Communities in Bohemia and Moravia, and the American Jewish Joint Distribution Committee (AJDC or "Joint") provided modest aid in money and goods in addition to supplying information on recent arrivals and people who had perished; his mother and siblings could have been among them. Willi was allocated a small but cozy one-room flat, a *garçonnière,* in an apartment building situated on a tree-lined street in one of the nicest Prague quarters; he also found a job in a firm that traded wood, a business he knew well. Ruth commented later that her father was not savvy enough to get something better, but to have managed a roof over his head in such a short time after arrival was a feat amid postwar scarcity, bureaucratic rigmarole, people pushing ahead of another in the line to secure housing, and—even with the war against the Jews now over— the perennial anti-Semitism. The economic devastation of Czechoslovakia was serious even without wholesale bombing. On recovering control of the state, the Czechoslovak government scrambled for cash, freezing prewar bank accounts. Returning exiles or concentration camp survivors received a pittance in exchange for their prewar assets.[2]

In a hopeful mood, Willi joined the Communist Party in 1946. After the horrors of fascism, the vaguely imagined communism or socialism that promised to restore justice and harmony among people and nations seemed to be an alternative to a regime that had caused the suffering of millions during the war. Ruth arrived shortly after her father. She had been demobilized from the military service on August 23, 1945; her discharge certificate from the RAF graded her character as "very good" and her proficiency as a linguist "satisfactory." She applied for repatriation the following day. Since reuniting with one's family took precedence over any other reason to be repatriated, Ruth declared that she wanted to be with her mother, "who returned from the concentration camp in Belsen." While she waited for transportation to Czechoslovakia, she received some money from the Ministry of Social Welfare to tide her over until she reached Prague.

FIGURE 6. Vilém (left) and Anna (right) Ornstein in Prague after the war.

Ruth left England with a trunk and two suitcases in October. Having already made one trip through Germany on her way to Bergen-Belsen, the present voyage through a country reduced to ruins and ashes did not shock her. Two weeks later, she and her father stood at the railway platform to await her mother's homecoming from Sweden. The train pulled into the station. The descending Anka looked aged but was elegantly dressed, wearing perhaps a hat and matching gloves, pearl earrings, and a matching necklace, beautiful as ever.

After six years of separation, Willi (forty-nine years old) and Anka (five years younger) settled in their cozy apartment, mourning dead parents, sisters and brothers, cousins, aunts and uncles, and so many friends. Ruth never overcame the feeling of being abandoned by her mother when the latter stayed behind in Czechoslovakia, feeling that if she hadn't done so, she would have spared herself the hardships that she underwent in the camps and the anxiety she caused Ruth and Willi. Anka, like the other returnees, received aid from the Jewish community and the AJDC. Did she recover any of the possessions that she entrusted to friends and acquaintances before the war? Food was scarce but Anka had experienced worse. Back at work as a homemaker, Anka used to meet with her concentration camp friends. Ruth recalled how these women, who had looked death in the face, talked animatedly about life, recounting their memories and bursting unexpectedly into laughter recalling comical moments. Willi, sitting in the corner of the apartment, remarked tongue-in-cheek that listening to their cheerfulness one was sorry not to have been there with them.[3]

Ruth returned to Czechoslovakia a lost soul. She had grown into a twenty-year-old independent woman who matured in England under extraordinary circumstances. Settling down to a disciplined style of life was alien to her. Like the recent arrivals from exile, she looked well, was healthy and decently dressed, in contrast to the arrivals from the concentration camps, who were sick, weak, hungry, and in rags. Unlike other women who returned from emigration, hiding, or incarceration avid to make up for the lost time, Ruth was adrift. Those who had not finished their education before the war were eager to complete it now or hoped to renew careers on which they had embarked earlier. Ruth was not interested. Reuniting with the family brought happiness and healing to many. Ruth reunited with her parents in Prague but did not want to live with them or even to be close by. Wartime England had given Ruth's life a meaning that was missing on her arrival in Prague. She tried her hand at teaching English, but it did not interest her. The environment was unsettling.[4]

The German aggression that Czechoslovakia had suffered in 1938, in

1939, and during the occupation, together with Britain and France's complicity in mutilating the country, influenced Czechoslovak postwar domestic and international politics. The government's trust in the alliance with the Soviet Union went hand in hand with the decision to expel the German population from the country. The Soviet Union and the Allies had favored the move on the premise that endorsing a national state of Czechs and Slovaks compensated for the German aggression and was a way to secure Czechoslovakia's democracy and independence.[5]

The population census taken in 1930 was decisive in 1945. Then, before the Nazis came to power, German-speaking Jews and non-Jews could choose between adhering to the Czech or to the German nationality. Vilém, who was born and raised in the border region of the Sudetenland and spoke German before he learned Czech, chose the Czech nationality. Anka did so as well. Thus, in 1946, Willi, Anka, and Ruth successfully validated their Czech nationality and Czechoslovak citizenship and were thereby spared the anti-German legislation. But they could not avoid the anti-German atmosphere created by many Czechs who did not distinguish between one German and another. Anti-Semitism and avarice had survived the occupation; heated nationalism was readily on display and influenced the expulsion of the Germans in a maelstrom of fury, vengeance, jingoism, and popular rage, all taking place amid the waves of migrants and refugees drifting from one part of Europe to another and posing humanitarian and organizational challenges to countries that had just emerged from destruction, starvation, and death. In 1930 Germans had made up 25 percent of the Czechoslovak population; in 1950, after the expulsion, they comprised only 1.8 percent. The retribution against the Nazis and their domestic collaborators aimed also to legitimate the postwar regime, justifying its policies and delegitimizing its opponents in the name of national security and sovereignty.[6]

The cleansing of the German population from Czechoslovakia had other ramifications. Vilém had left in 1939 to escape persecution and returned to a country where individuals—fascists, but also antifascists or German-speaking Jews—were singled out for expulsion, often brutally; he might have known some of them. He could not have been indifferent to the ravaging of the borderlands, the stealing and the squandering of property that the Germans, branded collectively as Nazis and denied their civil rights, were forced to leave behind. German was his mother tongue, but it was unwise to speak it in public. He spoke Czech with a German accent, did not change his German-sounding last name, and could not erase his drawl. His prewar antifascism—confirmed by his wartime army service—spared him legal problems on his return to Czechoslovakia but made the reintegration into the changed society difficult. German was not just a language; it was part of one's being that was amputated.[7]

Ruth felt out of place in Prague. In March 1946 she applied for an extension of her passport's validity and for a visa to travel to England and back. She stated that the purpose of her trip was to arrange financial matters that she did not manage to settle after being demobilized and repatriated in 1945, and to get married.[8] The British embassy in Prague stamped her passport on May 8 for a two weeks' visit. It was remarkable that she received the permit at all when Britain was overwhelmed with refugees and displaced people and was reluctant to let anyone in, especially after she had been already repatriated. Ruth arrived at Dover on a ferry on May 22. Whom was she to marry? Or did she use her engagement as a pretext to get a British visa?

In London, proverbial for its impenetrable fog that could force traffic to a standstill, Ruth rented a room and found a temporary job as a typist. Even though London looked drab, England felt as close to being home as could be. If Ruth expected to get married, the wedding did not materialize. The British embassy in Prague had given her a couple of weeks to settle her affairs, a deadline she ignored. When she applied at the Home Office for an extension of her stay, the application was denied, forcing her to leave without delay. Had the British let her, Ruth would have remained in England. As it was, she took the train to Dover and crossed the channel on July 17. From Calais the train rattled to Strasbourg and on July 19 her passport was examined at the border between Germany and Czechoslovakia. During the trip, Ruth struck up a conversation with a man sitting in the same compartment. Repatriated from Palestine, he introduced himself as Kurt Groll.

Disconcerting Changes

When Ruth and Kurt arrived in Prague in July 1946, they went their separate ways but must have promised each other to meet again. Ruth rented a room and found a secretarial job with the Allied Control Commission of the American military authorities, which continued (together with the United Nations Relief and Rehabilitation Administration [UNRRA]) to oversee the transfer of the German population from Czechoslovakia. It was an eye-opening experience and a lesson in institutionalized anti-Semitism, as Jews who had suffered the German onslaught and survived it were lumped together with German Nazis and collaborators. Distressed Germans and German-speaking Jews—some leaving against their will, others because they could not bear the hostility toward them in the border regions anymore—streamed into the office Ruth was managing. Some tried to bribe her with scarce goods such as furniture, begging her to ensure that they be transferred to Munich or anywhere else in the Allied-occupied zone in Germany except the Soviet sector. Those who had relatives in the Western zones could settle there; those that did not were bound for the Soviet sector. Ruth followed instructions to the letter. The job must have ended with the closing of the resettlement agencies in the middle of 1947.[9] By then her life had taken another radical change.

Ruth's and Kurt's courtship had been brief; they shared passion for music, a sense of humor, their peculiar Jewishness and chain-smoking; they had in common their emigration ordeals and sorrows for the deaths in the family while counting their blessings to have found survivors. Kurt was even-keeled, liked good wine and beer. Ruth, on the other hand, was an exuberant socialite, lacking even the elementary domestic skills. And so, the twenty-one-year-old Ruth announced to her mother that she was getting married to the thirty-eight-year old Kurt. Anka, who had lost any authority over her daughter, responded by slapping her face, signaling her disapproval of Ruth's choice of a husband.[10]

FIGURE 7. Ruth and Kurt's wedding in Prague in 1946

Ruth and Kurt married at the Prague registrar's office in the Old Town on December 21, 1946. The country was in chaos after six years of German occupation; shops were empty and what clothes they sold were of bad quality, unattractive and available only with state-issued coupons. Ruth wore a dark wool suit and shoes in which she could wade through the snow. Posing for a photograph outside the historic building, Kurt wore a winter coat. Both sported hats: Ruth's covered her abundant short, black wavy hair, Kurt's his bald head. Both wore glasses. Anka attended the wedding, as did Kurt's sister and brother-in-law. On the photograph, Ruth and Kurt wear smiles on their faces. Anka looks aloof.

Initially, the newlywed lived in a shared apartment because of shortage of accommodation, until they were allocated their own in April 1949. While food was difficult to get and there were lines outside grocery stores, it was nonetheless possible to get theater tickets and good health care. Ruth was unprepared for home life; her growing up in the boarding school for refugee children in England had not taught her the skills needed to run a household. Kurt may not have had much talent for domestic life either, after having lived an ascetic life of a prisoner. But Ruth arrived in Czechoslovakia with skills rare in a woman, which she had acquired as a clerk specializing in listening, translating, and transcribing Morse-code messages that required her to be alert and quick at rendering German into English.

After working for the Allied Commission, Ruth found a job with the Czechoslovak Airlines as a secretary, with English and German as her assets. In 1947 she joined the Communist Party at a time when this was not compulsory and when many other young people also enrolled, including people she knew from England, some having become prominent communist leaders. She did so because the communists promised a better democratic world, and the noncommunist president as well as the Communist Party secretary underwrote that pledge together. Unbeknown to the ordinary people, the communists were preparing to seize state power.[11]

The Soviet Union would have preferred to preserve the wartime alliance with the United States and Great Britain while at the same time carving out a sphere of influence over the neighboring countries and expanding its territory further than what the Security Council of the recently created United Nations had agreed to. However, European geopolitics was altered after the powerful 1945 demonstration of the atomic bomb, which the United States had and the Soviet Union did not. The USSR had a mighty army at a time when the Western countries were demobilizing theirs, but it was powerless against the atomic bomb. Concerned that another war might break out, Stalin took measures such as a military buildup and the subordination of the neighboring countries to the Soviet Union's discipline. Step by step, overseen by the Soviet envoys to Czechoslovakia, the communists were taking control of various ministries, such as the interior, which gave the party authority over the police and the security forces, power to grant or withhold licenses to print newspapers, and deciding influence in major industrial trade unions.[12]

The year 1947 was momentous. The wartime alliance of the Soviet Union and the Western powers had disintegrated. The Soviets and therefore Czechoslovakia as its ally rejected the US-designed Marshall Plan. The latter was conceived as a measure to prevent the European economy from collapsing after the devastating war and to dissuade the population from seeking alternatives that would erode the liberal economic system and government. It attempted to integrate Eastern European countries into the Western European economy and thus halt the expansion of the USSR. But the Soviet leaders did not distinguish the plan from an offensive designed to subvert their security, and even though they initially proposed accepting the aid to sabotage the Marshall Plan from within, Stalin canceled the maneuver at the last minute. In mid-1947 the two sides abandoned the prospect for cooperation and reconstruction of a new common European political order; confrontation ensued. Eastern Europe and the Western world were now separated by the ideological "iron curtain."[13]

Once again, Czechoslovak sovereignty was subordinated to the will of another state's political designs. After the war, Stalin agreed to the Czechoslovaks forming a multiparty government while at the same time the secret police was penetrating public institutions, and the communists were whipping up popular frenzy against the noncommunist opposition. Leaders of the political parties who had adhered to the system of parliamentary democracy, taking it for granted, lacked an effective plan for the entire country, failing to present themselves as viable combatants in the power struggle. Parliamentary democracy was doomed.[14]

The communist takeover in February 1948 was accomplished by a well-prepared course of action based in deception. Their stratagems made it look as inevitable, as demanded by the "people," the workers, and the People's militias (the Communist Party's army), all within the power vacuum left by the ineffectual opposition parties. Once the takeover was accomplished, the center of power was transferred from the government and its institutions to the party organs, which from then onward controlled all spheres of public life and, gradually, private life as well. By February 1948 the sovereign state of Czechoslovakia was incorporated in full into the Soviet bloc. As the Soviet Union was building a new realm in Europe, the British and the French were losing their colonial empires, affecting the European and world constellation of political and military forces.[15]

A few months into her wedded life, Ruth became pregnant. I was born on January 19, 1948. The Communist Party took over the country's institutions several weeks later. Both Ruth and Kurt were simple bystanders to these events, assuming a wait-and-see attitude while profound changes were taking place in all aspects of life. Instead of democratic coexistence among citizens, the regime propagated "class struggle" against "class enemies." Frenetic persecution and sweeping arrests contradicted the promised peace; the swell of "proletarianism" and the offensive against intellectuals were menacing. There were no pogroms such as the violent anti-Jewish riots in Poland, but the simmering poisonous anti-Semitism was affecting Jews who had wanted to assimilate or forget the horrendous past and to form new bonds in the postwar society. Kurt and Ruth took it personally when men and women who had served in the British army were targeted as imperialist traitors. How was it that their own country now diminished and wanted to obliterate Ruth's war effort and Kurt's suffering for the Allied cause, which contributed to Czechoslovak liberation? After all, before repatriation Ruth had been assured that her service in the Allied army was an act of patriotism and her disposition to contribute to the common cause of the Allied nations "will be duly appreciated by the government authorities of the republic."[16]

By the middle of 1948, disillusioned about the promises made by the new regime, Kurt and Ruth made up their minds about the political course on which the country had embarked and applied for emigration. Both had joined the Communist Party when it was voluntary, but now party membership was binding them to a regime that contradicted their expectations and beliefs in a free, democratic, and thriving society. Kurt, who had experienced instability and violence in Palestine in 1945 and 1946, knowing how difficult it was to start a business or find a job, had no desire to emigrate to the Jewish homeland after it was created in 1948, even if it was a country imagined to be free of anti-Semitism. Instead, on September 22, he submitted his application to the Council of Jewish Community in Prague to emigrate to Australia. The council forwarded his file to the AJDC Prague office, which sent a copy to its branch in Paris and the original to the Australian Jewish Welfare Society in Sydney. Both Kurt and Ruth spoke English well and the emigration agency considered them as ideal candidates. He was forty-one-years old, Ruth was twenty-four, and their child just a year and a half old.[17]

Months went by. The approval for their emigration to Australia reached the Paris office in September 1949 before it was sent to Prague. It was too late. By then the AJDC personnel knew that its days were numbered and its offices were to be closed. Indeed, at the end of the year, the government clamped down on emigration and travel from Czechoslovakia, denying what in 1948 the United Nations Declaration of Human Rights had elevated to the status of human right. The AJDC's activities on Czechoslovak soil were stopped in January of the following year.[18]

The year 1950 brought more desolation to Ruth and Kurt. Ruth decided to terminate their marriage. The age gap was insurmountable. Ruth at twenty-five was full of life, bored with the middle aged man she had wed but who remained a loyal friend after the divorce and a doting father till the end of his days. In September, Ruth's father was due to have prostate surgery. While on the operating table receiving anesthesia, his heart failed and he died. He was fifty-four years old. It was a stroke of luck that the apartment which Anka and Willi had occupied was so small that given the acute shortage of living space the authorities could not evict her for something more suitable for only one person.

Left by herself, Anka had to start earning her living. In Terezín she had acquired basic nursing skills, which now came in handy. She took courses and qualified as a nurse. Anka did not earn enough money to keep up with her tastes for face creams and nice clothes, but she had a knack for elegance and was able to turn old apparel and a few yards of material into modern outfits. She wore gloves and hats and always enhanced her outfits with earrings and a necklace. Like during the war, she lived largely on potatoes but now she could butter them. Anti-Semitism bothered Anka to the point that she tried to erase her Jewishness with rhinoplasty, although she never removed the tattoo on her arm.

Tribulations

Despite the disappointments that Ruth had suffered following the wartime, she found a dream job in the English section of the Czechoslovak radio network—the most powerful form of mass communication—and discovered her vocation as a translator and interpreter. The fact that she was hired at all suggests that her endeavor to emigrate and its failure did not reach the notice of the Ministry of the Interior even after paranoia set in and the government saw "enemies of the people" everywhere. The job appointment does not testify to freedom and independence of the Czechoslovak radio: more likely it was an oversight before the radio fell under complete Communist Party control.

Ruth's job as a translator and anchor started on November 1, 1949. A year later she was hired to a full-time position. This was probably due in part to her obligatory engagement in the young communist movement, and in part to the quality of her work—which brought her to the attention of the head of the short-wave broadcasting service and a labor union functionary, Vladimír Tosek, years later Ruth's second husband. He recommended her for promotion to the position of a reporter, translator, and news editor for the English broadcasts and suggested an increase in her salary.[19] That was in 1951. In April 1952, Ruth was fired from her job.

To consolidate the submission of Eastern Europe to the Soviet Union, Stalin and his henchmen devised the same sort of purges and show trials that they had practiced in the Soviet Union during the 1930s and continued after the war. They dispatched secret police advisers to every capital in the bloc to accelerate the hunt for the "enemies of the people." As the persecution of high party and government officials got underway, with their trials including torturing them into compliance, wholesale dismissals from ministries and government departments were taking place for all kinds of charges: for forging and disseminating food coupons; for resisting collectivization of agriculture; or for allegedly sabotaging the planned economy. Priests were accused for being in cahoots with the Vatican; the boy scouts excoriated "for endeavouring to keep the illegal scouting movement active."[20] Falsely accused of terrorism against the allegedly peaceful reconstruction of Czechoslovakia, thousands of men and women were condemned to prison terms ranging from several months to some years; one such case was for shooting a gun at the portrait of the president. In the process, the persecutions eliminated any effective opposition to the regime.[21]

The Slánský trial, so named for the general secretary of the Czechoslovak Communist Party Rudolf Slánský, was the most notorious violation of state's justice. It involved a concoction of false accusations against him and thirteen framed accomplices. They were charged with committing crimes against the nation for which eleven of them received the death penalty. Their "confessions" had been manufactured by the Ministry of the Interior; the defendants had to learn them by heart and regurgitate them in front a phony supreme court. The trials were a monstrous example of law-breaking that had a powerful negative impact on the history of communist Czechoslovakia.[22] Ruth's life spiraled because she knew them and was close to one of the defendants.

On November 24, 1949, deputy minister for foreign trade Evžen Loebl was arrested "in the name of the law," without any warrant or explanation.[23] A year later, Otto Šling, the party secretary in Brno, never returned home after work. What Loebl and Šling had in common was their exile in England during the war as Jews and dedicated communists. Both were engaged in communist propaganda in England, which earned them an investigation by the British secret service. Both used their membership and leadership in the Czechoslovak-British Friendship Club as a cover. Both returned to Czechoslovakia in 1945 to build the communist future. In prison in Prague, they were interrogated about their past, accused on false charges, tortured to confess, and indicted; the accusations included espionage, sabotage, treason, individualism, authoritarianism, bourgeois nationalism, Trotskyism, Zionism, having lost contact with the masses, and a litany of other fabricated self-serving conspiracies. In November 1952, Loebl was condemned to life in prison, Šling to death by hanging.[24]

Ruth's turn came on April 7, 1952. In the morning, she arrived at her workstation in the building of the Czechoslovak radio. Her superior, Aleš Suchý, did not wait for her to take off her coat, demanding that she leave the building immediately. It emerged later that the minister of information and propaganda, Václav Kopecký, had sent Suchý a list of Jewish employees to be dismissed. Had that order been carried out, the foreign radio broadcasting would have had to close, Suchý retorted; subsequently, the number of people who had to go was reduced, but Ruth was among those selected. The document she had to sign to terminate her contract said that her dismissal complied with the interests of the state and took place after a mutual understanding.[25]

Incriminating evidence against Ruth included her acquaintance with Loebl and Šling in England , in addition to being a Jew, having served in the western Allied army, and having foreign friends. Taken together these factors made Ruth an unreliable individual. Before joining the WAAF in 1943, she had worked as an office hand in the Czechoslovak-British Friendship Club, when Loebl was the secretary and Šling an assiduous visitor for a cup of coffee and debate about world affairs. Ruth's dismissal from her job was a breach of contract, but she was impotent against the decision. There was nowhere to appeal, no court or independent institution that would protect her against an arbitrary resolution based on flimsy arguments. But all things considered, she got off lightly. Others in similar circumstances were arrested.

Unknown to Ruth while she was looking for another job, the noose tightened around the accused. In preparation for his trial, Loebl was instructed to draw other innocent people into the web of invented crimes. He was forced to brand as an enemy the British-funded Czech Refugee Trust Fund, which had saved the lives of many persecuted communists and Jews before the German onslaught by spiriting them to England and then helping them to settle there, including Loebl, his wife and son, Ruth, and her father. He had to characterize the trust fund as the breeding ground of spies and imperialist agents for the British intelligence service. It was in the trust fund, Loebl was instructed to memorize as one of his felonies, that he learned the spying trade.[26]

Ruth and her father had left Czechoslovakia in the spring of 1939 by the same route as Loebl. But in his confession, Loebl claimed that many refugees were recruited for espionage in Kraków—where they received aid from the British Committee for Refugees from Czechoslovakia—in preparation for the postwar subordination of Czechoslovakia to western imperialism. As a deputy chairman of the Czechoslovak-British Friendship Club in London, Loebl kept on smearing himself in his false confession, claiming he betrayed the Communist Party and used the club in service to the exiled government and the reaction: "I betrayed the Communist Party and the idea of making the club into a centre of mutual cooperation."[27]

In November 1952, loudspeakers around the country broadcast daily the confessions of eleven high-ranking communists and government functionaries who admitted having committed heinous crimes. Šling confessed, "I admit that during my stay in England from 1939 to 1945 I was engaged in hostile, opportunist activities," establishing espionage contacts with British officials and seeking "to build up a good position for myself among the emigres." He returned from Britain to Czechoslovakia in 1945 as an imperialist agent. The trust fund, which pretended to be a British charity organization for aid to emigres, was in fact an espionage center, training agents to carry out a plan concocted by the government in exile to establish a military dictatorship in Czechoslovakia with the help of the Anglo-American imperialists.[28]

Loebl and Šling, like the rest of the indicted men, had been forced to participate in their own destruction, and they knew it. "With hindsight I am most pained by the fact that at the time I did not feel like a human being any longer," wrote Loebl in his memoirs. The humiliation tormented him for years to come. The fabricated confessions of defendants in these trials were so outrageous that people who had been their friends, colleagues, and acquaintances questioned their honesty.[29]

Listening to the admissions of guilt by men whom Ruth had trusted and who now reviled themselves turned her world upside down. Had she been deceived by Loebl, her mentor in England? Had she been bamboozled by Šling, who had endorsed her party application in 1947? Ruth's friend and former colleague in the British section of the radio suffered a breakdown and quit her job after hearing the confession given before the supreme court by the man with whom she was in love, and who was condemned to death. Like her, he was a communist and a comrade; could he have betrayed her and the cause?[30]

The brutality of the trials was crippling; the persecutions, the violence, and the repression had a profound impact on millions of citizens who from then on were forced to live their lives in fear and conformity; not only the opposition but the creative spirit of Czechoslovak society was largely smothered for years to come. This involved both poetry and music. Composers like Bohuslav Martinů, Igor Stravinsky, and Béla Bartók were considered decadent by the communist regime; playing Martinů at an exam exercise in the Academy of Performing Arts in Prague in 1951 was a guarantee that a student would not pass.[31]

Ruth started a new job in June, selling holiday tickets for the Czechoslovak travel agency. She did not last long on the job: she was bored and badly paid. In March 1953 Stalin died, followed a few days later by the Czechoslovak little Stalin, Klement Gottwald, in Prague. Most people sighed with relief, some shed tears. The death coincided with the governments of the countries in the Soviet sphere of influence being under pressure from their disgruntled populations. Living standards had worsened, all while the people been deprived of free access to creativity in the arts, in thinking, and contacts with the outside world. Industrial workers revolted openly against the regime in Eastern Germany but were repressed in one swoop by the Soviet occupation forces stationed there; in Poland and Czechoslovakia the discontent against the status quo simmered. When it erupted in a rebellion in the industrial complex of Plzeň, the workers' movement was crushed without mercy. Reform was needed, but while the forced collectivization eased, the monetary reform of May 1953 hit the people's pockets hard as their savings disappeared overnight. To give the appearance of change, on Soviet impulse and with the help of the state-controlled police apparatus the communist government lowered prices and increased salaries in order to maintain calm in the country.[32] It was in these circumstances that Ruth sought a way out of her dismal situation.

An opportunity arose in 1953 to join the International Union of Students (IUS) as an external interpreter. IUS was founded on Soviet initiative in Prague in 1946 as a representative body of students from Britain, France, and the United States as well as the countries of the expanded Soviet sphere of influence. Officially, its aim was to preserve coexistence and cooperation with the capitalist and the colonial world; its unspoken goal was to amplify the IUS's membership worldwide so as to sway its members

FIGURE 8. Daniela Spenser (first row, black sweater) in kindergarten in 1953, with the obligatory portraits of the president Klement Gottwald and the Soviet supreme leader Josef Visarionovich Stalin on the wall

to the Soviet anticapitalist and anticolonial outlook. It also created and disseminated propaganda to promote the Soviet Union and the emerging Eastern bloc's alleged social advantages over the capitalist West.

Ruth's boss was Jiří Pelikán, the IUS's general secretary. Pelikán was a seasoned member of the Communist Party, who had a knack for combining ideological zeal with common sense and diplomatic skills. His devotion to the party led him to participate in the practice of cleansing universities of people who were not its members, destroying their careers. Apart from hectoring anyone who would listen about peace and the Soviet Union's accomplishments, Pelikán helped students from the colonial countries to obtain scholarships to study at Czechoslovak universities. In a country in which uncontrolled international exchanges of ideas was next to impossible, Pelikán encouraged them. Obstacles to organizing international student symposia came not only from the countries of popular democracies, as they were called, but also from IUS's opponents, who rightly considered it to be a Soviet front organization. But Pelikán saw beyond the Cold War rhetorical conundrums on both sides of the divide, trying to inject freshness into the sleep-inducing dialogues. Quick minded, multilingual, with a disarming smile, he was always ready to initiate revelry with folksongs and dances in the middle of the night. Under his leadership, IUS conferences provided opportunities for mixing with all kinds of colorful people from around the world and for romances, friendships, and spontaneous merry evenings.[33] Ruth relished the change in her circumstances.

The Czechoslovak welfare system had at its core the goal to help women to integrate into the workforce in order to boost production, to allow them time for relaxation after work, liberating them from the worries of caring for a child in the most suitable environment possible. Boarding schools were deemed a better solution than entrusting children to grandmothers. Assisting the working mothers had the additional goal of integrating them and their children into the organized socialist structures; the subjectivity of a child was not part of the debate.[34] So living in the whirlwind of her work and desperately looking for a partner, Ruth took advantage of the socialist amenity for women, placing me at the age of five into a weekly boarding school. From its walls, portraits of the president Klement Gottwald and of Joseph Stalin looked down on the children until both communist leaders died in quick succession in 1953.

Freed from domestic chores, Ruth had time at her job at IUS to socialize with foreign communists or sympathizers from all over the world whose speeches she had to interpret at conferences, giving her the opportunity to imbibe lessons in practical international politics. She had to also translate the IUS's wooden resolutions and propagandistic articles for its organ *News Service*. Cabin interpretation was a specialized job, which required not only knowledge of languages but alertness and a capacity to think on one's feet. Ruth had learned those skills during the war as a listener at the intercepting stations of the Royal Air Force and with practice was getting better at her job.

Because Ruth was in regular contact with foreign citizens whose ideas might have been corrupting and was a Jew who had served in the British army, the secret police suspected her of disloyalty. An informant named "Jana" reported in 1954 to her handler "Kasal" that she had not seen Ruth after they had known each other in England and so could only report snippets on her life. To get hold of meaty information, she inquired about Ruth and Kurt from their landlord before they had divorced. There she found out that the couple wanted to emigrate to Palestine, she wrongly informed "Kasal," adding that Ruth was living with an Italian comrade.

"Jana" reported furthermore that "Comrade Chytilová" told her, in confidence, that Ruth made no secret about having been "schooled" by Otto Šling in England, which was the reason why she had been sacked from her job. The shadow of suspicion that Ruth had collaborated with the British intelligence still hung over her but could not be proved.[35]

The trials and the loss of her job had quenched Ruth's sympathy for the regime, but she did not know how to escape it. After four years at IUS, she learned to discern the political wheat from the ideological chaff in an environment of flourishing satire, expressed in cartoons and jokes: "Socialism might be ok, but should not they have tried it on animals first?" "Is it possible to build socialism in one country? Yes, but it's better to live in another." "Capitalism is the exploitation of man by man. In socialism it is the other way round."[36]

Entrapped

Prague was dubbed the "Communist Geneva" because it hosted numerous international organizations: IUS, the International Organization of Journalists, and the journal *Problems of Peace and Socialism*, known also as *World Marxist Review*.[37] From 1956 Prague accommodated the World Federation of Trade Unions (WFTU) after it was expelled from Vienna and before that from Paris. Cold War animosities toward the Soviet Union intensified in Western Europe in the late 1940s and the WFTU was one of its casualties.

What IUS represented for students, WFTU meant for the labor unions east and west in the Cold War divide. It had a similar origin, trajectory, and goals. Theoretically, WFTU brought together communist and noncommunist unions for the lofty tasks of destroying fascism, expanding democratic rights, supporting employment policies, and seeking to better jobs and wages, fair workdays, social security, and health care. Labor unions were encouraged to suggest common organizing issues, including the defeat of Franco's fascist government in Spain.

The WFTU was founded in 1945 as an organization committed to international economic reconstruction. Its consolidation worldwide was important for the Soviets because it conferred respect, making it possible to influence workers' movements beyond their geographical sphere of influence, engage in anti-capitalist propaganda, and defend Soviet domestic and foreign policies. But the noncommunist members of the WFTU rejected Soviet attacks on their capitalist governments. The division between the two camps sharpened in October 1947 when the Soviet government opposed the Marshall Plan for the reconstruction of Europe and all communist parties had to follow suit.

Louis Saillant, the WFTU's French general secretary, considered the Marshall Plan to be a reactionary scheme and an expression of US monopoly capital. In opposing the plan, he placed the WFTU in an awkward position, since he seemed to be against European recovery. One British trade union leader charged that in the hands of its president, the WFTU had become an instrument of Soviet policy. The original WFTU disintegrated in 1948 on the initiative of the West European partners. In 1949 it was reconstituted, now comprising only nations friendly to the Soviet Union.[38]

The WFTU settled in Prague in 1956 and needed a staff, including interpreters. Ruth was hired in February 1957. The organization was a babel of languages where Ruth, who acquired languages almost by osmosis, soon incorporated French into her arsenal. Now she could interpret from Czech, German, Italian, and French into English, which was her expertise. Besides being sought after as an interpreter and translator, Ruth had no difficulties navigating in the men's world. The war had steeled her into seeing herself as an equal to male colleagues. Due to her exceptional talents, her salary was also equal or higher to those of most men around her. She liked the good life and needed money to pay for it. Ruth was one of the first owners of a television set at a time when one had to stand in line the whole night to buy the rare commodity and she was also a car owner. She drove her dark blue Fiat on the sleepy streets of Prague as well as the lonely roads to ski resorts in northern Bohemia. The car made her the envy of neighbors, who hurled anti-Semitic slurs at her. Through her job, Ruth also traveled on assignments to neighboring countries, as well as to China and African nations.

Ruth's trips abroad and daily mingling with foreigners drew the attention of the state secret police (StB, for its abbreviation in Czech). The StB had started a file on her in the early 1950s, and at some point it reclassified her from an object of surveillance to a potential recruit as an informer. In August 1958, it approached her: Josef Kořenek, a specialist on England at the Ministry of the Interior, interviewed Ruth on August 28. He recommended her as a useful collaborator because of her daily contact with foreigners, her knowledge of languages, and travels abroad: "During the interview she seemed positively inclined, knowing what her duty is and whenever necessary we can turn to her." Kořenek was satisfied with this highly intelligent catch who had a wide political overview, social skills, an extraordinary vitality, and alertness due to her work as a cabin interpreter. With adequate guidance and control, he could get good results. Apparently, Ruth volunteered to contact people she knew at school in England and in the British army. She was sworn to state secrecy and given the alias of Soňa.[39]

Ruth knew that contacts with foreigners from the capitalist countries was a minefield in Czechoslovakia. She was not supposed to have them. But she did because it was part of her job. From the evidence available, Ruth tried to play their game. The Interior Ministry's officers were interested in her foreign contacts and so she made out reports on them. Overall, the interrogators complained about her lack of enthusiasm to supply the sumptuous material to which she supposedly had privileged access.

Because the ministry destroyed everything Ruth had reported, we have only the secret police operatives' reports on her. In 1958, while she was being recruited, the police operator wrote about her intimate relationship with someone named TOSEK, in capital letters, from the Czechoslovak television. Their contact was confidential because Tosek was married. The Ministry of the Interior did not trust her entirely, so it looked for some compromising material to trap her into its network unreservedly. All it found were letters that Ruth mailed for her friends on a trip abroad so that they would arrive faster and circumvent mail censorship. It was wrong, she admitted. Then and throughout Ruth's collaboration with the StB, her pragmatic ex-husband recommended fake cooperation, giving useless information and adapting to the evils of the regime to preserve her employment.

In September 1960, two days before her thirty-fifth birthday, the results of Ruth's collaboration were evaluated. There were no tangible results, the interrogator complained. Ruth was an opportunist, seeking only personal goals, feigning her positive attitude toward the system; she was completing her tasks superficially and showed no initiative unless there was a prospect of a trip abroad. First Lieutenant Farský ended his evaluation with a recommendation and a threat, which he underlined: that either she collaborate properly with the Interior Ministry or her travels would be forbidden and "in that way she will lose her job at the WFTU." In the future, she was to report on all foreigners she knew and on all close contacts she had in the WFTU. Farský wanted to be present at the next meeting.[40]

In October 1962 Ruth-Soňa was up for another evaluation. Lieutenant Dvořák was either content with the results of Ruth's work or she changed her tactic. She was straightforward in her dealings with the ministry and was willing to admit her mistakes; however, she lacked a "critical approach" and the initiative to glean valuable information for which she was well placed. Still, she did provide some interesting news items regarding foreigners. Her command of languages was notable, even better than when she was recruited. The handler was impressed and even exaggerated Ruth's abilities because she did not speak Russian or Spanish as the assessment stated. Her travels abroad, to the capitalist as well as to the socialist countries, her participation in the most important conferences, international negotiations, and youth festivals, were mentioned as giving her access to venues from which she could bring useful information. In the next evaluation, it would be decided whether she could be put into contact with foreign counterintelligence. It was going to take place in 1963; we don't know whether the meeting took place or not because there is no mention of it in the archive.[41]

Ruth was assessed again on December 22, 1964, by a first lieutenant who introduced himself as Had Alvi. He concluded that Ruth's performance was mediocre despite her excellent potential. It was not known whether she had divulged her collaboration with the Interior Ministry to anyone, she was intimate with Tosek, and she owned a car. When abroad, she liked to postpone her returns for a day or two. It was necessary to keep a check on her. In November Ruth had gone to Budapest to a conference and upon her return provided useful analysis of WFTU's internal workings. The StB considered again the value of her day-to-day contacts with foreigners, her social skills, and knowledge of languages. Based on the material she had provided and despite the previous complaints about her negligence in reporting on her colleagues, Ruth was proposed for promotion to an agent-informer.[42]

Everything changed in 1966 when Ruth quit her job. Her health had deteriorated. From October on she was on a sick leave. As far as the secret police was concerned, Ruth became expendable because she ceased to be in regular contact with foreign nationals. Collaboration was to end and her file was to be stored in the archive of the ministry for five years. Her handwritten reports were recommended for destruction.[43]

Ruth had played their game of reporting on her colleagues as little as it was possible until she could no more. She left WFTU voluntarily to get the police off her back even though it meant a substantial decrease in her exceptionally high salary. She had developed painful stomach ulcers, which could have originated in the stress stemming from the collaboration with the secret police and the existential insecurity with which they had been constantly threatening her. Ruth had discussed leaving Czechoslovakia with Kurt but did not carry it out because it would have required a lot of planning to escape with a child when legal emigration was next to impossible. She was still going to conferences as an interpreter and did translations to compensate for her reduced salary at her new job in the Czechoslovak News Agency, where her assignment was sorting out photographs, putting captions under them in English to be sent or sold to foreign news agencies.

Taken all together, it seems that she quit her well-paid job to escape the prison her life had become and to recover her health. Ruth's tribulations were about to be offset when Vladimír Tosek—her boss at the radio station, a longtime colleague from the interpreters' booth, and then a dashing television journalist (who had been divorced in 1960)—became the love of her life.

FIGURE 9. Vladimír Tosek, the dashing television journalist

9

The Journalist for a Better Tomorrow

Vladimír Tosek was born one year after Czechoslovakia became a sovereign nation in 1918. His parents, Adolf Tosek and Zdenka Tosková, etched their belonging to the Slavic nation into his name. Assimilated Prague Jews, patriotic, enlightened, and prosperous, they did not spare effort and money to advance Vladimír's education. He was a gifted child who absorbed knowledge and languages in stride. Unsuspecting of the tragedy to come, his parents sent him on a study trip to England in 1938, at the last possible moment. They perished in Auschwitz. Their names are emblazoned on the wall of the Pinkas synagogue in Prague together with those of seventy-seven thousand other Holocaust victims: line upon line of tidy writing, names, dates, places, in alphabetical order from ceiling to floor. "Nothing at all except the unaccountable names of the dead."[1] Vladimír was burdened by their tragic disappearance for the rest of his life.

The Family

Vladimír, his sister, their parents, and aunts and uncles belonged to the stratum of society that in the 1950s was designated with the derogatory epithets "bourgeois" and "class enemies." Adolf Tosek, born in a town close to Prague in 1875, became a businessman after graduating from a technical school. He imported and sold wine supplied by his Italian relatives living in Trieste, eventually becoming a representative of the major European wine and spirit manufacturers. He was a man of short statue, with thin lips above which he wore a carefully trimmed mustache and bushy eyebrows lining his oval face. When in Prague in 1909 he married Zdenka Wittlerová, twelve years his junior, both declared themselves to be without Jewish faith. Looking at their photographs, it is apparent how Zdenka's look changed markedly with the style of the times, from the elaborate hairdo and a frilly chemise in 1915 to short hair simply combed and a white blouse adorned only with a brooch a few years later. Her delicate features remained the same. It could have been before the marriage that Adolf changed his Jewish last name Taussig to the Czech Tosek. Thus, it was a sign of the perennial anti-Semitism in Czechoslovakia that the communist police authorities referred to Vladimír consistently as "formerly Taussig." He never bore that last name.

Vladimír and his older sister, Helena, were both well-groomed and widely traveled. They had crisscrossed Europe several times, visiting relatives in Trieste, the enchanting countryside and villages of Switzerland and Austria, the French Riviera, and the Italian beach of Rapallo as well as the museums of Paris and Rome. Educated first in a Czech school, Vladimír, or Dada as the family called him, concluded his middle school in a French gymnasium before his parents decided to send him to England to continue his studies.[2]

By 1938, the nineteen-year-old Vladimír had already mastered several languages. Tall, handsome, broad-shouldered with dark brown wavy hair and green eyes, he inherited his father's thin lips and his mother's delicate features. Despite the anti-Semitic atmosphere of neighboring Germany spilling over into Czechoslovakia in the 1930s, Vladimír's father was optimistic that life would go on as usual. Helena had been married happily to a non-Jewish entrepreneur since in 1935 and business flourished. When Vladimír's parents committed to sending him to Manchester for a two-year course of study at a commerce academy, they could provide him with a modest monthly stipend.

In 1939 Adolf Tosek was sixty-four years old, his wife fifty-two. Many Jews had left Czechoslovakia before the German occupation in March 1939, and others were getting ready to leave now that it had occurred. But emigration was a complex decision: generational, financial, and psychological. From Manchester, Vladimír urged his parents to leave, but his father was reluctant not only because train trips had been cancelled, he wrote, but because emigration was possible with only one suitcase in hand and without any money. Before the occupation, one could send furniture ahead but not anymore. Business was still doing fine. If it were not for the back pain, life was all right. Helenka dropped in periodically for a cup of coffee.[3]

But not all was normal; Adolph's letter to Vladimír from March 25 had been opened in search of illegally sent money or postal stamps. The Aryanization of Jewish property was proceeding unresisted because "J. were resigned to their destiny," wrote the senior Tosek laconically about his Jewish neighbors. The parents' greatest satisfaction was that Vladimír was spared their existential anxiety; they, old people, were not so relevant. Adolph believed they would reunite one day. In the meantime, they were expecting new regulations for Jews, like those implemented in the Reich and some in places in Czechoslovakia already: a famed popular Prague restaurant and café had signs hanging on its wall declaring "non-Aryans are not welcome." Adolph was busy, his wine and spirit distribution business was still doing well, "so nothing to worry."[4] That was in April 1939.

With time, letters between Vladimír and his parents became sparse and their language cryptic. They were mainly about money, missing letters, and expropriation of Jewish property, including jewelry: "It's a good thing that it doesn't concern us," wrote Vladimír's father, trying to sound cheerful. He hoped that Vladimír would continue his school into the second year. To better illustrate the atmosphere at home, he included in one of his letters a newspaper clipping stating that in one provincial town, Jewish shops had to display in their shopwindows in Czech and German that they were *Židovský obchod* or *Jüdisches Geschäft*: "Jewish shop." Other establishments had to announce that the business was in the hands of non-Jews. For the time being, the atmosphere toward the Jews was without hate. "We have to await what comes next." The separation was hard on all of them.[5]

Pessimism was penetrating their lives. Vladimír's father could not send money anymore because the bank did not answer Jewish requests for withdrawals. In June 1939 Vladimír turned twenty years old, an occasion that was celebrated with only a phone call. His mother especially regretted that she did not have her beloved son close to her. Did he have enough money, socks, shoes, food? If not, father and mother would send some; "We'll manage somehow," they wrote, despite new regulations that changed every day. And there was not enough information about what to expect. "I wish us to reunite all healthy really soon and in the hope that this is just an episode in our life but one that may end happily for all."[6] Soon thereafter, Adolf Tosek had to give up his job and his business was aryanized. It could have been bought by an honest purchaser or by an anti-Semitic speculator profiting from the aryanization of Jewish assets. The good news was that Vladimír ended his first year at the commerce academy successfully. Helena, who was twenty-eight years old in 1939 and married to a non-Jew, could no longer travel and the couple was subjected to ignominious pressure meted out on non-Jews to divorce their Jewish spouses, which was out of the question. Still, she was spared the worst anti-Jewish persecutions.[7]

Even fewer letters reached Vladimír's parents after war broke out in September, which made them despair. Was he ill? Vladimír was well, but his life was taking a different course from the one that his parents had prognosticated for him, and he could not share it in writing. To become a businessman was not his calling. He abandoned the school. In Manchester he befriended other Czechoslovak emigrants, many of whom belonged to the clandestine Communist Party, and they drew him into their orbit. To earn his living, he worked for different firms and for a short time as an agricultural laborer. The Czechoslovak-British Friendship Club, the domain of the communists, had branches throughout Great Britain and one in Manchester. Vladimír became active writing articles for their journal, *Mladé Československo* ("Young Czechoslovakia"), and speaking in public. Through the club he liaised with British progressive organizations and with German and Austrian youth groups, all to orchestrate the support for beleaguered Czechoslovakia.

In the Army

It was not until Hitler betrayed the nonaggression pact he had signed with Stalin in August 1939 and attacked the Soviet Union in June 1941 that the Communist Party gave the green light to its members and fellow travelers like Vladimír to join the England-based Czechoslovak army. He relocated from Manchester to one of the army's headquarters in Leamington Spa, some thirty kilometers southwest from Birmingham, and was assigned to the armored brigade as an artilleryman.[8]

Vladimír was not the military type, but his talents were not wasted. He excelled as a private engaged in consciousness raising among the rank and file, inculcating discipline among the soldiers through lectures and speeches on history and current events with the restoration of Czechoslovakia's sovereignty in mind. It was not an easy job to keep the multicultural Czechoslovaks together. Ideology and prejudices stood in the way of the cohesion of Czechs, Slovaks, Jews, and anti-Semites, Sudeten Germans, radical nationalists, anti-capitalist and anti-imperialist communists, but training in the army helped to bind them together building a formidable military machine. The communists collaborated with the exiled government in London but at the same time kept their distance from it. Holding the government responsible for the capitulation before Hitler and for the Western powers' complicity in destroying Czechoslovakia, the communists were already thinking postwar reconstruction country and their role in it.[9]

There is a blank in Vladimír's military history between 1941, when he joined the army, and the deployment of the Czechoslovak Independent Armored Brigade during the siege of the Nazi pocket on the beach of Normandy in 1944. Vladimír himself described those years as uneventful, until finally in June 1944 his unit was transported to northern France on an old warship that could navigate in shallow waters. There the brigade got stuck for three weeks, waiting for better weather conditions and orders to continue inland. Finally, the brigade entered the fray, fighting locally from farm to farm until the German capitulation in May 1945.[10]

Vladimír's return trip to Czechoslovakia after seven years of absence was moving. He did not know what he would find when he mounted the vehicle that mapped the way for the convoy that followed, making sure to avoid the destroyed roads and mines. They arrived in Plzeň, a Czech town in southwest Bohemia, sometime in the middle of May. Vladimír went to the local radio station to broadcast his search for the Tosek and Mařík families. One of the helping hands at the station was the twenty-one-year old Libuše Zykmundová, who made a lasting impression on Vladimír, then twenty-six years old. Shortly after having met her, he had to leave the town and proceed to Prague. His health had suffered the consequences of unhealthy living conditions in the army: he was diagnosed with paratyphoid and hospitalized for several weeks. After leaving the hospital and before being demobilized, Vladimír was granted a week of vacation. He went to Plzeň. One can find no other reason for him to spend a week there than to see Libuše again.[11]

Soon after his first arrival in Prague, Vladimír rang the bell at the apartment in which he had spent his childhood and adolescence with his parents and sister. Helena opened the door with a baby boy in arms. She had the sad duty to tell him about their parents' murder in Auschwitz.[12] Vladimír had nowhere to live and moved in with his sister and brother-in-law until he found a place for himself. It seems that he did not apply then or later to any of the institutions helping Jews returning from exile, the army, or concentration camps to get assistance in finding an apartment. He considered himself ineligible for privileges that more needy people deserved. At the end of May 1945, he witnessed one of the many military parades in Prague celebrating the liberation from the German occupation. For him and Helena the cost of peace was high.

On the Short Waves

Vladimír did not join the Communist Party of Czechoslovakia in England because the party only existed underground there and lacked the official apparatus to enlist new members. Still, to all who knew him he proved to be a reliable comrade. So, when he arrived in Prague, he was recommended by the communists with whom he had cooperated in England to become a party member. Moreover, two prominent party functionaries, Otto Šling and Evžen Loebl, invited him separately to work with them at their ministries. It was fortuitous that he declined both offers of employment. Had he accepted, he would have suffered the fate of their collaborators during and after the Slánský trial, which cost many of them their positions. Vladimír had other plans.

In England he had become a skilled communicator and now he wanted to join the Czechoslovak radio to learn the craft of journalism. He also wanted to study philology and enrolled into philosophy faculty of Charles University. He knew the radio station's new director, Bohuslav Laštovička, from England; for his part, Laštovička knew Vladimír's qualities from his engagements in propagating communist ideas among the British public and in the army. Thus, Vladimír was considered ideologically reliable when the communists were filling important positions in public life and institutions on their road to power.[13]

In his application for a job in the monitoring service of the Czechoslovak radio as an English and French translator, Vladimír extolled his linguistic qualities and patriotic engagements in England in both Czechoslovak and British organizations. He was hired almost immediately and needed a few days before starting the job to arrange personal matters such as securing an apartment, procuring clothes, and taking care of his parents' affairs but otherwise he was eager to begin straightaway. Anticipating that university studies would require time off work, he applied for shorter hours and unpaid holidays before exams. He hoped to graduate by the summer of 1947. However, his fragile health obstructed this plan; he was often on a sick leave, suffering from chronic stomach, duodenal, and intestine afflictions.[14] Together with party assignments, this meant he could not continue the university studies.

Vladimír's capability on the job must have been appreciated, because on March 8, 1946, the general director nominated him the head of the short-wave radio broadcasts. Four days later, Vladimír married Libuše Zykmundová, the young woman he had fallen in love with at first sight on arrival to Czechoslovakia in May 1945. When party ideologues questioned him about his past, he extolled Libuše as a like-minded partner with whom he could found a family and build the socialist motherland. He had an inquisitive mind and was so esteemed at work that in 1947 he was sent to France and England to study the technicalities of short-wave radio broadcasting, which in Czechoslovakia was still in its infancy. On December 23 of that year, their first son was born.[15]

Vladimír did not need any convincing about the correctness of the course that the Communist Party of Czechoslovakia took when it seized power in February 1948. The radio building and broadcasting of the events as they unfolded were key to the success of the takeover and had to be defended. Some employees slept in the offices to shield the building with their bodies and perhaps weapons. "Forward with the left, not a step back" was one of the slogans transmitted to listeners at home and abroad. Vladimír oversaw the daily short-wave broadcasting to thirty-six countries on five continents in nineteen languages, including Esperanto, explaining the meaning of the events as they were unfolding. Later, when his loyalty to the regime was questioned, Vladimír claimed the broadcast had a huge following and enjoyed great resonance among workers in the capitalist countries. He successfully carried out his job, "sometimes exaggerating it," according to one malicious report on his behavior during the heady days in February 1948.[16]

Vladimír was an unwavering supporter of the Communist Party despite the bureaucratization and the centralization of the decision-making at the radio station, which led to the decline in the variety and attraction of the programs broadcast and to listeners' turning to foreign stations. In this ideologically charged atmosphere, when Vladimír was criticized, it was not for his lack of zeal but for displaying initiatives independent of his superiors' orders. He did not have to be told what was politically right and wrong but had a critical mind of his own, which his superiors found difficult to tame and conform to theirs.

While Libuše was employed as a social worker, a nanny looked after their first son. Vladimír quit Charles University in 1949, compelled by the radio directorship to attend a yearlong training course at the University of Political and Economic Sciences. This educational setup was managed by the cultural and propaganda department of the Central Committee of the Communist Party of Czechoslovakia, aiming to improve the Marxist instruction of its students. After he returned to his job in April 1950, Jan, his second son, was born a few months later. The nanny left and the children were sent to nurseries. It was a time of ideological profiling in search of "class enemies," "bourgeois" elements, and suspicious individuals, who were sacked from their jobs with no explanations given. Communist leaders were disappearing from public sight. By then, Vladimír's sister had emigrated to France with her husband and their son, which must have been a blow to a man who had dedicated his life to the construction of a system that she now rejected. He severed relations with her.[17]

The Cold War spy mania reached Vladimír in 1950. The Ministry of the Interior requested several of his acquaintances and friends to give their assessments of his character. His boss at the radio station reported that Vladimír was talented, ambitious, and stubborn, at times ultra-radical, interpreting the party line according to his own criteria. His friend Dr. Bedřich Rattinger, who also knew him in England and was instrumental in drawing him to the communist circles when Vladimír "was still under the influence of all kinds of bourgeois liberal ideas," assessed him favorably. Another colleague reported that Tosek was conceited and curt, having an "academic" attitude toward the people.[18] Many interpreted his self-confidence as arrogance.

Like many other communists, by now Vladimír had come to believe that genuine Marxism-Leninism was being deformed by Stalinism and the misuse of state power. He believed in fighting for justice wherever he saw it being violated. As a boss, he defended his colleagues' rights to a decent life and demonstrated an appreciation of their performance on the job. Thus, when he was Ruth's superior, recognizing her talents, he recommended her for promotion and a better salary; he helped a Spanish comrade in exile in Czechoslovakia from Franco's Spain, as well as an English colleague when he believed she was treated unfairly by the radio administration.[19]

His communist credentials were impeccable by the party standards; his professional expertise was beyond criticism; his treatment of colleagues was fair. As much as the secret police probed into his purported Zionist activities, it did not find any. Even his marriage was exemplary, as he reported without naming Libuše: "I succeeded in attracting her to our cause in such a way that in March 1946 she joined not only the marriage union but also the party." He was a caregiver for his children, living in a "comradely environment" with Dr. Rattinger, a deputy in the national assembly, so that his wife was "growing politically all the time."[20]

None of Vladimír's ennobling qualities mattered when, on the last day of May 1951, he was dismissed from his job and his contract was rescinded with the euphemism "after a mutual agreement."[21] The order came from the nerve center of power, the Central Committee of the Czechoslovak Communist Party. Vladimír was thirty-two years old, had two sons and one on the way, although it was Libuše who bore the brunt of their care. She, too, suffered the consequences of his dismissal by being denied the job to which she was aspiring and by having the secret police probe into her private life.[22]

The incriminating factors outweighed Vladimír's qualities at a time when Czechoslovak society and institutions were under the party's scrutiny for alleged ideological blemishes. He was a Jew, suspicious because a strong undercurrent of Marxism associated Jews with capitalism and the bourgeoise; he had served in the British army during the war and had relatives in capitalist countries, including his sister. Vladimír's concocted sins comprised cold-blooded calculation to advance his career, "objectivism," "westernism," sarcasm, venom, lack of "Bolshevik methodology," and smug superiority. His phenomenal memory for such technical details as times and waves on which the short-wave radio broadcast aroused suspicion among his colleagues. As Czechoslovak radio was falling under the total party control, aided by the institution's employees, Vladimír's conduct provoked misgivings among his adversaries who seemed to have slung mud at him out of spite.[23]

After his dismissal from the radio, having been thoroughly screened, Vladimír found a job as a deputy editor of the publishing house of the Czechoslovak agriculturists' organ *Brázda* (*Furrow*) in November 1951. It was not an ideal assignment, but Vladimír accepted it without remonstrations. Agricultural science was then dominated by the Soviet pseudoscientist Trofim Lysenko, whose discredited theories included a denial that genes existed and the claim that geneticists were enemies of socialism. It was not a safe job: Vladimír, who had to travel to the countryside, requested and was granted a pistol for personal defense.[24]

Knowledgeable about the theoretical underpinnings of the current course of history, Vladimír soon became a leader in the local party organization and a threat to others who made sure that he would not last long on the job. Through machinations of which the details are unknown, he was dismissed in July 1952. Vladimír did not protest; it might have been just as well because the environment at *Brázda* was not conducive to any creative work, although Vladimír managed to teach himself Russian.

Now that he was unemployed again, the labor bureau offered him a job as a miner. It was a relief to find a job at the Orbis publishing house, editing and translating works of literature and travelogues into foreign languages, subjects that were close to his interests. One of his jobs was completing the second edition of the travelogue of the celebrated travelers, explorers, and filmmakers Jiří Hanzelka and Miroslav Zikmund. Hanzelka and Zikmund, elevated to the status of state celebrities for putting socialist Czechoslovakia on the world stage, were honored with a lavish edition of their *Afrika snů a skutečností* (*Africa, Dream and Reality*). The book enjoyed high-quality binding, design, and paper, black-and-white photographs, glossaries of foreign names and terms, and maps, all with a print run of 50,400 and subsequent reprints.[25] It must have been an aesthetic and cultural joy to be the book's editor.

A less enjoyable task was to oversee the translation into several languages of the published protocol of the 1952 fabricated trials and confessions extracted from the tormented victims of the party leaders. Orbis published the complete record of the so-called Slánský trial in 1953 in an edition of 75,400 copies. What did Vladimír think about the trials, an investigator named "Sokol" from the state secret police asked one day when he visited him at his home. "Tosek did not express himself one way or another," the investigator reported later. Indeed, he knew the men in question and did not understand the whole affair. So as much as the Interior Ministry investigated Vladimír, it never found him off guard, never found anything punishable in his behavior or speech, and eventually shelved his file.[26]

Neither the personal nor the political trials instigated by the state and the party against innocent people corroded Vladimír's convictions that Czechoslovakia was on the right path. He was not blind to the institutional violations of justice but believed that with time they would be put right. He was far from pursuing a career or seeking a position in the party hierarchy. His ideology did not stand above his morality; he was a cultured man and honesty went with defending his worldview. His mind was captivated by socialism as a project, by Marxism as the scientific teaching method, and by the Communist Party as the instrument to carry out the project. There was no other way. His conundrum was how to reconcile the often-absurd directions from above with his creative spirit without ever deviating from the overall political and ideological design of achieving socialism.

The TV Celebrity

Vladimír applied for a job at and was hired by the Czechoslovak television when membership in the Communist Party was a condition to join the team and when employees who were not party members were dismissed. The budding journalist was appointed at the end of 1956, after his predecessor fell under the suspicion of disloyalty and jailed. These were extraordinary times. In February 1956 the Soviet leader Nikita Sergeyevich Khrushchev revealed to the high echelon of the party that during Stalin's long reign, he had committed criminal acts against millions of citizens, including the comrades from his rank. The earth-shattering revelation provoked an easing of the state's political strictures, and the impression gleaned by Western observers was that a new era had dawned. However, the hopeful expectations were overshadowed in October by the Hungarian popular uprising against the communist regime, brutally repressed by the Soviet army. One of the questions Vladimír was asked during his job interview was his position on the Hungarian events, to which he replied with the politically correct answer: it was a counterrevolution. The answer was satisfactory; he got the job.

He signed his contract in January 1957. Vladimír knew what his obligations as a worker on the ideological front were and was mindful of what the regime demanded of intellectuals. Television broadcasting was meant to be an educational instrument for the masses, one that had to transmit the successes in the construction of socialism, highlight the leading role of the Communist Party, the struggle against liberalism, bourgeois democracy, and nationalism. The medium was new—the broadcasting system had only been founded in 1953—and there were not many owners of television sets. Radio broadcasting surpassed it by far as the means of reaching large audiences, but television was enhanced by images. Vladimír had learned a great deal from his years on the radio, observing his experienced colleagues' collection of information and their style of communication. He caught on to the difference between the radio and the television fast, blending images and narratives effectively to stimulate the audience's interest. His colleagues looked up to him.[27]

Vladimír was hired as a commentator of international news, not as a national news reporter. This had an advantage. As more and more households were acquiring television sets, Vladimír was unique in regularly bringing images of the world that they could not see for themselves into their living rooms. Reporters of internal events had a harder time. The political secretariat of the Central Committee of the Czechoslovak Communist Party had its team of censors, watching closely to prevent reporters from straying into areas of social reality that were to remain hidden from the public view at a time of economic stagnation, a descent into corruption, and growing cynicism, despite Czechoslovakia's being the most egalitarian country in Communist Europe. Thus, television news, delivered in a droning voice, was dull. It broadcast dignitaries—men and (rarely) women—milling at airports and in companies' boardrooms, hugging, kissing, and shaking hands: events enlivened by young pioneers giving away bouquets of flowers. News reels reported on happy factory workers overcoming the fixed production quotas, celebrations of this or that victory, the signing of this or that treaty, infinite images of Soviet dignitaries; other favorite news items included images of healthy children and sport games.[28]

Vladimír sought to break out of the constraints imposed by the censorship, resorting to his imagination to turn an official event into an interesting story. In 1957, for instance, the Czechoslovak airline connection between Prague and London was renewed. Vladimír was not on that first flight, but he used the occasion to take the viewers on a trip to London, Windsor, and Oxford, to show them British architecture, the double-decker buses, the underground stations and transport on the river Thames, people wandering on the streets, and many historic landmarks. The actual program has not been preserved by the Czechoslovak television's archive, only its description, but one can imagine that Vladimír accompanied the images with the relevant historical background and poignant narrative to take the viewers into a society and culture that he knew well.[29]

He always had his audience in mind. The daily press used to review his programs. It expressed the opinion that he allowed his viewers to participate in interesting dialogues with witty commentary, logical and on a high level, avoiding platitudes. There was not a journalist of that quality commenting on domestic news. But if he succeeded in preserving a degree of independence, it was in part due to his talents, in part because he might have applied self-censorship, never losing sight of the role that television had to play in increasing the ideological education of the viewers and as an instrument of socialist development.[30]

In a similar manner as Ruth, Vladimír's professional success brought him to the attention of the state secret police (StB). The Ministry of the Interior knew him from years past as a target of government spying, but now he was viewed as a potentially useful police informant. On May 25, 1958, Jiří Čermák, a police investigator, reported to his superior, "I have established a personal acquaintance with comrade Tosek Vladimír, Prague television journalist. I met Tosek through another television journalist, who is our informant, and was introduced as the informant's friend." Čermák was impressed by Vladimír's intelligence and love for his family. Tosek seemed to be the type of person who fulfilled "our requirements to become a collaborator." His recruitment would not be a problem, because he was "rationally and I think emotionally on our side." His tasks as an informant were to be in the area of "westerners," foreigners arriving in Czechoslovakia; he was to be asked to report on people who worked in the foreign section of the Czechoslovak radio. He could be trusted and would be recruited "on the strength of his ideology," his belonging to the party, and "devotion to the popular democratic regime."[31]

Although Vladimír was compromised by his previous personal contacts with people liquidated during the Slánský trial in 1952, relationships with people who had escaped from Czechoslovakia after the communist takeover in February 1948 (including his sister), and by having served in a Western army during the war, Čermák believed that Vladimír would be a loyal collaborator. Tosek "understood correctly the state security political tasks and committed himself to work with us." He promised to communicate information he gleaned from contacts with foreigners and was ready to reestablish written contacts with people he knew from his wartime emigration. In his favor was the fact that during the Hungarian uprising of 1956, a year of the communist crisis, "he stood uncompromisingly against the counterrevolution." Vladimír may have believed that in joining the secret police network, he was aiding in the construction of a system of which the secret policing was an instrument of rule to pursue enemies within the state and abroad.[32]

His recruitment took place in February 1959. He met Čermák in a wine cellar in the center of Prague at one o'clock in the afternoon; the room was almost empty, so they could talk undisturbed. Vladimír confided in the police officer information about his family or so the officer reported it: his first wife's infidelity and his reluctance to grant her a divorce for which she was asking—because of the four children they had together—troubled him. After an exchange of pleasantries, according to the officer, Tosek (or, as the officer continued to deride him, "formerly Taussig") offered his unconditional collaboration. Given his character and linguistic skills, "here is a total guarantee of a good collaborator." His code name was to be Cornel.[33]

In early November Vladimír was asked to profile some female announcers and other Czechoslovak television colleagues. He obliged. In an interview in November 2017 with one of them, Kamila Moučková, the former news presenter abounded in glowing compliments about Vladimír and the entire television team that she had joined in 1957. She might have never learned about Vladimír's report about her; it might have had no impact on her career or, if she knew, she might have forgotten it.[34]

Yet, Vladimír described Moučková as someone who came from a communist family but whose political profile was questionable: "In her attitude to life and work she lacks communist spirit. She is a typical petty bourgeois lady, too interested in money and trying to work as little as possible—and for that in different engagements to earn as much as possible—and at times she conceals her hypocritical feelings with hysterical outbursts even during party meetings at which she tries to simulate her abundant awareness. She deceives some people, not all." About another news anchor he had little to say, and in order to say anything he relied on information provided by a third party. One announcer, he reported, was politically uneducated and only interested in her looks, while the third one, one of the best and recently divorced, was politically passive. Of the fourth one he knew nothing, wrote Vladimír, alias Jiří Váňa.[35] There was no malice in his report, but it is fair to say that it was dosed with self-righteousness.

Vladimír found 1959 to be a difficult year personally; he left home and his divorce proceedings were underway. A handsome man with a roving eye, forty years old, he was a public figure and a face known from the television screen. When promenading on a street, people recognized him, turning their heads. By then he was visiting Ruth regularly in our apartment. Fearing a scandal if his extramarital affair was known, my mother found no better way to avoid my meeting him in our tiny flat than locking me in my room.

No personal troubles obstructed Vladimír's work. Even though the editorial contents of the television programs were supervised or produced by the ideological department of the Central Committee of the Czechoslovak Communist Party, Vladimír tried to overcome the constraints imposed by the censorship, choosing as subjects for his programs issues that were politically unassailable and interesting at the same time. The interview with Paul Robeson is a case in point.

Vladimír was enamored of Robeson, an accomplished Black American singer and actor. As a boy, in 1936, he had seen the film *Show Boat*, in which Robeson sang in his seductive deep-toned voice the moving song "Ol' Man River," about working on the Mississippi River. The song made a lasting impact on him. Born in 1898 in Princeton, New Jersey, the son of a slave, Robeson studied law at Columbia University though he never practiced the profession. He came to Prague in 1949 as a guest of the Communist Party and to attend the musical festival Prague Spring. Vladimír was in the audience. When Robeson returned to Prague in June 1959 for a brief stopover during another of his European tours to attend the Congress of Socialist Culture, the television journalist jumped at the opportunity and arranged an interview in the studio.

Vladimír was a tall man, but when they stood next to each other, Robeson towered over him. The American singer addressed the audience with the disarming "jak se máte," Czech for "how are you." He professed love for the Czech people, the Soviet Union, China, socialism, and, above all, Czech music. With a grand piano standing on one side of the studio, Robeson sang his celebrated repertoire, accompanied by his pianist: Negro spirituals, a Mexican lullaby, American folk songs, and Bedřich Smetana's "Píseň svobody" or "The Song of Freedom." This Czech patriotic song evoked the revolutionary spirit of 1848, a broad popular revolt against the Habsburg monarchy that might have reverberated with some of the listeners: "From the foreigners, there are no gifts! / Czech glory, Czech honor, / In Czech lands only the Czech is the Lord!" Robeson ended his performance with "Ol' Man River." Vladimír, and the television staff in their working clothes, brought flowers and shook hands with the celebrity in the studio. More interviews with interesting individuals followed.[36]

Vladimír's attraction to Robeson was esthetic as well as ideological. He saw him as the embodiment of a fighter for international solidarity with all oppressed people, a denunciation of slavery, segregation, racism, colonialism, and imperialism. Like himself, Robeson was devoted to the idea of socialism. We don't know what the viewers thought of the performance. When I asked a Czech musicologist who was inspired by the genre of spirituals for his opinion, his answer was that he was not motivated by Robeson when he founded "Spirituál kvintet" in 1960. He saw inauthenticity in Robeson's trained voice, in his singing popular songs and presenting himself as the symbol of peace in a country where peace was a convenient shibboleth of the regime. Was Robeson aware that freedom and creativity were stifled in Czechoslovakia and that African students at Czechoslovak universities were subjected to racial discrimination?[37]

Interviews became one of Vladimír's preferred journalistic genres, even though they could not be spontaneous encounters with his guests and had to follow an approved script. This was nowhere as evident as in the interview that he conducted with the legendary Argentinian Ernesto Guevara, *El Che*. The arrival of the bearded revolutionaries into Havana and the flight of the Cuban dictator Fulgencio Batista to Miami in January 1959 had inspired the young generation worldwide. It must have been around that time that Vladimír learned Spanish and became a leading commentator about the Latin American political movements on Czechoslovak television.

The twelve-minute repartee with one of the leading figures of the Cuban revolution, visiting Prague in 1960 as part of the Cuban government's economic delegation, was carried out in the television studio. The decorations were sparse, comprising only the Cuban flag draped behind Guevara and a table with an ashtray standing in the middle of the studio. As was appropriate, El Che wore a khaki outfit. Vladimír, wearing a simple suit, posed questions in Czech and then in Spanish. Guevara gave readymade answers, which Vladimír translated word for word with no commentary. The Cuban revolution was making an astonishing progress, the Argentinean stated matter-of-factly, inspiring fear among the American imperialists by its speed. Vladimír followed a script that lay on his lap hidden under the table. What was the importance of revolutionary Cuba for the world? El Che answered with humor: by being a "bad example" for Latin America. From Prague, Guevara traveled to Brno, where he visited a tractor plant. A photo taken of him sitting behind the driving wheel shows him puffing on a cigarette with a smiling entourage of factory comrades behind him. After Guevara, Vladimír interviewed the Brazilian communist Luis Carlos

Prestes and the Chilean communist writer Pablo Neruda, who had taken his last name from the Czech nineteenth-century poet.[38] When Vladimír traveled to Cuba in May 1961, where he labored in a brigade shoulder to shoulder with El Che, he added an interview with Fidel Castro to his repertoire.

In February 1960 Vladimír finalized his divorce. He loved his children and took it upon himself to guide them through the world of culture, history, and natural wonders while Libuše continued to work in an office and simultaneously played the role of homemaker and nurturing parent. The children were aware that they had a famous father. Some of them liked it, others less, but they regularly watched his television appearances on a TV set, which the family owned earlier than most Czechoslovak households.[39]

On April 17, 1961, a US-sponsored invasion force landed on the Cuban shore of Playa Girón in the Bahía de los Cochinos (Bay of Pigs), in a failed effort to topple Fidel Castro's regime. Vladimír was best suited to report on the American debacle, but he was prevented from doing so. A storm was provoked by a previous program in which he had contrasted the Soviet cosmonaut Yuri Gagarin's orbit in space, considered a socialist accomplishment, to the trial of the Nazi leader Adolf Eichmann in Jerusalem, a symptom of capitalist decadence. It was the wrong contrast. Vladimír juxtaposed, albeit negatively, the Soviet Union and Israel, Czechoslovakia's nemesis. Captured in a suburb of Buenos Aires in May 1960, Eichmann was flown to Israel and brought to trial on April 11, 1961, for committing crimes against the Jewish people, crimes against humanity, and war crimes. Vladimír was enraged that he could not cover the story of the US-backed invasion of Cuba and took his case to the television Communist Party meeting, convinced that both the Bay of Pigs fiasco and Eichmann's trial in Jerusalem were his to report and analyze.

Without thought for the consequences, Vladimír began his powerful protest by reminding his colleagues and bosses that after four and a half years on the job, three years out of which he had dedicated to international political affairs, he had appeared close to two hundred and fifty times on the screen, having covered the most important world events. Viewers' correspondence testified to the fact that they were grateful for his attractive and newsy program's clarity and conviction. He was popular, his programs carried a weight that was now held against him. Vladimír claimed that the television audience was waiting for his commentary on the happy end in Cuba, which he was not allowed to make. Instead, he was asked to show some documentary material about Cuba without his face or voice. His blood boiling, Vladimír refused to participate in this charade:

"For two and a half years I tell the people that revolutionary Cuba is unbeatable with our support, and when it is confirmed, I am not allowed to speak. Try to understand my situation." He felt that he was attacked from below the hip without knowing where the attack came from: "That applies to anyone from the Central Committee to the City Committee to the District Committee all the way to here," meaning from the uppermost echelons of the Czechoslovak Communist Party to the local party committee. "I can assure you, that I am used to fighting; during the war I was in danger of my life and I did not care, and nothing worse than what happened to my parents could happen to me again; not even the losses and defeats in my personal life later; nor any of the 'defensive' and 'preventive' measures from the different organs can bend me. I can terminate this work right now. The satisfaction that I have attracted from children to grandmothers for the communist cause is something to be proud of." Vladimír could not be accused of "ideological deviation," so he was blamed for "coldness" and "individualism." It was absurd to reproach him for detachment in commenting on Eichmann's trial for no other reason than the fact that "among the people, who Eichmann gassed, broke, and incinerated in the furnace were my father and my mother."[40] He anticipated that this would be his last commentary. It was not.

Where did the animosity toward him come from? In an environment of chicaneries practiced among colleagues, envies, jealousies, including perhaps anti-Semitism, Vladimír's prestige grew because he was uniquely endowed with the qualities necessary for the job of commentator of international events on Czechoslovak television. He would have liked to work in a team, but collaboration with him was not easy. Without intending it, he put people down and therefore turned them off. But his professionalism was generally recognized.

For one, the StB asked him to stay on the job. We don't know what happened behind the scenes, but in May he was allowed to travel to Cuba. His secret police handler requested him to be on the lookout for information without giving him any specifications. He may not have brought back anything useful for the StB but he managed to interview Fidel, which increased his prestige.[41]

In addition to his television work, Vladimír lectured in factories about the world situation and socialism. While traveling abroad was out of bounds for most of the population, he acted as an interpreter at international conferences in Tunisia, Morocco, and Iraq, as well as visiting countries closer home. The StB was always interested in his journeys, hoping that he would bring back important information on the behavior and ideas of potential foes of the country. Often, they were disappointed. He was not cut out for spying; what interested him most during his travels was to capture local scenes from the lives of ordinary people, set in their natural environment in ways that he could bring onto the television screen.

New opportunities arose for television broadcasting when the Central Committee of the Czechoslovak Communist Party unexpectedly nominated Jiří Pelikán as the television's studio chief in June 1963. He and Vladimír were old acquaintances from the International Union of Students' conferences at which Vladimír had acted as an interpreter. Pelikán's long-time participation in the party and close ties to the highest echelons were now useful. He brought fresh air to the asphyxiated medium, favoring a personal approach to journalists' work, some limited freedom of expression, and mild criticism of the political system's failures. Daring as it was, Pelikán believed in a dialogue with power, in speaking truth. The relative thaw that had taken place at the time of his nomination was short-lived, however. It ended with Khrushchev's ousting and Leonid Brezhnev's ascendancy as the general secretary of the Soviet Communist Party. Censorship hardened again.[42]

This was the ambience in which Pelikán conceived an unprecedented dialogue between Prague and Vienna, hoping to construct a telebridge between speakers from different political parties and worldviews, between the Czechoslovak communist intellectuals and members of the Austrian Social Democratic and Christian Democratic parties, all public figures. Vladimír was to act as the simultaneous interpreter of the event, set to take place on September 24, 1964.

It was a fiasco. From the evidence available, the dialogue failed because the Czech communists were constrained by a preordained script that prevented the participants from a freewheeling debate, while the Austrians were at liberty to talk as they thought fit. The Czechs were tongue-tied because they had to defend and propagate the communist way of thinking without expressing any criticism. There was more. At the last minute, Vladimír refused to be the interpreter of the event because his immediate boss, not Pelikán, denied him an honorarium that he believed was his due. He flew into rage. "Kiss my ass" was his reaction as he turned his back on his boss and the event. He later apologized, but the harm was done. The interpretation of the discussion was inadequate. Viewers complained that the Austrian participants were censored to the point that they could not be properly understood. Pelikán had to bear the brunt of the party's scathing criticism and was requested to draw adequate "political-personal conclusions from this case dealing with the workplace in the television studio."[43]

Pelikán was depressed by the unexpected result of his initiative. In preparing the innovative dialogue, constructing a bridge between two cities, two political cultures, he proceeded using his common sense. He feared that the failures of such experiments might provoke the party and the government authorities to stop them altogether. Even though "the true guiding role of the party for television" was paramount in his mind, he wanted to introduce creative changes in the studios. Vladimír contributed to the experiment's failure. Reading between the lines of Pelikán's long personal letter to him, Vladimír subordinated the larger political significance of the attempt to puncture the wall between the east and the west and let ideas circulate to his sense of superiority and pride.[44]

Vladimír's punishment was eviction from Prague to Plzeň for a year to monitor German television, starting in February 1965. The StB summoned him to a meeting before he left. The controller reported that the journalist had been a willing informant but did not go out of his way to provide information except for the few occasions when he snooped on his television colleagues or provided political analysis from conferences at which he acted as an interpreter. In May he reappeared in Prague and met with his StB controller to let him know that he would be back soon and that in Plzeň he had no contact with foreigners, so there was nothing to report on of strategic weight. The next meeting was scheduled for September. By then, the secret police were losing interest in him. It could have been after Vladimír's return to Prague that he moved in with my mother and me. His children met "Aunt Ruth" and gradually accepted the social and family dynamics that went with the relationship.[45]

Vladimír was back at his desk in the television studio at a time when the Czechoslovak arts were bursting with creativity. There was the new wave of Czech and Slovak films, plays performed in small intimate theaters, and novels written in new idioms. But unlike writers, filmmakers, and song composers who could resort to metaphors, double meanings, and satire to stir the stale air, journalists had a more difficult task because they worked with facts and facts were censured. Some television journalists ventured into critical investigative programs as a window on the reality lived by ordinary people or programs that intended to ventilate long silenced social, political, and economic problems. Most of the time, the programs were censured before being put on air or were scuttled altogether and their creators accused of revisionism.[46]

Vladimír did not raise polemical issues in his televised programs; he did not participate in any form of defiance of the government and party rule and hence was not subject to any reproach from the high-ups for "ideological instability" the way some of his colleagues were. He fulfilled the party's motto that journalists were "first and foremost active agents in accomplishing the goals and the politics of the Party."[47] He was not ready to criticize the regime, not until his party gave him the green light to do so. After all, criticism was considered pessimism and augured political destruction.[48]

He dealt with the limits imposed on creative journalism by making his prime-time Saturday night programs as attractive and meaningful as could be. "Dear Friends," Vladimír used to address his audience, lifting his face from the written script in front of him to make eye contact with his viewers; from there, he unrolled interesting, knowledgeable narratives on the international subject at hand. He was at his best when he guided the viewers through historical landmarks, unusual scenery. and people from different cultures, drawing on his love of nature, geography, and the arts; and he was most dreary when on occasions he described which of the political bigwigs met whom, using party platitudes. Vladimír played down the Cold War rhetoric and debates that stemmed from such hot-button issues as the construction of the Berlin Wall in August 1961 or the Cuban missile crisis in October 1962.

Vladimír never underwent self-criticism of his past, bourgeois or otherwise; he did not feel the need to subject himself to any ideological and moral contrition like so many of his contemporaries. Or perhaps he did so only in the intimacy of his thoughts. He knew that he was participating in a perversion of the ideal in which he believed but that did not deter him from remaining faithful to it all his life. They were responsible for corrupting it, not him. Even when during the 1960s the media poured a wave of criticism, he went about his business as usual. His conflict with the government and the regime was not over the long-term values and goals, but rather over the bureaucratic forms of governing, authoritarian rule, and the arbitrary interventions into the work of a well-meaning journalist.[49]

In 1966, the journalist's business was to report on the war in Vietnam. In one program that aired before he traveled to Vietnam in April of that year, Vladimír sarcastically referred to the US president and his secretary of state as losers—his favorite idiom. And when he returned, he brought back colorful stories for his children, such as the amazement of hairless Vietnamese people at seeing a man whose hands were covered with thick hair. He showed the television viewers a piece of airplane shrapnel as a war trophy, claiming to confirm thereby that the United States was the loser and the heroic Vietnamese people the winners.[50]

Vladimír's three-part program about Czechoslovakia's participation at the Expo 67 crowned his years as a journalist before the momentous year of 1968. The television studio sent him to Montreal in the summer of 1967 to cover the International and Universal Exposition, the world's fair. It turned out to be an unmitigated success for Czechoslovakia on the competitive international scene and for him as a reporter. The Czechoslovak pavilion was visited by hundreds of thousands of sightseers, all considering it unique. Vladimír's favorite cameraman, Jan Eisner, followed him; milling among the crowds with a microphone in hand, the journalist asked variably in English and French what the visitors liked best. All were enchanted. For example, film director Elia Kazan noted that the exhibits were organized in such a way that they breathed the cultural spirit of the country, not selling goods like so many of the other pavilions. Czech baroque art was exhibited together with imaginative artifacts made from glass. Czech experimental theater and the multimedia cinema attracted audiences in large numbers. Czech and Slovak food and beer were served to the delight of émigrés from afar, who drank beer and sang their favorite songs like in the old times before economic scarcity or the repressive regime drove them into emigration. Expo 67 succeeded also as an economic endeavor; behind the scenes, contracts were signed with American and Canadian firms. It was Czechoslovakia at its best in quality and most imaginative organization. If only Czechoslovakia could function like that pavilion, Vladimír sighed.

Neither Vladimír nor anyone else that he interviewed from the Czechoslovak team mentioned socialism. It was not because its construction in Czechoslovakia was not prime on his mind. There was no need to dwell on it. Expo 67 harmonized talents, goodwill, cooperation, patriotism, superb organization, and plans for enlarged international trade, imbuing Vladimír with optimism that a different Czechoslovakia was possible, one that could live side by side with capitalism peacefully and prosper. And that was the spirit with which Vladimír impregnated the series Expo 67, aired at the end of the year and the beginning of the next.[51]

There were other ways that 1967 was significant. What started as a dalliance with Ruth became a hard-solid partnership in travels and translations. After he returned from Montreal, Ruth and Vladimír were married in September. They were a notable couple, known for their extraordinary linguistic expertise, which was in high demand. The also stood out when seen side by side: Ruth was petite, while her husband a tall man whose shoulder she barely reached; not given to style and appearances, she never tried to compensate for the difference by wearing high-heeled shoes. Her wedding attire did not change much from when she had married Kurt in

1946; the same kind of suit, shoes to fit in color, a hat. Her mother was at the wedding, dressed in a classically cut suit. This time, she was pleased with Ruth's choice of a partner, regretting only that he had to be such a staunch communist. Vladimír's oldest son, almost twenty, attended it as well as. I was nineteen years old, trying life on my own in England.

FIGURE 10. Ruth and Vladimír's wedding in Prague in September 1967

Shortly before they were married, Ruth and Vladimír moved to an upscale villa on a quiet tree-lined street in one of Prague's suburbs sitting on a hill above the embankment of the Vltava River. Ruth was settling into domesticity she had not known before. She admired Vladimír for his intellectual breadth, affectionately hanging on his every word. And he was unique in tolerating her chain-smoking. Ruth would have liked to have a child fathered by him, but the four children he already had filled his quota and Ruth was past her prime child-bearing years anyway.

They had much in common, although it was unlikely that they ever shared their respective experience of collaboration with the state secret police. They had belonged to the same milieu: the non-Jewish Jewish world expressed by telling jokes and using the odd Yiddish cultural reference, but never celebrating any Jewish rituals; the painful experience of the Holocaust through the annihilation of family members; war years in England in which both engaged with the deep conviction of their political and moral obligation to stand up to Hitler; the tribulations resulting from the anti-Semitic, repressive 1950s, which both suffered with existential losses. But whereas Vladimír did not lose faith in the communist system and fought on for its improvement, Ruth learned to navigate amid adversities. Even though she did not share Vladimír's loyalty to the Communist Party and its brand of socialism, Ruth's commitment to him gave her a sense of belonging and kept her grounded.

10

Shattered Hopes

The Prague Spring of 1968 engulfed the entire country. It was one of the most exhilarating and most devastating events of the twentieth century. It lasted only eight months, from January to August, but it left an indelible mark on Czechoslovakia and the world. For some, the movement meant reform from above to democratize the communist one-party system together with decentralizing the economic management, increasing productivity, satisfying the needs for popular consumption, and ending the unhealthy balance of payments; others expected the full-fledged restoration of democracy. The Soviet military's invasion on August 21 truncated this unprecedented nonviolent internal confrontation. It changed Ruth's and Vladimír's lives in a radical way. It was a rude shock to those who endorsed the policy of détente.

Broadcasting the Illusion

At the end of 1967 Vladimír squeezed a trip to Sicily into his busy schedule. An amateur cameraman and a gifted scene setter, he had a special interest in visiting the small town of Sambuca di Sicilia. When he was back in Prague finishing the documentary, southern Italy was struck by a devastating earthquake. The biopic he produced, with additional shots from the life-saving efforts in Sicily, was broadcast in April 1968. It expressed Vladimír's political credo. Avoiding lambasting phrases, he documented one day in the life of the communist mayor Guiseppe Montalbano, known to the townsfolk as Pipo.[1]

Vladimír reveled in making the documentary. It allowed him to go deep into the antique history of the Greeks and the Romans, the geography of the peninsula, and its variegated populations; he shot the magnificent homes of the rich to contrast them with the shabby dwellings of the workers, many of whom were forced to migrate to Germany to earn their living. But the main point of the film was to portray Pipo Montalbano, who day in and day out stood shoulder to shoulder with his neighbors, debating their problems, making collective decisions, and consequently enjoying their trust. Thanks to Pipo's dedication, the local Communist Party repeatedly won the elections. The subliminal message to the television viewers, at the time of the national debate about whether the Czechoslovak Communist Party should remain as the leading force in the society, was that the party had to deserve that role. It had to win the hearts and minds of the population by deeds and not by force or decree.[2] But Alexander Dubček, who became the general secretary of the Czechoslovak Communist Party in January 1968, had before him a mightier task than Giuseppe Montalbano.

Replacing a dinosaur with the kind-looking Slovak Dubček as the head of the party nomenclature was a political earthquake in Czechoslovakia. Haltingly at first, the removal of a Stalinist relic opened the floodgate for questions and debates about the past, the present. and the paths to follow. Vladimír, like his colleagues in the television and the radio stations who until then had been covering the international scenes, switched their attention to the fast-unfolding domestic events. Democratic socialism became the watchword. Turning the bureaucratic authoritarian system into an open society was the goal. Few had a clear idea what it should look like or how open it should be. Though the discussion was initiated from above, gradually the society joined the discussion. As weeks and months passed, the public acquired divergent and opposing positions that with time crystallized into various social groupings. Even though political parties existed within the national front, they were dominated by the communists, making the front look more like an office than a functioning political institution. In the subsequent months, the different factions engaged in a debate with the communists (as did the communists among themselves) about their right and ability to continue monopolizing state power.[3]

Most of the old-time communists doubted that the regime changes could be carried out without the dominating role of their party, although they admitted that plurality of opinions was possible. There lay one of the contradictions of the reform process: how to square the leading role of the communist party with freedom of opinions, which the citizens craved, and how to reconcile the citizens' impetus to organize into interest groups that could grow into political parties and the reluctance of the existing elite to allow political pluralism. There were other conundrums. How could one turn the badly planned and led national economy into an efficient market one within the structure of state-controlled relations of production, ownership of property, distribution of goods and services? How could they make enterprises based on professional knowledge and endowed with autonomous decision-making effective without engendering aspirations to privatize? And, last but not least, how could the Czechs convince the "fraternal" neighbors that the Czechoslovak road to socialism was not jeopardizing the cohesion of the block and the global balance of power?[4]

Vladimír threw himself headlong into the whirlwind of those debates. But in 1968 he had one debt to pay. Paul Robeson was seventy years old in April and Vladimír wanted to celebrate the occasion with the television audience. When he did, he cut a different figure on the screen from when he recorded his interview with the American celebrity in 1959. Whereas in 1959 he had worn an ill-fitting gray outfit, now Vladimír wore a dark designer suit, stiff shirt collar, and an elegant tie. He reminded his viewers who Robeson was and had the entire footage recorded nine years before replayed as a tribute to the musician, to the fighter for freedom and socialism, and to a friend, then ill and in retirement.[5]

Unlike Vladimír's subsequent shows, this one did not provoke any controversy. But from then on, he did not shy away from polemical issues, which he believed had to be discussed in public to enhance the reform process in order to achieve the desired democratic socialism. How much freedom should the government allow the media, how much freedom should the media adopt to act responsibly, and how much freedom could society bear, unaccustomed as it was to openness of the press, radio, and television? These questions occupied him throughout the eight months of the Prague Spring.

It was a feat that when the elite functionaries and public figures were reluctant to appear on live television without rehearsed questions and answers, Vladimír managed to bring three of them together for a discussion at the television studio. Old-time communists, the three men were among the architects of the reform process. They met in the studio one day in March, after factory workers from an industrial plant in Prague, or those who spoke on their behalf, questioned in strong words the sudden flood of news and critical opinions on the political, economic, and cultural situation in the country. Accustomed to a situation where an individual had no voice but spoke on behalf of the collective—party, government, factory, union, television studio—the workers were dismayed to hear so many dissonant voices. They were "confused," the cacophony disoriented them; they felt it was a breach of discipline to speak publicly about the party's internal problems, the more so by people who did not even belong to it, meaning journalists. The workers put together a resolution, clamoring for punishment for those who violated alleged party discipline.[6]

Vladimír opened the live debate reading excerpts from the resolution.

He entitled the program appropriately "What It's All About." It was early March; the reform process that had begun in January still lacked specific contours. Announced as the "Action Program," it was still unknown, which was unsettling. The discussion mirrored the inquisitive mood of the society and the optimism of the party's functionaries that all the problems, past and present, would be resolved successfully within the limits of the existing socialist structure, never doubting that it would be respected outside of Czechoslovakia. So, what was the workers' commotion all about?

One sticking point of the discussion was the leading role of the Communist Party; all agreed that if the party wanted to retain that role, it had to represent the whole of the society, communists as much as noncommunists. It had to attract young people who had repudiated the party's cadre politics because it guaranteed members positions of responsibility irrespective of their qualifications. Return to capitalism? "Nonsense," Dr. František Kriegel exclaimed in English. Here was a medical doctor with many battles on his record from the Spanish Civil War to China during the Second World War, who would play a major role during the subsequent months as one of the reform program's resolute stalwarts. The new economic policy would not mean unemployment and low wages; it would be led by experts, but experts endowed with the right political preparation. Unity, unity, unity was one of the shibboleths of the discussion. Should the party be criticized for its past mishandling of justice, Vladimír asked them? Of course, but that must happen together with the recognition of the party's "conquests" accomplished since 1948. The rehabilitation of the people wronged by the justice system during the 1950s was an obligation of the current government.

The subject matters that surfaced repeatedly in this and other debates concerned the relations between workers and intellectuals. The reform communists held that it was an artificial conflict, going back to the 1950s, when during the frenzy of the "class war" intellectuals were sent to factories and factory workers, educated overnight in party schools, replaced them and became the "vanguard" of the society. But were workers treated as the avant-garde in a political and economic system that had been installed from above without them? In the many debates over the following months among manual workers, government officials, and journalists the issue was an open wound. Workers complained that they had no say in the decision-making of the factories in which they produced goods, but they bore the responsibility for often catastrophic results and they, too, were often victims of the factories' malfunctions.[7]

Freedom of expression and transparency were other major items of the discussion. What could and could not be discussed in public, what should the public know about the inner workings of the party? Would too much freedom and information erode the foundations of the republic? And what about the criminal injustice committed against thousands of innocent men, women, and children by the same Communist Party that claimed its leading role was not in dispute? But it was early March and opinions were still in the making. For reasons of history and geopolitics, relations with the Soviet Union were unshakable and therefore not subjected to any debate. And finally, a quiz. Acting as a headmaster, Vladimír asked his guests their prognosis for March 1969: the Communist Party would be a leading force, albeit democratic, was the unanimous answer. Vladimír concurred, believing like his guests in the historical predestination of socialism as a higher order. But in May, Dr. Kriegel confided to a friend, "You know, I fear that one day we might meet somewhere in a faraway concentration camp."[8]

That was just the beginning of Vladimír's foray into provoking open public discussions. In April he introduced a novel weekly program on Czechoslovak television called *One from Among Us*. The idea was to interview ordinary people or well-known ones who had something interesting to say, to debate or to polemicize with them. The program was the run-of-the-mill in democratic countries but new in Czechoslovakia, where speaking truth and revealing flawed reality to the public was without precedence, unimaginable in the past because it was considered as aiding the "class enemy." A problem could be discussed only after the party had given the green light to do so. A publicist had no right to an opinion. Polemical programs had been made but if shown at all, quickly withdrawn by the censor.[9]

The program that Vladimír devised did not admit any censorship; each journalist was responsible for the content of the off-the-cuff interview. The main interest was the person in the studio. His or her identity was not known beforehand. After broadcasting each program, polemics continued on the pages of the press. Vladimír invited three of his colleagues to take turns. The opening of each interview was a theme played by a miniature piano music box to bring about an intimate atmosphere. It became one of the most popular discussion series.[10]

The first program was broadcast on April 9. The guests were Rudolf Slánský and Jan Šling. What these young men had in common was that their fathers had been victims of framed-up trials and were hanged in 1952. Both were Jews, but that was not the issue. Rehabilitation of their innocence was on the national agenda and was contained in the "Action

Program," finally made public in early April. Vladimír wanted to contribute to the creation of awareness about the crimes committed in the 1950s and to the restoration of justice as an inseparable part of the reform process. If the country was to move forward, it had to confront its past and make peace with it, which could be done only by repairing the injustices. Life and wasted existence could not be restored, but the perpetrators of the criminal injustice had to be punished.

It was remarkable to hear that the two men had not lost faith in either the communist system or Marxism as its guiding principle. Neither Slánský nor Šling held grudges against the political regime that had victimized their fathers and themselves (as sons of "traitors" their childhood had been a traumatic one). The broadcast has not been preserved but the reaction to it has, thanks to the debate in the press after it was aired and the letters that inundated the television studio. For some viewers, the program was eye-opening, exposing them to a previously hidden reality. Other viewers were appalled, sending anonymous anti-Semitic and otherwise vulgar letters to the television studio and to Vladimír or other TV anchors.[11]

"A dive into the human soul" was how one journalist described the television debate following the screening of the inaugural episode. After the transmission ended, a telephone rang; the man on the other side hurled invectives at Vladimír, telling him among other improprieties to stop dragging Jews onto the screen. In one unsigned letter an anti-Semite stated that he had liked Vladimír until he interviewed a "dirty Jew." One anonymous letter was particularly brutal: "I wish that your parents will end on the gallows and that a reporter would ask you to testify in front of a camera." Vladimír was saddened by the message but responded nevertheless: "I can assure the anonymous writer that his wish was fulfilled twenty-four years ago. Happy?" Vladimír referred to his parents' murder in Auschwitz, which the anonymous reader may or may not have understood. There were also appreciative letters. One came from a soldier who was present at the hanging and the incineration of the victims, wishing to get in touch with one of their sons. Vladimír facilitated the encounter.[12] This and other freewheeling television broadcasts broke the dam of public opinion. Censorship was swept aside in practice before being abolished by law in June.

Anti-Semitism showed its ugly face again in an interview that the journalist Ladislav Daneš conducted with the renowned Jewish writer Arnošt Lustig on the first anniversary of the war between Egypt and Israel in 1967, after which Czechoslovakia was obliged by the Soviet Union to break relations with the Jewish state. Lustig gave his opinion, which differed from the official interpretation of the Arab-Israeli war. All the countries from the socialist block had assumed an anti-Israel stand. Lustig argued that Israel had the right to launch the war to defend the country, since it was besieged by its Arab neighbors from its inception and suffered from a blockade in the south. While some viewers agreed with his opinion, others did not.

Before Daneš, who was not Jewish, opened the interview with his next guest weeks later, he showed the viewers a stack of letters that he had received after speaking with Lustig. While some of their authors were grateful to hear another point of view about the war, some letters spewed anti-Semitic venom, thus annulling any possibility for an exchange of opinions. The interview has not been preserved, only the viewers' reaction. For example, one viewer wrote, "Mister Daneš, when in the future you want to spoil our evening, invite another Jew." One letter extolled President Władysław Gomułka for chasing Jews out of Poland. Facing his viewers, Daneš posed a rhetorical question: Do such citizens deserve democracy? What would they do with it if they had it?[13]

It so happened that the guest sitting in the studio, waiting to be interviewed while Daneš was addressing his audience, was a Jew. I was the guest. In February 1968 I returned from England after a year of working as an au pair to learn English. On my return, I was hired by the Barrandov film studio in Prague to work as a translator for William Cartwright, the editor of the Hollywood film *The Bridge at Remagen*. This World War II drama depicted the final months of the war in Germany during which the German and American troops faced each other at the Ludendorff bridge over the Rhine River close to the town of Remagen. The film was being shot on sets close to Prague where the Vltava River substituted for the Rhine; a plywood church and watchtowers were built on the river's banks. Wehrmacht and American tanks served as props and would become a minor casus belli together with other Soviet accusations that a counterrevolution had been planned in Czechoslovakia. In August 1968 the Soviets invaded, cutting short the film's production. It was finished in West Germany and Italy and screened in 1969 but not in Czechoslovakia.

Daneš did not ask me about my current job. He was interested in my experience in England, my adaptation to a different country at the age of twenty, and my future plans. It was a friendly, innocuous conversation, which also covered my discovery of a British society dedicated to the conservation of nature. Shortly after the program was aired, Daneš received more anti-Semitic and vulgar letters, threatening him and his family.[14]

When it was Vladimír's turn again, he interviewed the recently appointed minister of the interior, Josef Pavel. It was May, flowers bloomed in the garden in which Vladimír and his cameraman met Pavel and his wife next to their country house. The documentary opens with an idyllic scene of a dog running about, Pavel sharpening a sickle, his wife potting around the garden. Pavel, a legendary veteran of the Spanish Civil War, had (like Vladimír) participated in the Czechoslovak Independent Armored Brigade in England and in the siege of Dunkirk. But Vladimír did not know that they were in the same army unit because Pavel had used his Spanish nom de guerre, Franta Šustr.[15]

The interview skirted the dark history of the 1950s, in which General Pavel had played a prominent role as an implementer of the communist government's repressive policies as the head of the People's militia—the party's army—before eventually becoming one of their victims. The same government that he had served loyally jailed him for three years as it persecuted imaginary enemies. But Pavel never signed any confession, even while he was starved of food and tortured. Nothing could break him, he told Vladimír. He disciplined himself even to control his anger and hate for the people who were destroying him.[16]

Due to his past and to his known rectitude, the new Czechoslovak prime minister approached Pavel in 1968, asking him to consider the post of minister of the interior. Pavel knew that he was agreeing to head a discredited ministry, a poisoned chalice, with well-oiled links to the Soviet state secret service, the KGB. He knew that he had to make sweeping personnel changes at the ministry, that individuals with criminal record had to be removed from their posts, and that illegal practices had be stopped. Were telephones still being tapped and mail intercepted, Vladimír asked him? Pavel vehemently denied it. If there were such cases as the press had recently reported, they represented remnants of the past. And what about the political prisoners and their rehabilitation, why was it taking so long to liberate them and to restore their rights? Because, Pavel responded, the people in charge of executing justice were the same ones who had committed the illegal acts.[17] Much remained to be accomplished.

But Pavel did not have the entire ministry under his control. His deputy minister was Viliam Šalgovič, Dubček's trusted friend. In June the StB was separated from the public service (SNB) and put under Šalgovič's command. And Šalgovič used his power to sabotage the removal of the old cadres from the ministry while collaborating with the KGB and the East German secret police, with fatal consequences for the reform process. Even before this separation of the StB and the SNB took place, the minister could not share all his concerns with Vladimír. One might have been that the Prague Spring liberalizers would not go as far as dismantling the machinery of coercion (indeed, Dubček insistently pledged to the Soviet leaders he would not carry this out). The policy toward the StB exemplified the limits, self-imposed or not, of the government's liberalizing intentions.[18]

Even before settling down to his job, Pavel conducted a diagnosis of the country's national security. In May 1968 he sent a long, alarming report to Dubček and to the Central Committee of the Czechoslovak Communist Party. In the interview with Vladimír, Pavel appeared to be a steely soldier who entered the political fray to cleanse the country of its nefarious past and set it on a new road, but in the report to the party he called for the need to defend the principles on which the whole system stood—one party rule and state direction of all public affairs in the face of destabilizing tendencies accompanying the democratization process. He referred to leaflets attacking the Czechoslovak Communist Party, its leading role and political leaders, socialism, and the alliance with the USSR: some of these read, "The horrendous Bolshevik government is coming to an end"; "It is a shame and crime to be a member of the KSČ," the abbreviation in Czech of the Czechoslovak Communist Party. Pavel noted that monuments were erected to honor Tomáš Garrigue Masaryk, the first Czechoslovak president, and that one leaflet called on the Czech nation to rise and defend itself against total economic, cultural, and moral decline and to remove "the brutal dictatorship of servants of foreign power, who for 20 years had terrorized our nation without mercy, destroyed its international respectability, assassinated and impoverished its people etc."[19] This revolution would triumph when streets were strewn with the "Bolshevik plebeians." In the same report, Pavel mentioned calls by communists and workers demanding that the government safeguard the socialist fatherland from a revisionist group in the party and the state administration. According to these complaints, the television, press, radio, and literature had demoralizing effect on the people, seeking to separate them from the Czechoslovak Communist Party and socialism. The media did not engage in constructive criticism but represented the "bourgeois liberal demagoguery," isolating the workers from the intelligentsia, wanting to end the leading role of the working class and the party in society, liquidate it, and sound the death knell of the socialist conquests. Together with the justified criticism of past errors committed by the security organs in the 1950s, Pavel concluded, the current security organs were suffering from scandalous attacks, their secrets being revealed in an atmosphere of increasing violence.[20] Such libels could well have been manufactured in the StB's workshops to smear the reform process, which Pavel never mentioned.

Given the minister's diagnosis of the state of the nation's security, his loss of authority in the StB, the prominence of the old cadres in the Communist Party's national and local organizations, the secret police's past methods employed against alleged class enemies or people suspected of plotting continued unhampered. Unwittingly, Vladimír became entangled in the StB's machinations.

Georges Penchenier was a French journalist, working in 1968 for Radio-Television-Luxembourg. Like so many of his associates, he was attracted by Czechoslovakia. Something entirely new was happening: socialism was being reformed by the architects of its deformation. Penchenier, who was fluent in Czech, had spent time in Czechoslovakia after the war and was expelled around February 1948. Like in the old times, in 1968 the StB shadowed foreign journalists, including Penchenier. An StB officer visited the hotel where the Frenchman was staying and infiltrated his room, photographing his diary and a telephone address book. In them he found Vladimír's name as a person to contact, with the proviso that Tosek was not reliable because, as somebody had told Penchenier, "he retained a bit of the old style." Nevertheless, Penchenier set up a meeting with Vladimír for July 23 in a café. Tosek did not arrive, but they met the following day for lunch. It could have been Vladimír who facilitated Penchenier's meeting with Pavel, duly recorded in the French journalist's police file and used against Vladimír when it became convenient.[21]

The ministry's counterintelligence routinely tracked the activities of foreign embassies and diplomats. Among others, they targeted the British press attaché Cyril Jonsen. Tosek and other journalists used to meet him and apprise him, as a colleague, of their interpretation of the events taking place in Czechoslovakia. This became another incriminating piece of evidence against Vladimír later, when he was falsely accused of passing national secrets to Jonsen.[22]

By the time Vladimír and his colleagues organized an open debate with workers from a factory assembling photo cameras, the ambience in Czechoslovakia had taken a new turn. Gone was the optimistic prognosis that the reform process would continue unhampered. The government could not restrain the political skirmishes that were taking place on all levels: in the local party organizations, in the media, in factories, in the national assembly, in the Central Committee of the Czechoslovak Communist Party, and most ominously among the "fraternal" countries engaged in disinformation campaigns and worse still planting a cache of arms on the border as a supposed provocation by West Germany and the United States. The publication of the article "Two Thousand Words" in major dailies on June 27 added fuel to the fire. The article certainly provoked a hysterical reaction in the Communist Party. Penned by the writer Ludvík Vaculík and conceived by a group of scientists and intellectuals, it expressed the thoughts of millions of citizens. It was a call for the creation of an active civil society, one that refused "to be shouted down."[23] On an appropriate occasion a few days later, Vladimír used the article to illustrate the seriousness of the threats against the reform process.

Czechoslovakia was much more unsettled than television broadcasting projected to its viewers. Dubček and his reform-minded comrades asked journalists to tame their enthusiasm for free expression, in other words to help the reformers to consolidate their ascendance over their opponents in the Communist Party by not publishing critical articles about the past twenty years and the Soviet Union. They also asked the journalists to refrain from demanding military neutrality for Czechoslovakia. Some media heeded the admonishment, others did not.[24] This time, Vladimír was not part of the disciplined core. Debates in the squares, in the cafés, and the pubs continued to be rowdy, as part of the public refused to acquiesce to Dubček's plea for restrain. This was democracy, wasn't it?

One sunny Friday afternoon on July 12, Vladimír, along with two male and two female colleagues, gathered outside the Meopta factory in a small town northeast of Prague, facing a sizeable group of workers. A fifty-minute documentary was produced from that debate. First, the black-and-white film introduced the viewers first to the town's environs, the fields and the sleepy streets, country houses, and a man on a bicycle (to highlight the customary form of transportation). Then the camera focused on the appliances and the workers, mainly women, assembling and packaging photographic equipment. It then followed them when their shift was over, leaving the precinct of the factory, all smiles, dispersing in several directions. Just an ordinary day in the life of Meopta workers. But the debate that took place that sunlit afternoon was not ordinary by any means.

The first salvo was fired by a woman, reading a prepared statement. All workers were supposedly equal before the law, but some were more equal than others; members of the Communist Party were the privileged few. Her coworker added that discredited cadres had not been removed from their positions; at best they were recycled to diplomatic posts. It was true that the architect of the new economic policy, Ota Šik, explained its premises to the public, but what was the position of the factory directors on whose decisions the workers' lives depended and who had proven untrustworthy and incompetent? When would qualifications replace undeserved privilege and nepotism? To the question of why more public figures did not appear on television and talk to the workers directly without intermediaries, one journalist replied that they were invited but it was not always easy to convince the higher-ups to appear, and when they did agree, to talk sincerely. And then there was the perennial propaganda about the leading role of the proletariat. The workers did not believe they were leading anything; quite the opposite, their interests were being systematically ignored.[25]

Vladimír expected that the recently published article "Two Thousand Words" would spark off a debate, and came prepared. The article-turned-manifesto reflected the budding civil society's alarm at the permanence of the old guard in the party, some of whom Dubček defended as reformable individuals whom he trusted or otherwise as people who could not be removed for fear of creating enemies within. Their continued presence in the echelons of power antagonized that part of the society that was willing to give the Communist Party leaders and the regime the benefit of the doubt. The manifesto was a response to the lukewarm fulfillment of the reform program, whose architects seemed unable or unwilling to respond to the unexpected and unanticipated movement of a society that could no longer be controlled administratively, not even by Dubček's well-meaning cautionary tales.[26]

The manifesto—addressed to workers, agriculturists, bureaucrats, artists, and society more broadly—was not only a diagnosis but also an indictment. "Parliament no longer debated, the government no longer governed and the directors no longer directed," it stated.[27] Elections had no meaning and laws had lost their weight. The greatest achievement up to that point was freedom of expression. It was true that the reconstruction of the country could not be accomplished without or against the communists. But the weight of the social and political life had to shift from the central organs to the local ones, which were better suited to control power to oversee the economy, and to eliminate the damaging elements in society without resorting to violence. The Prague Spring was an opportunity to return the common good to the nation and to build socialism corresponding to national traditions.

The text was bold but far from being a call to create an opposition to the government; rather, it insisted that the reform process should accelerate and leadership act according to the democratic demands that the government upheld and could implement only with the participation of the society. But anything that smacked of autonomous initiatives from below was a red line that the communist leadership was not willing to overstep. The article provoked a hysterical reaction not only among the high party functionaries and some intellectuals but also among the communist leadership of the neighboring countries. A Czech prominent reform leader was reported to shout, "Do you know what this means? Tanks, tanks will follow this!!!"[28]

The manifesto united the leading communists, who considered it as an attack on their positions. Dubček did not say anything until he reflected on the article's consequences. When he did, he considered its publication a national catastrophe, the end of the democratization process, believing that it would inspire the conservatives to stage an attack on the new party course, which they did. The article became a pretext for accusation that the counterrevolutionaries were attempting to seize power in Czechoslovakia.[29]

Vladimír thought that the manifesto would trigger some controversy among the workers of Meopta, but it did not. Their relative lack of interest in it showed that uppermost on the workers' minds were their own grievances, not words. One participant from the audience mentioned the manifesto, giving Vladimír the opportunity that he was waiting for to read from an East German newspaper in order to show the way the article's content was distorted by a journalist from the neighboring country to make it seem an anti-state anarchist call to arms against socialism.

All in all, it was a good discussion. The proverbial rift between manual workers and the intelligentsia was overcome in this context. People said what was on their minds, except for the party members present, who kept silent. The workers trusted that the television journalists would make their grievances heard around the country. The debate was commented on in letters to the television channel, anonymous as well as signed. What did anonymity reflect, asked one journalist, trying to explain the phenomenon after the event in Meopta and more generally? In principle, anonymous letters belonged to the wastepaper basket. But in the circumstances of Czechoslovakia, they reflected the last twenty years of administrative-bureaucratic form of government, an anonymous system requiring anonymous conformity, leading to anonymous criticism; and they reflected society's moral crisis. Anonymity also meant the persistence of local "pashas," inspiring fear when democracy required openness, tolerance, and argumentation.[30]

The environment in Czechoslovakia was brittle, and not only on account of the controversial article. The country's leaders and journalists assumed a defensive posture about the reform program, which was now attacked from within and from without. "We shall not abandon our course," was the headline of one daily in early August as the Czechoslovak leadership was drilled by the "fraternal" countries on the wrong course that Czechoslovakia had taken.[31] Dubček enjoyed popular trust like no politician in the world, television viewers were told by one of his followers. A change of course was unthinkable. Czechoslovak affairs were to be determined by the country's leadership democratically. But neither Dubček nor his associates were willing to speak openly about the growing encirclement in which Czechoslovakia was finding itself; nor would they discuss Dubček's exhaustion thanks to the systematic attacks by the Soviet leadership. They did not rule out an intervention to stop the reform process but considered the Prague Spring different from the Hungarian revolt in 1956. Few considered that what made the Prague Spring more threatening to Moscow was the fact that this time the impetus for revolt came from within the party.[32]

On Tuesday, August 20, it was Vladimír's turn to conduct another interview program. When it was over, he left the television studio unaware that it was his last one. Like most nights, he, Ruth, and their likeminded friends, gathered to analyze the current situation and discuss what was to come. At the back of their minds loomed the possibility of an occupation, but that night they deemed it a remote prospect.

Broadcasting the End of an Era

The humming sound of the arriving airplanes bringing the invading army and the accompanying hardware could be heard from any part of Prague during the early morning hours on August 21. Telephones rang in most households in the middle of the night to awaken people to the horrendous reality that Czechoslovakia was being occupied. It was a profound shock, to the point that some believed that it was a joke; it was not. An anecdote soon circulated that the invasion was some kind of swap: seven thousand tanks for two thousand words. In what would be a futile act of resistance, the radio broadcast the Czech and Slovak anthems, attempting to glue the fragmented country into one resisting whole against the occupiers.[33]

At daybreak, Vladimír left home not knowing what was to come next. Trams were not running. When he reached the gas station, there was already a line, but people recognized his face and allowed him to jump ahead, fill his tank, and drive off. Like his colleagues, he went to the main television studio in the center of Prague. He encountered streets filled with angry, dismayed, and weeping people, shouting at the bewildered soldiers on top of the tanks—who did not even know which country they had come to suppress the alleged counterrevolution—to go back to where they came from. Ruth, on her way to the office at the Czechoslovak Press Agency (ČTK) where she worked in the English language photo feature section, approached disconcerted foreign tourists who did not understand what was happening. Switching from language to language, she explained to them the reasons for the commotion. Once in the office, she quickly selected photographs of the invasion that reporters had brought in to send to news agencies abroad.

When Vladimír arrived at the studio, the broadcasting had already begun despite the minister of communication's effort to thwart it. From having supported the legitimate government, the minister switched sides, acting on behalf of the interventionists. He wanted to prevent the transmission of the legitimate government's message to the nation condemning the invasion and replace it with a broadcast of a fake appeal to the Warsaw Pact countries legitimizing the invasion as fraternal assistance aimed at containing anarchism. His attempt at subversion ended in failure. Around eight o'clock in the morning the radio transmitted President Ludvík Svoboda's message condemning the invasion and appealing to the population not to mount resistance to the foreign army. Truth will prevail, socialism will prevail, the anchors' reassured the dumbfounded but defiant citizens.[34]

The television channel continued broadcasting until about half past eight, when armed soldiers violently entered the studio, cut the cables, and damaged the equipment. For seven days, a cat and mouse chase ensued as the television technicians and journalists attempted to keep on broadcasting and the occupiers to frustrate them. Alternative studios sprang into action time and again, allowing the reform leaders to maintain communication with the nation for at least a short while. The popular slogan at this time called out, "For Dubček or Svoboda, not a drop of water for the occupiers."[35]

Some of the television staff, including Vladimír, moved to a transmission tower close to Prague at about ten in the morning on August 21 to renew broadcasting after another studio was detected and kicked off the air. The broadcast lasted for over an hour until the occupying forces discovered it, aided by the Interior Ministry's employees. The cameraman managed to capture on film a tank that emerged from the woods behind the hut that held the transmission equipment and to film the escape of the journalists. This makeshift studio was silenced but others were soon made operational.[36]

The television and radio staff worked together. Following the abduction of the Czechoslovak leaders to Moscow on August 23, amid reports of dead and injured, and unable to broadcast on television, Vladimír addressed listeners on the radio. He told the audience that Dubček and people close to him had been kidnapped and flown to Moscow together with traitors who did not represent anyone. Until Dubček was heard from again, all acts and words from the occupiers and their hired murderers were illegal and damaging to the people of Czechoslovakia.[37] Strong words.

Collaboration with the invading force was despicable, making resistance that much more complicated. By the decision of the government, on August 24 Minister Pavel stripped the turncoat Šalgovič, who supported the invasion, of his post, invalidating all directives that he had issued after August 20 and ordering the national security forces under his command to protect the radio installations. By then the station of the occupier, Vltava, had begun transmitting from East Germany. Laden with grammatical errors, faulty pronunciation, and bad syntax in Czech and Slovak, the station broadcast the Czechoslovak government's supposed invitation to the Soviet Union, in which the regime allegedly plead for military help because the republic was threatened by counterrevolutionary and antisocialist elements.

Meanwhile, popular culture flourished. Graffiti and handbills proclaimed slogans such as "Lenin wake up, Brezhnev went mad"; "Kolja, what is a counterrevolution? That is when you don't agree with Lenin"; "How do the Russians visit their friends? In tanks"; "How do the Czechs know that the Earth is round? In 1945 the imperialists were driven out to the west and in 1968 they returned from the east"; "What is the shortest and most beautiful Czech fairy tale? They left"; "Which is the most neutral nation in the world? Czechoslovakia. It does not interfere in its own internal affairs"; "What is the most secure country in the world? Israel, because it has no friendly neighbors"; "What is black and knocking on the door? The future."[38]

The makeshift studios did not cover large swaths of the country and so several had to transmit simultaneously to extend the communication radius. One transmission tower was in southwest Bohemia, sitting on a mountain called Klet', in an area controlled by the Czechoslovak army. Close to the Austrian border, it was a convenient place from which to smuggle film recordings of the occupation out of the country so that the whole world could watch the events in Czechoslovakia as they were unfolding. The television staff brought the material from Prague and entrusted it to people willing to carry it across the border.[39]

The history and memory of these remarkable days, as witnessed by all who had experienced them, may be only approximate, but they retain the flair of the events. On the afternoon of August 23, a car equipped with sound and video cameras left Prague for Klet' to build a provisional transmission studio on a hill next to a transmitter tower. It was a dramatic operation. Cars were being inspected on the roads, and so a plan was hatched to transport the journalists in a coffin but even a hearse could be inspected, and the idea was dropped. Still, the car managed to get through, and from August 23 to 26, transmissions from Klet' were secured at intervals of two hours. Vladimír and three other journalists appeared on the screen, showing footage delivered to them and broadcast as far afield as the reception would go. The district Communist Party and the army unit assisted the television team, reinforcing the security of the area with soldiers and armed vehicles. The television team received military uniforms and a hut to sleep and eat in, close to the transmitter. On August 25 the television aerial in a nearby town was disabled. This signaled to the men and women at Klet' that something similar could happen there soon. Only the difficult access to the transmitter on top of the hill allowed transmission for some time longer despite the occupying forces' admonitions to the local army personnel to interrupt it. But on August 26 the television crew was advised to leave. They abandoned the location and moved to a village at the bottom of the hill. The technicians returned to Prague with the equipment while Vladimír opted for leaving Czechoslovakia.[40]

Several of the journalists crossed the frontier at a point known only to the border patrol. The plan was to meet in Austria with a television team from Brno and to continue broadcasting from there. Apparently, Austrian television offered Tosek and his colleagues the possibility of transmitting from a steamer anchored on the Danube, but this did not take place. To get to the border, Vladimír took off the military uniform, put on a fireman's garb, and was taken to the frontier hidden in a fireman's cistern truck. There he took off this outfit and was driven in his civilian clothes to a wire wall; a border patrol official unlocked the wall and then accompanied the fugitives to the Austrian border crossing.[41]

Before Vladimír left Klet', he asked one of his colleagues to let Ruth in Prague know that he was going to the home of Oskar, a codename of a friend they had in Vienna, and that she should join him. Crossing the border at an unofficial point meant that his passport was not duly stamped. This fact became a casus belli a few months later. The border patrol came under the Ministry of the Interior, so the state security organs had detailed information about who had been on call during the days of the broadcasts from Klet' and who from among the border patrol officers helped the journalists cross the border. Later these men were interrogated and punished for facilitating the journalists' escape. The same ministry had infiltrated a secret police agent into the team of the television workers, to record their activities.[42]

Safe in Vienna, Vladimír listened to Dubček's speech on his return from Moscow. Suppressing tears, Dubček addressed the nation on August 27. He appealed to the population to renew its trust that not everything from the reform course was lost, that there remained hope, and that he was the person to realize it. But could he, the listeners mused? True, the tanks and the soldiers left the main squares, becoming less visible. But even the undying optimist president of the National Assembly, Josef Smrkovský, did not find adequate words to express what had transpired in Moscow during the abduction of the communist leaders and what was in store for Czechoslovakia. When the official communiqué was broadcast, it was like a bucket of tepid water. It contained nothing but empty phrases. There was no indication of a clear reassuring path forward. The Prague Spring leaders came back alive but with their hands tied.[43]

The president, the prime minister, the general secretary of the Czechoslovak Communist Party, the president of the National Assembly, the president of the National Front—all Dubček's associates, kidnapped by the Soviets and flown out of the country on military airplanes—had been held incommunicado at an unidentified police property in the Carpathian Mountains before being transferred to the Kremlin. There, they met with the Czech and Slovak conspirators who had participated in the military occupation, and with whom they had governed until a few days before. During a chaotic exchange about what was possible and what each side was unwilling to accept in the new state and party arrangements in Czechoslovakia, the "Moscow protocol" was formulated. Dr. Kriegel, known for his resolve, was not admitted into the hall where the discussions took place; Dubček was absent after suffering a breakdown. The final document justified the military intervention, did not mention anything about the departure of the foreign army, made no reference to the reform course of the Czechoslovak Communist Party, and rejected the nominations to the highest state and party positions that had occurred at the extraordinary national party congress (which had been planned for September but met immediately after the occupation to choose trusted popular representatives in free elections). President Ludvík Svoboda was the first to sign the Soviet dictate. As an army general, he had seen bloodshed before and feared it now. Others followed, except for Dr. Kriegel.

The Dubček leadership capitulated. Even though countless people died, the world seemed indifferent to the Czechoslovak catastrophe. The Western powers responded passively to the invasion. Great Britain's response reflected its traditional attitude toward Eastern Europe, emphasizing stability rather than self-determination; France continued cultivating its ties with the Eastern bloc regimes; US president Johnson was preoccupied with Vietnam and arms control talks with the Soviets; Willy Brandt worked to improve West Germany's relations with the Soviet bloc and strengthen diplomatic ties with the German Democratic Republic. After a brief outrage in the summer of 1968, all reverted to the business as usual. It did not help that Western radicals despised the bourgeois democracy that for their Czechoslovak counterparts would be a dream come true.[44] The Prague Spring was over.

Part IV

11

At a Crossroads

At the crack of dawn on August 28, 1968, Ruth sat in her red car, with me next to her, both of us with a suitcase to make it appear as if we were going on a holiday. The previous day, Dubček had returned from Moscow with his head down and pleading with the nation to accept the impossible: the Soviet occupation of Czechoslovakia. Ruth drove south to the Austrian border. Not knowing the constellation of the invading armies around the country, her dominant thought was to get to the border before the Russians. After several hours of driving on winding roads along the undulating hills of southern Bohemia, she came across a colony of tanks, trundling on a two-lane road in the same direction as us. One by one, Ruth overtook them, driving underneath the tanks' cannons stretched over the width of the road. It was nerve-wracking.

The border town of Gmünd was swollen with Czechs and Slovaks, whom the friendly guards let across on foot carrying suitcases, pushing prams, driving cars, or riding motorbikes. A radio crew was waiting for a scoop. One journalist pushed a microphone at Ruth. Shaken by the dramatic days in Prague and the harrowing journey to the border, she found that talking about it released her pent-up tensions. Back in the car, she cruised on toward Vienna to meet Vladimír, as agreed.

In Limbo

At the end of summer 1968, Vienna was a beehive of refugees from occupied Czechoslovakia, some scurrying from embassy to embassy in search of the most suitable country for emigration; others staying put, waiting to see if the situation back home would take a turn for the better, that is, if the government and the Communist Party leaders would take a firmer stand vis-à-vis the occupiers, or whether they would implement Moscow's dictate.[1]

Whether awaiting one outcome or the other, reading the news, or exchanging information with friends and acquaintances, every refugee saw the future differently, had different fears and dreams. Vladimír and Ruth looked for temporary jobs. Ruth, a jack-of-all-trades, found one in Vienna at the bureau of United Press International working as desk editor and performing other office duties. Her linguistic capacities made her a flexible partner who could accommodate herself to many European countries and settings. It was Vladimír who had to decide what to do and where. "I am only his appendage," Ruth thought to herself. I had it easier. Helped by the Jewish Joint Committee, I flew to London as soon as I could to start university studies that the British government made available to Czechoslovak students.

Among other demands, the Soviets had ordered the resignation of Jiří Pelikán, the director of the national television service. He left Czechoslovakia in September. Sheltered at the Czechoslovak embassy in Rome, he was helping everyone he could thanks to his many acquaintances in the European media networks. He rescued Vladimír from inactivity and anxiety by finding him a temporary job in Mexico City to engage in the logistics before and during the Olympic Games on behalf of the European Broadcasting Union. While this was nothing spectacular, it kept Vladimír busy for six weeks with no spare time to see anything of the country or the games. In early November, he turned up in Paris, anxious to find a job that would entitle him to the extension of his legal permit to stay abroad. Vladimír kept on writing letters left, right, and center to different European press and broadcasting agencies, but to no avail. Bidding for time, he applied to his employer for unpaid holidays. He did not want to sever relations with either the Czechoslovak television or the country, nor would he repudiate what he had stood for all his life: being a Czechoslovak journalist and a communist publicist. Should he return to Czechoslovakia and stand shoulder to shoulder with his colleagues who defied the occupiers and their collaborators in the media? But gloom was overtaking him and Ruth as they watched the events across the border.[2]

In October, on the fiftieth anniversary of the founding of Czechoslovakia, protests had erupted in most of the country's major cities; in Prague the police tried to persuade the throngs to disperse but in the end resorted to truncheons. On the anniversary of the Bolshevik revolution in November, small groups in Prague pulled down and burned Soviet flags; once again the government deployed police with truncheons, fire hoses, and reinforcements from the People's Militia. As November 17 (the International Students' Day) was approaching, and with it the anniversary of the Nazi murder of the student Jan Opletal, the communist leadership feared that the media might inflame the atmosphere, cause protests, and so lead to another mobilization and deployment of Soviet troops that had by this time retreated from the cities. Thus the regime opted to crackdown on journalists accused of inspiring the disorder and to adopt a "firm course." In his opening speech at the November plenum of the Central Committee of the Czechoslovak Communist Party, Dubček warned in hackneyed phrases against the "rightist danger"; in the same breath, he urged people not to succumb to skepticism that the post-January course of the party had been abandoned. Citizens, he exhorted, should "remain optimistic but disciplined."[3]

Ruth clearly did not want to return to Czechoslovakia, while Vladimír, despite being nauseated by what he saw on television, heard, on the radio and read in the newspapers, was tempted to join the turmoil with his colleagues. At the same time he was aware of the already imposed restrictions on freedom of speech and of more to come. Their friends urged them to return and join the ranks of those opposing the usurpers who controlled the country and help support the weakened reformers by any means available. Pelikán in his capacity as cultural attaché in Rome, on the other hand, was helping Vladimír all he could to find a job. One possibility was the Radiotelevisione Italiana (RAI), although the Italian labor unions might be unwilling to hire a foreigner, he wrote. Just as Pelikán was drafting this letter, Vladimír received a ray of hope by way of an invitation from Fabio Borrelli, the socialist director of RAI's foreign relations, offering him a plane ticket to go to Rome for an interview.[4]

Vladimír made the trip on January 8, 1969. RAI offered him a one-year contract as an external collaborator, with a salary equivalent to an Italian journalist and a starting date in the middle of February. The work content was not specified, but it was agreed that he would collaborate in tasks related to television journalism and documentary production and make use of his linguistic skills in international relations. Neither his face nor his name would ever appear in public; he wanted to remain a Czechoslovak journalist with legal residence abroad, among other reasons so that his children could visit him.

Before he could travel to his destination in Italy, he needed to go to Prague to arrange practical matters, above all to replace his soon to expire passport with a new one. Vladimír hoped to legalize his stay in Rome with the blessing of the Czechoslovak television management that, after Pelikán was dismissed, still had a decent director. In a letter to the prime minister in January 1969, Vladimír assured him, "I am and remain a Communist journalist"; the Italian job would not compromise him, as neither his name nor his face would appear publicly. Furthermore, he wrote, his work would not contradict his obligations as a loyal Czechoslovak journalist who would never speak critically of the regime.[5]

Shortly before Vladimír's trip, the atmosphere in Prague turned tragic after the twenty-year-old Czech student Jan Palach set fire to himself on January 16, 1969, in Wenceslas Square and died three days later of his wounds. His act aimed at the conscience of the people at home and abroad, calling for life in dignity, truth, and freedom. His burial on January 25 turned into a peaceful mass protest against the Soviet occupation and against the regime's restrictions on the media; the demonstration also called for the prohibition of the Soviet-sponsored mendacious newspaper *Zprávy*.[6]

Given the circumstances, going to Prague was risky, but it was the only alternative Vladimír had if he wanted to legalize his stay abroad. There were other reasons to be concerned. Vladimír and Ruth's permits to stay abroad and private passports were soon to expire; he sent them to Prague with the application for their renewal but was notified that their permits had been denied and their passports retained by the authorities. Fortunately for both, they still had their official passports designed for business trips. Vladimír's only chance to obtain a legal stay abroad was an assignment from the Czechoslovak television. And if it was denied, he noted dryly, "it would mean an artificial production of emigrants and moreover of people who had no such intentions."[7] He was aware of the changes taking place in the Czechoslovak television: some of the prominent journalists were removed from their responsibility in programming, others were prevented from appearing on the television screen, while still others were summarily fired. Reportedly, Vladimír's fate was on the line as well.[8]

He crossed the border on February 6, 1969, while Ruth stayed in Vienna. The Ministry of the Interior went on the alert. His arrival in Prague was preceded by the first of *Zprávy*'s several diatribes against him. The paper accused him of collaboration with the British diplomat and press attaché Cyril Jonsen in August 1968. Even though "jk," the author of the smear, claimed not to know the details of the contacts, Tosek allegedly supplied Jonsen with information on party and government positions. "jk" continued with allegations regarding Ruth's working for a Jewish organization and Vladimír's organizing a group of journalists in Vienna, most likely participating in the broadcasts of Radio Free Europe, and spreading damaging materials about Czechoslovakia. The anonymous author also insinuated that the way they had crossed the border was unknown.[9] Most likely, "jk" was an unscrupulous hack of the Interior Ministry, in charge of planting false information.

Vladimír had legal documents when he crossed the border in August 1968 and Ruth was not working for a Jewish organization but for the United Press Agency. Facts did not matter. The culture of slanders and anti-Semitism that the critical media had confronted head-on in 1968 reappeared. The canard was disseminated throughout the country.[10] What incensed Vladimír most was that "jk" referred to him as a "former" employee of the Czechoslovak television. It was a bad omen.

The television director obliged Vladimír's request and applied to the Interior Ministry for his and Ruth's new passports and exit permits. On February 19, Vladimír was summoned to the Toscan Palace for an interview with officials whose job it was to issue new passports. The interview turned into an interrogation. The interrogators, Major Ťupa and Major Bárta, questioned Vladimír on the circumstances of the broadcasting the previous August. They wanted to know names, but most importantly they asked how he crossed the border on August 26, 1968, claiming that the crossing was illegal because Vladimír could not produce the obligatory stamp on his exit permit. Then they wanted to know who he knew from his travels abroad. He replied that he knew many people but would not name names. The next thing his interrogators did was to take away his official passport. Their insistence on the illegality of the border crossing, Vladimír thought, was intended to disqualify the work of the Czechoslovak television team's broadcasting during the heady days after the occupation, delegitimizing the 1968 reforms and their leadership.[11]

After this harrowing experience, Vladimír penned a provocative newspaper article titled "How I Went for Wool and Returned Sheared," narrating the details of the interrogation that crushed his expectations to obtain a passport. He didn't suspect that his sparring with the Ministry of the Interior would cause even further problems. *Zprávy* continued inventing facts, for example that Vladimír had a brother who worked for the BBC and that Vladimír was seeking to join him. People like Tosek "are in fact carrying out antisocialist and anti-Soviet, counterrevolutionary politics," claimed the paper.[12]

The daily paper *Práce* published Vladimír's narrative and asked the Czech interior minister Josef Grösser for a comment. There was no reply until April 11. It arrived as a tape recording that the newspaper transcribed and published in full. The recorded voice belonged to Lieutenant Zdeněk Rajchart, chief of the department of passports and visas at the Ministry of the Interior. A man of intelligence and cunning, probably he was selected for the task as likely to be on the same level as a seasoned publicist and because the busy minister had "certain allergy" to ultimatums addressed to government functionaries. If Vladimír asked for explanations about the conversation at the ministry, Rajchart could provide it thanks to a careful study of that interview, which the ministry recorded without Vladimír's knowledge. Rajchart charged that Vladimír had not crossed the border at a designated crossing point on August 26, 1968. It was true that he had the right documents but on crossing the frontier to Austria, his papers were not stamped. But all these were minutiae.

There was nothing strange about questioning Vladimír; it was in the interest of the country to safeguard its security, wasn't it? Rajchart knew who had helped him to cross the border and much more. He knew for instance that when the Soviet tanks were approaching the hill at Kleť where the television team was broadcasting between August 23 and 26, the military commander offered Vladimír and the crew a shelter on the Czechoslovak side of the border, but "Tosek was so anxious and fearful, and for that reason insisted on an immediate departure abroad." However, Rajchart's central point was not that the transmission from Kleť was illegal, and it did not bother him that Vladimír crossed the border the way he did. What mattered was that Tosek spoke to his interrogators from a moral high ground and with arrogance, in response to their daring to treat him as if he were a delinquent.[13]

Rajchart had a trump card hidden up his sleeve. In a well-calculated move, he showed his hand: "But you know, don't you, that you did not always have such a negative attitude to the Security [organs] as you assume now," he said, referring to Vladimír's collaboration with the StB between 1959 and 1966. The officers who had interrogated him did not act arbitrarily, considering Vladimír's previous good relations with the Ministry of the Interior. "I think that I don't have to convince you about the principles of conspiracy," Rajchart rubbed in the insult. Could it have been the case that Vladimír's attitude now was an attempt to atone for his sins from the past? Reverting to the role of the good cop, Rajchart concluded, "Now that the whole affair has been clarified, you will be given the exit permit."[14]

But in fact, nothing was clarified. The revelation of Vladimír's collaboration with the Interior Ministry's secret police was a well-aimed retaliation for his participation in the Prague Spring, his clandestine broadcasting of the occupation, and his steadfast defense of the 1968 reform process. It was intended to erode public's trust in a well-known journalist.

Vladimír must have been stunned by the revelation but remained defiant. His friends and acquaintances were dumbfounded. Numerous readers of *Práce* requested further explanations; the newspaper tried to get his reaction, but did not reach him or find him at home. Vladimír was concerned about the effect that such a "recommendation" might have on his colleagues and readers at home and abroad. He thanked the many citizens who conveyed support, trust, and encouragement, whether personally or in writing.[15] But the damage was done.

Before Vladimír left Prague, he wrote a rebuttal to Rajchart's article. He objected to the reference to his supposed fear when the Soviet tanks were drawing near the transmitter. Furthermore, "even more illustrative were the intimations repeated several times made by Colonel Dr. Rajchart about my 'alleged relations with his ministry.'" In his defense, Vladimír pointed out that during the fifties he was accused of collaboration with the British, American, and other foreign organs, and that he had been recently smeared on the pages of *Zprávy*. But Rajchart knew where it hurt most. The ministry issued Vladimír's and Ruth's passports and exit permits, attempting to clear the ministry's reputation before the public after it had created an air of doubt around Vladimír as an honest communist journalist and a Prague Spring reformer.

Práce would have liked to but could not publish Vladimír's response to the Ministry of the Interior. The article was about to be printed when the chief of the internal political section of *Práce* received instructions that Tosek's response must not be published because it "could hamper the preparations and the session of the Central Committee of the Communist Party of Czechoslovakia" that was to take place a few days later; only official news could be printed.[16]

Vladimír's rebuttal was published in the fortnightly *Filmové a televizní noviny* on April 30, 1969, an organ of the television station that by then had been subjected to censorship. It required some courage for the editors to publish the article when no other newspaper dared to do so. Vladimír denied any previous connection with the secret police and with a heavy heart left Prague on April 24. As when he arrived in February, the Ministry of the Interior was put on the alert. Around 5 o'clock in the morning, he reached the border to Austria by train. The search by the border patrol was light until the officials from the Ministry of the Interior took over. They went through all his belongings, especially printed matter; they took letters out of their envelopes and read them, and leafed through journals and magazines packed in his luggage. The train for Vienna was delayed due to this search.[17]

In 1990 Vladimír's close friend the journalist Karel Kyncl recalled the circumstances of Vladimír's sparring with the Ministry of the Interior in 1969. At the time, Kyncl had been working for the newspaper in which Vladimír had published his article in March and could not publish his response in April. Kyncl recalled that after the "velvet revolution" of 1989, when Vladimír was no longer alive, Ruth returned to Prague from England. Among her belongings was a chest with personal documents: "In it lies the archive from the Prague years of her husband. So perhaps we shall learn something. Even the author of this narrative is aware of how many questions have emerged from this episode and how much has remained unclear. Perhaps future historians of journalism will be able to provide clear answers. After all it's not only about the outstanding Czech journalist Vladimír Tosek."[18] Kyncl was right. Vladimír was an outstanding journalist who personified a whole generation of intelligent and well-intentioned men and women in thrall to an ideal, representing an entire era. By joining the reform movement in 1968, he sought to correct the system's vices, which, as we now know, could not be corrected. His dream in tatters, in 1969 Tosek negotiated his legal status with a government and a party closely supervised by the Soviet occupiers, which punished him brutally for daring to defy the system during the spring of 1968. It wrought revenge on him by reminding him of a past that he would rather have consigned to archival dust.

Emigration

"What a terrible world it is in which you can choose between a homeland that promises suffering and suffering that afflicts those who choose to renounce their homeland."[19] With these words, the writer Ivan Klíma spoke for many. But Vladimír and people like him had an additional reason to agonize. The ideology to which they had dedicated their lives, which they had made personal sacrifices to build and reconstruct, was smothered by the invading army. They had served that system, and some were now tormented by their responsibility in having brought about the catastrophe of August 1968. Emigration, at least for some, was not about saving their skin. Only by leaving, they believed, they could continue what they had begun during the previous years and months, some within the framework of the socialist or communist ideology, others gradually freed of it, but all with the goal to continue striving toward democracy, justice, and pluralistic thinking with its many different interpretations. Many remained committed to democratic socialism.[20]

Vladimír and Ruth never characterized their emigration as exile, which for all intents and purposes it was. Had they remained in Czechoslovakia, they would have lost their jobs, Vladimír would have been expelled from the party, and their professional lives would have been destroyed like those of most of their colleagues who did not leave. But Vladimír's dilemma was not simple; he considered himself a communist come what may. "I maintain that I belong to that no matter how proscribed the association—even though in the past and for so long I was blind to the point of compliance and defense of all of its mistakes and crimes—and so I, who is conscious of it all, belong to it, and they are the usurpers," he wrote.[21] He allied himself with the party during the war against Nazism; his faith in communism was reinforced after the war in part because his parents had perished at the hands of the Nazi; whatever steps the Communist Party took against him were its responsibility.

Vladimír and Ruth had been living in Rome since May. He had nominal employment but no actual work. The Italian television was in political and organizational turmoil, so nobody had time to assign him concrete tasks. It was frustrating. The upside was that his four children could visit him, and he had time to show them the Roman antiques and museums. The children came and went, but one refused to return to Czechoslovakia. Jan was eighteen years old in 1969 and was soon due to carry out his obligatory military service. He found the idea that as a soldier he could be called to repress street demonstrators, who might include his sister and brothers, unacceptable.[22]

With free time on their hands, Vladimír and Ruth did translations for whoever offered them a job. He was fifty years old; Ruth was forty-four. Both were full of energy but with no prospects. Emigration was hard on them. Ruth was separated from her friends and from me. She did not share Vladimír's political zeal but respected his steadfastness in following his star. He suffered from nostalgia for Czechoslovakia, Prague, and the music of the language that had been his work tool. Ruth did not suffer from such quandaries. What finally led them to take the step of no return was the brutal police repression on the first anniversary of the invasion in August 1969 and the reappearance of the accusation in the media that Vladimír had been passing national intelligence to Mr. Jonsen, the British cultural attaché in Prague, accompanied by the label "a traitor of the people."[23]

Left alone in Prague, Anka was helping Ruth and Vladimír with practical matters like arranging subscriptions to newspapers and magazines, transfers of money, and contacts with people with whom they needed to be in touch. But Anka was desperately lonely; she survived the hell of the concentration camps partly because of luck but in good measure because the extreme circumstances called for connectedness, solidarity, and friendship among the prisoners. Now she did not have any of this. Ruth had never been protective of her war-tormented mother's well-being, physical or emotional. Kurt had his family: a sister, a niece, a nephew, and a brother-in-law. He did not care about politics. When as a member of the Communist Party he was asked about the invasion, he replied that he was against the 1968 reforms and favored the help of the fraternal parties to stave off "the counterrevolution." He could not care less. All that mattered to him was that he could visit me in England where I studied at the university and was now married to the actor Jeremy Spenser.

Anka had no one. Kurt used to visit her but did not want to burden Ruth with the weight of any responsibility and did not report on how abandoned her mother felt. I wrote to my grandmother every fortnight, but those letters were no substitute for the missing hearth. Anka would have been allowed to visit Ruth in Italy if Vladimír had not been sacked from the television studio in November 1969, leading to the expiration of their legal status abroad. Furthermore, the doctor had diagnosed her with cirrhosis of the liver, which had been damaged during the years of privation in the concentration camps, and her health began to decline. As she was seized by bouts of fever, a good neighbor brought her food. She contemplated committing suicide and in January 1971 carried it out. After so much suffering, she refused to suffer any more. She was seventy years old.[24] Kurt apprised Ruth with no extra words. Despite having seen the horrors of Bergen-Belsen, Ruth continued to resent her mother for abandoning her in 1939, for causing her and Vilém go through the agony of thinking she was dead; all of this made her incapable of feeling Anka's despondency.

After Ruth had divorced him, Kurt remained a bachelor for the rest of his life. Never an ambitious man, he worked as a salesman in a socialist state-administered firm, exporting ceramic products until his retirement. The job took him repeatedly to Holland. The few photos in my possession show him potbellied, jovial in the company of his business partners, drinking beer, and eating herring. For practical reasons, he was a member of the Communist Party all his life; when asked questions about current politics, he always responded with the right answer, seeking only to be left in peace. Kurt enjoyed life: good food and music, imported drinks. Dressed with studied elegance, he liked to wear fashionable tailormade three-piece suits and matching ties, white shirts with stiff collars, and elegant cufflinks. An inveterate cigarette chain-smoker, after he retired, he used to meet with his pals at a tavern close to his home to alleviate loneliness. He died in Prague in 1975 from prostate cancer, not yet sixty-seven years old, taking his wartime experience to the grave.

Ruth and Vladimír had their own uncertainties to deal with. Emigration required endurance of repeated failures and nightmares. Ruth had a recurring dream that her husband had knowingly lost his wedding ring. Emigration meant responsibility, especially if the person in question was a leading personality during the reform movement. So, if their sufferings were to be worth it, life had to have meaning. It took time, but eventually they would find it in carrying the torch of the Prague Spring. For the time being, they had existential problems to resolve.[25]

Their longtime friend Jiří Pelikán believed genuinely that exile was not an individual act but a decision concerning "our entire collective," which in his mind included Ruth and Vladimír. He explained his motivations to choose exile in October 1969 in a letter to the London *Times*. "This decision was difficult, even tragic, for me personally, but politically it was inevitable," he wrote. The Czechoslovak leadership had repudiated the policies that Dubček symbolized between January and August 1968, calling them antisocialist and antirevolutionary. Despite Dubček enjoying the support of most of the population, the regime falsified facts, "returning gradually to the methods and language of the dogmatic Stalinist period."[26] It was a return to the all-embracing bureaucracy that combined terrorizing and chivying, rewarding and punishing.

Pelikán wrote the article in the major British newspaper with fervor and faith. Silence and inactivity were not an option; "the main front of this fight is naturally at home in our country," which he wanted to help it along from outside. Considering later attempts on his life, Pelikán was prescient when he wrote, "I am not concerned with my personal security which is as vulnerable abroad as it is at home." To speak truth as a communist and as a patriot on the world stage about Czechoslovakia was paramount on his mind, no matter what came out of his decision to emigrate. These were not hollow statements.

The Czechoslovak authorities took them seriously; Pelikán's declaration provoked an outburst of lies and vulgarities about his past, uttered on Czechoslovak television by people with whom he had been in the same party for decades. The outrageous smears included references to Vladimír, whose Italian sojourn Pelikán had allegedly arranged so that they could direct illegal activity together from Italy. "So there is nothing left for us but to initiate the illegality for real! What do you say, Vladimír?" Pelikán joked.[27]

Pelikán's concern was how his exile would be considered by his friends at home. His goal was to continue the post-January politics while remaining a communist. In the end, his exile was a struggle in defeat. Aware of the existential persecution of people at home and the loss of jobs, Pelikán took it upon himself to help boosting the courage of individuals in opposition to the regime in Czechoslovakia and to inform the world about them. "As soon as it is possible to express and defend these opinions publicly at home, I shall return to submit an account of my activities," he wrote.[28] True to his word, Pelikán tried to fulfill his promise; after the 1989 "velvet revolution" he returned to Czechoslovakia, but by then few people were interested in hearing what he had to say.

Throughout their exile, the intellectual diaspora that adhered to the tenets of the Prague Spring and democratic socialism was a thorn in the flesh of the normalization regime, especially since they called themselves a socialist opposition. The regime in Czechoslovakia and the Soviet government did all they could to make sure that its existence was not recognized either by the Western powers or, more importantly, by the Western communist parties. Its presence was an indictment of the system that had engendered that diaspora. Making the cultural, the political, and the scientific camps persecuted at home known outside of Czechoslovakia contributed to questioning the country's authoritarian regime in the West. Paradoxically, the same socialist political exiles were a nuisance for the countries in which they settled, because they kept on disturbing the conscience of a world that wanted to preserve the status quo.[29]

In addition to the old questions about exile and emigration, debating the loss of motherland to gain freedom or what was freedom's worth without homeland, the newly minted exiles repeatedly asked where they were more useful to their country, at home or outside of it? Some justified exile by helping opposition movements at home by providing them with information and study material and maintaining their contacts with the outside world. But there was a pull in the opposite direction, as some opponents of the regime felt that preserving the balance between thinking people at home and abroad required staying put. Going abroad, one critic observed, was playing into the hands of the powerholders; leaving made it easier for the regime to govern. On the other hand, the same critic admitted that "we could not do 99% of things we did. Exile after 1968 saved the cultural survival of this nation."[30]

In the fall of 1969 Vladimír reached his lowest point. Unlike many of his friends and acquaintances, he had an income but no work since arriving in Rome in May. His contract in the Italian television was to expire the following spring. The uncertainty and anxiety was only magnified in Ruth. Financial security was important but not the goal. Unlike Ruth, Vladimír took his unshakable conviction in socialism's future into exile; it was a goal that he never abandoned, even if he knew it had no realistic prospects in the near term: "I am sorry of course that for such a long time I stuck to the illusions, but it speaks in my favor that I have overcome many."[31] No, Vladimír had not lost faith in socialism as a historically predestined higher order.

Knowing that the end of the contract in Rome was in sight, out of despair Vladimír wrote letters to universities in Europe and the United States, offering himself as a teacher of languages and literature. He had the knowledge but not the right qualifications and his applications were rejected one by one. Fortunately, both Ruth and Vladimír had exceptional linguistic skills that were politically neutral and made them readily employable, even if it was not at their dream jobs.

Toiling in Caversham

One of the things that pained Vladimír about the separation from his homeland was the loss of contact with its culture, the television audiences, the shared unique tongue. He would have liked a job as a full-fledged journalist at Reuters or at the BBC, doing programming or broadcasting for the listeners at home. But there were no vacancies in a field overpopulated by previous and current waves of competent and competing emigrants.[32] So, when Pelikán suggested the option of working for the BBC monitoring service, where there were openings, Vladimír accepted the proposition. He was screened for his background, passed all the tests, and was offered a position as a Russian monitor. So, in April 1970 the family packed their belongings in Rome and relocated to England, Vladimír driving with his son Jan and Ruth going by train with the luggage that did not fit into the red car.

The BBC monitoring service situated in Caversham Park a few kilometers north of Reading in Berkshire was formed in 1939 to provide the British government with access to foreign media and propaganda, producing valuable information during World War II, particularly about places where foreign journalists were banned. From its beginning the service was an interception station monitoring foreign radio transmissions with an easy connection with the War Office, a hotline link to Prime Minister Churchill, and another to the FBI offices in the United States. It continued after the war as a listening station focusing on open sources rather than military, diplomatic, or restricted networks. It housed one of the most comprehensive radio centers in the world, with outstanding engineering facilities. Housed in a Georgian marbled mansion, it operated on a round-the-clock schedule in one hundred and twenty foreign languages from all over the world.[33]

The BBC monitoring service hired multilingual monitors who could switch from one language to another as the need arose. The incoming radio broadcasts, in languages that ranged from Albanian to Zulu, were translated, summarized, and sent to the BBC, foreign and commonwealth departments, the Ministry of Defense, the intelligence service, the FBI, and subscribers. The service's uniqueness lay in its ability to learn of crises and coups in a split second.[34] After several secretarial jobs, Ruth found an employment as a monitor as well, listening to the Czech and East German news broadcasts day in day out and translating them into English.

The Caversham jobs paid the bills. They bought a detached house on a quiet street in Reading, for which they received a loan from the bank. A mortgage was a new concept in their lives; taking care of a house was another. Luckily, they had Vladimír's son living with them. Neither was good at manual tasks, leaving Honza to resolve many house-related mishaps. In front of and behind the house were small gardens that the English tradition required to be kept tidy. Gardening was not their métier; mowing the grass was a nuisance, and the garden, separated by a low wood fence from their neighbors, could not hide the permanently overgrown shrubs and weeds.

Aside from their regular jobs, Vladimír and Ruth were in demand to do translations of material coming out of Czechoslovakia or of foreign languages works unavailable to Czech readers. They wished to be surrounded by as wide a circle of friends as could be but that proved difficult after they had moved to Reading to be close to work. The move also cut them off from the vibrant London cultural scene.[35]

Despite the fact that both Ruth and Vladimír knew England from their wartime years and did not feel like complete outsiders, exile sapped Vladimír's morale and led to his withdrawal from any public engagement. The man Ruth had admired was no longer there. She tried to prop him up and make him speak in public, but Vladimír refused. Even after Pelikán founded the journal *Listy* in 1971 (about which more later), Vladimír took a back seat. He helped with translations but did not take an active role in the journal. He did make a political statement, however, by translating into Czech the provocative reflection of the Soviet dissident Andrei Amalrik (who had been in and out of Soviet jails), titled *Will the Soviet Union Survive until 1984?* And he undertook the task of translating from Russian into Czech Arnošt Kolman's monumental memoirs, comprising a manuscript of over five hundred typewritten single-spaced pages, smuggled from Moscow to Sweden. Kolman's uniqueness lay in his trajectory as a Prague Jew, a mathematician, and a philosopher who had dedicated his life to fighting hot and ideological wars for communism. He spent a good part of his life in the Soviet Union. After the invasion of Czechoslovakia in 1968, he put pen to writing his memoirs about a generation that had devoted life to a degenerated ideal. The text was published in Germany in 1979 and in the Czech Republic only in 2005. By then, it did not have the potency that it had had when it appeared first, though not in Czechoslovakia where it was needed most. Vladimír assumed the undertaking because he identified with Kolman's dreams, trials, and frustrations. But Ruth hoped that her husband would do more than vent his dejection through translations; if only Pelikán could engage him in the journal's editorial activity, Vladimír might cease to be so withdrawn and become active again, she entreated him. We shall never know what effect the revelation of his association with the StB had on his intellectual and emotional disposition, but it might have weighed on him profoundly.[36]

Periodic respites from the dullness of work, isolation from friends and family, and nostalgia for home came from periodic travels during their winter and summer holidays. Not great skiers, Ruth and Vladimír enjoyed the sight of the snowcapped mountains in the Swiss Alps, sliding on easy slopes. During the summers, they used to go camping in France or Italy. After visiting a string of museums, churches, art galleries, and castles, they usually drove to stay at the seaside. Arrangements could always be made to meet friends scattered around the world, or to see his sister Helena in the United States, with whom he reconnected in emigration. More tentative were their furtive get-togethers with Vladimír's children living in Prague, which required a lot of organizing and coded telephone communications facilitating meetings in Hungary and Yugoslavia.

Always hungry for knowledge, in 1975 Vladimír enrolled at Reading University to read Russian and German language and literature. It gave him enormous satisfaction. Ruth supported him in his endeavor but while Vladimír was writing essays or cramming for exams, she felt lonely. The work was not so interesting, and she felt cut off from friends and from London's cultural vibrancy. But the year 1977 changed all that. The catalyst occurred when in January the BBC broadcast an interview about her war years with the British intelligence in one of the episodes of the series *The Secret War*.[37] And then, Charter 77 burst into the public domain in Czechoslovakia and beyond.

In 1975, Czechoslovakia was one of the first countries to sign the accords that crowned the Helsinki conference on security and cooperation in Europe. In doing so, the country recognized respect for citizens' rights and duties. As the accords agreed to respect the coexistence of the different political systems and abide by the principles of nonintervention—to the satisfaction of the Soviet bloc—the signatory states conceived the accords as a confirmation of the geopolitical status quo for decades to come. But the communist regimes underestimated the impetus that the conference gave to the opposition in East European countries, which took advantage of the legal provisions of the Helsinki accords to demand that the respective states fulfill the rights enshrined in its text as fundamental human rights. In an indirect way, the Helsinki agreement engendered Charter 77, a broad-based conglomerate of people opposed to the oppressive regime in Czechoslovakia and the other countries of the communist bloc. Furthermore, it not only expressed the mood at home but was also a turning point in the exile community.[38]

When Charter 77 appeared in January 1977, the regime immediately began to search for its originators, both at home and abroad. It remembered Vladimír in a forty-five-minute-long TV program about the alleged crimes committed by the British intelligence service in Czechoslovakia during 1968, branding him a traitor. At this point, Vladimír threw all the reservations and precautions he had held since 1968 to the wind and began to engage in defense of the loosely defined democratic principles in Czechoslovakia as expressed by the chartists. For her part, Ruth had no reservations whatsoever about being active publicly. From then on, they participated in demonstrations, spoke on the radio, and engaged in denouncing the illegitimate normalization regime. For example, Ruth traveled to Lancaster to talk to university students about the meaning of Charter 77. She was nervous but in her element. Their activism acquired more vigor by the tenth anniversary of the invasion in 1978, as they participated in events in England and on the European continent. Vladimír addressed an open-air mass meeting in Brussels, participated in press conferences, and gave interviews on British radio and television, recalling the courageous days after the Soviet-led occupation when broadcasting was menaced by the Soviet tanks. Inevitably, in 1979 the Czechoslovak authorities stripped them of their citizenship for their "antisocialist" activities. The government attributed to Ruth and Vladimír all sorts of power and intentions they did not have, accusing them of being enemies of the socialist regime and in cahoots with Pelikán to destroy the international labor movement.[39]

Vigilance beyond the Border

The Ministry of the Interior let Vladimír and Ruth leave the country in 1969 but tailed them throughout the years of emigration, virtually to Vladimír's grave in 1987. The ministry knew that they had left Rome in April 1970, that he and his son drove to London in the same red car in which we had left Czechoslovakia in August 1968 and with the same Czech license plates. While Pelikán warned Vladimír and Ruth repeatedly that the StB was on their heels in London and that it had informants "among our people," Vladimír and Ruth were unconcerned.[40]

On arrival in London, their car (a Škoda, from the Czech automobile company) needed to be serviced. Vladimír arrived at the Škoda mechanic's shop, gave his particulars and left. The serviceman was an StB informant and so Vladimír's data—like his employment at the BBC monitoring service, his salary and friendships—made it into his police file, which the Ministry of the Interior had reopened. This time his alias was "Topol." The StB collaborator was instructed to keep the relationship with Tosek alive even after the car was repaired. Pelikán was right: there was an informant from the ministry's "foreign agency" who most likely belonged to the narrow circle of Vladimír's and Ruth's acquaintances, for only few people knew about their arrival.[41] That was just a beginning of the police harassment.

The loosely organized exile socialist opposition, which the Ministry of the Interior dubbed the "right-wing post-August emigration" and which coalesced around Pelikán to keep the ideals of the Prague Spring alive, maintain active contact with a wide spectrum of likeminded people in Czechoslovakia, and supporting them as much as possible, was a thorn in the flesh of the normalization regime. By being vocal abroad, they promulgated a version of the Prague Spring's meaning in stark contrast to the government's effort to modify the memory of 1968. And what better medium than national television to construct an alternate history that suited the government's goals to consolidate the regime? Loyal journalists, script writers, and filmmakers were on hand to do the prescribed job after the new television director had cleansed the studio of all the critical minds, the "right-wingers." Journalists who had left Czechoslovakia, like Pelikán and Tosek, were tarnished as globetrotters "to whom socialist patriotism was evidently alien and proletarian internationalism just a convenient membership card for their personal careers."[42]

The Czechoslovak television and film studios made a genre out of smearing such people, who had no means of defending themselves. Hackneyed teams of producers, script writers, and directors manufactured propaganda films and documentaries, portraying journalists and public figures from the time of the 1968 Prague Spring and the reform process as being responsible for the present day catastrophic economic situation and the moral decline of the Czechoslovak people. To legitimize the regime, they had to delegitimize the reformers. Thus the protagonists in these broadcasts were portrayed not only as antisocialist and antipatriotic but also as immoral, traitorous, criminal, or dissolute. Vladimír became one of their prime targets.

Za volantem nepřítel ("Enemy behind the Wheel," 1974) was a case in point. In the film, a distorted picture of the reform process of 1968, the real Vladimír appears in a scene in which a communist functionary listens with scorn to the reform-minded journalist insinuating that the workers deluded themselves that they were the leading class in society. Disgusted by what he was hearing without listening to the end of the transmission, the functionary switched off the set. The programmer did not bother to replicate Vladimír's real voice on the screen.

Many television viewers still remembered Tosek's face. In the film he was portrayed as being among those reformers who sought revenge on the old-style communists and wanted to hang them from streetlamps. In the scene, the aforementioned functionary sneered at their claim that theirs was a socialism with a human face. "But we put up with it," he said self-critically, implying that the invasion was justified to put an end to it all. The film made the point that the reform movement was a humbug at best and a criminal endeavor at worst. In the original script, the film was going to end with a scene in which the thunder of bombers flying over Prague on the night of August 21 was transmuted into an optimistic song, but the filmmakers took it out as possibly too provocative to the viewers.[43]

Třicet případů majora Zemana ("Thirty Cases of Major Zeman") was a popular political thriller shown on Czechoslovak television between 1976 and 1979. The regime was concerned about the political education of the young generation that had no historical memory of the events that had transpired during the time covered by the series between 1948 to 1973. Was the journalist Ivo Holan, prominent in the series until he was assassinated, meant to represent Vladimír Tosek? Quite possibly he was. The show was conceived by the Ministry of the Interior's editorial department, staffed with former policemen full of piquant stories. And then the ministry had archives at its disposal. The material on which the film is based happens to coincide with Vladimír's file in the ABS archive. What was left to the imagination of the script writers was to dramatize the material, presenting a distorted interpretation of the period, contriving situations and implausible coincidences. Emigrants in particular were portrayed as real or potential traitors.[44]

If many of the protagonists of the series were likeable figures with whom one could identify, Holan was not one of them. He was portrayed as an unprincipled scheming character who sold Czechoslovak scientific secrets to the West for a few thousand dollars. In a cloak-and-dagger narrative shrouded in Cold War context, Holan was punished for his double-dealing by being assassinated and tossed into the Baltic Sea in 1963. The message was that individuals such as Holan, a careerist television journalist during 1960s who traveled abroad freely, was untrustworthy, willing to betray his profession for money. And individuals like him were the movers and shakers during the Prague Spring. Did the viewers make the connection between Holan and Tosek when looking at the actor stroking his girlfriend's legs as the couple watched a recorded commentary made by Vladimír about the Cuban missile crisis of 1962? Vladimír's daughter did.[45]

Retrospectively, the series cast a long shadow over television journalists and on the year 1968; it was riveting, exotic, and had all the features of a crime film while the political message was not forced down the viewers' throat. Viewers might have "identified with the state-approved characters played by state-approved actors."[46] If indeed Holan impersonated Tosek (notably, he wore a turtleneck sweater, which was one of Vladimír's favorite garments), Vladimír's StB file was thick with material for a portrait of a journalist who was the exact opposite of Holan. Tosek was never for sale. And that might have been the point: to denigrate a popular journalist representing the Prague Spring by tarnishing his stellar reputation.[47]

Unaware of the negative rendering of his persona on Czechoslovak television, Vladimír was content when in 1979 he obtained his university degree with flying colors and at the age of sixty retired happily from the BBC monitoring service. He took a job with Amnesty International, where he had to take a bird's-eye view of the world's human problems, which suited him well. He found the job meaningful and was sorry that he had not retired earlier. Ruth continued at hers, albeit grudgingly, until she, too, could retire. By then the technology was changing at the BBC monitoring service, as satellite monitoring was replacing the earth-based systems. It meant an increasing traffic of information that Ruth found hard to cope with, adding to her misery. She had been suffering from depression for which the doctor ordered electroshock therapy, but the medicine proved worse than the illness. She was so unhappy: she missed me, but I was a long way away. Our relationship had been damaged long before and we lacked the tools to repair it. Honest introspection or some form of psychoanalysis was no one's strength.

However, doing difficult translations brought Ruth money and some satisfaction. In Prague the regime staged a trial of some dissidents that the BBC television wanted to dramatize with Ruth's help. She was also translating theoretical texts about the experience of the Prague Spring, riddled with citations from Lenin and Marx, which was hard work. True, after Vladimír graduated from the university and retired from the BBC, they moved to London to be closer to friends, theaters, and concert halls. But then Ruth had to commute to Caversham in her minicar—it was tiring, particularly when she had night shifts. Both Vladimír and Ruth hoped for a closer but paid collaboration with Pelikán and the journal *Listy*. This would happen only after Pelikán was elected a deputy to the European Parliament on behalf of the Italian Socialist Party's branch in Milan in 1979 and had extra money to spend. Ruth resigned from the BBC and in March 1982 a new chapter began in their lives.

With a caravan attached to their car, they sped through the Brennen Pass and then south on the *autostrade del sole* on their way to Rome to take charge of the journal. Vladimír would be in his element as a journalist; Ruth, who thrived on public relations and fraternizing with like-minded people, felt that her life was moving beyond the humdrum as the journal's administrator.[48] The Czechoslovak Ministry of the Interior took note of their relocation.

12

A Bridge over the Frontiers

Jiří Pelikán and his closest associates were convinced that exile was justified on condition that they support fellow citizens at home in their resistance against the ruthless regime seeking to control or destroy their lives. Pelikán had a plan. But how to formulate it and convey it back to Czechoslovakia across the barrier that the normalization regime erected between those in exile and in the homeland? Settled in Rome after a protracted search for a permanent home, busy with television and radio interviews explaining the meaning of the Prague Spring from the communist standpoint, Pelikán found the time to summon a handful of people he trusted for a two-day get-together at Lago di Como. The meeting, held at one of the most scenic Italian resorts in Bellagio near Milan, was to be a hushed affair comprising seven to ten guests who would travel there mindful of possible shadowing by the Czechoslovak secret police. In the spring of 1970, on the banks of the lake, the "Como" group conceived the regular publication of the journal *Listy*. The name revealed the editor's intention to continue in the spirit of a journal censored in Czechoslovakia after the invasion. Vladimír and Ruth, in transition to their new life from Italy to England, were not among the journal's founders, but their life in exile was determined by its existence and by their belonging to it first as its invisible cohort and later as active members.

Listy began to circulate in January 1971. It was not a secret that it was produced in Rome, smuggled to Czechoslovakia, and that Pelikán headed the operation. In no time, the regime activated resources to combat the journal in Czechoslovakia as well on the other side of the border. Anyone who possessed a copy of the journal, anyone who was found reading it, and anyone distributing it or copying its articles was accused of undermining the republic, damaging the world socialist system, attacking peace, and violating the constitution. In truth, between 1971 and 1989 *Listy* documented the state of the national cultural and political catastrophe while fighting to overcome it.

FIGURE 11. Jiří Pelikán holding the journal he founded

The Mission

"Why cannot we remain silent?" was *Listy*'s opening salvo. The journal addressed readers in Czechoslovakia first and foremost, assuring them that it would continue upholding the values of the Prague Spring and democratic socialism after the Soviet occupiers and their underlings had silenced the free press and suppressed any intellectual and literary expressions that did not conform to the government's dictated norms. The journal was the voice of the Czechoslovak socialist opposition in exile and at the same time a forum for society at large to express its antagonism to the abnormal regime. Every issue included the legend "read and pass on to your acquaintances." Just reading *Listy*, which the government had proscribed, was an act of resistance and defiance against the authoritarian communist regime.[1]

But Pelikán could not manufacture and distribute the journal by himself. The group that coalesced around him was composed of men in their forties or early fifties; except for Ruth, women came in later. Before emigration all the men had been prominent in politics or the media, longstanding members of the Communist Party, and active in the 1968 reform movement. The initial rumbling about forming a political party was abandoned as impractical in fighting for regime change. Their armory was made up of ideas—their sponsorship, production, and circulation—all to preserve and disseminate culture that in Czechoslovakia could be created only under painfully difficult circumstances.

Through articles and interviews in the countries in which they had settled, Pelikán and his friends, well-informed about the events taking place in Czechoslovakia and the countries of the Soviet bloc, sought to explain to governments, political leaders, East-Central European friends, and Western communist parties' general secretaries what the Prague Spring was, refuting the Czechoslovak government's propaganda against it. They deemed international solidarity and alliances fundamental to eventually undermine the Soviet Union's grip over the nations of East-Central Europe. Whenever signs of solidarity occurred, *Listy* relayed their significance back home in order to inspire optimism and to make such events intelligible within the larger international context of the Cold War.

The journal averaged forty pages per issue in 1971 but had doubled in size by 1988. It was issued bimonthly, usually printed in Italy. It attempted to strike a balance between articles written at home, expressing what their authors there could not write about there, and articles informing readers at home about events relevant for Czechoslovakia to which the readers had no other access. Theory and polemics were excluded most of the time in favor of an exchange of vital information. Because its articles were written in Czech and occasionally in Slovak, *Listy*'s impact on readers outside of Czechoslovakia was limited. To assure that the most important articles were known more widely, Pelikán had some of them translated and published in English, French, German, and Italian. Ruth and Vladimír, working at their BBC monitoring service job, were willing translators in their spare time.

Throughout *Listy*'s existence in exile, the journal's goal of reaching as many readers in Czechoslovakia as possible was difficult to achieve. Under challenging circumstances, the editors had to communicate with authors, organize the delivery of information and articles across the border, and assure that money was available to pay for the operations, all of which were complicated and delicate issues. It took time for the circulation mechanisms to be established, tested, and then maintained. Care had to be taken that the provenance of the Czech articles was not discernible and that people's lives were not endangered. The persecution of citizens active in the opposition to the regime and of *Listy*'s collaborators was relentless and conspirational methods and tactics were paramount in order to manufacture and distribute the journal. How Pelikán obtained and used money to run the operation was his domain.[2]

What did *Listy* mean to its readers in Czechoslovakia? Pelikán always asked that question, to which there was no reliable answer as no surveys could be conducted. But on the journal's tenth anniversary in 1980, Jiřina Šiklová who had been deeply involved in the conspiracy of *Listy*'s distribution as well as in the circulation of its articles inside and across the borders (for which she was arrested a year later), gave some answers.

A sociologist prohibited by the regime to work in her profession, Šiklová was a frequent contributor to the journal under pseudonyms taken from the names of various rivers. Her assessment highlighted the important fact that people read the journal and, once they had done so, passed it on to others. Participating in the prohibited sphere defied the normalization regime. To lend *Listy* meant overcoming one's fear, demonstrating one's belonging to a suppressed community, and showing trust in the person to whom one was lending it. In reading the journal one gleaned information that contradicted the regime's lies. The government's persecution of its victims with no legal recourse was so disproportionate that it was a small satisfaction that *Listy* recorded the absurdities, such as being interrogated for articles that a person published in 1968. Difficult as it was, the journal carried out a dialogue across the border, reflecting contrasting interpretations of events even while the interlocutors faced the Ministry of the Interior's vigilance and repression. Šiklová appreciated those articles that took note of what the Communist Party's organ *Rudé právo* did not write about. *Listy*'s ideas reached even the government corridors where economic issues or the politics of the Soviet Union were discussed. In an unpredictable way, *Listy* invigorated its readers, amalgamated people of different ideological persuasions, and provided them with moral support. If only more issues could be sent, to circulate and be read.[3]

Pelikán's collaborators had jobs; some were better paid than others, but nobody was compensated for their editorial work. Whatever money Pelikán procured that did not go into the production of the journal was sent to authors in Czechoslovakia. The drawback was that *Listy*'s articles were edited in people's spare time, and since they were all working, they had little of it to spare. Nevertheless, for most of them writing and collaborating with the journal filled an intellectual and political void brought about by their emigration. *Listy* became their medium of communication, of exchanging ideas, binding them to like-minded people in exile and at home not only intellectually and politically but also emotionally. It allowed them to preserve old friendships. Association with *Listy* gave many of them a sense of belonging and without any prescribed organizational ties.[4]

Writing for *Listy* or for any publication proscribed by the regime in Czechoslovakia was not simple. An author would write an article and had to deliver it to a specific address. On the way he or she could be followed, perhaps be forced to destroy the article for fear of being intercepted, return home, and if that happened, have to write it all over again at night and repeat the odyssey in the hope that the article would make the journey across the border to Vienna, Rome, or London. When a person was found with an article deemed antisocialist, its author or bearer could end up in jail. And having made it to Rome, not all typewritten articles were legible because they could have been one of many duplicates, had to be retyped, entailing time and expense. Messages transmitted verbally between foreign couriers and contacts at home could suffer from miscommunications when one of the parties had insufficient knowledge of the language used. *Listy* did not have a team of copyeditors or fact-checkers. To turn an article into a suitable text required that Pelikán or his closest and trusted friends do the editorial work.[5] Vladimír was one of them, while Pelikán, the editor in chief, had the last word about what was or was not published in the journal.

Listy upheld the spirit of the 1968 reform movement at a time when many Europeans in both halves of the continent were turning away from or against ideological politics and Marxism. But just how deeply the brutal suppression of the Prague Spring had destroyed any hopes for socialism with a human face or of reforming the Stalinist inhumane system was not evident to the reformers in exile. Nor were they aware that Marxist revisionism had been crushed and smothered under the Soviet tanks. Pelikán was an intellectual but a practical politician first and foremost and *Listy* was his instrument. He was hoping that Czechoslovak citizens would gradually elaborate a viable political platform and not just join sporadic protests. For this reason, he insisted that the journal should avoid polemics, and he maintained that he didn't have the right to criticize anyone. Disagreements over tactics, strategies, and the future of socialism existed but were voiced rarely in *Listy*'s pages.[6]

The unexpected turn in European politics energized the rudderless opposition at home, which the government tried to mollify with material improvements. To no avail: the regime's opponents took advantage of the new situation, espousing the human rights of the Helsinki Accords. Their adoption crystalized into Charter 77 two years later.[7]

The regime did not tolerate opposition in Czechoslovakia and found it unacceptable that it had a voice representing it outside. The problem was all the more serious because the emigrants had been members of the Communist Party, had held high positions, and were known internationally. As much as the regime maligned them, it could not write them off. Pelikán was singled out as one of the main instruments of anticommunism and deemed an obstacle to legitimizing the normalization regime. The existence of the Czechoslovak emigration was dangerous because it was also influencing some sectors of the population at home, fostering their hope that a new Prague Spring could return.[8]

Thus, *Listy* had to be stopped. One way was to spread false information about Pelikán, claiming that he had collaborated with the Gestapo during World War II (in fact the Gestapo had arrested him for antifascist activities) and sowing suspicion about him through the dissemination of fabricated messages that he allegedly wrote. The Czech government bribed Italian postmen to photograph Pelikán's letters and pressured the Vatican to remove him from its premises, where he lived in one of its buildings. On February 4, 1975, Pelikán received a warning: an envelope with a book from Milan was delivered at his door. It had a more elaborate wrapping than other packages. He unwrapped it with care; on opening it an explosive device was activated and the envelope caught fire. He threw it into the corridor; only his curtains suffered from the flames. The aim was not to kill him but to frighten him into silence. Pelikán wrote to Ruth and Vladimír as well as to the rest of his collaborators, "I can assure you that it is not a pleasant feeling to hold a little object, which suddenly starts to buzz, smoulder and then burst into flames—I threw it away from me and I lay on the floor, in expectation of an explosion, which did not happen."[9] In haste Pelikán penned his autobiography, in case they really killed him. The book had also a political goal: vindicating his generation, which had matured in war as antifascist, endured Stalinism, and remained socialist.[10]

Pelikán was not silenced and *Listy* went on relentlessly. In 1975 the journal published Alexander Dubček's letter to the Federal Assembly of Czechoslovakia and the Slovak state council and Václav Havel's letter to Gustáv Husák, the man who had demoted Dubček and replaced him in 1969 as the first secretary of the Czechoslovak Communist Party.[11] Husák, Slovak like Dubček and jailed during the 1950s for alleged bourgeois nationalism, assumed the task of implementing the restoration of the neo-Stalinist regime, owing his accession to power to the invasion.

Some individuals could not endure the unrelenting oppression. Vilém Prečan, a historian and coauthor of the book *The Seven Prague Days* documenting the invasion week as it unfolded, suffered harassment as a consequence. By 1976 he had enough of the regime's bullying. He lost his position, as did over one hundred other historians, and was forced to live from hand to mouth working odd jobs to support his wife and three children. When he applied for emigration, the regime gladly obliged, happy to get rid of an irksome intellectual. Prečan packed as much of his archive as he could and with a heavy heart said goodbye to friends. Once he crossed the border, he sent the news to Pelikán. They had known each other as partners in the clandestine labor of getting printed material and messages across the border in both directions. Pelikán trusted Prečan, letting him have a secret postal address in Rome.[12] The historian became one of *Listy*'s pillars; he and his wife Helena were an addition to Ruth's as much as Vladimír's circle of friends.

Charter 77

The news of the charter's appearance was a bombshell. "We believe that CHARTER 77 will help to enable all the citizens of Czechoslovakia to work and live as free human beings," the document said.[13] By the time the text appeared in the first issue of *Listy* a month later, Charter 77 was known around the world. It had seeped into public consciousness in Czechoslovakia without being able to appear in the press thanks to the government's furious reaction, snatching the text wherever it was found and subjecting its spokesmen to interrogation and jail. *Listy* published the text together with the entire list of its signatories and the three undeniably brave spokesmen. If at the end of 1976 Pelikán had doubts about *Listy*'s future, Charter 77 injected it with a new energy and revived its mission. Furthermore, Charter 77 broke the myth propagated by the regime that its consolidation was successful.

With two hundred and forty-one signatures collected secretly from around the country at the end of 1976, Charter 77 denounced the government's violation of the constitution and the international laws like the United Nations' Universal Declaration Human Rights and the Helsinki Accords to which it had subscribed. It did not seek to consolidate the opposition in one organization but to defy the government in order to win basic human rights for all citizens, including the right to share responsibility for the state of the nation. The government's reaction was frenetic, demanding a condemnation of a document that no one was allowed to read. By March some four hundred citizens had added their signatures. *Listy* registered each name. Signing the manifesto was an act of courage that the government undermined through police surveillance, telephone interference (or cutting the service altogether), disallowing the Charter 77 signatories' children to study at universities, and other petty nuisances intruding into normal daily life.[14]

Pelikán understood Charter 77's political significance instantly, even if he was leery of its declaration that it did not aim to become an organization and a base for political activity in opposition to the regime. He and his colleagues deemed Charter 77 a triumph of national historical importance, unlike many fellow citizens in Czechoslovakia who sympathized with it but thought it to be a quixotic moral gesture. Since the regime would not comply with its demands, Pelikán thought that "a small action program" should be elaborated, with realistic demands, such as the freeing of political prisoners, an end to discrimination against students to punish their fathers or mothers for opposing the regime, the restoration of religious freedom, the return of qualified people to their jobs, the end to travel restrictions, and tangible workers' rights in labor unions and in the administration of enterprises. Pelikán had ten thousand leaflets with the charter's text printed to send home and for distribution among Czechoslovak tourists abroad.[15]

The regime saw in Charter 77 a call for the destruction of socialism and the restoration of capitalism. The *Listy*'s group, on the other hand, identified the charter with an embryonic political force that ideally would evolve into a movement for the restoration of democratic socialism in Czechoslovakia. It would have liked to exert influence over its evolution, but it could not. Charter 77 and the milieu in which it was born and grew had a life of their own. In response to the government's control over the chartists' lives and that of the society as a whole, the chartist movement defied the party and the state at an enormous personal cost; and although they existed on the margins of the society, some believed they managed to create the semblance of an alternative society, a parallel polis, both political and personal. Havel, who had grown into Charter 77's leading voice, conceived it as a moral force, inviting people to an active participation as citizens in hopes that it would lead to the birth of independent political structures deriving from conscience and not from any calculation.[16]

Pelikán never criticized Charter 77 for its discursive insistence on apolitical politics, not even in his private correspondence. He viewed it and the chartists as an organic outgrowth of the existing society. He was closer to some and more distant from other of its signatories. It is perhaps not accidental that Pelikán and Havel never established an epistolary relationship, even though both of them both wrote regular letters to many other friends (and Havel to other *Listy* collaborators); nor did either mention the other, at least not in their published correspondence. Was it evident to Pelikán and his associates in exile that it was Havel's and his friends' actions rather than the *Listy* group who were influencing the course of history? Perhaps. But in any case, *Listy* remained a steadfast messenger and disseminator of the suppressed culture, publishing and making authentic documents from Czechoslovakia available to the European and American audiences in translation by Vladimír, Ruth, and many others, defending the persecuted and the jailed in the world press, pointing incessantly at the regime's violation of human rights, and drawing attention to the wider East European phenomenon of repressive regimes dominated by the Soviet Union. It could not do more.

It is true that in its origin Charter 77 involved not only Havel but also the revolutionary firebrand Petr Uhl, the Catholic Václav Benda, and the former party apparatchik Zdeněk Mlynář, in addition to many other voices contradicting and complementing each other while a young generation was growing up in their shadow. Due to the government's persecution of Charter 1977's signatories, including a sexual assault on one woman, numerous chartists were forced to or decided to emigrate. The aforementioned woman was one of them. Another founder of Charter 77 lost to emigration was Mlynář. A member of the party elite and a theoretician, Mlynář described himself as a reform-minded communist as opposed to a noncommunist democrat. In September 1969 he was expelled from the Central Committee of the Czechoslovak Communist Party and in March 1970 from the party. Until his emigration, he belonged to a group that identified itself as expelled communists opposed to the government. While Charter 77 was in the making, Mlynář supported the undertaking, bringing dozens of signatures to endorse it.[17]

Mlynář emigrated to Austria in June 1977. Here was a figure well-known among the communist higher-ups and in foreign government circles on both sides of the curtain, who could advance *Listy*'s goal by gaining access to additional rungs of the European Left and to various statesmen. Mlynář stated that his goal was not the remaking of the political exile community but to find his own place inside it. But he was steeped in the style of Communist Party politics, which he never abandoned and which rubbed many of the original core group the wrong way. During the Prague Spring he believed in the need to correct the deformations of the system but was dismissive of spontaneity and popular movements. He propounded changes but insisted they had to be regulated politically, meaning from above, including democratic politics.[18]

The incorporation of Mlynář into the group affected its trajectory. Not only did he want to steer *Listy* toward a defined ideological and organizational reformist socialist line—which was not fundamentally different from Pelikán's goals—but he wanted to take a leading position. The group rejected this idea. Nobody could replace Pelikán, who was respected by all: the man was endowed with a sense of humour, a genuine interest in others, and great generosity. His sense of solidarity was matched by his savoir vivre. Power and money did not interest him. Mlynář, on the other hand, was tough: he was gifted, knowledgeable, intelligent, a strong personality, used to swaying others to his positions, but without the congeniality at which Pelikán excelled. Mlynář lacked the merits and did not have the trust of the group that had been built over the years; moreover, his ideas about how to achieve democratic socialism were not shared by all. But he was without a doubt an intellectual asset. For example, he set up a research project called "Crises in Soviet-Type Systems," compiling short analytical texts by experts. Several members of the *Listy* group participated in the project. Subsequently, he published *Mráz přichází z Kremlu* ("Nightfrost in the Kremlin"), an autobiographical journey through socialist Czechoslovakia all the way to 1968, including his participation in the August Moscow negotiations that ordered the occupation. The book became an instant bestseller among people interested in the subject.[19]

Charter 77 affected Vladimír as well as Ruth. Like the others in the group that put out *Listy*, they, too, were energized by the turn of events. Why did Vladimír change his mind and decided to become fully involved as a writer from then on? His moral and ideological universe may have been thrown into disarray after any hope for democratic socialism was shattered by the Soviet occupation. The revelation in 1969 of his previous collaboration with the secret police, just as he was seeking to legalize his status as a Czechoslovak communist journalist abroad, was a hard blow to overcome. Emigration itself was a traumatic experience. He could have been concerned that his name on the pages of *Listy* might affect his children in Czechoslovakia, who by 1977 had grown to adulthood.

Having weighed the odds, Vladimír seems to have decided to make a weightier contribution to *Listy*, but uncertain of its impact on the lives of his children, he did so under the pseudonym Julián Slatina. His articles pilloried the official press and were ironic, resorting to sarcasm as his shield and his sword; he wrote glosses rather than reflections. They were oddly self-referential: Vladimír was present in most of them, as if he needed to vindicate his long silence and absence from the press even though readers did not know who Slatina was.

Ruth, free of Vladimír's intellectual and existential agonies, shared his concerns as much out of love as out of her own beliefs. Her view of the world was more pragmatic; ever ready to use her skills to good purposes, she organized *Listy*'s meetings and translated Charter 77's documents as needed, banging the translations out with two fingers on a typewriter. Both Vladimír and Ruth offered solidarity to chartists in distress after some of them had been forced or decided to emigrate to England.

Periodically, *Listy*'s friends and collaborators went through soul-searching exercises. What was *Listy*'s and the exiles' role? To energize the opposition movement at home? Were they to create a movement for free democratic socialist Czechoslovakia abroad or at home? It was true that in the eyes of the population the reform process had been largely discredited by the capitulation of the party leadership in 1968, albeit under military pressure. By accepting the Moscow protocol, the leadership had paved the way for the normalization affecting millions of people. It was also true that the instruments of repression had hardened and that the occupation had warned the other countries of the bloc against attempting democratization. All these irrefutable facts led to feelings of powerlessness, to an inclination toward passivity, waiting for new developments in Moscow without which any attempts at a change seemed useless. But passivity was not an option.[20]

Listy had no alternative but to try to become an actor in the programmatic formation of a new socialist Czechoslovak opposition, insisted Mlynář. He felt the journal should be a forum for analyzing problems of socialism and democracy conceptually, not only rehashing past experiences. *Listy* should break two taboos: "not to interfere in the disputes at home and not to take a position on the disputes of the Western European left."[21] Pelikán shared Mlynář's political concerns but not at the cost of undermining the cohesion of the *Listy* group. In the conclusions drawn during a meeting in Cologne in November 1979, the group did not adopt Mlynář's proposition for a deeper and wider political engagement at home and among the European Left. The prevalent position was that a change in the existing international system was not on the horizon, that there was no relaxation of the Soviet domination in East-Central Europe and that the division into opposing camps could not be overcome. *Listy*'s mission would remain "to inform the world public about the real circumstances in Czechoslovakia and about the struggle of the Cz. democratic opposition," which did not preclude a theoretical political discussion about perspectives for democratic socialism in Czechoslovakia.[22] The group's unity was preserved.

And then in August 1980 the Polish workers organized an independent trade union, Solidarity, and dockers struck in Gdansk's shipyards.

The union rapidly grew to ten million members in virtually every workplace in Poland, in one of the great labor upsurges of modern history. The Czechoslovak press undertook an intensive campaign against the independent labor unions, branding them as antisocialist and counterrevolutionary and calling for "fraternal help." For close to two years, until the workers suffered military defeat by General Jaruzelski, *Listy* lent its pages unreservedly to the Polish efforts to extricate the country from Soviet hegemony and its Polish underlings. It was on everyone's mind that events in Poland had far-reaching consequences for Czechoslovakia and the countries of the entire Soviet bloc. The workers' opposition to the communist regime was different from the Prague Spring. It was an opposition from below, not controlled by the Communist Party, as laborers refused to put up with the unpopular regime. The workers' insurrection demonstrated that under certain circumstances the system could be challenged and *Listy* examined those circumstances and the actions of the leaders of the revolt. The declaration of martial law in December 1981 to forestall Soviet military intervention was a bitter pill to swallow. To top it all, it was disappointing to read a German social democrat assuring people that the situation of the detained activists was satisfactory, relying on the report of a deputy minister of the People's Republic of Poland. With a dose of sarcasm, some in Czechoslovakia concluded that "now the only salvation is [US president Ronald] Reagan."[23] That was a somber conclusion coming from *Listy*'s collaborators, who perceived an immutable Soviet power established inside the bloc and frozen relations between the East and the West.

Besides being *Listy*'s editor, Pelikán had become an Italian politician, elected in 1979 to the European parliament on behalf of the Italian Socialist Party. It was a unique position, which allowed him to keep Czechoslovakia on the radar of the international community. The task was to keep on insisting before the parliamentarians that Europe would not enjoy peace until East and West were united and human rights were respected.[24]

As a parliamentarian, Pelikán traveled constantly between Rome, Brussels, and Strasbourg and consequently could not devote as much time to *Listy* as he would have liked to. Vladimír and Ruth had offered to collaborate with him and the journal before, provided he could supplement their pensions. He could not until he had become a member of the European Parliament, and his income allowed him to fill the holes to support *Listy*. So, in 1982 he invited them to Rome to take charge of the journal's everyday business. Vladimír became its editor and Ruth the administrator while the final decision about what to include in each issue remained Pelikán's.

Vladimír was never easy to work with: he was stubborn and sometimes pedantic and vain; soon he crossed swords with *Listy*'s other collaborators and even with Pelikán. It was lucky that their political ideas coincided. Both were firm in their conviction that socialism was the only path for humankind to follow and that they were to return to Czechoslovakia to restart the course of democratic socialism, which was interrupted by the 1968 occupation. Arguing with Vladimír could be stressful, so when Pelikán was on the campaign trail for reelection to the European parliament in 1984, he let Vladimír make all the decisions regarding the journal, "because I don't have the nerves to haggle with him."[25] On occasions authors objected to Vladimír's shortening their article or altering their grammar. But above all, noted Prečan, the journal lacked vitality under his direction: "Vladimír is not the person who could give the journal a character and infuse it with grace."[26]

Was Vladimír aware of the grumblings about his style and dispositions? Whatever the case, in Rome he was in his element again, as a guide to anyone interested in its antiquities, palaces, museums, and the history and architecture that he knew so well. He loved Italy from an early age, but this time his and Ruth's sojourn in the country was not easy. Vladimír's diabetes had worsened; he was injecting himself with insulin several times a day, which did not prevent him from falling once into a diabetic coma. In addition, the couple was traumatized by two burglaries of their apartment in early January 1984, just as *Listy*'s publication deadline was approaching. In both cases the intrusion looked like an ordinary break-in. Not even the cautious Pelikán suspected that the incident could have been anything else but a vulgar robbery, even though *Listy*'s office was ransacked over Christmas in 1982. Then the thieves stole a typewriter with Czech letters, hardly a coveted market commodity. From the evidence available, the burglary was a professional job by the secret police. In Vladimír's file in the archive of the Ministry of the Interior there is a hand-drawn floor diagram of the robbed apartment situated at number 15 Via Guglielme Ciamarra.[27]

Pelikán was worried. "By the way, I have a great problem with the Toseks (and they with Rome): they were burgled twice in succession and Ruth had hysterical attacks and her stomach ulcers reappeared and with that insomnia and it's a vicious circle, we have to be patient with them at this point and I don't even know, if I can persuade them to remain in Rome, because Ruth wants to go back to England."[28] If Pelikán were to lose them, *Listy*'s smooth running would be jeopardized. But Vladimír and Ruth set the date to leave Italy for 1986.

Shortcomings and criticisms notwithstanding, *Listy* continued to carry out its mission as an unconditional conduit for Charter 77's documents, for silenced writers in Czechoslovakia, and for writers in exile. However, from Pelikán's point of view, no matter how voluminous the published and disseminated material and intellectual production from Czechoslovakia in the journal, the undertaking was not meeting the desired political aims. At the meeting of the editorial board at the beginning of 1984, Pelikán again posed the questions regarding the journal's nature and future. It remained a journal of Czechoslovak socialist opposition, maintaining continuity with the ideas of the Prague Spring under new conditions of development at home and worldwide. Should *Listy* remain an organ generating ideas about reforms and communicate with those at home who identified with it, or should it gradually move away from these concerns and address those of the younger people? Should the journal's initiatives seek changes at home, including partial reforms such as those implemented in Hungary? Or should it advocate "pure democracy?" Or do nothing? Should *Listy*'s creators seek their replacement? But by whom? There was always the nagging question of how to overcome the dejection that prevailed among the journal's collaborators, restore their trust in *Listy*'s mission, and get them to continue dedicating their free time to it.[29]

The Gorbachev Phenomenon

Pelikán welcomed the dawn of 1985 with pessimism. The immobility in Moscow and Prague weighed on him heavily. True, Brezhnev had died of a heart attack in 1982, Yuri Andropov, the head of the KGB, succeeded him only to die in February 1984 of renal failure. He was replaced by Konstantin Chernenko, who belonged to the same cohort committed to preserving the status quo. But there was a new generation of leaders angling their way into the power structure at a moment when the need for economic restructuring of the Soviet Union was evident. The appearance of a small but vocal group of Soviet dissidents, calling for the repudiation of the Helsinki conference as a historical fraud and asking Western governments to stop this hypocritical game, was unexpected. It would be good news, Pelikán wrote to a friend that January, "if Chernenko died and was replaced by Gorbachev and if in Moscow some change and movement was to take place, at least personal and generational." Indeed, the octogenarian Chernenko died in March of emphysema and the party central committee members acclaimed the fifty-four-year-old Mikhail Gorbachev, an up-and-coming regional party boss, to replace him, some with enthusiasm, others with concealed enmity.[30]

The arrival of Gorbachev at the helm of the Soviet Union in March, his proposed policies of perestroika and glasnost, reconstruction and openness, provoked many and contradictory reactions. Some people were optimistic that something was moving in the Soviet Union; the pessimists considered the system unchangeable and believed that one man would make no difference. The *Listy* group was also affected. Some of its members stayed faithful to the reform era of 1968, others took the view that society had evolved and there was no return. The Gorbachev phenomenon infused the adherents to the Prague Spring with the confidence that the Communist Party could still play a role in a renewed reform movement and that democratizing socialism was possible.

Zdeněk Mlynář was best suited to explain the significance of Gorbachev, who was at this point still a largely unknown entity. When Mlynář studied in Moscow in the 1950s, he and Misha Gorbachev were close friends. Mlynář trusted him and took it upon himself to explain Gorbachev's intentions even before the Soviet general secretary began to put them into practice. Here was a man who had belonged to the system all his life but for whom power and politics were not ends in themselves; rather, he intended to use them to reform the Soviet Union. On April 9, Mlynář wrote an article for the Italian Communist Party's organ *L'Unità*, republished in *Listy* as "The End of Stagnation," in which he extolled Gorbachev's virtues. It so happened that the Italian prime minister Bettino Craxi went to Moscow on a state visit. He took the article with him and handed it to Gorbachev, but the Soviet leader was concerned that people might find out that he had a friend who personified the Prague Spring and pretended he did not know who Mlynář was.[31]

Speculations about the structural changes in the Soviet Union and the countries of Central and Eastern Europe abounded in Czechoslovakia. While the Czechoslovak powerholders were nervous because they owed their political existence to the Soviet suppression of the reform movement, the fundamental question people asked was, Would Gorbachev repudiate the Soviet-led occupation and the installation in the Czechoslovak government of individuals who contradicted the very principles on which Gorbachev based his hope for success in the Soviet Union, namely, democracy, economic restructuring, and freedom of speech? Gorbachev called the representatives of the bloc to Moscow in March 1986; during the meeting, he talked about equality among the partners, respect for sovereignty, independence of each country, collaboration, and the responsibility of each party for developments in its specific country. "The partners agreed. But did not take it, it seemed to me, all that seriously," Gorbachev wrote in his memoirs. The past weighed heavily on them. In October 1986 the Soviet politburo accepted the notion that the East-Central Europeans could follow their own paths and renounced the use of military force to intervene in these countries.[32] But that still did not satisfy the expectations of Czechoslovak citizens.

The moment of truth came in April 1987 when Gorbachev visited Prague. Before his arrival, Charter 77's spokespeople sent him a letter, signed by a few courageous men and women, surely not expecting a reply. "Mister General Secretary," they wrote, without mentioning all the insignias that came with the post. They did not expect Gorbachev to resolve the calamities caused by the occupation; it was up to the Czechoslovak society itself to do so. If he really wanted to normalize relations between the two countries and have a positive influence on Czechoslovak and European conditions, it was in his power to withdraw the Soviet army and the nuclear war heads from Czechoslovak territory. Granting freedom and democracy where the Soviet Union had denied them would help the democratization process in the Soviet Union as well. "Mister General Secretary, accept this letter as an expression of our openness and sincerity," they entreated.[33]

On his arrival to Prague for a three-day visit, Gorbachev and Husák kissed and hugged like all their predecessors, ritualizing the eternal friendship between Czechoslovakia and the Soviet Union. The Czechoslovak *nomenklatura* hastened to declare that it stood behind the need for changes, but it was not clear who would carrying them out after all the reformers had been purged from their jobs and public life. Gorbachev did not show any discomfort when dealing with the gravediggers of the Prague Spring. Let the process take its natural course to avoid any destabilization of the Soviet bloc, was Mlynář's view of Gorbachev's perplexing silence on the question of the Soviet occupation. Mlynář concluded that his friend was still a hostage to the Brezhnev doctrine of limited sovereignty in the countries of the Soviet bloc. It was unwelcome to hear Gorbachev's highlighting the economic successes of Husák's government when the ordinary citizens felt the economic stagnation in their lives, brought about by the regime's inefficient economic policies, "the economics of shortage," as the contradictory operations of Soviet-style economies were called. On his return to Moscow, Gorbachev reported to his colleagues from the politburo on his message to the Czechoslovak leadership: "I told them that right now we are moving from formulating the concept of perestroika to practicing it. If there is something that works for you, take it. The only thing we are counting on is solidarity. In the international arena we will firmly hold to equality, even though we are big and you are small." Gorbachev was not imbibing any inspiration from the Prague Spring reforms as Mlynář and others had claimed; still more importantly, "I let it be understood that we have no intention of reconsidering our position on 1968."[34]

Havel was saddened by some of his fellow citizens' unwarranted enthusiasm for Gorbachev, engendered by the belief that he would bring them freedom and solve their problems by liberating them from Husák: "The visit of the czar-reformer in its province where they govern thanks to the intervention of their antireform's predecessors was such a piquant event—at least as far as expectations were concerned—that a really unexpected number of journalists flocked to Prague." When Gorbachev came out onto the street after attending a performance at the National Theater, Havel was walking his dog along the bank of the Vltava River. He watched with curiosity the spectacle of "a frenetic roaring crowd" waving at the leader. What an unreformable nation this is, he thought; and what could be said about the Westerners, who "thaw like an iceman in a stove, as soon as an eastern bigwig sends them a charming smile!"[35]

Unlike Havel, Pelikán, Vladimír and Ruth and most of the *Listy*'s group supported Gorbachev. In perestroika and glasnost, they saw the rehabilitation of the Prague Spring. True, there were many differences between the two movements, but thanks to Gorbachev change was in their air. What was still missing was an unequivocal declaration by the Soviet leadership that the intervention in August 1968 was a "political error" made by Brezhnev's government; such a declaration would guarantee "that similar manifestations of the great power hegemony will not be repeated in the future."[36]

This view was not shared by all readers and some collaborators of *Listy*. Prečan (vocally), Uhl (in a letter from Prague), and others (in silence) criticized this glorification of the past. Indeed, a true reckoning with the past meant dealing with the demise of the Prague Spring and the moral catastrophe that followed due to the constant ceding of power to the occupiers' lackeys until in August 1969 Dubček himself signed the "rubber truncheon law" outlawing any protest against the invaders.[37]

The twentieth anniversary of the 1968 invasion was approaching. The *Listy* group met in Cologne in November 1987 to prepare for the occasion. Mlynář prepared a discussion paper, postulating among other ideas for the future that the Czechoslovak leadership of the Communist Party should assist reforms from below by implementing them from above. Havlíček was appalled by the idea. Like everybody else, he watched Gorbachev's politics with interest but restraint, anticipating that in time the normalization regime would end but feeling that the Soviet-engendered perestroika and glasnost were not appropriate lessons for Czechoslovakia. What if, retorted Havlíček, the Soviet political shift had no other goal than strengthening the Soviet Union's threatened superpower position? He objected to Mlynář's unreflective affirmation that Czechoslovak citizens desired nothing other than socialism. To advocate that the Communist Party of Czechoslovakia be the vehicle for implementing the reforms after all the harm it had caused was ridiculous; it deserved "to be disbanded and its activists held accountable." He also objected to Mlynář's party jargon. Others did not agree with Mlynář's text, either. Prečan attended the meeting and advocated for the leading role of the party to be put to rest for good. Despite such protests, Mlynář's conception prevailed and was published in the February 1988 issue without any fundamental change. In protest, Havlíček resigned from the *Listy* group.[38]

The same November that the group met in Cologne, Adolf Müller, one of its members, founder and editor of the Index publishing house, invited ten intellectuals in exile to reflect on the year 1968 as well as on the current prospects for change in Czechoslovakia with Gorbachev's reforms in mind. Some of those who replied were members of the *Listy* group, some were friends and contributors with radically different positions. The fault lines ran between those who cherished hopes and those skeptical that Gorbachev's policies could influence Czechoslovakia's political course. Pelikán, Prečan, and Vladimír were among the men interviewed; there were no women. Each man could freely choose how to answer the questions. Most believed that Gorbachev's reforms had lessons to teach that might facilitate reforms in Czechoslovakia. In his written presentation, Vladimír went over his entire life before expressing hopes for a future that would result not from manna falling from the sky but from the work of each and every citizen; Gorbachev had created the conditions for change. None of those supporting Gorbachev attributed any meaning to the Soviet leader's sojourn in Czechoslovakia in April 1987, during which he did not disassociate himself from his predecessor's fatal military invasion and the thousands of Soviet soldiers still occupying the country nor from Soviet responsibility for the Czechoslovak calamity of the past twenty years.[39]

And then *Listy*'s life came to a standstill. Ruth and Vladimír had, after four and half years in Rome, returned to London in October of the previous year, to seek better medical treatment for his diabetes. But on December 8, at the age of sixty-eight, Vladimír died. Pelikán put everything on hold and flew to London. So did I with my son. A helpful Foreign Office staff member activated the British embassy in Prague so that Vladimír's children, Zdenka and Lubomír, could obtain exit permits—but not before showing to the authorities a letter from the hospital doctors that Vladimír was in intensive care. They arrived in London in time for the funeral.[40] The journalist Karel Kyncl, also living in exile in London, expressed his feelings about the loss of his long-time friend with a poem by the English bard John Dunne: "No man is an Island, entire of itself; every man is a piece of the Continent, a part of the main; if a clod be washed away by the sea, Europe is the less, as well as if a promontory were, as well as if a manor of thy friends or of thine own were; any man's death diminishes me, because I am involved in Mankind; And therefore never send to know for whom the bell tolls; It tolls for thee." Ruth was devastated; momentarily she lost her bearings. At sixty-two years old, she was left alone in London; with good friends scattered in different countries and with my son and me living at the time in Chapel Hill, North Carolina, she had no one to lean on in her distress. Ruth was determined to continue work with *Listy*, finding solace from the pain of bereavement in its activities. It was high time to switch from using a typewriter to learning the mysteries of a personal computer. She mastered the task.

Changes were taking place in Eastern Europe, but the Czechoslovak government was paralyzed by the Gorbachev phenomenon. Set in their dictatorial ways, the powers-that-be did not know how to react to the shifting world at home, where new and independent initiatives entered the political fray, demanding freedom for all, and where people were taking to the streets fearless of consequences. The Soviet bloc was tottering, but the government did not feel threatened as long as the Soviet leaders did not condemn the 1968 invasion. When challenged, the authoritarian regime reacted wielding the traditional weapons of power.

Charter 77, with Havel at the head, was planning a seminar assessing the twenty years following the 1968 occupation but the event was going to be more than that. The number 8 seemed to be inscribed in Czechoslovak historical trajectory: besides 1968 and 1988, 1918 was the year of the foundation of the republic; 1938 was etched into people's memory as the year of the Anglo-French betrayal and 1948 as the fatal communist takeover. The seminar was planned as an international event with prominent national and foreign participants. Prečan and Havel feared that because it had not been prepared well intellectually, the symposium might turn out to be a mere publicity stunt; but Havel thought that even if it were just that, it was important to push Charter 77's boundary of freedom inch by inch.[41]

One of the guests, the English historian Timothy Garton Ash, left a testimony of the event. As the Western guests were assembling in Prague, their Czech hosts were locked up or placed under house arrest. Havel went into hiding to avoid either fate. On November 11, the guests gathered at

Hotel Paris: academics, writers, human rights activists, parliamentarians from Western Europe and the United States, and the press. Then, at nine o'clock in the morning, Havel walked in, striding along the marble corridor. Before the police bundled him away in front of the German and Austrian television cameras, he declared the symposium open and added, "Well, in this moment I am arrested."[42]

A female secret police officer with a bouquet of flowers in her hand, who went by the name "Lieutenant Novotná," tendered an envelope to each person in the hotel lobby with the warning that the symposium *Czechoslovakia 88* was illegal. Ash and others drafted a statement protesting the violation of the Helsinki Accords, pointing at the government's flagrant contempt for the elementary human rights. The whole of Czechoslovakia learned of the event within hours from the BBC, Radio Free Europe, and the Voice of America. Western diplomats deplored the Czechoslovak authorities' action, but the government was unmoved by the opprobrium.[43]

That December Ruth, too, decided to test the regime's flexibility. It was the anniversary of Vladimír's death. The Czechoslovak embassy in London stamped her British passport with a visa valid for four days. Ruth took the British Airways flight from London to Prague, landing at Ruzyně airport. The regime's watchdogs were waiting for her. On seeing her passport, the inspection officer handed it to two policemen standing nearby who took her aside and up to the fourth floor of the airport building. It did not happen often that somebody from *Listy*'s group turned up in Prague, they said with sarcasm. They had evidence that she carried important messages. Whom was she planning to visit and who were the communications for? Ruth refused to answer any questions. The police did not allow her to make any phone calls, so she turned around and took the next plane to London. A year later, Ruth was back in Prague to witness the revolution.

Part V

13

Back to the Native Land

For most Czechs and Slovaks, Europe was an imagined community that would guarantee them political and economic security, normality provided by the rule of law. Determined to abjure the Warsaw Pact, they trusted the North Atlantic Treaty Organization would secure them military safety. To return to Europe meant getting out from under the Soviet hegemony, recovering sovereignty, freedom of expression, and freedom to travel, and getting to know the countries from which they had been barred for decades. The model to imitate was liberal capitalism and parliamentary democracy in an undivided world and an integrated Europe. Few believed that any other way was possible. But of what kind of Europe were the Czechs and Slovaks hoping to be part? The welfare state was poorer than they had imagined and was under attack, modernity as the path to social progress was being questioned while ecological concerns, climate change, feminism, and human rights had been integrated into the new Left or had replaced or rivalled leftist thinking.

Living in that Europe, most members of the *Listy* group were yearning to go back home after they had labored for Czechoslovakia's return to democracy and creative freedom. They believed that their understanding of the Western way of life, participation in democratic institutions, and publication of books and magazines with modern technologies could be put to good use by the new leaders and intellectuals at home. But their integration into a country that was changing radically proved problematic. For twenty years, the group had been advocating democratic socialism, which the 1989 revolution swept aside as an obsolete political and economic project.

1989: Annus Mirabilis

This wondrous year was charged with contradictions and dangers, tensions and uncertainties, fears and courage, defiance and violence, steps taken forward and retreats, improvisation and helplessness at times, but it was also festive (carnivalesque, some claimed). It was a miracle that the contending parties, groups, and movements vying to gain or retain visibility or power came out of the skirmishes peacefully, overthrowing the communist regime with no roadmap toward democracy. It was a miracle that whereas in January 1989 Václav Havel was a prisoner of a police state, in December of the same year he became a president of a free country, embarking on an unknown path toward new political, economic, state-building, and social arrangements. It seemed a miracle that the nuclear-armed Soviet Union watched as its outer empire dwindled without intervening. The fast moving events were breathtaking. The men and women in exile were impatient.[1]

Envisioning the future as he would like it to be, Pelikán composed *Listy*'s 1989 first issue. On a split title page, he and Havel appeared together. It was a literary synergy with political undercurrents, illustrated by eloquent photographs. The die had been cast, wrote Havel; civil society had woken up, unwilling to continue enduring the imposed conditions in apathy, determined to do something for its freedom other than just sitting by the radio, sympathizing quietly with Charter 77, exchanging samizdat literature under the table, and applauding meaningful plays in the darkness of the theater auditorium. The powerholders saw it, too, but they held on to their cards in the only way they knew, which was keeping the totalitarian structures intact and saying no to any dialogue. But society demanded pluralism and freedom for all. And, as Havel's jailer once told him, "Truth is on your side!"[2]

Following Havel's exposition of the domestic conundrums, Pelikán wrote about the international scene. Gorbachev had made great strides in liberalizing the Soviet Union, but national conflicts in the Soviet republics and growing state and party antagonism to the reforms he introduced with no corresponding support coming from the workers, were debilitating his policies. Pelikán saw as hopeful the relations between the Soviet Union and the United States in questions of disarmament and Gorbachev's commitment to withdraw Soviet troops from Afghanistan. However, nothing could replace "a return to active politics." It was undeniable that Charter 77 was a wide platform, but the new situation required the creation of active groups and clubs with opinions on the state of public affairs, the elaboration of concrete programs to prepare the soil for real pluralism, allowing voices ranging from new socialist trends to Christian-democratic and other currents to contribute to the development of society. Pelikán wanted to be part of the anticipated democratizing process to which he had been committed since he had chosen exile in 1969. What was needed now was a tolerant debate with no exclusions, not even of the communists as long as they did not impose their "leading" role and respected the opinions of others. He counseled neither struggle for power, nor return to the past.[3]

The articles were illustrated with a drawing of Havel, posed against the silhouette of Prague's spires, and revealing photographs. One showed the police in full gear standing on Wenceslas Square on January 15, facing rows of young people gathered to honor the memory of Jan Palach who had immolated himself there in January 1969, followed by images of police brutality against them. Havel himself was a victim of the police violence there, taken to custody, interrogated, and jailed for being one of the many citizens who gathered to remember the anniversary of Jan Palach's "absolute sacrifice," as he put it, while protesting the occupation of Czechoslovakia. Havel was accused of inviting others to join the commemoration and of using foreign radio stations to broadcast his message.[4]

Pelikán understood that his imagined project for free and democratic Czechoslovakia after the communist regime was gone was unthinkable without Havel's central role, his accumulated wisdom, prestige, experience, and following. But in his projection for the future, he also believed it unthinkable without Alexander Dubček, who was indeed waiting in the wings to return to active politics. When Havel was freed from jail in May, following an international uproar to liberate him, Dubček was most likely sincere when he made the gesture of being among the well-wishers to welcome him home. *Listy* registered the encounter of the two men holding hands, with a smiling Olga Havlová looking on.[5]

In the same issue, Pelikán highlighted Dubček's triumphant trip to Italy in November 1988, where the former secretary general of the Czechoslovak Communist Party received an honorary doctorate from Bologna University and was welcomed by the Italian communists and Pope John Paul II while the regime still held him its hostage. It was not made public at the time that he decided that his wife better should stay at home when the authorities refused to give him the assurance that they would not be barred from returning to Bratislava. Dubček met with the socialist prime minister Bettino Craxi in an inconspicuous way so as not to antagonize the communists. Fearful that he was shadowed by the secret police and seeking to assure the success of the occasion and his return home, Dubček and Pelikán met at night. It may have been then that they designed a plan to bring Dubček back to the public limelight. Indeed, Dubček's trip was a well calculated political stunt, giving him the opportunity to defend the 1968 reforms and vindicate himself on the world stage. According to his close friend Michal Reiman, who met him in Vienna on his return trip to Bratislava, Dubček rehabilitated himself as the legitimate leader of Czechoslovak perestroika.[6]

Pavel Tigrid, the long-standing editor of the prestigious journal *Svědectví* published in Paris, and with whom Pelikán had been collaborating closely in exile, was alarmed after he read *Listy*'s 1989 first issue. Tigrid saw in the articles written by and about Dubček in Italy a call for the return of reform communists and their program of 1968, considering them a fatal step back. He saw the articles as Pelikán pushing Dubček to the political antechamber. Tigrid and Pelikán belonged to the same generation, born in 1917 and 1923 respectively, but while Pelikán had become a communist at an early age and remained faithful to the ideology's fundamental tenets, Tigrid was a conservative democrat all his life, indeed being forced to emigrate after the communist takeover in 1948. Tigrid did not accord Dubček any moral right to reenter Czechoslovak politics after the debacle of the Prague Spring. That right belonged only to Havel.[7]

Why put Havel and Dubček into opposition with each other, asked Pelikán in his reply to Tigrid? Both had merits. Dubček had not sold his soul to the normalization regime; what was needed then was tolerance to achieve national reconciliation. But perhaps Pelikán's reading of the present moment was too idealistic, failing to fathom the depth of the yearning to make the Communist Party accountable for the injustices of the past, the devastation of the last forty years in personal lives, the desolation of the economy, and the destruction of the environment.[8]

Segments of society spearheaded unprecedented actions. New opposition groups and manifestos had been adding their voices to the nascent but clandestine plurality complementing the well-established Charter 77. The "Club for Socialist Reconstruction," OBRODA (Renewal), for example, was composed of expelled communists and some signatories of Charter 77. The club adhered to the Prague Spring and to Gorbachev's democratization process in the belief that this was the start of a new era of socialism, reconstructing communist parties and regimes in Eastern Europe and converging with groups in other countries in a pan-European socialist movement. They considered themselves Dubček's heirs, including his idea that the Communist Party was the guarantee of a progressive socialist development. *OBRODA* found home on the pages of *Listy*, but Pelikán did not share its belief that it would be the dominant actor in Czechoslovakia's future. Other associations or manifestoes that sprang into being included "A Few Sentences," "The Society for a Merrier Present," "The Left Alternative," "Most" (Bridge), and "Democratic Initiative." *Listy* registered them all.[9]

While new initiatives were being born in Eastern Europe, in June the Chinese government brutally repressed the student protest for democracy on Tiananmen Square while Gorbachev's perestroika faced fierce opposition in the Soviet Union. Once again Poland surprised its neighbors when in June's elections the communists lost dramatically and a noncommunist Catholic intellectual, Tadeusz Mazowiecki, the spiritual leader of Solidarity, won the post of the prime minister, sending shock waves through the socialist camp. While the Tiananmen Square massacre was a cautionary tale and a confrontational strategy to be avoided, the result of the Polish elections was inspiring for the opposition.[10]

Pelikán's reaction to the events around him was to throw his previous reservations about not engaging in politics in Czechoslovakia to the wind. Democratic reforms and pluralism must be enforced from below but also with allies within the existing power structure, which he did not consider an undifferentiated group. But who were the allies? The demonstration to remember the 1968 invasion on Monday August 21showed that the regime was unwilling to cede an inch of its power. The demonstrators on the streets invoked Charter 77, Havel, Dubček, freedom, and Poland; they intoned the national anthem while receiving brutal police blows, giving the men in uniforms kicks in return and labeling them Gestapo. The regime experienced local pandemonium and international embarrassment on August 21, 1989.[11]

Havel lived in a whirlwind. As his stature had grown nationally and internationally, more demands were made on him inside and outside of Czechoslovakia. With his tongue in his cheek he wrote, "The situation is beginning to be dramatic. One part of the society wants to make me as its leader, the other part (a smaller one) wants to annihilate me as fast as possible. I don't know, which one of the two would be better."[12] While Havel was still in prison, he was nominated for the Nobel Peace Prize. He did not win it but in October was awarded the peace prize at the Frankfurt book fair presented by the German book sellers' association. In his acceptance speech, titled "Words on Words," Havel reflected "on the mysterious link between words and peace, and more generally on the mysterious power of words in human history." In Czechoslovakia words landed people in prison. His point was corroborated many times over. The German actor Maximilian Schell read Havel's speech because he was prevented from delivering it himself. The Czechoslovak authorities did not allow him to receive the prize, nor did they allow his wife to travel to Germany to witness the ceremony. The German president Richard von Weizsäscker as well as the Chancellor Helmut Kohl attended the occasion.[13]

By November, Eastern Europe was experiencing a commotion: the Berliners hammered down the wall; crowds yearning for freedom cut the wires on the border between Hungary and Austria so that people could move from east to west undeterred; trains loaded with East German citizens who had stormed the West German embassy in Prague were taken to the Federal Republic through their country for all to see their resolve to be free, leaving behind the cars in which they had arrived. The Czechoslovak regime made one last attempt at displaying its illegitimate power, using truncheons once again to repress a student protest on November 17. This time the police violence did not break the students' determination to go all the way in getting rid of the regime, supported by thousands of citizens. The events that followed became a legend.[14]

The revolutionary weeks started with the crushing of the demonstration on November 17, followed on November 19 by the formation of the Civic Forum headed by Havel—an umbrella association of many voices yearning for free and democratic Czechoslovakia—and its counterpart the Public against Violence in Slovakia—until the government resigned on November 24 under the pressure of the unrelenting crowds on the streets, followed by a general strike and several mammoth demonstrations. In all these events, Havel and Dubček stood side by side. Gorbachev's long overdue condemnation of the Soviet invasion of 1968 finally convinced Pelikán that the moment had arrived "at last!"[15]

Listy's title page from the December 1989 issue carried a photo of Dubček and Havel holding hands again and Dubček waving at a roaring crowd in his "return to history." Pelikán's dream came true, at least symbolically. He anticipated that soon the journal would not have to be smuggled to Czechoslovakia but could be distributed freely in bookshops and newspaper stands at home, where it had always belonged.[16]

The last act performed by President Husák before resigning was to nominate on December 3 a new government in which communist ministers remained in the majority. The Civic Forum in the Czech lands and its Slovak counterpart, which in the meantime had become the most powerful forces of citizens in revolt and with which the decayed regime had to deal, rejected it. The evidence is inconclusive, but the reason why Zdeněk Mlynář was whisked to Prague from Vienna one night in the Czechoslovak ambassador's vehicle might have been to help whatever could be salvaged of the falling regime. He participated in a televised debate on December 7, after he had already appeared in a solo dialogue with the television station director on December 1. Mlynář argued that it was premature to sweep aside the disintegrating power structures while the population's emotions were raw. He felt that it should be done once the revolutionary fervor died down and new ones could be designed; he proposed to give the recently nominated government a chance to show what it was capable of in terms of governing.[17]

The viewers were appalled; critical letters flooded Mlynář's and the television studio's postbox: "I don't know where you got the nerve today, in the middle of a still unfinished struggle for power in this country, to give us advice and lessons." Mlynář was one of those who made it possible for Charter 77 to appear, but soon after he left Czechoslovakia while people like the author of the letter went to jail. A group of forty expelled communists from the town of Roudnice were disgusted that Mlynář dared to give the party a new lease on life: "For us the former members of the Czechoslovak Communist Party your action is laughable and despicable." A. Hajská wrote to Mlynář that he confirmed before the whole nation that he had not been missed while in exile. The exception was Václav Soukup. In 1968 he was eighteen years old, lamenting the demise of the Prague Spring. He wanted to leave the country a year later, but "thanks to the vigilance of our border organs," he was stopped because he had all his personal documents on him. Seven years later, he joined the Communist Party, beseeched by a comrade who was expelled in 1970 to replace him. The subsequent years were full of contradictions, too complicated to be recounted. He spent the beginning of November in Moscow and so he understood Mlynář, who like him was in favor of coordinating Czechoslovak internal politics with "our partners." On his last day at his job as a party functionary in a railway construction firm, writing on the party's stationary, Soukup exhorted Mlynář to continue the good work "because we need your objective and unbiased stands" and the dissemination of enlightened ideas. If Mlynář needed somebody to help him with gathering material or with dental care, Soukup and his wife, who worked in a dental laboratory, were at his service now that he had time on his hands, as he had no more party obligations and had been expelled from the Central Committee of the Czechoslovak Communist Party's political university.[18] For all to see, except Soukup and his ilk, Mlynář was the wrong messenger of a wrong message at the wrong time.

The negotiations between the Civic Forum, the Slovak Public against Violence, and the regime communists that followed—guided by moral principles on one side and the desire to attain power or to retain it on the other—showed that the weight of ethical authority was prevailing over the state's instruments of control and that the Prague Spring and Dubček had to take a subordinate role given the revolutionary momentum. Havel became the head of the state and Dubček the head of the Federal

Assembly. Thus, on December 29, 1989, in the coronation hall of Prague Castle, Dubček led the ceremony in which Havel was elected to the presidency of the Czechoslovak Socialist Republic.[19]

In London, Ruth had been watching on television the throngs of people jangling keys, marching with lit candles, and experimenting with freedom. She wanted to be present at the jubilation. All flights to Czechoslovakia had been sold out, so she flew to Frankfurt and took the train to Prague. While she was standing in an overcrowded wagon, the train jerked, and she fell and broke her leg. After it was put in cast in a Prague hospital, Ruth hobbled on the streets undeterred by her injury, imbibing the euphoric atmosphere.

The Arrival

The emigrants, who had left Czechoslovakia without breaking ties with their country, longed to return. The reform communists among them, now in their sixties, were not ready to retire in 1989. They had been waiting for this moment for twenty years, contributing to it, and ready to participate in the renewal of democratic Czechoslovakia. From their geographical distance but emotional and intellectual proximity they watched the fall of the regime and the negotiations to build a new one. Their activities in exile to aid the opposition in their fight against the unacceptable normalization regime had been invigorating and they did not want to give them up. They hoped that they would be welcome.

Vilém Prečan had been *Listy*'s ardent collaborator in exile but he belonged to a different category than the group itself. He had abandoned any illusions about the Prague Spring and socialism long before 1989. He and Václav Havel talked on the phone on December 26. By then the dissident playwright was an inch away from the presidency. What were Prečan's wishes, he asked? The president's blessing of the documentation center that Prečan had created in exile, he replied, to also reward his devoted collaborators. He also wanted to remain the organizer of Havel's political writings. "I know that everything takes me a long time, but in return my work is quite thorough." And any post? No: the historian's dream was to be able to create an institute to study modern history. And so as early as February 1990 Prečan was able to lay the founding blocks for the Institute of Contemporary History to help put right the desolate state of Czechoslovak historiography.[20]

František Janouch, a physicist by profession, had divided his life in exile between scientific conferences and raising money for the opposition at home. When Havel became president, Janouch hurried to Prague to put himself at his disposal wherever the president would need him. Havel nominated him one of his foreign advisors. It was an honorary designation. Janouch was satisfied: "I have no personal political ambition—my only ambition is that it works for us, that we overcome problems as fast as possible and with the minimum of obstacles which inevitably await us in the course of the transition toward the pluralistic, modern and developed society and a functioning market economy." Janouch watched the difficult birth of the new country from the outside and on occasional visits to Czechoslovakia. He observed for instance President Havel's neglect of Slovakia and counseled him on the need to repay debts to those who abroad had engaged in defending human rights in Czechoslovakia. And then he regretted the painful division of Czechoslovakia into two countries, which Havel could not stop. Janouch, like all the exiles, was proud to be Czechoslovak and grateful to Havel for elevating the country's profile in the world.[21]

It was a shock when in 1992 Janouch found out that the Ministry of the Interior suspected him of being a KGB agent because of his frequent travels to the Soviet Union before it collapsed. The ministry requested that his collaborator in the Prague office of Charter 77 Foundation, which Janouch had created in 1978 in Sweden and moved to Prague after 1989, inform on him. Janouch was outraged: "I did not dedicate almost thirty years of my life to help creating a regime, which after less than two years will create a new network of snitches around my person. I am sad, mister prime minister. With your pardon, wanting to throw up."[22] Gradually, Janouch was moved aside by Havel's younger entourage; he was humiliated after all he had done for Charter 77 and Havel. Still, in October 2001 the president awarded him the medal for Merits of First Grade.[23]

The scholar of German literature Eduard Goldstücker's return was determined by his belonging to the 1968 generation and the Communist Party, which disqualified him in the eyes of those who were seeking a reckoning with the past and bent on dismantling the socialist regime root and branch. As a result, this academic renowned at European universities was barred from returning to Charles University to continue where he left off in 1968: teaching German literature.[24]

The architect of the economic reform of 1968, Ota Šik, was seventy years old in 1989. He had emigrated to Switzerland after the invasion and become a university professor. After the revolution, Šik returned briefly to Czechoslovakia, hoping to renew the fight for the "third way," fusing socialism and market economy, social justice, and private property. To no avail. His theory suffered vicious attacks and was caricaturized. He realized that his time for struggle was over. Painful as it was, Šik decided not to return to Czechoslovakia and to devote time to his painting, a hobby that gave him enormous satisfaction.[25]

The economist Jiří Kosta was euphoric in 1989, comparing his happiness at the fall of the opprobrious regime to his escape from the death march at the end of the war in 1945 and again to the spring of 1968. At the age of sixty-eight, Kosta and his wife chose to live between the two worlds, Germany and the recovered homeland, realizing that it was possible to have a universal identity rather than only one nationality. For his part, *Listy*'s collaborator Dušan Havlíček was able to transfer his long-time experience in the operation of private commercial television broadcasting in Switzerland to Czechoslovakia. His counsel was to reduce dependence on state's finances to the minimum so that television did not have to be beholden to the state in any way and could live on its own resources; he stressed the importance of serious viewer surveys, to guarantee sponsors' advertising. He, like many, was saddened by the attacks on the 1968 generation, on Charter 77, and the Civic Forum by the up-and-coming stalwarts of the new country who only yesterday were part of the normalization regime. Havlíček believed that the emigrants deserved a better welcome after fighting the communist regime for several decades. For others, returning to Czechoslovakia was another emigration, although friends were irreplaceable and family could be the decisive factor in the choice to move back or stay put in the adopted country.[26]

Karel Kovanda, remembered by his comrades from the 1960s as Che Kovanda, returned to Czechoslovakia in 1990 with an expertise in private business management: "I was heading home without any expectations. No property to be regained, no political aspirations, no advice to hand out. I returned to serve the country. How many of us were there? Perhaps a few of those who served Havel directly—Pavel Tigrid, Ivan Medek, Karel Schwarzenberg. There's not many. And furthermore—I had a group of friends in Prague from the time of our student activism of the sixties. These people helped me find my bearings in the new Czechoslovakia and ushered me in my diplomatic aspirations, including leaning on Minister Dienstbier to see me. These then are the two points thanks to which my return was successful: I didn't expect anything from anyone; indeed, on the contrary, I sought to contribute. And, I had a solid safety net of friends whom I could lean on."[27] In 1991 Kovanda began to pen contributions to the Prague daily *Lidové noviny*, called "I and My Money," which became popular with the readers. Kovanda's short, well informed, and witty articles provoked an instant dialogue with his audience. The articles dealt with the unfamiliar Western capitalist conundrums such as saving, investing, loans, spending, inflation, and buying and selling on a free market.[28]

On the whole, the exiles had collaborated for over two decades in relative harmony but broke lances on their return. The political, ideological, and even personal differences that had been subsumed by the common goal to contribute to the democratization of Czechoslovakia reappeared; their visions on the future of Czechoslovakia divided them. Mlynář stood out. Here was a prominent politician from 1968's reform movement, a signatory of Charter 77, a European intellectual, pursuing his agenda for socialist reconstruction with relentless passion as before, now in an environment of growing postcommunist anticommunism. Even though his presence was marginal, it was not dead as some had anticipated after his disastrous December 1989 television appearances. Mlynář was convinced that the Prague Spring and Gorbachev had lessons to teach. Until his death in 1997, he did not care that he was swimming against the tide. Living between Prague and Vienna, he published books, wrote articles, corresponded with admirers and detractors, and even entered the political fray in the elections of 1996 on behalf of the "Left Bloc" with the slogan "neither the government of tanks nor the government of banks." The electoral result was negligible. To make sure that his star did not come back to shine, in 1992 Mlynář was included in the nefarious group of government functionaries accused of high treason for abetting the invasion of August 21, 1968. No incriminating evidence was found against Mlynář, and he was exonerated in 1995.[29] But the damage to his reputation had been done.

What a paradox, Pelikán ruminated, that the new Ministry of the Interior, which was staffed with people who knew better, resorted to smearing the exile, like their predecessors had. How to explain it? Were the new power holders, former oppositionists among them, afraid of the possible return of communism under the leadership of the former reform communists? In ways that mixed facts with fantasy, Pelikán was one of the frequent targets of the press because of his communist past, his alleged collaboration with the Gestapo, and his role as the television station's director during the 1960s (it was claimed that he used his position "to idiotize" the nation). Rhetorically, Pelikán asked whether it was worth returning. He also lamented that the new government "was unable to take advantage of the intellectual potential and those experiences of contacts and knowledge of life in the West" that the returning exile had offered on their arrival. True, President Havel formed a group of advisors, but it had disintegrated not because it was unable to council him but because it was never summoned, thus demonstrating his indifference to the experience of the exile. And then the thorny rumor that Pelikán was an agent of the secret police was difficult to disavow without the Ministry of the Interior's making incriminating archive documents available.[30]

Pelikán could not overcome the many barriers that stood in his way to return to active politics because no one was interested in his experience in exile and because he was identified with the Prague Spring (in an environment of ongoing historical reckoning, the Prague Spring's many adversaries deemed it a fiasco or a swindle); his engagement in the fight for the renewal of democracy in Czechoslovakia while in exile did not make up for those alleged iniquities.[31] But while Pelikán could not integrate into the postcommunist environment, *Listy*, his brainchild, moved to Czechoslovakia and adapted to the new milieu successfully. President Havel welcomed the journal with gratitude: "I salute Listy's editorial group on its 20th year. I do not forget the enormous work which you accomplished for Czechoslovak democracy. During the long years you informed truthfully about the situation in our country and published documents from Charter 77, information from VONS and in general independent literature which could not be published at home. Thank you."[32] So it was *Listy* that became Pelikán's instrument to influence the hearts and minds of the public. The 1990 first issue, still printed in Germany, sold out its thirty thousand copies in two days. Evidently, there was a market for the journal; at the same time, at an exhibition of samizdat and exile literature at the Museum of Czech Literature in Prague, a lonely issue of *Listy* lay in the corner near the bottom in one of the exhibition's eight big halls. *Listy* still had to find its "key to home."[33]

Pelikán found a way. To begin with, he did not follow any fashionable trend. *Listy* became a political and cultural journal that examined the Prague Spring and socialism critically, arguing that to discard the experience of the 1968 movement was to liquidate the valuable intellectual potential of that generation. *Listy* came to represent one kind of leftist persuasion, rooted in reform communism, inspired by the Prague Spring, but enriched by the European and world experience of practicing democracy in combination with the lessons derived from the catastrophe of 1968. It was a paradox that the proponents of the new Left, which historically had struggled against the social consequences of capitalism, had before them the task of helping liberal capitalism to stand on its feet with an accent on social justice, now that the "third way" had been rejected.[34]

Pelikán's and his friends' major concern was democracy. The implementation of economic reforms, of Europe without borders was important but not enough when chauvinism and racism were rising their ugly heads in contradiction to the desired postcommunist visions. Free and fair elections were vital except when there lurked the danger that they could turn into an anticommunist plebiscite. Pelikán reiterated that the rules of democracy were tolerance and listening to the opinions of others. He reminded people of Masaryk's dictum that democracy was a discussion. Charter 77 spokespeople also warned in the pages of *Listy* that the newly acquired freedoms could be squandered by egotism, hypocrisy, and falsehoods. *Listy* continued in the spirit of Charter 77 and the democratic opposition because democracy depended on the citizens giving the conservative Right or the progressive wing of the Civic Forum a mandate through votes. But while the civic movement was moving to the center of the political spectrum, the Communist Party was longing for the lost past, considering 1989 a defeat and dreaming about future revenge and retaliation. Democracy was a choice of alternatives without violence, without striving for utopias, through free and fair elections.[35]

Another inveterate communist without a party, Eric Hobsbawm, put the same idea in a different way: "Can humanity live without the ideals of freedom and justice, or without those who devote their lives to them? Or perhaps even without the memory of those who did so in the twentieth century?"[36]

In mid-1994, Pelikán pondered *Listy*'s mission again. Should it remain tilted toward the liberal Left, continue the legacy of Charter 77 and the dissent, and maintain some continuity with the Prague Spring or change the direction toward a more pronounced socialist orientation? Pelikán must have thought that this was needed, that the liberal Left had fulfilled its mission and that the much-weakened socialist Left had to be revived. There was no leftist journal to be found in Czechoslovakia, even though he believed there was a "market" for it. With the help of Petr Uhl, known for his persistent socialist beliefs, Pelikán hoped to fill the void "to contribute to the creation of a strong democratic left opposition, capable of presenting itself as an alternative to the current government."[37] That did not mean ceasing to be pluralistic and becoming intolerant of opposition opinions; it meant that it was necessary to remain a critical observer and a commentator on the Czech Republic's trajectory from a firm left-wing point of view.

In addition to being pluralistic and providing space for free thought, offering information, sharing inspiring ideas, and being affordable, *Listy* was successful because it kept its independence from any political party or influence, even though Pelikán retained the right to decide whom "to cheer," whom to invite to the pages of the journal, and whom to address.

Similar ventures had begun after 1989 and collapsed soon after because they did not have a clear purpose and considered publishing a financial enterprise, the success of which depended on rich sponsors and advertising. *Listy* integrated into Czech cultural life because it embraced the entire social and political spectrum without losing sight of its underlying goal, which included contributing to the shaping of the post-totalitarian culture. The democratic socialism in which he continued to believe with every fiber of his being remained its mission. The original editorial board and contributors, with exceptions, were gradually replaced by a generation that had no ties to the Prague Spring or to the emigrants. What Pelikán could not do as a politician, he achieved in *Listy* as an intellectual: reconnecting the post-1989 experience with the historical experience and thinking of 1968, remaining inclusive of all currents of thought deemed progressive, democratic, and patriotic. Pelikán's *Listy* remained faithful to its other calling, which was to uphold Czechoslovakia, the Czech Republic from 1993 on, in its efforts to be tied inextricably to Europe and the world. His merits were never rewarded. Pelikán's name was canvassed before Havel for the Tomáš Garrigue Masaryk Award, but the anticommunists in the Czech National Council allegedly blocked his nomination.[38]

Pelikán died in June 1999. His longtime friend Jan Štern, *Listy*'s Czech editor who used the pseudonym "Bohemicus," wrote what could have been an epitaph: "Perhaps it sounds grandiose, but in my imagination *Listy* is a kind of a bridge linking the Prague Spring of 1968 and November 1989."[39] Pelikán would have been pleased to read Štern's appreciation because it precisely captured the legacy he wanted to bequeath to the coming generations.

Epilogue

"Communism in Eastern Europe had been the wrong answer to a real question."

—Tony Judt, *Postwar*

Ruth arrived in Prague in 1990, tied to *Listy* almost organically. At sixty-five years old, she was brimming with energy; work made her life meaningful. But first she had to find a place to live and to recover her Czechoslovak citizenship, of which she was unlawfully stripped by the normalization government. The city had changed; and while she noted that the trams did not run under their old numbers along the routes that she knew, Ruth did not register the deeper meaning of the passage of time. As under socialism, she believed that she was entitled to an apartment. In her letters of application to the mayor of Prague and to the district housing department, she justified her right with the argument that all these years in exile she had worked with Mr. Pelikán for *Listy*, the journal of socialist opposition that published Charter 77's documents. It did not occur to her that a government functionary may not have been acquainted with a proscribed journal, an underground movement, and an exiled politician, or did not care. But Ruth never ceased to live in the glory of the Prague Spring and the valiant exile. Not getting anywhere with her search for a suitable place to live, Ruth decided to buy one in a building that, given the shortage of living space, the local government put on sale for emigrants like her, mainly retired, who wished to return to Czechoslovakia. There she reunited with friends coming back from exile who wanted to savor free Czechoslovakia, reunite with families and friends. The building lay on the outskirts of Prague, surrounded by woods, far from the bustling center. Ruth was not fond of taking walks, so the beauty of the woods was wasted on her; she preferred to sit at her desk in front of a computer and to answer telephone calls.[1]

Initially, Ruth's skills were in high demand. The English language was still a rare commodity in the early 1990s and Ruth had plenty of work translating books and articles, earning a few bylines. She teamed up with her friends and together they translated a book by Zdeněk Mlynář, and collaborated with Czech historians and the Harvard scholar Mark Kramer on a book documenting the history of the Prague Spring and its demise. Ruth was in her element helping foreign journalists find their way in the chaotic but exhilarating post-wall environment, in addition to helping with *Listy*'s administration and organizing conferences. Even after her capacities slackened, Pelikán kept her name as *Listy*'s permanent collaborator out of loyalty to a friend and an old-timer. Gradually, a new generation of English-speaking translators and interpreters replaced her.[2]

Ruth's public engagements declined but her private life in Prague had a lot to offer; besides the rich variety of theaters and concert halls, she had friends with whom to laugh and rekindle memories of Vladimír. When life on her own became too demanding or she was lonely, Ruth would fly to her other home in London or visit me and my son Daniel in Mexico until she could no longer crisscross the world. On one of her visits, Ruth spoke to a class of undergraduates in my course on European history, giving testimony of her experience during World War II. It was a memorable occasion for my mother as well as for the Mexican students, who asked many questions.

Ruth's life in Prague attracted the attention of newspapers and magazines, the sociologist Marta Marková and the documentarist Olga Sommerová. All that attention opened the floodgates of her suppressed memory, reconnecting the past and the present, albeit selectively. The Czech sociologist interviewed Ruth in 1990, describing her as a small white-haired woman: when "one looks into her face perceives only her big brown eyes and Dior red on her lips." Ruth talked about her emigration with her father to England in 1939, expanded on her experience as an interpreter of war intelligence at the Royal Air Force, and delved into the harrowing encounter with her mother in Bergen-Belsen, mixing heroic pathos of almost epic proportions with a sense of adventure. She said not a word about her intention to emigrate from Czechoslovakia in 1949 or her collaboration with the state secret police. Here, as always, Ruth swept unpleasant memories under the carpet. Her return to Czechoslovakia in 1990 was different from her return in 1945, she said: then the enemy were the Nazis, toward whom one felt nothing but revulsion; this time the return was unnerving because the defeated enemy were her compatriots. Ruth was still grieving Vladimír's death, recalling the trauma that the 1968 invasion had caused him: "What did the Russians, whom we loved, what on earth had they done to us?"[3] She was sorry that Vladimír's yearning to return home was unfulfilled. Her recurrent dreams were of the two of them walking the Prague streets hand in hand.

At the age of sixty-eight, in 1993, Ruth applied for a pension in the Czech Republic. She had to fill a questionnaire about her wartime service. She wrote, "I advanced with the British units through northwestern Germany (Hanover, Celle) and in April 1945 I was there during the liberation of the Bergen-Belsen concentration camp."[4] She was not. Ruth served in the air force, and the camp was liberated by the British and the Canadian army. She arrived a fortnight or so after Bergen-Belsen had been freed. But Ruth's wartime service gave her a satisfaction like no other pursuit in her life. The moment at war's end when she found her mother was such a profound experience of the Nazi treatment of Jews that it needed to be recounted over and over. After all, during the deadly fifties the communist regime did not recognize her participation in the war effort, which she undertook not for personal gain but for the greater good, including on behalf of Czechoslovakia's liberation. Fearing her wartime merits would be disregarded again, she stretched the truth and magnified the events because she deserved to receive the pension.

Ruth recounted with relish her role in intercepting the communications between the Luftwaffe pilots and their ground controllers, to make them fly to where the British pilots could shoot them down. She loved bragging (corroborated by evidence) that "they flew to where I told them." She evidently did not look on the war as a time when she was no more than a cog in a death machine; rather, she remembered it as her life's finest moment.

In 1996 Ruth reflected on her entire life in front of a camera during a series of four interviews conducted by the Shoah Visual History Foundation in Prague. She had just turned seventy-one years old; from the first moment that the camera focused on her, it was evident that she was eager to give her testimony. She sported a striking red jacket, her hazelnut brown eyes, augmented by the lenses of her glasses, looked livelier than ever. Ruth's wavy hair, always the envy of her female friends, was not as abundant as it used to be and was now discolored from nicotine smoke. Ruth followed the interviewer's script but highlighted those moments and reflections on her life that meant most to her. She regretted that she had no roots, that her Jewishness was shallow, but at the same time she cherished the ease with which she could adapt to many cultural milieus, indeed her cosmopolitism, in the face of rising nationalism and chauvinism around her.[5] Her thoughts always came back to the painful subject of family, of which Ruth lamented that she had only fragments. The older she was, the more she mourned those who had perished in the Holocaust.

Feeling desolate at times, she was sorry that she had no faith. Vladimír's offspring, their partners, and children partially substituted for her missing family. I shuttled across the Atlantic Ocean from Mexico, sometimes with my mother's beloved grandson, to accompany her for brief periods of time. My cousin Věra spent gin and tonic happy hours with her, lighting one cigarette off the butt of the other.

Ruth spent the last months of her life in Hagibor, the smart Jewish rest home in Prague where she could smoke on the balcony or inhale fresh air while rolling in a wheelchair through its tree dotted garden. One morning she did not wake up.

FIGURE 12. Ruth with Daniela Spenser in Prague at Hagibor in 2013. Photo by Petr Balajka.

Notes

Preface

Epigraph. André Gide, *Le traité du Narcisse* (Paris: Mercure de France, 1899).

1. Zuzana Slobodová, "Ruth Tosek Obituary," *Guardian*, October 6, 2013.

2. Timothy Garton Ash, *Homelands: A Personal History of Europe* (New Haven, CT: Yale University Press, 2023), 144.

3. Tony Judt and Timothy Snyder, *Thinking the Twentieth Century* (New York: Penguin, 2012), 276–78.

Chapter 1

1. John J. Hartman and Jacek Krochmal, eds., *I Remember Every Day . . . : The Fates of the Jews of Przemyśl during World War II* (Przemyśl: Towarzystwo Przyjaciøł Nauk, 2002), 9; David R. Semmel, *11th of Av* (North Charleston, SC: CreateSpace, 2010), 5–20; Mark Mazower, *What You Did Not Tell: A Russian Past and the Journey Home* (London: Allen Lane, 2017).

2. "Janek Zimmermann," in Hartman and Jacek Krochmal, *I Remember Every Day*, 31–32; "Teodora Zimmermann-Miller," in *I Remember Every Day*, 39; "Fred Wahl," in *I Remember Every Day*, 57–59; "Ignacy-Izaak Felder," in *I Remember Every Day*, 66–67; "Sidonia Lewin-Lax," in *I Remember Every Day*, 108–13; Semmel, *11th of Av*, 5.

3. "Janek Zimmermann," 31–32; "Teodora Zimmermann-Miller," 39; "Fred Wahl," 57–59; "Ignacy-Izaak Felder," 66–67; "Sidonia Lewin-Lax," 108–13; Semmel, *11th of Av*, 5.

4. Petr Kaplan, "The Sudeten Germans and the Twilight of the First Republic," *Czech Journal of Contemporary History* 1, no. 1 (2013): 153; Jan Kilián, *Teplice: Historie, kultura, lidé* (Prague: Lidové noviny, 2015), 217–18.

5. Kilián, *Teplice*, 225–31; Lenka Burgerová and Radek Spála, *Židé v Teplicích—600 let historie* (Teplice: Jan Zykmund, 2014), 185–86; Bondy, *"Elder of the Jews,"* 22–23.

6. Kilián, *Teplice*, 240–42.

7. John Haag, "Knights of the Spirit': The Kameradschaftsbund," *Journal of Contemporary History* 8, no. 3 (July 1973): 133–53; Kilián, *Teplice*, 245–60; Bondy, *"Elder of the Jews,"* 25.

8. Ruth Tosková, interviewed by Anna Lorencová, Prague Jewish Museum, Prague, Czech Republic, 1996, cassette 016 (hereafter cassette 016, PJM).

9. Kilián, *Teplice*, 261–62.

10. Kilián, 266.

11. Tosková, interviewed by Lorencová; Saul Friedländer, *When Memory Comes* (New York: Other Press, 1978), 14–15. The 1930 census recorded 356,000 Jews in the country, representing 2.4 percent of the population.

12. Ruth Tosková, interviewed by Eva Benešová, Prague, Czech Republic, Septem-

ber 23, 1996, University of Southern California, Shoah Foundation Institute (an impression gained by looking at photographs); Olga Sommerová, dir., *Sedm světel*, 2007, YouTube video.

13. Mark Mazower, *Dark Continent: Europe's Twentieth Century* (London: Penguin, 1999) 69–70; Bondy, *"Elder of the Jews"*, 40–44; Norman Davies, *Europe: A History* (New York: Harper, 1998), 966–67.

14. Peter Demetz, *Prague in Black and Gold* (New York: Hill and Wang, 1997), 342–43; Jan Láníček, *Arnošt Fischer and the Jewish Politics of Early 20th-Century Europe* (London: Bloomsbury, 2017).

15. Tosková, interviewed by Lorencová.

16. Madeleine Albright, *Prague Winter: A Personal Story of Remembrance and War, 1937–1948* (New York: HarperCollins, 2012), 62–83; Peter Longerich, *Goebbels: A Biography* (New York: Random House, 2015), 367; Petr Kaplan, "The Sudeten Germans and the Twilight of the First Republic," *Czech Journal of Contemporary History* 1, no. 1 (2013): 149–54; P. E. Caquet, *The Bell of Treason: The 1938 Munich Agreement in Czechoslovakia* (London: Profile Books, 2018), 90–91.

17. Longerich, *Goebbels*, 367–69.

18. Longerich, 374–79, cited in Adam Hochschild, *Spain in Our Hearts: Americans in the Spanish Civil War, 1936–1939* (Boston: Houghton Mifflin Harcourt, 2016), 312.

19. Longerich, *Goebbels*, 380–87.

20. Christopher R. Browning, "Giving in to Hitler," *New York Review of Books*, September 26, 2019; Albright, *Prague Winter*, 88–94; Gordon Skilling, *Listy z Prahy* (Toronto: Sixty-Eight Publishers, 1988), 100–101; Friedländer, *When Memory Comes*, 24–25.

21. Stefan Zweig, *The World of Yesterday* (Lincoln: University of Nebraska Press, 2013), 439–44.

22. Tim Bouverie, *Appeasing Hitler: Chamberlain, Churchill and the Road to War* (London: Penguin Random House, 2019); Albright, *Prague Winter*, 97–108; Jörg Osterloh, "Sudetenland," in *The Greater German Reich and the Jews: Nazi Persecution Politics in the Annexed Territories 1935–1945*, ed. Wolf Gruner and Jörg Osterloh (New York: Berghahn Books, 2015), 72–74; Milan Hauner, "Beginnings of the Czechoslovak Government in Exile 1939–1941," in *Exile in and from Czechoslovakia during the 1930s and 1940s: The Yearbook of the Research Centre for German and Austrian Exile Studies*, vol. 11, ed. Charmian Brinson and Marian Malet (New York: Rodopi, 2009), 102–32; Géraldine Schwarz, *Those Who Forget: My Family's Story in Nazi Europe* (New York: Scribner, 2020), 108.

23. Wilbur Carr, the Minister in Czechoslovakia to the Secretary of State, Prague, Czech Republic, January 26, 1939, *Foreign Relations of the United States* 1939 (hereafter FRUS), vol. 1., 760.62/1911, telegram, 34–35; Osterloh, "Sudetenland," 75; Livia Rothkirchen, *The Jews of Bohemia and Moravia Facing the Holocaust* (Lincoln: University of Nebraska Press, 2005), 90.

24. Laurent Binet, *HHhH* (London: Harvill Secker, 2012), chapter 77; William Bullitt, the Ambassador in France to the Secretary of State, Paris, France, March 13, 1939, FRUS, 860F.00/608, telegram, 37.

25. Longerich, *Goebbels*, 411; Geist, the Embassy Chargé in Germany to the Secretary of State, Berlin, Germany, March 14, 1939, FRUS, 860F.00/614, telegram, 38.

26. The German Chargé Thomsen to the Secretary of State, Washington, United

States, March 17, 1939, FRUS, 860F.00/756, 45; Irving Linnell, consul general to the Secretary of State, Prague, Czech Republic, March 25, 1939, FRUS, 860F.00/768, telegram, 60; Linnell, consul general to the Secretary of State, Prague, May 23, 1939, 860F.00/863, 63–64; Albright, *Prague Winter*, 112; Longerich, *Goebbels*, 12; Mazower, *Dark Continent*, 75.

27. Friedländer, *When Memory Comes*, 24–25.

Chapter 2

1. Foreign Office to Sir N. Henderson in Berlin, cypher telegram, October 26, 1938, NA (National Archive), CO 323/1607/9 (Commonwealth Office); Tara Zahra, *The Great Departure: Mass Migration from Eastern Europe and the Making of the Free World* (New York: W. W. Norton, 2017), 143–48.

2. Laura E. Brade, "Networks of Escape: Jewish Flight from the Bohemian Lands, 1938–1941" (PhD diss., University of North Carolina, 2017); Jana Burešová, *The Dynamics of Forced Female Migration from Czechoslovakia to Britain, 1938–1950* (Oxford: Peter Lang, 2019), 21–23.

3. Ruth Tosková, interviewed by Anna Lorencová, PJM, 1996, cassette 016.

4. Daniela Gleizer, "La política mexicana frente a la recepción de refugiados judíos (1934–1942), in *México, país refugio: La expereincia de los exilios en el siglo XX*, ed. Pablo Yankelevich (CDMX: Plaza y Valdés, Conaculta, INAH, 2002), 119–40.

5. Livia Rothkirchen, *The Jews of Bohemia and Moravia: Facing the Holocaust* (Lincoln: University of Nebraska Press, 2005), 101.

6. "Tiskopis na žádost o cestovní pas," March 30, 1939, Police directorate in Prague, Czech Republic, Ministry of the Interior, National archive, box 8165, fond 0347/11; Doreen Warriner, "Winter in Prague," *Slavonic and East European Review* 62, no. 2 (April 1984): 209–40; Hana Velecká, "Britská pomoc uprchlíkům z Československa od okupace do vypuknutí války v roce 1939," *Soudobé dějiny* 8, no. 4 (2002): 659–91; William Chadwick, *The Rescue of the Prague Refugees 1938–1939* (Leicester, UK: Matador, 2010), 31–33.

7. Tosková, interviewed by Lorencová.

8. Warriner, "Winter in Prague," 240; Tosková, interviewed by Lorencová; A. J. Drexel Biddle, US ambassador in Poland to the Department of State, Warsaw, Poland, March 23, 1939, FRUS, 1939, file 740.00/671, telegram, 96; Velecká, "Britská pomoc," 671; R. Kopecký, *Československý odboj v Polsku v r. 1939* (Rotterdam, Modrá Revue, 1958), 15–19; Clare Hollingworth to Margaret Clayton, Katowice, March 27, 1939, National Archives, Home Office, file 294/56; Jana Barbora Burešová, *The Dynamics of Forced Female Migration from Czechoslovakia to Britain, 1938–1950* (Oxford: Peter Lang, 2019), 30.

9. Tosková, interviewed by Lorencová.

10. Tosková, interviewed by Lorencová; Kopecký, *Československý odboj v Polsku*, 16–18; Velecká, "Britská pomoc," 673; Eduard Goldstücker, *Vzpomínky 1913–1945* (Prague: G Plus G, 2005), 124–28; Margaret Layton to Clare Hollingworth, London, April 18, 1939; Clare Hollingworth to Margaret Layton, Katowice, June 18, 1939; Clare Hollingworth to Acland Allen, Katowice, June 16, 1939, NA, HO, file 294/56.

11. Clare Hollingworth to Margaret Layton, Gdynia, March 21, 1939; Margaret Layton to Clare Hollingworth, London, April 13, 1939; Clare Hollingworth to Allen Acland, Warsaw, July 2, 1939, NA, HO, file 294/56.

12. Tosková, interviewed by Lorencová; Clare Hollingworth to Margaret Layton, Katowice, June 19, 1939, NA, HO 294/56.

13. Burešová, *Dynamics of Forced Female Migration*, 33–34; Tim Bouverie, *Appeasing Hitler: Chamberlain, Churchill and the Road to War* (London: Penguin Random House, 2019), 59–60; Louise London, *Whitehall and the Jews, 1933–1948: British Immigration Policy, Jewish Refugees, and the Holocaust* (New York: Cambridge University Press, 2003), 142–68; Martin Gilbert, "British Government Policy towards Jewish Refugees," *Yad Vashem Studies* 13 (1979): 127–67.

14. Tosková, interviewed by Lorencová; Vera K. Fast, *Children's Exodus: A History of the Kindertransport* (London: I. B. Tauris, 2011), 41–42; Mark Jonathan Harris and Deborah Oppenheimer, *Into the Arms of Strangers: Stories of the Kindetransport* (London: Bloomsbury, 2017), 199–201; Laura E. Brade and Rose Holmes, "Troublesome Sainthood: Nicholas Winton and the Contested History of Child Rescue in Prague, 1938–1940," *History & Memory* 29, no. 1 (Spring/Summer 2017): 3–40.

15. See chapter 8 in this book.

16. "British Committee for Refugees from Czechoslovakia," case no. 6678, May 22, 1939. The Czech Refugee Trust Fund, Friendly Aliens. Documents kindly provided by Richard Gaskell.

17. "British Committee for Refugees from Czechoslovakia," case no. 6678, May 22, 1939. The Czech Refugee Trust Fund, Friendly Aliens. Documents kindly provided by Richard Gaskell; Jana Burešová, "The Czech Refugee Trust Fund in Britain 1939–1940," in *Yearbook of the Research for German and Austrian Exile*, vol. 2 (Amsterdam: Rodopi B.V., 2009), 133–46.

18. Bouverie, *Appeasing Hitler*, 418–21.

19. Ian Buruma, *Their Promised Land: My Grandparents in Love and War* (New York: Penguin, 2006), 153–54; Peter Longerich, *Goebbels: A Biography* (New York: Random House, 2015), 438–39; Bouverie, *Appeasing Hitler*, 380; Madeleine Albright, *Prague Winter: A Personal Story of Remembrance and War, 1937–1948* (New York: HarperCollins, 2012), 142–43; Brian Urqhhart, *A Life in Peace and War* (New York: Harper & Row, 1987), 33–41.

20. Kent Education Committee, Springfield, Maidstone to the Secretary, Board of Education, London. October 11, 1940, NA, ED 35/473; Tosková, interviewed by Lorencová.

21. Hedy Fromings, interviewed by Ian Willoughby, Prague Czech radio, part 1, October 24, 2006; Burešová, *Dynamics of Forced Female Migration*, 31–32.

22. Inka Vostřežová, interviewed by Daniela Spenser, Prague, Czech Republic, December 20, 2013; Burešová, *Dynamics of Forced Female Migration*, 134–36.

23. Michael R. Hoare, "In the Beginning: A Memoir of Boyhood and an Extraordinary Family," unpublished undated manuscript; Burešová, *Dynamics of Forced Female Migration*, 136.

24. Franz to the children, May 17, n.p. and London, December 9, 1940, p.a. It's not clear who Franz was. Vera Gissing, *Pearls of Childhood: The Poignant True Wartime Story of a Young Girl Growing Up in an Adopted Land* (London: Robson Books, 1994), 69–70.

25. Tosková, interview by Lorencová; Andrea Hammel, "'Why Is Your Czech So Bad?' Czech Child Refugees, Language and Identity," in *Exile in and from Czechoslovakia during the 1930s and 1940s: The Yearbook of the Research Centre for German and Austri-*

an Exile Studies, vol. 11, ed. Charmian Brinson and Marian Malet (New York: Rodopi, 2009), 215–28; Vostřižová interview; Miriam Darvas, *Farewell to Prague* (Isle of Man, UK: MP Publishing, 2015). The book is a mixture of history and fiction. Loebl, Eugen, NA, KV2/309, file closed.

26. Jan Němeček, "Československý londýnský exil a židovská otázka," in *Terezín Studies and Documents*, ed. Jaroslava Milotová and Eva Lorencová (Prague: Terezín Iniatitive Institute, 2002), 324–40; Jan Láníček, "The Powerlessness of Czechoslovak Jews during the Second World War," *East European Jewish Affairs* 44, no. 1 (2014): 21–50.

27. Tosková, interviewed by Benešová.

28. Tosková, interviewed by Lorencová.

29. Vilém Ornstein, Soldier's registration no. 255/1946, Vojenský ústřední archiv; London, *Whitehall and the Jews*, 181; Tosková, interviewed by Lorencová.

30. "Czech State Schools," NA, Fond Sb. CS-VB, box 1, file 300.04.

31. Burešová, *Dynamics of Forced Female Migration*, 38; Ruth to Hedy, no date or place, p.a.; Tosková interviewed by Benešová, reel 1.

32. George S. Wood to Cumberland Education Committee, Brampton, Cumberland, n.d., copy in ABS, fond 425, file 425–48–35.

33. Tosková, interviewed by Lorencová; Longerich, *Goebbels*, 528–31; Tosková, interviewed by Benešová.

Chapter 3

1. Poster, National Archives (NA), Inf. 3/119; "WAAF Pre-entry Training," September 13, 1941, NA, AIR 2/6187; Penny Summerfield, "'Heroes' and 'Stoics': War Work and Feminine Identity," *Reconstructing Women's Wartime Lives* (Manchester, UK: Manchester University Press, 1998), 77–114.

2. Ruth Tosková, interviewed by Anna Lorencová, PJM, 1996, cassette 016; Bořivoj Srba, *Můzy v exilu: Kulturní a umělecké, aktivity čs. exulantů v Londýně v předvečer a v průběhu druhé světové války, 1939–1945* (Brno: Masarykova universita, 2003), 687–837.

3. Jan Křen, *Dvě století střední Evropy* (Prague: Argo, 2005), 469–72.

4. Tosková, interviewed by Lorencová; Srba, *Můzy v exilu*, 452–55; Jana Barbora Burešová, *The Dynamics of Forced Female Migration from Czechoslovakia to Britain, 1938–1950* (Oxford: Peter Lang, 2019), 186–87; Rosemary Kavan, *Freedom at a Price: An Englishwoman's Life in Czechoslovakia* (London: Verso, 1985), 5.

5. Eleanor Rathbone to Sir Henry Bunbury, London, March 16, 1940, NA, HO 294/638.

6. Georgi Dimitrov, "19 July 1941," in *The Diary of Georgi Dimitrov 1933–1949*, ed. Ivo Banac (New Haven, CT: Yale University Press, 2003), 182; Bohuslav Laštovička, *V Londýně za války: Zápasy o novou ČSR 1939–1945* (Prague: Svoboda), 1978, 86.

7. "Kašpar," Czech Group of the C.R.T.F.," November 3, 1941, Otto Šling, NA, KV 6/74; Extract from B.2. London report re the Czech-British Friendship Club, March 27, 1942, Loebl, Eugen, NA, KV 2/3090.

8. Ruth to Hedy, London, n.d. 1942.

9. David Reynolds, *From the World War to Cold War: Churchill, Roosevelt, and the International History of the 1940s* (Oxford: Oxford University Press, 2006), 117.

10. Ruth Charlotte Ornstein, Royal Air Force register no. 2148419; Karolina Ste-

gurová, *I ženy chtěly bojovat: Československé ženy v britských armádních pomocných sborech ATS a WAAF za druhé světové války* (Prague: Academia, 2021), 110–28.

11. Ruth Ornstein, service sheet, RAF, no. 2148419.

12. Doreen Luke, *My Road to Bletchley Park: The Memories of WAAF* (London: M. & M. Baldwin, 2003); Stegurová, *I ženy chtěly bojovat*, 78.

13. Dalma Darnley Taylor, "WAAFs in 'Y' Service," *BBC WW2 People's War*, March 14, 2004, YouTube video.

14. Taylor, "WAAFs in 'Y' Service"; Stegurová, *I ženy chtěly bojovat*, 128–41.

15. Tosková, interviewed by Lorencová.

16. Ruth Tosková, interviewed by Eva Benešová, Prague, Czech Republic, September 23, 1996, University of Southern California, Shoah Foundation Institute, reel 1.

17. Sinclair McKay, *The Secret Life of Bletchley Park: The WWII Codebreaking Centre and the Men and Women Who Worked There* (London: Aurum, 2010).

18. Aileen Clayton, *The Enemy Is Listening* (New York: Ballantine, 1980), 39–40; Tosková, interviewed by Lorencová.

19. Tessa Stone, "Creating a (Gendered?) Military Identity: The Women's Auxiliary Air Force in Great Britain in the Second World War," *Women's History Review* 8, no. 4 (1999): 605–24; Military Department, J.A.G.'s Office, MI19, November 28, 1945, NA, WO 311/632.

20. Ruth's military service sheet; Mark Mazower, *What You Did Not Tell: A Russian Past and the Journey Home* (London: Allen Lane, 2017).

21. Clayton, *The Enemy Is Listening*, 47–83; Helen Fry, *The M Room: Secret Listeners Who Bugged the Nazis in WW2* (London: Marranos Press, 2012), 34–39; Geoffrey Pidgeon, *The Secret Wireless War: The Story of MI6 Communications 1939–1945* (Richmond, UK: Arundel Books, 2008); Sinclair McKay, *The Secret Listeners: How the Y Service Intercepted German Codes for Bletchley Park* (London: Aurum, 2012), 6; Benito Operation Report no. 7, NA, AIR 40/2242; "Signal intelligence or Y service," NA, AIR 40/2239; Group Captain Sgd. C. S. Caddell, "Y Intelligence for combined operations; " Military Department, J.A.G.'s Office, MI19, November 28, 1945, NA, WO 311/632; Kevin Jones, "From the Horse's Mouth: Luftwaffe POWs as Sources for Air Ministry Intelligence during the Battle of Britain," *Intelligence and National Security* 15, no. 4 (2008): 60–80.

22. Taylor, "WAAFs in 'Y' Service."

23. Beryl E. Escott, *The WAAF: A History of the Women's Auxiliary Air Force in the Second World War* (London: Shire, 2003), 20–27; Stone, "Creating a (Gendered?) Military Identity," 605–24; Tosková, interviewed by Lorencová.

24. Max Hastings, *The Secret War: Spies, Ciphers, and Guerrillas 1939–1945* (New York: HarperCollins, 2016), 47–53.

25. Escott, *WAAF*, 27–36; Tosková, interviewed by Benešová, reel 2.

26. McKay, *Secret Listeners*, 10–14, 99–100; Tosková, interviewed by Lorencová.

27. Tosková, interviewed by Lorencová.

28. Ruth Tosková interviewed by Olga Sommerová, Prague, Czech Republic, 2007; Ruth Tosek in Brian Johnson, Dominic Flessati and John Groom, writers, *The Secret War*, documentary, BBC and Imperial War Museum, January 5–February 9, 1977, available on YouTube.

29. Peter Longerich, *Goebbels: A Biography* (New York: Random House, 2015) 567–

615; Niall Ferguson, *The War of the World: Twentieth-Century Conflict and the Descent of the West* (New York: Penguin, 2007), 510–22.

30. Geoffrey Roberts, *Stalin's Wars: From World War to Cold War, 1939–1953* (New Haven, CT: Yale University Press, 2006), 192–210; Křen, *Dvě století střední Evropy*, 474.

31. Edvard Beneš, "Z Moskvy—po podpisu sovětsko-československé smlouvy (21. prosince 1943)," in *Šest let exilu a druhé světové války: Řeči, projevy a dokumenty z r. 1938–1945* (Prague: Orbis, 1946), 215–22.

32. Gottwald in conversation with Dimitrov, "14 December 1943," in Banac, *Diary of Georgi Dimitrov*, 289; Eduard Goldstücker, *Vzpomínky 1913–1945* (Prague: G Plus G, 2005), 136–45; Laštovička, *V Londýně za války*, 81–87.

33. Longerich, *Goebbels*, 627–29.

34. Clayton, *Enemy Is Listening*, 317–33; Madeleine Albright, *Prague Winter: A Personal Story of Remembrance and War, 1937–1948* (New York: HarperCollins, 2012), 289–98; Tosková, interviewed by Lorencová.

35. Clayton, *Enemy Is Listening*, 327; Longerich, *Goebbels*, 632–34.

36. Tosková, interviewed by Lorencová.

37. Tosková, interviewed by Sommerová.

38. Tosková, interviewed by Lorencová; Robin Geiss, "Name, Rank, Date of Birth, Serial Number and the Right to Remain Silent," *International Review of the Red Cross* 87, no. 860 (December 2005): 721–35; Stephen Tyas, "Allied Intelligence Agencies and the Holocaust Information Acquired from German Prisoners of War," *Holocaust and Genocide Studies* 22, no. 1 (Spring 2008): 1–24.

39. Military Deputy J.A.G., CSDIC Reports, October 31, 1945, NA, WO 311/632.

40. Ian Buruma, *Their Promised Land: My Grandparents in Love and War* (New York: Penguin, 2018), 273.

Chapter 4

1. Helena Krejčová and Anna Hyndráková, "Postoj Čechů k židům: Z politického zpravodajství okupační správy a protektorátního tisku v letech 1939–1941," *Soudobé dějiny* 2, no. 44 (1995): 578–605; Franci Rabinek Epstein, *Franci's War: A Woman's Story of Survival* (New York: Penguin, 2020), 24–25.

2. Laura E. Brade, "Networks of Escape: Jewish Flight from the Bohemian Lands, 1938–1941" (PhD diss., University of North Carolina, 2017), 235–36; Jaroslava Milotová, "Ústředna pro židovské vystěhovalectví v Praze: Geneze a činnost na počátku roku 1940," in *Terezínské studie a dokumenty*, ed. Miroslav Kárný and Margita Kárná (Prague: Academia, 1997), 22; Bohumil Černý, "Emigrace židů z Českých zemí v letech 1938–1941," in Kárný and Kárná, *Terezínské studie a dokumenty*, 61.

3. Krejčová and Hyndráková, "Postoj Čechů k židům," 586–88.

4. Anna Ornsteinová, Prague, December 18, 1945, p.a., Ministry of National Defense, *Vojenský ústřední archiv*, file no. 255/46; Vojtěch Blodig, ed., "Z deníku Evy Roubíčkové," *Terezínské listy*, no. 20 (1992): 67–97; Ruth Bondy, *"Elder of the Jews": Jakob Edelstein of the Theresiendstadz* (New York: Grove Press, 1981), 249–76.

5. Hannelore Brenner, *The Girls of Room 28: Friendship, Hope, and Survival in Theresienstadt*, Audiogo, September 15, 2009, 11 CDs; Anna Hájková, "Řekla jsem si, že se prostě musím nějak přizpůsobit: Mladé ženy v ghettu Terezín," *Soudobé dějiny* 18, no. 4

(2011): 603–26; Zuzana Ružičková and Wendy Holden, *One Hundred Miracles: A Memoir of Music and Survival* (London: Bloomsbury, 2019), 103–28.

6. Anita Tarsi, "Práce v pasti: Ústředna práce v prvním roce existence ghetta Terezín," in *Terezínské studie a dokumenty*, ed. Miroslav Kárný and Eva Lorencová (Prague: Academia, 2000), 127–40; Bondy, *"Elder of the Jews,"* 253–73; Michael Gruenbaum and Todd Hasak-Lowy, *Somewhere There Is a Sun: A Memoir of the Holocaust* (New York: Aladdin, 2015), 262–90.

7. Anna Hájková, *The Last Ghetto: An Everyday History of Theresienstadt* (Oxford: Oxford University Press), 66–67, 86–88.

8. Zdeněk Lederer, *Ghetto Theresienstadt* (London: Edward Goldston, 1953), 53; Wendy Holden, *Born Survivors: Three Young Mothers and Their Extraordinary Story of Courage, Defiance, and Hope* (New York: Harper, 2015), 106.

9. Hanuš H. Sladký, "Epizody ze života přeživšího," in *Terezínské studie a dokumenty*, ed. Miroslav Kárný, Margita Kárná, and Eva Lorencová (Prague: Academia, 1998), 296–97.

10. Bondy, *"Elder of the Jews,"* 338–53.

11. Miroslav Kárný, "Výsledky a úkoly Terezínské historiografie," in *Terezín v konečném řešení židovské otázky*, ed. Miroslav Kárný and Vojtěch Blodig (Prague: Logos, 1992), 23–33.

12. Lederer, *Ghetto Theresienstadt*, 113–5; Epstein, *Franci's War*, 79–80. In Terezín, thirty-four thousand people died; eighty thousand others were sent from the ghetto to their death. See Ruth Bondyová, "Humor jako zbraň," in Kárný and Kárná, *Terezínské studie a dokumenty*, 228–43.

13. According to Yad Vashem's website, Transport Eb took prisoners from the Theresienstadt ghetto in Czechoslovakia to the Auschwitz Birkenau extermination camp in Poland in May 1944: "In the morning of May 13, 1944, the inmates chosen for this transport received written notice ordering them to report to the assembly site, the 'Schleuse' located at the Hamburg Barracks, on May 15. They were allowed to bring with them up to 50kg of luggage. The inmates, who had received identification numbers upon their deportation to Theresienstadt, were now given new ones. After they were counted, they were taken to the Theresienstadt train platform, where they were loaded onto the waiting train. This transport, designated 'Eb,' left Theresienstadt on May 18, 1944, and was the last of three transports that left Theresienstadt that month, prior to the inspection of Theresienstadt by the Red Cross delegation. On board were 2,500 men, women and children. Historian Danuta Czech maintains that the transport arrived in Auschwitz-Birkenau the next day, on May 19. However, according to survivor testimonies, it arrived during the night between May 19 and May 20."

14. Ruth Bondy, "Women in Theresienstadt and the Family Camp in Birkenau," in *Women in the Holocaust*, ed. Dalia Ofer and Lenore J. Weitzman (New Haven, CT: Yale University Press, 1998), 316; Holden, *Born Survivors*, 161.

15. Epstein, *Franci's War*, 80–85.

16. Epstein, *Franci's War*, 80–88; Ota Kraus and Erich Kulka, *Továrna na smrt* (Prague: Naše vojsko, 1964), 95; Primo Levi, *Survival in Auschwitz* (New York: Collier, 1993), 27–28; Anita Lasker-Wallfish, *Inherit the Truth 1939–1945: The Documented Expe-*

riences of a Survivor of Auschwitz and Belsen (London: Giles de la Mare Publishers, 1996), 71–72; Heather Morris, *The Tattooist of Auschwitz* (London: Zaffre, 2018).

17. Truda Bartková, "Očima vzpomínek, 1943-prosincový transport," *Terezínské listy*, no. 21 (1993): 102–5.

18. R. K., interviewed by Anna Lorencová, November 4 and 11, 1994, cassette 374, Prague Jewish Museum, Prague, Czech Republic.

19. Francine Prose, *Anne Frank: The Book, the Life, the Afterlife* (New York: Harper-Collins, 2009), 173.

20. Hermann Langbein, *People in Auschwitz* (Toronto: Fitzhenry and Whiteside, 2005), 50–177; Primo Levi, *The Drowned and the Saved* (London: Abacus, 1989), 74–82; Michaela Wolf, ed., *Interpreting in Nazi Concentration Camps* (New York: Bloomsbury, 2016).

21. Langbein, *People in Auschwitz*, 400–401; Levi, *Survival in Auschwitz*, 91; Bondy, "Women in Theresienstadt," 324; E. P., interviewed by Anna Hyndráková, Holešov, March 3, 2002, casette, 965, Prague Jewish Museum, Prague, Czech Republic; Bondy, *"Elder of the Jews,"* 409–140; Tadeusz Borowski, *This Way for the Gas, Ladies and Gentlemen* (New York: Penguin, 1976), 70.

22. Epstein, *Franci's War*, 101–3.

23. Ruth Tosková, interviewed by Anna Lorencová, PJM, 1996, cassette 016; Epstein, *Franci's War*, 114–15; Göran Rosenberg, *A Brief Stop on the Road from Auschwitz* (New York: Other Press, 2012), 99.

24. Longerich, *Goebbels*, 597–652.

25. Longerich, 649–73.

26. Rudolf Höss, *Death Dealer: The Memoirs of the SS Kommandant at Auschwitz*, ed. Steven Paskuly (New York: Da Capo Press, 1996), 168–72.

27. GB, cassette 916; EZ, cassette 996; VS, cassette 918; HT, cassette 229; HW, cassette 679, Prague Jewish Museum.

28. Kurt Wehle, "Očima vzpomínek. Tam někde musí být židovská obec," *Terezínské listy*, no. 22 (1994): 109–21; Anna Hájková, "Between Love and Coercion: Queer Desire, Sexual Barter and the Holocaust," *German History* 39, no. 1 (2021): 112–33; Epstein, *Franci's War*, 117–64; E. K., interviewed by Anna Lorencová, Prague, May 29, 2009, cassette 1126 a–c, Prague Jewish Museum, Prague, Czech Republic; Ruth Tosková in Olga Sommerová, dir., *Sedm světel*, 2007, YouTube video.

29. GB, cassette 916; EZ, cassette 996; VS, cassette 918; HT, cassette 229; HW, cassette 679, Prague Jewish Museum; Hájková, "Between Love and Coercion," 120–29.

30. Epstein, *Franci's War*, 164.

31. Tosková, interviewed by Lorencová.

32. Tosková, interviewed by Lorencová.

33. Lt.-Col.R. I. G. Taylor, Report on Belsen Camp, NA, WO 219/3944A; Mark Celinscak, "At War's End: Allied Force at Bergen-Belsen," (PhD diss., York University, 2012), 37–42; Paul Kemp, "The British Army and the Liberation of Bergen-Belsen, April 1945," in *Belsen in History and Memory*, ed. Jo Reilly, David Cesarani, Tony Kushner, and Colin Richmond (London: Frank Cass, 1997), 134–48.

34. Dick Williams, "The First Day in the Camp," in *Belsen 1945: New Historical Perspectives*, ed. Suzanne Bardgett and David Cesarani (London: Vallentine Mitchell,

2006), 27–30; Joanne Reilly, *Belsen: The Liberation of a Concentration Camp* (London: Routledge, 1998), 10–18.

35. Captain P.S.O. Farmer, "Bergen-Belsen Concentration Camp," May 21, 1945, appendix 6 in Bardgett and Cesarani, *Belsen 1945*; Truda Bartková, "Očima vzpomínek. Osvobození v Bergen-Belsenu a návrat domu," *Terezínské listy*, no. 23 (1995): 101–12; Ružičková and Holden, *One Hundred Miracles*, 245–61.

36. Michael John Hargrave, *Bergen-Belsen 1945: A Medical Student's Journal* (London: Imperial College Press, 2014), 13.

37. Ben Shephard, *After Daybreak: The Liberation of Bergen-Belsen, 1945* (New York: Schocken Books, 2005), 144–45; Hargrave, *Bergen-Belsen 1945*, 13–17, 57–80.

38. Tosková, interviewed by Eva Benešová.

39. Tosková, interviewed by Lorencová.

40. Tosková, interviewed by Lorencová.

41. Tosková, interviewed by Lorencová.

42. R. T. cassette 016, PJM; Zdenka Fantlová, *Klid je síla řek' tatínek* (Prague: Primus, 1996), 260–61; Elfriede Schulz, International Tracing Service, Bad Arolsen, ref. no. T/D-7002952; Klaus Tätzler in Bergen-Belsen museum pointed me in the right directions; Marie Hakansson provided me with Anna's medical record on her arrival in Sweden.

Chapter 5

1. Ladislav Baletka, *Židé v dějinách Valašského Meziříčí, Vsetín* (Valašské Meziříčí: Publikace Šoka Vsetín, 2004), 54–55; Kateřina Čapková, *Češi, Němci, Židé? Národní identita Židů v Čechách, 1918–1938* (Prague-Litomyšl: Paseka, 2005), 141–44; Assaf Sharon, "This Obstinate Little Man," *New York Review of Books*, November 4, 2021. Valašské Meziříčí has been fictionalized in Alena Mornštajnová, *Hana* (Brno: Host, 2017).

2. Jaroslava Milotová, "Ústředna pro židovské vystěhovalectví v Praze: Geneze a činnost od počátku roku 1940," in *Terezínské listy a dokumenty*, ed. Miroslav Kárný and Margita Kárná (Prague: Academia, 1997), 10–29; Géraldine Schwarz, *Those Who Forget: My Family's Story in Nazi Europe: A Memoir, a History, a Warning* (New York: Scribner, 2020), 44.

3. Martin Gilbert, "British Government Policy towards Jewish Refugees," *Yad Vashem Studies* 13 (1979): 127–67.

4. Roger Adelson, review of *Ploughing Sand: British Rule in Palestine 1917–1948*, by Naomi Shepherd, *American Historical Review* 106, no. 4 (October 2001): 1504–5; Undersecretary of State, Sumner Welles to President Roosevelt, Washington, United States, January 9, 1939, FRUS, 867N.01/1365, 694; J. Rives Childs, "Memorandum of conversation," Division of Near Eastern Affairs, Washington, United States, January 10, 1939, FRUS, 867N.01/1391, 696–700; Herschel V. Johnson, the Chargé in the United Kingdom to the Secretary of State, London, February 11, 1939, FRUS, 867N.01/1441–2, 707–9; Aide-Mémoire from the British embassy to the Secretary of State, Washington, March 17, 1939, FRUS, 867N.01/1593, 732–36.

5. Ian Buruma, "The Hell of Victory," *New York Review of Books*, November 24, 2011; Arieh J. Kochavi, "The Struggle against Jewish Immigration to Palestine," *Middle Eastern Studies* 34, no. 3 (July 1998): 146–67; Dalia Ofer, *Escaping the Holocaust: Illegal Immigration to the Land of Israel, 1939–1944* (Oxford: Oxford University Press, 1990), 3–7, 32.

6. Ofer, *Escaping the Holocaust*, 23–25.

7. George Wadsworth to the Secretary of State, Jerusalem, June 28, 1939, FRUS, 867N.4016/89, 778–80.

8. Dalia Ofer, "The Rescue of European Jewry and Illegal Immigration to Palestine in 1940. Prospects and Reality: Berthold Storfer and the Mossad le' Aliyah Bet," *Modern Judaism* 4, no. 2 (May 1984): 159–81.

9. Dr. František Weidmann, "Referát k poradě zástupců náboženských obcí Protektorátu Čechy a Morava," August 13, 1939, Prague Jewish Museum, Prague, Czech Republic; Ruth Bondy, *"Elder of the Jews": Jakob Edelstein of the Theresiendstadz* (New York: Grove Press, 1981), 141–48; Jan Láníček, *Arnošt Fischer and the Jewish Politics of Early 20th-Century Europe* (London: Bloomsbury, 2017), 56–66; Laura E. Brade, "Networks of Escape: Jewish Flight from the Bohemian Lands, 1938–1941" (PhD diss., University of North Carolina, 2017), 135, 230–32; Ofer, *Escaping Holocaust*, 98–103.

10. "Referát Dra. Arjeho," December 13, 1939, Židovská náboženská obec v Praze, Prague Jewish Museum, Prague, Czech Republic; William Perl, *The Four-Front War: From the Holocaust to the Promised Land* (New York: Crown, 1979), 271–72; Brade, "Networks of Escape," 224–35.

11. Viktor Schwarz, interviewed by Marek Bouda, Prague, Czech Republic, January 8, 1996; Valtr Kraus, interviewed by Jana Dráská, Prague, Czech Republic, April 25, 1996, USC Shoah Foundation Institute.

12. Schwarz, interview.

13. Kraus, interview.

14. Stephan E. C. Wendehorst, *British Jewry, Zionism and the Jewish State, 1936–1956* (Oxford: Oxford University Press, 2012), 156–58; Mordechai Naor, *Haapala: Clandestine Immigration 1931–1948* (Israel: Ministry of Defence and IDF Museum, 1987), 8–10; Avishai Margalit, "The Spell of Jabotinsky," *New York Review of Books*, November 6, 2014; Hillel Halkin, *Jabotinsky: A Life* (New Haven: Yale University Press, 2014).

15. Vojtěch Blodig, ed., "Z deniku Evy Roubíčkové," *Terezínské listy*, no. 20 (1992): 67–97, n. 39; Valtr Kraus, interviewed by Marek Bouda, April 25, 1996, Prague, Czech Republic, Survivors of the SHOAH, Visual History Foundation.

16. Ofer, *Escaping the Holocaust*, 71; Eri Jabotinsky, *The Sakarya Expedition: A Story of Extra-Legal Immigration to Palestine* (Johannesburg: Newzo, 1945), 1–2. I received a copy of the travelogue from the archivists at the Jabotinsky Institute in Tel Aviv.

17. Judy Cohen, *Song of the Silent Bell: My Parents' Memoir: Their Separate Roads to Survival during the Holocaust Era* (Bloomington, IN: Universe, 2016), 38–39; Eric Felix, interviewed by Lorrie Fein, Queens, United States, April 21, 1998, US Shoah Foundation Institute; Bedřich Utitz, *Kaleidoskop mého století* (Prague: Academia, 2013), 38–45; Perl, *Four-Front War*, 271–92; Ofer, *Escaping the Holocaust*, 83; Jabotinsky, *Sakarya Expedition*, 33.

18. Ofer, *Escaping the Holocaust*, 45–46; Perl, *Four-Front War*, 329.

19. Ofer, *Escaping the Holocaust*, 81–82; Jabotinsky, *Sakarya Expedition*, 19–23; Kraus, interview.

20. Presidency of the New Zionist Organization to Viscount Halifax, Secretary of State for Foreign Affairs, "Illegal Jewish Immigration into Palestine," February 1, 1940, NA, FO 371/25239; Perl, *The Four-Front War*, 330–31; Vladimír Jabotinsky to Sir Archibald Sinclair, London, January 24, 1940, NA, FO 371/25239.

21. Sir R. Hoare, Bucharest to Foreign Office (hereafter FO), "Proposal that European Danube Commission should meet to discuss the plight of the Jewish refugees marooned on the Danube," January 19, 1940; Sir R. Hoare to FO, "Illegal immigration into Palestine: S.S. Sakarya," Bucharest, January 27, 1940, NA, FO 371/25239.

22. Sir Archibald Sinclair, House of Commons, to Lord Halifax, January 29, 1940; "Jewish Refugees," *Parliamentary Question*, House of Lords, February 13, 1940, NA, FO 371/25239; Gilbert, "British Policy towards Jewish Refugees," 159–62; Naomi Shepherd, *Ploughing Sand: British Rule in Palestine 1917–1948* (New Brunswick, NJ: Rutgers University Press, 1999), 215.

23. Perl, *Four-Front War*, 316–18; Jabotinsky, *Sakarya Expedition*, 27; Jan Rovenský, interviewed by Tatiana Pelíšková, Brno, Czech Republic, October 11, 1996, USC Shoah Foundation Institute.

24. Valtr Kraus and Helena Krausová, interviewed by Jana Dráská, April 25, 1996, Prague, Czech Republic, Survivors of the SHOAH, Visual History Foundation.

25. Jabotinsky, *Sakarya Expedition*, 36.

26. Jabotinsky, *Sakarya Expedition*, 36; Jan Martinec, *Bastard* (Prague: Klub čtenářů, 1991), 141–62; Cohen, *Song of the Silent Bell*, 44; Foreign Office to Mr. Beard in Asunción, London, January 31, 1940, NA, FO 371/ 24239.

27. Jabotinsky, *Sakarya Expedition*, 3–4, 37–40; Cohen, *Song of the Silent Bell*, 43; Walter Stamberger, interviewed by Jan Jelínek, Horní Ždár, Czech Republic, February 6, 1997, USC Shoah Foundation Institute; Utitz, *Kaleidoskop mého století*, 52–55.

28. Valtr Kraus, notes from his trip on the *Sakarya* in the private archive of his daughter Eva Turner; Ofer, *Escaping the Holocaust*, 80–82.

29. Leni Yahil, "Select British Documents on the Illegal Immigration to Palestine (1939–1940)," *Yad Vashem Studies* (1974): 241–76; Perl, *Four-Front War*, 335–37; Schwarz, interview; Rovenský, interview; Jabotinsky, *Sakarya Expedition*, 45–49.

30. "Proposal to extend the powers of the High Commissioner for Palestine to enable effective action to prevent illegal immigration of Jews," February 13, 1940, NA, FO 371/25238.

31. "Jewish Illegal Immigration into Palestine. Memorandum prepared by the Foreign Office and Colonial Office," December 1939–January 1940, January 17, 1940; Malcolm MacDonald to Edward Halifax, Colonial Office, February 14, 1940, in Yahil, "Select British Documents"; Mr. Downie, Colonial Office to Mr. Carvell, "Regulations governing illegal immigration into Palestine," February 2, 1940, NA, CO 733/425/12.

32. Jabotinsky, *Sakarya Expedition*, 45.

33. Kraus and Krausová, interview.

34. Jabotinsky, *Sakarya Expedition*, 39–43; "Jewish Refugees," *Parliamentary Question*, House of Lords, February 13, 1940; Harold MacMichael, the High Commissioner for Palestine, to Sir John E. Shuckburgh, Undersecretary of State at the Colonial Office in London, Jerusalem, December 15, 1940, NA, CO 733/425/12.

35. To Sir R. Hoare in Bucharest, February 15, 1940, deciphered and decoded telegram, NA, FO 371/25239.

36. Jabotinsky, *Sakarya Expedition*, 47.

37. Erich Kulka, *Židé v Československém vojsku na západě* (Prague: Naše vojsko, 1992), 24, 83–86.

38. Verena Buser, "In Detention: Memories of Jewish Refugees Interned in Atlit near Haifa," in *British Internment and the Internment of Britons: Second World War Camps, History and Heritage*, ed. Gilly Carr and Rachel Pistol (London: Bloomsbury, 2023), 189–206.

39. Rovenský, interview; Perl, *Four-Front War*, 6; Ofer, *Escaping the Holocaust*, 84; Schwarz, interview; Jiří Boehm, interviewed by Marek Bouda, Prague, Czech Republic, March 27, 1996, USC Shoah Foundation Institute.

40. Lord Robert Cecil, House of Lords, to Malcolm Macdonald, Colonial Office, London, May 8, 1940; J. E. S. to Sir C. Parkinson, June 26, 1940; Sir Maurice Bonham Carter, Downing Street, London, July 1940; Jeanne (Ania) Jabotinsky, telegram, to Rt. Hon. Josiah Wedgwood, May 1, 1940; Jeanne Jabotinsky to Lord Lloyd, Secretary of State for the Colonies, London, July 28, 1940; M.I. 12 for M.I. 5, June 11, 1940; To Sir J. Shuckborough, August 5, 1940; MacMichael to Sir J. Shuckborough, Jerusalem, December 14, 1940, NA, CO 733/425/12; Margalit, "Spell of Jabotinsky."

41. Felix, interview; Ofer, *Escaping the Holocaust*, 139; Cohen, *Song of the Silent Bell*, 47; Jabotinsky, *Sakarya Expedition*, 49; J. M. Kadlec, *Svatá Země v Československém odboji* (Prague: Orientální ústav, 1947).

42. Kraus, interview.

Chapter 6

1. Kurt Groll, Prague, Czech Republic, December 2, 1947, Ministry of National Defense, Military historical archive (Vojenský historický archiv, hereafter VHA).

2. Josef Kadlec, *Svatá Země v Československém odboji* (Prague: Orientální ústav, 1947), 33–34.

3. Monty Noam Penkower, *Palestine to Israel: Mandate to State, 1945–1948* (New York: Touro University Press, 2019), vii.

4. "Poměry na Středním Východě," written in 1945, VHA) 19–1/49; Alois Bloch and Jiří Bolách to the Cz. general consul, Sarafand, August 5, 1940, VHA, 19–7/2, f. 18; Karel (illegible), Jindřich Kerpell, František Weinstein to the General consulate of the Czech Republic, Atlit, April 27, 1940, VHA, 19–20; Dr. Josef Rufeisen to Kadlec, Tel Aviv April 23, 1940, VHA, 19–21/29.

5. Mjr. Jaroslav Petr, "Židé v Československé armádě v střední východ," Jerusalem, November 19, 1941, National archive, MNO, MV-L, box 92, folder 2–3/28; Petr was the pseudonym of major J. Havlíček. Kadlec to MNO, telegram, Jerusalem, July 17, 1940; Kadlec to General Sergei Ingr, "Organizace čsl. vojenského oddílu v Palestině," Jerusalem, August 9, 1940, VHA, 19–7/2; Erich Kulka, *Židé v Československém vojsku na západě* (Prague: Naše vojsko, 1992) 73–76; Karel Klapálek, *Ozvěny bojů* (1968, repr.; Prague: Naše vojsko, 1987), 32; J. M. Kadlec to Leo Baltuch, "Povolávací rozkaz," Jerusalem, August 2, 1940, VHA, 19–21/29; Josef Kadlec, general consul in Palestine, to General Sergei Ingr, Minister of national defense, Jerusalem, August 9, 1940, VHA, 19–7/2, and 20–26; Kadlec to Ingr, Jerusalem, September 20, 1940, f. 28; Kadlec, *Svatá Země*, 11 and 107–110; Magdalena Sedlíčková, "Antisemitismus v československé zahraniční armádě" (thesis, Charles University, 2012), 55–61; Kadlec to General Ingr, Čsl. vojenský oddíl v Palestině, "Ukončení náborové akce v Palestině," Jerusalem, September 10, 1940, VHA, 19–21/29.

6. "Jewish Volunteers in the British Army in W.W.II 1939–1945," Israel War Veterans League, Imperial War Museum (hereafter IWM), K. 96/1468, ms. 1–33.

7. "Inter-service lessons learnt in the campaign in Greece," Commanders in Chief Committee, March to April 1941, March 12, 1942, NA, CAB 44/120.

8. "Supplement to The London Gazette," War Office, July 3, 1946; "Operations in the Middle East from 7th February 1941 to 15th July 1941," General Sir Archibald P. Wavell, Commander in Chief in the Middle East to the Secretary of State, September 5, 1941, NA, WO 201/167; Matthew Willingham, *Perilous Commitments: The Battle for Greece and Crete 1940–1941* (Staplehurst, UK: Spellmount, 2005), 19–55; Robin Higham, *Diary of a Disaster: British Aid to Greece 1940–1941* (Lexington: University Press of Kentucky, 1986), 1–10; Steinhardt, US Ambassador in the Soviet Union, to the Secretary of State, Moscow, March 2, 1941; MacVeagh, US Minister in Greece, to the Secretary of State, Athens, March 3, 1941, Greece, The Axis War against Greece, FRUS, 740.0011, 653–54; General Alexander Papagos, *The Battle of Greece 1940–1941* (Athens: J. M. Scazikis "Alpha," 1949), 362–84.

9. Private Papers of H. E. Grocock, IWM, box 01/30/1; Eduardo D. Feingold with Juan Buchas, *The Kalamata Diary: Greece, War, and Emigration* (Lanham, MD: Rowman and Littlefield, 2010), 47–147.

10. MacVeagh, US Minister in Greece, to Secretary of State, "German Invasion of Greece," Athens, April 14, 19, 20 and 23, 1941 FRUS 740.0011, 718–23.

11. Willingham, *Perilous Commitments*, 85–103; Papagos, *Battle of Greece*, 362–84.

12. Private papers of C. Hamersma, "Princess Alice," Imperial War Museum (hereafter IWM), box no. 05/68/1.

13. Hamersma, "Princess Alice"; IWM, box no. 05/68/1; "From a Geneva correspondent," Geneva, July 2, 1941, NA, CAB 44/120; Yoav Gelber, "Palestinian POWs in German Captivity," *Yad Vashem Studies* 16 (1981): 89–137.

14. Hamersma, "Princess Alice," IWM, box no. 05/68/1.

15. Adrian Gilbert, *POW: Allied Prisoners in Europe, 1939–1945* (London: John Murray, 2006), 47; private papers of R. Holme, "Adventures of a 'Brown Job,'" IWM, box no. 99/82/1, 25.

16. Joseph Robert White, "'Even in Auschwitz . . . Humanity Could Prevail': British POWs and Jewish Concentration Camp Inmates at IG Auschwitz, 1943–1945," *Holocaust and Genocide Studies* 15, no. 2 (Fall 2001): 266–95.

17. Private papers of H. E. Grocock; "Affidavit in the matter of German war crime and in the matter of the shooting of private J.R. Gambrill," N.Z.M.C., Military Department, Judge advocates general's office, London, May 29, 1945, NA, WO 311/936.

18. Private papers of H. E. Grocock, IWM, box 01/30/1.

19. Ted Lees, "Life as a Prisoner of War," StalagVIIB/344 Lamsdorf Prisoners of War, accessed April 8, 2020.

20. Holme, "Adventures of a Brown Job," IWM, box no. 99/82/1, 34.

21. Holme, "Adventures of a Brown Job," IWM, box no. 99/82/1, 37.

22. "Stalag VIIIB 344 Lamsdorf," StalagVIIB/344 Lamsdorf Prisoners of War, accessed April 8, 2020.

23. Ruth Tosková, interviewed by Anna Lorencová, PJM, 1996, cassette 016.; Vasilis Vourkoutiotis, "What the Angels Saw: Red Cross and Protecting Power Visits to

Anglo-American POWs, 1939–1945," *Journal of Contemporary History* 40, no. 4 (October 2005): 689–706.

24. "Deník vojína Irvinga Georga Becka: Váleční zajatci v Muně," accessed April 10, 2020; Jon Jay, *Facing Fearful Odds: My Father's Story of Captivity, Escape and Resistance '1940–1945* (Barnsley, UK: Pen and Sword), 2014.

25. Holme, "Adventures of a 'Brown Job,'" IWM, box no. 99/82/1, 34–42.

26. Gilbert, *POW*, 197.

27. Zdeněk Konečný and František Mainuš, *British Prisoners-of-War in Czechoslovakia, and Silesian Territory during the Second World War* (Brno: Sborník prací filozofické fakulty Brněnské univerzity, 1966), 153–57; Private papers of J. J. Andrew, IWM, document 17366; Joan Beaumont, "Prisoner of War in the Second World War," *Journal of Contemporary History* 42, no. 3 (July 2007): 535–44; Noel Barber, *Prisoner of War: The Story of the British Prisoners Held by the Enemy* (London: George G. Harrap, 1944), 40.

28. Jonathan F. Vance, "The Politics of Camp Life: The Bargaining Process of Two German Prison Camps," *War & Society* 10, no. 1 (1992): 109–26.

29. Sybille Steinbacher, "East Upper Silesia," in *The Greater German Reich and the Jews: Nazi Persecution Policies in the Annexed Territories 1935–1945*, ed. Wolf Gruner and Jörg Osterloh (New York: Berghahn, 2015), 257; Bella Gutterman, *A Narrow Bridge to Life: Jewish Forced Labor and Survival in the Gross-Rosen Camp System, 1940–1945* (New York: Berghahn, 2008); Arieh J. Kochavi, *Britain and the United States and Their POWs in Nazi Germany* (Chapel Hill: University of North Carolina Press, 2005), 2–5.

30. Peter Hayes, "Forced and Slave Labor: The State of the Field," in *Forced and Slave Labor in Nazi-Dominated Europe: Symposium Presentations* (Washington, DC: United States Holocaust Memorial Museum, 2004), 1–9; Wolf Gruner, "Jewish Forced Labor as a Basic Element of Nazi Persecution: Germany, Austria, and the Occupied Polish Territories (1938–1945)," in *Forced and Slave Labor in Nazi-Dominated Europe*, 35–48; Gilbert, *POW*, 213.

31. Kurt to Anna, Tel Aviv, September 27, 1945; Gilbert, *POW*, 217; Konečný and Mainuš, "British Prisoners-of-War"; Steinbacher, "East Upper Silesia," 239–66; Géraldine Schwarz, *Those Who Forget: My Family's Story in Nazi Europe* (New York: Scribner, 2020), 81, 124.

32. Private papers of Holme, "Adventures of a 'Brown Job,'" IWM, box no. 99/82/31.

33. Private papers of Holme, "Adventures of a 'Brown Job,'" IWM, box no. 99/82/31, 44–47.

34. Gerald H. Davis, "Prisoners of War in Twentieth-Century War Economies," *Journal of Contemporary History* 12, no. 4 (October 1977): 623–34; Franz C. Liemert to the Headquarters of prisoners of war camp, Stalag VIII B in Lamsdorf, Niklasdorf, May 26, 1942; Captain Larscher to Stalag VIII B, Fryvaldov, August 10, 1942. Documents supplied by Roman Janas; "Complaints from the POW camps: British camp leader, Stalag VIII Teschen, June 2, 1944; Senior British medical officer, Stalag VIIIB hospital; Hauptvertrauensmann to the Commandant Stalag VIIIB, April 3, 1944, the Wiener Library documents section 546.

35. Kurt to mother and Anna, Tel Aviv, September 27, 1945; Kurt to Anna, Tel Aviv, November 18, 1945; Konečný and Mainuš, "British Prisoners-of-War," 159–60.

36. Private papers of H. E. Grocock, IWM, box 01/30/1; Jay, *Facing Fearful Odds*, 34.

37. Private papers of Holme, "Adventures of a 'Brown Job,'" IWM, box no. 99/82 /77–78.

Chapter 7

1. Kurt to Aninka, Tel Aviv, November 18, 1945. Other recent examples of sons and daughters searching for their families' wartime experience are Göran Rosenberg, *A Brief Stop on the Road from Auschwitz* (New York: Other Press, 2002); John Jay, *Facing Fearful Odds: My Father's Story of Captivity, Escape and Resistance 1940–1945* (Barnsley, UK: Pen and Sword, 2014); Betty O'Neill, *The Other Side of Absence: Discovering My Father's Secrets* (Edgecliff, Australia: Impact Press, 2020); Ariana Neumann, *When Time Stopped: A Memoir of My Father's War and What Remains* (New York: Scribner, 2020); Rita Benn et al., eds., *The Ones Who Remember: Second Generation Voices of the Holocaust* (Westport, CT: City Point Press, 2022). While in Palestine, Kurt was awarded the Africa Star, a military campaign medal first created by the United Kingdom on July 8, 1943, and given to British and Commonwealth forces who served in North Africa between June 10, 1940, and May 12, 1943, during World War II.

2. Daniel Blatman, "The Death Marches January–May 1945: Who Was Responsible for What?" *Yad Vashem Studies* 28 (2000): 155–201; Arieh J. Kochavi, *Confronting Captivity: Britain and the United States and Their POWs in Nazi Germany* (Chapel Hill: University of North Carolina Press, 2005), 203–18; Jiří Kosta, "Pochod smrti-osvobození-návrat. Gliwice-Blechheimmer-Medzilaborce-Praha," *Terezínské listy a dokumenty* (2005): 15–24; Yehuda Bauer, "Death Marches," *Modern Judaism*, no. 3 (1983): 1–21.

3. Ian Kershaw, "Calamity in the East," in *The End: The Defiance and Destruction of Hitler's Germany 1944–1945* (New York: Penguin Press), 2011, 167–206.

4. Lesley Loughlin, "The Long March to Freedom." The song is based on the account of Bernard Loughlin, written for his son Hugh, Lesley's husband.

5. Susanne Urban, "'Unknown Dead': Unsettling Finds from the Archive of the International Tracing Service," *Yad Vashem Studies* 40, no. 1 (2012): 197–216.

6. Private papers of R. Holme, "Adventures of a 'Brown Job,'" IWM, box no. 99/82/1, 80–84; Private papers of H. E. Grocock, IWM, box 01/30/1.

7. Bauer, "Death Marches," 10; Jay, *Facing Fearful Odds*, 47.

8. Guy Dirkin, *Missing the Boat: War Stories of Thomas Alan Dirkin* (n. p., 2018).

9. The image is borrowed from Ben Shephard, *The Long Road Home: The Aftermath of the Second World War* (New York: Anchor Books, 2012), 63; testimonies from the forced march and the liberation have been collected by Sean Longden, *Hitler's British Slaves: Allied POWs in Germany 1939–1945* (London: Constable and Robinson, 2005); Peter Longerich, *Goebbels: A Biography* (New York: Random House, 2015) 681; Ian Buruma, *Their Promised Land: My Grandparents in Love and War* (New York: Penguin, 2006), 95; Sébastian Farré, "The ICRC and the Detainees in Nazi Concentration Camps (1942–1945)," *International Review of the Red Cross* 94, no. 888 (Winter 2012): 1394–97.

10. Kurt Groll to the Czechoslovak repatriation commission, Keele-Hall, Newcastle under Lyme, July 2, 1945; Czechoslovak repatriation mission to Kurt Groll, London, July 11, 1945, Jewish Joint Distribution Committee archive. I would like to thank Jeffrey Edelstein for providing the documents.

11. Monty Noam Penkower, *Palestine to Israel: Mandate to State, 1945–1948* (New

York: Touro University Press, 2019), 3–4; Arieh J. Kochavi, "The Struggle against Jewish Immigration to Palestine," *Middle Eastern Studies* 34, no. 3 (July 1998): 146–67.

12. "Prime Minister to President Truman, Personal and Top Secret," September 16, 1945, NA, CAB 120/660; "The Palestine Problem," G.S.I. (14), G.H. Q. M.E. F. October 1945, NA, WO 201/192.

13. Naomi Shepherd, *Ploughing Sand: British Rule in Palestine 1917–1948* (New Brunswick, NJ: Rutgers University Press, 1999), 223–25; Kochavi, "The Struggle against Jewish Immigration to Palestine," 146–67; "Likvidace a repatriace—dotazy a návrhy Ministerstva národní obrany (MNO) v Košicích," Jeruzalém, May 1, 1945, VA, Střední východ, generální konzul podplukovník Novák, VHA, 19–3, ff. 24–99; Saul Friedländer, *When Memory Comes* (New York: Other Press, 1978), 148–49.

14. Rabbi Dr. S. Arje to the Cz, military mission, Jerusalem, September 24, 1942; Curriculum vitae of Hanuš Rebenwurzel, VHA, 19–40, ff. 93, 94; Schwarz, interview, reel 2 and 3; "Likvidace a repatriace-dotazy a návrhy," to MNO in Košice, Jerusalem, May 1, 1945, VHU, 19–3, ff. 75–81.

15. Kurt to Aninka, Haifa, September 6, 1945.

16. Joža Karas, *Music in Terezín 1941–1945* (New York: Beaufort Books, 1985), 179–80; Vojtěch Blodig, "Poslední dny války, první měsíce míru: Terezín v roce osvobození," *Terezínské listy*, no. 23, (1995): 7–23; Muller and Piechocki, Alice's Piano, 239–42.

17. Kurt to Aninka, Tel Aviv, September 18, 1945; personal email communication with Judith Lipschitz, May 15, 2022.

18. Dr. Flek, Prague, June 28, 1944, Zentralregistratur, Kurt Groll Israel, document provided by Jeffrey Edelstein, JDC.

19. Kurt to Aninka, Tel Aviv, September 18, 1945. Seven hundred kilometers is equivalent to about 435 miles.

20. Kurt to mami and Aninka, Tel Aviv, September 27, 1945.

21. Kurt to mami and Anča, Tel Aviv, October 18, 1945; "Příkazání bytu pro osoby bez přístřeší a osoby z koncentračních táborů," Hlavní město Praha, June 30, 1945..

22. Kurt to his mother and the Weinsteins, Tel Aviv, October 26, 1945.

23. Kurt to his mother and the Weinsteins, Tel Aviv, October 26, 1945; Dita Kraus, *Yo, Dita Kraus: La bibliotecaria de Auschwitz* (Barcelona: Roca Editorial, 2021).

24. Kurt to mami, Tel Aviv, November 17, 1945; Kochavi, "Struggle against Jewish Immigration to Palestine," 146–67.

25. Kurt to Anča and Arnošt, Natanya, February 20, 1946; Kurt to Anča and Arnošt, Tel Aviv, April 28, 1946; Kurt to Anča and Arnošt, Natanya, May 10, 1946.

26. Kurt to Anča and Arnošt, Natanya, February 20, 1946; Kurt to Anča and Arnošt, Tel Aviv, April 28, 1946; Kurt to Anča and Arnošt, Natanya, May 10, 1946.

27. "Czechoslovak consulate in Jerusalem to Kurt Groll," Jerusalem, November 18, 1945, Kurt Groll, VHA.

28. "Likvidace a repatriace-dotazy a návrhy" to MNO in Košice, Jerusalem, May 1, 1945, VA, Střední východ, generál konzul podplukovník Novák, 19–13 and 24–99.

29. "Likvidace a repatriace-dotazy a návrhy," to MNO in Košice, Jerusalem, May 1, 1945, VA, Střední východ, generál konzul podplukovník Novák, 19-13.

30. Podplk. J. M. Novák, "Směrnice pro přesuny. Repatriace ze Středního Východu do vlasti," Jerusalem, June 9, 1945, VHU, 19–7/3, 42–62.

Chapter 8

1. J. W. interviewed by Anna Lorencová, Prague Jewish Museum, Prague, Czech Republic, March 17, 1998, cassette 724; Jan Láníček, "The Postwar Czech-Jewish Leadership and the Issue of Jewish emigration from Czechoslovakia," in *Postwar Jewish Displacement and Rebirth, 1945–1967*, ed. Françoise Ouzan and Manfred Gerstenfeld (Leiden: Brill, 2014), 76–96; Dita Kraus, *Yo, Dita Kraus: La bibliotecaria de Auschwitz* (Barcelona: Roca Editorial, 2021), 186–87; Ariana Neumann, *When Time Stopped: A Memoir of My Father's War and What Remains* (New York: Scribner, 2020), 275–88.

2. Melissa Müller and Reinhard Piechocki, *Alice's Piano: The Life of Alice Herz-Sommer* (New York: St. Martin's Press, 2012) 247–48; Ruth Tosková, interviewed by Anna Lorencová, PJM, 1996, cassette 016; Heda Koválыová and Erazim Kohák, *Na vlastní kůži: Dialog přes barikádu* (Toronto: 68 Publishers, 1973), 69; Ruth Tosková, interviewed by Olga Sommerová, Prague, Czech Republic, 2007.

3. Tosková, interviewed by Lorencová; D. B., interviewed by Adéla Skálová, Prague Jewish Museum, no place, Czech Republic, January 16, 2014, casette 0124.

4. Susan Groag Bell, *Between Worlds: In Czechoslovakia, England, and America* (New York: Dutton, 1991), 139–40; Gerta Vrbová, *Betrayed Generation: Shattered Hopes and Disillusion in Post-War Czechoslovakia* (Cambridge, UK: Zuza Books, 2010) 42–68; Zuzana Ružičková and Wendy Holden, *One Hundred Miracles: A Memoir of Music and Survival* (London: Bloomsbury, 2019), 41–42.

5. Karel Kaplan, *Poválečné Československo: Československo, 1945–1948, národy a hranice* (Munich: Národni Politika, 1985), 5–6, 14–22, 130–58.

6. Chad Bryant, "All the Germans Must Go," in *Prague in Black: Nazi Rule and Czech Nationalism* (Cambridge, MA: Harvard University Press, 2009), 208–52; Kateřina Čapková, "Between Expulsion and Rescue: The Transports for German-Speaking Jews of Czechoslovakia in 1946," *Holocaust and Genocide Studies* 32, no. 1 (Spring 2018): 66–92; Benjamin Frommer, "Retribution as Legitimation: The Uses of Political Justice in Postwar Czechoslovakia," *Contemporary European History* 13, no. 4 (2004): 477–92.

7. Bradley F. Abrams, "Morality, Wisdom and Revision: The Czech Opposition of the 1970s and the Expulsion of the Sudeten Germans," *East European Politics and Society* 9, no. 2 (Spring 1995): 234–54; Mark Dworjetski, "Adjustment of Detainees to Camps and Ghetto Life and Their Subsequent Readjustment to Normal Life," *Yad Vashem Studies* (1963): 193–219; Tomas Sniegon, *Vanished History: The Holocaust in Czech and Slovak Historical Culture* (New York: Berghahn, 2014).

8. Ruth Ornšteinová to the Interior Ministry, Prague, Czech Republic, March 12, 1946, NA, Policejní výpis.

9. Tosková, interviewed by Lorencová; Čapková, "Between Expulsion and Rescue," 78–83.

10. Tosková, interviewed by Lorencová.

11. Vrbová, *Betrayed Generation*, 87–91; Bell, *Between Worlds*, 87.

12. David Reynolds, *From World War to Cold War* (Oxford: Oxford University Press, 2006), 274; Eduard Goldstücker, *Vzpomínky, 1945–68* (Prague: G plus G, 2005), 16–22; Tony Judt, *Postwar: A History of Europe since 1945* (London: Penguin Books, 2006), 130–31.

13. Klaus Larres, "Churchill's 'Iron Curtain' Speech in Context: The Attempt to Achieve a 'Good Understanding on All Points' with Stalin's Soviet Union," *International*

History Review 40, no. 1 (2018): 86–107; Scott C. Parrish, "New Evidence on the Soviet Rejection of the Marshall Plan, 1947," *Cold War International History Project*, working notebook 9 (March 1994).

14. Prokop Drtina, *Československo můj osud* (Toronto: 68 Publishers, 1982), 421–22; István Deák, "Could Stalin Have Been Stopped?" *New York Review of Books*, March 21, 2013; Vít Smetana, "Pod křídla Sovětů. Mohlo se Československo vyhnout 'sklouznutí' za železnou oponu?" *Soudobé dějiny* 15, no. 2 (2008): 276–302; Goldstücker, *Vzpomínky 1945–1968*, 26–27.

15. Karel Kaplan, *The Short March: The Communist Takeover in Czechoslovakia 1945–1948* (New York: St Martin's Press, 1981), ix, 2–5, 105.

16. Karel Kaplan and Pavel Paleček, *Komunistický režim a politické procesy v Československu* (Prague: Barrister & Principal, 2001), 33–36; Judt, *Postwar*, 806–8; Jan Bečko, Minister of Social Welfare, London, February 20, 1945, National archive, Czechoslovak army, fond PMR-L, file.

17. Kurt Groll to AJDC, Czechoslovakia, Prague, September 23, 1948; Helen Kohn, emigration director, AJDC in Czechoslovakia, Prague, Czech Republic, January 5, 1949, ABS, fond 425, file 425–48–35; Kurt Groll and Ruth Groll to the Federation of Australian Jewish Welfare Societies, n.d., ABS, fond 425, file 425–48–35; Jeffrey Edelstein, "Piecing Together a Puzzle with Newly Received Digital Collections: Paris and Prague Materials Provide Answers to a 70-Year-Old Mystery," *JDC Archives*; Láníček, "Postwar Czech-Jewish Leadership," 76–96; Jana Svobodová, *Prague* (Prague: Ústav pro Soudobé dějiny, 1994), 26–47.

18. Kurt Groll to AJDC, Czechoslovakia, Prague, September 23, 1948; Helen Kohn, emigration director, AJDC in Czechoslovakia, Prague, Czech Republic, January 5, 1949, ABS, fond 425, file 425–48–35; Kurt Groll and Ruth Groll to the Federation of Australian Jewish Welfare Societies, n.d., ABS, fond 425, file 425–48–35; Edelstein, "Piecing Together a Puzzle; Láníček, "Postwar Czech-Jewish Leadership," 76–96; Svobodová, *Prague*, 26–47.

19. Závodní rada skupiny ROH, March 28, 1951; Vl. Tosek to personal department, March 28,1951; Ladislav Novák and Vladimír Tosek, "Ruth Grollová: návrh na zařazení redaktorky," April 25, 1951, Czechoslovak radio archive, file Ruth Grollová.

20. Mr. Braodmead to Foreign Office, Czechoslovakia: information summary, April 7–20, 1952, April 21–May 4, 1952, Mr. Kirk to FO, June 16–29, 1952, June 30–July 13, 1952, FO 371/ 100379.

21. Anne Applebaum, *Iron Curtain: The Crushing of Eastern Europe 1944–1956* (London: Penguin, 2012), 293–318.

22. Igor Lukeš, *Rudolf Slánský: His Trials and Trial*, Cold War International History Project, Woodrow Wilson International Center for Scholars, working paper no. 50.

23. Eugene Loebl, *Sentenced and Tried: The Stalinist Purges in Czechoslovakia* (London: Elek, 1969), 10.

24. Mr. Thomas to Northern Department, "The Case of Otto Šling," February 19, 1951, NA, FO 371/ 94483; Marian Šlingová, *Truth Will Prevail* (London: Merlin Press, 1968), 47–51; Loebl, Eugen, NA, KV2/3090.

25. Richter to Ruth Grollová, April 21, 1952, Ruth Grollová file, Czech radio archive; Tosková, interviewed by Lorencová.

26. Loebl, Eugen, NA, KV/3091; Šling, *Truth Will Prevail*, 55.

27. Loebl, *Sentenced and Tried*, 187–92; Ministerstvo spravedlnosti, *Proces s vedením protistátního spikleneckého centra v čele s Rudolfem Slánským* (Prague: Ministry of Justice, 1953), 306–7.

28. Otto Šling, NA, KV 6/75; On Šling's activities in England, NA, KV 6/74; Melissa Feinberg, *Curtain of Lies: The Battle over Truth in Stalinist Eastern Europe* (Oxford: Oxford University Press, 2017), 18–26.

29. Loebl, *Sentenced and Tried*, 187–92.

30. "Jana," the cover name of a secret police informer, November 24, 1952, Czech radio archive, file Ruth Grollová; Melissa Feinberg, "Fantastic Truths, Compelling Lies: Radio Free Europe and the Response to the Slánský Trial in Czechoslovakia," *Contemporary European History*, no. 1 (February 2013): 107–25.

31. Ružičková and Holden, *One Hundred Miracles*, 48–51.

32. Christian Ostermann, "'This Is Not a Politburo, but a Madhouse.' The Post-Stalin Succession Struggle, Soviet Deuthschlandpolitk and the SED: New Evidence from Russian, German, and Hungarian Archives," *Cold War International History Project Bulletin* 10 (March 1998): 61–72; Galina P. Murášková, "Mocenská vertikála a nálady v československé společnosti v padesátých letech 20. století. Pohled sovětských diplomatů v Praze," *Soudobé dějiny* 20, no. 4 (2013): 605–27.

33. Jiří Pelikán to Dr. Václavík, Prague, April 13, 1956, NA, fond MSS, uncataloged; Peter Waterman, *From Coldwar Communism to the Global Emancipatory Movement* (Helsinki: Into Kustannus, 2014); Jiří Pelikán and Antonio Carioti, *Jiří Pelikán—nepohodlný exulant: Rozhovor s Antoniem Cariotem* (Prague: Novela Bohemica, 2015), 19; Applebaum, *Iron Curtain*, 474–517. Jiří Pelikán to comrade Vecker, Prague, Czech Republic, April 3, 1956, NA, MSS archive; Pelikán, Příspěvek předsedy MSS Jiřího Pelikána pro Informační bulletín, 1958, Archivo storico, Camera Dei Diputati, Fondo Jiří Pelikán, box 2; Joël Kotek, *Students and the Cold War* (New York: St. Martin's Press, 1996), 86–106; Francesco Caccamo, *Jiří Pelikán a jeho cesta socialismem 20. Století* (Brno: Doplněk, 2008), 17–20.

34. Jiří Knapik, *Děti, mládež a socialismus v Československu v 50. a 60. Letech* (Opava: Slezská universita, 2014).

35. "Kasal," "Grollová Ruth, rozená Ornšteinová," February 11, 1954, ABS, fond 302, file 302–102–2.

36. Ben Lewis, *Hammer and Tickle: A History of Communism Told through Communist Jokes* (London: Weidenfeld & Nicolson, 2008).

37. Mikuláš Pešta, "Journalists as Communism's Fellow Travellers? A New Look at the International Organization of Journalists," *Soudobé dějiny* 28, no. 3 (2021): 787–90.

38. Daniela Spenser, *In Combat: The Life of Lombardo Toledano* (Leiden: Brill, 2020), 261–67.

39. "Věc: Grollová, Ruth-předání svazku," signature illegible, July 25, 1958; Grollová, Ruth, "Prohlášení," Prague, Czech Republic, August 20, 1958, First lieutenant Josef Kořenek, "Grollová, Ruth-záznam o pohovoru," Prague, Czech Republic, August 28, 1958; Kořenek, "Návrh na verbovku," Krajská správa Ministerstva vnitra, 11. Odbor, 1. Oddělení, ref. Anglie, August 29, 1958, ABS, fond 302, file 302–102–2. See stories like Ruth's in Zdena Salivarová-Škvorecká, *Osočeni: Pravdivé příběhy lidí z "Cíbulkova*

seznamu" (Brno: Host, 2000); Annemarie Sammartino, "We Are the State We Seek: Everyday Life in Czechoslovakia and East Germany, 1945–89," *Contemporary European History* 21, no. 3 (August 2012): 477–91; Petr Blažek and Pavel Žáček, "Czechoslovakia," in *A Handbook of the Communist Security Apparatus in East Central Europe, 1944–1989*, ed. Krzysztof Persak and Łukasz Kamiński (Warsaw: Institute of National Remembrance, 2005), 85–161; František Koudelka, *Státní bezpečnost 1954–1968* (Prague: Ústav pro Soudobé dějiny, 1993), 45–53.

40. Farský, "Vyhodnocení spolupracovnice Soňi," Prague, Czech Republic, September 6, 1960, ABS, fond 302, file 302–102–2.

41. Lieutenant Dvořák, "Spolupráce SOŇA-vyhodnocení," Prague, Czech Republic, October 22, 1962, ABS, fond 302, file 302–423–9.

42. First Lieutenant Had Alvi, "Vyhodnocení pracovníka 'Soňi,'" Prague, Czech Republic, December 22, 1964, ABS, fond 302, file 302–423–9.

43. First Lieutenant Stanislav Korák, "Návrh na uložení spolupracovníka 'Soňi,'" číslo svazku 21638, Prague, Czech Republic, April 4, 1967, ABS, fond 302, file 302–423–9. On the usefulness of the StB archive, see Prokop Tomek, "Svazek StB jako historický pramen," *Soudobé dějiny* 12, no. 2 (2002): 208–14.

Chapter 9

1. Eric Hobsbawm, *Interesting Times: A Twentieth Century Life* (London: Allen Lane, 2002), 178. In the 1970s, the Czechoslovak regime desecrated the memorial by painting out the inscriptions. Its excuse was that no particular group among the many victims of fascism ought to be singled out for special commemoration. Eroded by time and water, the inscriptions of the Holocaust victims were restored after the end of communism.

2. Lubomír Tosek, transcription of notes from a meeting with his father in Hungary in the summer of 1986, Prague, Czech Republic, June 10, 2019.

3. Adolf Tosek to Vladimír, Prague, Czech Republic, March 28, 1939.

4. Adolf Tosek to Vladimír, Prague, Czech Republic, March 28, March 31, April 9, 1939, April 11, 1939, April 17, 1939. In Czech: "Ž. se odevzdali do svého osudu."

5. Adolf Tosek, Zdenka Tosková, and Helena Maříková to Vladimír, Prague, Czech Republic, April 5, 1939.

6. Adolf Tosek to Vladimír, Prague, Czech Republic, June 4, 1939.

7. Miloš Mařík to Vladimír, Lausanne, Switzerland, August 5, 1939; see Ariana Neumann, *When Time Stopped: A Memoir of My Father's War and What Remains* (New York: Scribner, 2020), 91.

8. Lubomír Tosek, transcription of notes from a meeting with his father in Hungary in the summer of 1986, Prague, Czech Republic, June 10, 2019; Kulka, Erich Kulka, *Židé v Československém vojsku na západě* (Prague: Naše vojsko, 1992), 25–129. A distance of thirty kilometers is equivalent to about nineteen miles.

9. Eduard Čejka, *Československý odboj na Západě (1939–1945)* (Prague: Mladá fronta, 1997), 50–53; Kulka, *Židé v Československém vojsku na západě*, 165; Ladislav Kudrna, "Projevy antisemitismu v Československých pozemních a leteckých jednotkách za druhé světové války," *Terezínské listy*, no. 36 (2008): 59–88.

10. Lubomír Tosek, transcription of notes from a meeting with his father in Hungary in the summer of 1986, Prague, Czech Republic, June 10, 2019.

11. Dělostřelecký pluk, Dovolenka, Tosek, Vladimír, T-424, June 21 to 27, 1945.

12. Zdenka Tichotová, née Tosková, interviewed by Daniela Spenser, Prague, November 27, 2017.

13. Bohuslav Laštovička, *V Londýně za války: Zápasy o novou ČSR 1939–1945* (Prague: Svoboda, 1978), 77–81; Eva Ješutová, "Budovatelský rozhlas, 1945–1948," *Od mikrofonu k posluchačům* (Prague: Český rozhlas, 2003), 184–234.

14. Vladimír Tosek to the Czechoslovak radio, Prague, Czech Republic, July 12, 1945; Přiznání studijních úlev p. Vl. Toskovi, August 24, 1945, Czech radio archive.

15. Bohuslav Laštovička to Vladimír Tosek, Prague, Czech Republic, March 8, 1946, Czech radio archive; "Ustanovka," Leutenant Liška, Prague, Czech Republic, May 24, 1952, Ministry of the Interior, signatura MTH 21792, Czechoslovak State Security Archive (Archiv bezpečnostních složek, hereafter ABS).

16. Tom Dickins, "The Political Slogan in Communist Czechoslovakia (1948–89)," *Central Europe* 15, no. 1–2 (2017): 58–87; "Kádrový posudek na s. Vladimíra Toska," Hájek, Prague, Czech Republic, June 5, 1951, ABS, file MTH 21792.

17. Zdenka Tichotová, interviewed by Daniela Spenser, Prague, Czech Republic, November 7, 2017.

18. B. Laštovička, to the cadre department of the Czech radio, 1950; Dr. Rattinger to the cadre department of the Czech radio, Prague, Czech Republic, September 11, 1950, ABS, fond MTH/ 1. Sprava SNB, signatura MTH 21792.

19. Čestmír Císař, *Paměti: Nejen o zákulisí Pražského jara* (Prague: SinCon, 2005), 381–82; Kateřina Březinová, "Spanish Political Emigration in Czechoslovakia, 1948–1958: Cold War Transregional Mobilities," unpublished paper; Ruth Tosková, interviewed by Anna Lorencová, PJM, 1996, cassette 016.

20. Vladimír Tosek, "Rodinný a osobní život," Prague, Czech Republic, May 20, 1950, Kadrové oddělení, Czech radio archive.

21. Osobní oddělení, June 7, 1951, Czech Radio Archive.

22. Jar Veselý, "Vladimír Tosek-poznatky," Prague, November 27, 1951, ABS, file 12402–326; Zdenka Tichotová, personal communication to Daniela Spenser.

23. Dráždil, alias Sokol, "Vladimír Tosek-Taussig-zpráva," Prague, June 24, 1952, July 31, 1952; Jarmila Klenová, Ruth Majerovičová, and Jarmila Chytilová, to the Ministry of National Defense, Prague, August 3, 1951, ABS, file 43891; Rostislav Behal, "Rozhlas po nástupu totality 1949–1958," *Od mikrofonu k posluchačům* (Prague: Český rozhlas, 2017), 236–88.

24. Valery N. Soyfer, *Lysenko and the Tragedy of Soviet Science* (New Brunswick, NJ: Rutgers University Press, 1994), 27; Vladimír Tosek to the Regional directorship of national defense, Prague, Czech Republic, November 19, 1951, National archive, Policejní ředitelství, Vladimír Tosek file.

25. Jiřina Šmejkalová, "Command Celebrities: The Rise and Fall of Hanzelka and Zikmund," *Central Europe* 13, no. 1–2 (2015): 72–86; Lubomír Tosek, transcription of notes from a meeting with his father in Hungary in the summer of 1986, Prague, Czech Republic, June 10, 2019.

26. Sokol, "Navštěva u Vladimíra Toska," January 31, 1953; Likar, "Tosek, Vladimír—uložení osobního svazku do archivu," September 12, 1954, ABS, file 43891.

27. Jiří Knapík and Martin Franc, *Průvodce kultůrním děním a životním stylem v*

Českých zemích 1948–1967 (Prague: Academia, 2011), 201–3; Jarmila Cysařová, *Televize a moc, 1953–1967* (Prague: Ústav pro Soudobé dějiny, 1996), 22–28; Milan Bárta, "Cenzura československého filmu a televize v letech 1953–1968," *Securitas Imperii* 10 (2003): 5–57; Vladimír Železný and Přemek Podlaha, interviewed by Daniela Spenser, Prague, Czech Republic, December 9, 2013.

28. Tony Judt, *Postwar: A History of Europe since 1945* (London: Penguin Books, 2006), 425–49; from a review of television news in images without sound, 1961–1965, Czech television archive. The archivist Karel Sieber carried out the research in October 2017; Jarmila Cysařová, *Česká televizní publicistika: Svědectví šedesátých let* (Prague: Edice České televize 66, 1993); Karel Kaplan and Dušan Tomášek, "Zpráva ministra vnitra R. Baráka politickému sekretariátu ÚV KSČ o činnosti Hlavní správy tiskového dohledu," in *O cenzuře v Československu v letech 1945–1956* (Prague: Ústav pro Soudobé dějiny, 1994), 153–58. HSTD was in the words of Barák a carbon copy of the Soviet censorship institution GLAVLIT.

29. Vladimír Tosek, "Documentary film about London, Windsor and Oxford, traveling, city, English gothic, city transport," Czech television archive, 1957.

30. Cysařová, *Česká televizní publicistika*, 16–17.

31. Jiří Čermák, "Záznam o osobním poznání," Prague, Czech Republic, May 25, 1958, ABS, file 43891–020–0029.

32. Jiří Čermák, "Záznam o osobním poznání," Prague, Czech Republic, May 25, 1958, ABS, file 43891–020–0029.

33. Jiří Čermák, "Záznam o verbovce," Prague, Czech Republic, February 26, 1959, ABS, file 43891–020–0034.

34. Kamila Moučková, interviewed by Daniela Spenser, Prague, November 13, 2017.

35. Jiří Váňa, "Jako hlasatelky v Čs. Televizi v Praze účinkují," November 27, 1959, Prague, Czech Republic, ABS, file 43891–020–0053–55. Vladimír's reports are written in his unmistakable handwriting.

36. Vladimír Tosek, "K sedmdesátinám Paula Robesona," April 8, 1968, Czech television archive. The interview from 1959 was included in this 1968 program.

37. Jiří Tichota to Daniela Spenser, email, Prague, Czech Republic, August 20, 2021; Františka Schormová, "Stalinův černý apoštol: Afroamerický zpěvák Paul Robeson v Československu," *Soudobé dějiny* 28, no. 1 (2021): 183–213.

38. Vladimír Tosek with Guevara, Czech television archive. I would like to thank Michal Zourek for the document of Guevara in Brno; Hana Bortlová, *Československo a Kuba v letech 1959–1962* (Prague: Charles University, 2011), 62–63.

39. Jan Tosek, Lubomír Tosek, and Zdenka Tichotová, interviewed by the Daniela Spenser, Prague, November 2017.

40. Vladimír Tosek, Prague, Czech Republic, April 24, 1961, four single-spaced typewritten pages held in ABS, file 43891–020–096–100.

41. "Jiří Váňa," Prague, Czech Republic, August 11, 1961, ABS, file 43891–020–0107. The interview has not survived.

42. Martin Štoll, *Television and Totalitarianism in Czechoslovakia: From the Democratic Republic to the Fall of Communism* (New York: Bloomsbury, 2019), 168–70; Caccamo, *Jiří Pelikán a jeho cesta socialismem* 20, 22–23.

43. Jarmila Cysařová, "Svědectví pamětníků," in *Televize a moc*, 67–72; Captain Šmejkal, Vladimír Tosek z Čs. Televize—zpráva, Prague, Czech Republic, October 6, 1964, ABS, 43891-000-0177; V. Koucký, "Schůze předsednictva ÚV KSČ," October 15, 1964, NA, Archive of ÚV KSČ, fond 05/3, file 11; C. C. Parrott to Northern Department, Prague, Czech Republic, FO 371/182577, March 5, 1965.

44. Pelikán to Vladimír, Prague, Czech Republic, November 5, 1964, Camera dei Deputati, Archivo Storico, Fond Jiří Pelikán (1923–1999), box 2.

45. "Vyhodnocení spol. Cornela" (February 15, 1965), ABS, file 43891; František Koudelka, *Státní bezpečnost 1954–1968* (Prague: Ústav pro Soudobé dějiny, 1993), 17–19; Jan Tosek, Lubomír Tosek, and Zdenka Tichotová, interviewed by Daniela Spenser, November 2017.

46. Peter Hames, *Czech and Slovak Cinema: Theme and Tradition* (Edinburgh: University Press, 2009), 75–94; Miloš Forman and Jan Novák, *Turnaround: A Memoir* (New York: Villard Books, 1994); Pavel Kohout, *To byl můj život?* (Prague: Odeon, 2018), 692–93; Ivan Klíma, *My Crazy Century: A Memoir* (New York: Grove Press, 2010), 157–84.

47. Štoll, *Television and Totalitarianism in Czechoslovakia*, 170, 174.

48. Cysařová, *Česká televizní publicistika*, 100.

49. Klíma, *My Crazy Century*; Kohout, *To byl můj život?*; Jiří Růžička, "Poststalinismus jako (ne)stalinský projekt modernity? Možnost konceptuálního uchopení intelektuálních 'reformních' diskursů v období 1956–1968," *Soudobé dějiny* 25, no. 1–2 (2018): 208–28; Marci Shore, "Engineering in the Age of Innocence: A Genealogy of Discourse inside the Czechoslovak Writers' Union, 1949–1967," *East European Politics and Societies* 12, no. 3 (1998): 397–441.

50. Zdenka Tichotová, interviewed by Daniela Spenser, Prague, Czech Republic, November 14, 2017.

51. Vladimír Tosek, *Expo 67*, Czech television archive.

Chapter 10

1. Vladimír Tosek, "Den starosty Montalbana," April 12, 1968, Program 68, Czech television archive online.

2. Jiří Suk, "Je v pražském jaru 1968 alternativa k dnešnímu kapitalismu? Politická úvaha nad historickou interpretací," *Soudobé dějiny* 17, no. 3 (2010): 461–67.

3. František Janouch, Martin Groman, and Daniel Štěpánek, eds., *Na smutek není čas: Korespondence mezi Františkem a Rivou Krieglovými a Františkem Janouchem a Adou Kolmanovou (1974–1979)* (Prague: Nadace Charty 77, 2009), 21.

4. Jiří Suk, *Veřejné záchodky ze zlata: Konflikt mezi komunistickým utopismem a ekonomickou racionalitou v předsrpnovém Československu* (Prague: Prostor, 2016), 215–46; Jiří Lederer, *Touhy a iluze (vzpomínání do srpna 68)* (Toronto: Sixty-Eight Publishers, 1984), 175–213; Rosamund Johnston, "Red Tape and Hot Media: Radio, Politics and Socialist Celebrity in Czechoslovakia, 1945–1969," (PhD diss., New York University, 2019), 289.

5. Vladimír Tosek, "K sedmdesátinám Paula Robesona," April 8, 1968, Program 68, Czech television archive online.

6. Vladimír Tosek with Bohumil Šimon, member of the Central Committee of the Czechoslovak Communist Party (who oversaw the economic sector), František Kriegel, member of the Central Committee of the Czechoslovak Communist Party and a

deputy in the National Assembly. and Vladimír Madera, university professor, in "Oč vlastně běží?" March 12, 1968, Program 68, Czech television archive online; Eduard Goldstücker, *Vzpomínky 1945–1968* (Prague: G plus G, 2005), 145–47.

7. Jiří Svejkovský, "Tváří v tvář," March 14, 1968, Program 68, Czech television archive online.

8. Lederer, *Touhy a iluze*, 235.

9. Vladimír Tosek, "Mezi námi," *Reporter* (Prague), no. 14 (April 1968): 3–10. The censured programs were *Spor* and *Porota*, made in 1966. *Spor* was aired once and censored; *Porota* couldn't be aired until March 1968. See March 14 and 18, Program 68, Czech television archive online.

10. Jarmila Cysařová, *Televize a moc, 1953–1967* (Prague: Ústav pro Soudobé dějiny, 1996), 66; Ladislav Daneš, *Můj život s můzami, televizí a tak vůbec* (Prague: Malá skála, 2005), 89.

11. Vladimír Tosek, "Mezi námi," April 9, 1968, Program 68. Only a photograph of the three has been preserved. See also Eva Tomanová, dir., *Syn nepřítele státu*, Česká televize, 2022, 53:31, a documentary about Karel Šling.

12. Arnošt Frydrych, "Cesta do hlubin divákovy duše," *Reportér* no. 18 (May 1–7, 1968): 26–27.

13. Daneš, *Můj život*, 89; Ladislav Daneš, "Mezi námi," June 11, 1968. The transcription of the interview is in the ABS archive, file 614142.

14. Ladislav Daneš, interviewed by Daniela Spenser, Prague, Czech Republic, December 16, 2013.

15. Vladimír Tosek, "Mezi námi," May 7, 1968, Program 68, Czech television archive online.

16. Milan Bárta, "My jsme rozhodnutí zneškodnit každého, nikoho se nebojíme," *Paměť a dějiny* 4 (2012): 9–22.

17. Zdeněk Mlynář, *Mráz přichází z Kremlu* (Cologne: Index, 1981), 143; Simon Graham, "Internationalising the Intelligence History of the Prague Spring," *Cold War History* 20, no. 3 (2020): 293–310.

18. Čestmír Císař, *Paměti: Nejen o zákulisí Pražského jara* (Prague: SinCon, 2005), 789; Mlynář, *Mráz přichází z Kremlu*, 145; Graham, "Internationalising the Intelligence History," 301–4; Goldstücker, *Vzpomínky:1945–1968*, 156; Kieran Williams, *The Prague Spring and Its Aftermath: Czechoslovak Politics, 1968–1970* (Cambridge, UK: Cambridge University Press, 1997), 210.

19. Josef Pavel to Alexander Dubček, Prague, Czech Republic, May 14, 1968, and "Informace o současné státní bezpečnostní situaci v ČSSR," presented to ÚV KSČ, May 20, 1968, NA, ÚV KSČ, 4243/1968.

20. "Informace o současné státní bezpečnostní situaci v ČSSR," presented to ÚV KSČ, May 20, 1968, NA, ÚV KSČ, 4243/1968.

21. Georges Penchenier, "Agenturní zpráva," July 23, 1968, Náčelník 2; mayor Slavík Oddělení,, "Úřední záznam," July 30, 1968, and "Vyhodnocení signálu 'PAN,'" August 5, 1968; Vladimír, Matura, "Vyhodnocení signálu 'PAN,'" Prague, Czech Republic, September 17,1968, ABS archive, folder 616692.

22. "Informace čs. kontrarozvědky o některých tendencích v činnosti ZÚ kapitalistických států, cizích státních příslušníků i jednotlivých čs. občanů," Prague, Czech

Republic, June 30, 1968, NA, Hlavní správa [Main directorate] STB, OS-00210-/150–68, NA, UVKSC, 4571/1968.

23. Ludvík Vaculík, "Dva tisíce slov," in *Jaro 1968: Čítanka pro děti a mládež* (Cologne: 150000 and Index, 1988), 225–27; Dušan Havlíček, *Jaro na krku: Zážitky ze zákulisí sekretariátu ÚV KSČ od června do prosince 1968* (Prague: Ústav pro Soudobé dějiny, 1998), 77; Klíma, *My Crazy Century*, 231–32; Moritz Poellath, "Agents, Fascists and Provocateurs: Disinformation as an Instrument to Delegitimize Uprisings in Eastern Europe (1953, 1956, 1968) and Its Impact on the Politics of Memory," *Journal of Intelligence History* 22, no. 2 (2021): 1–23.

24. Zdeněk Mlynář, *Československý pokus o reformu 1968: Analýza jeho teorie a praxe* (Cologne: Index-Listy, 1975), 118–33.

25. Vladimír Tosek and Jiří Kantůrek, "Kam spějeme?" July 12, 1968, Program 68, Czech television archive online. The names of the other journalists are unknown.

26. Jiří Hoppe, *Pražské jaro v médiích: Výběr z dobové publicistiky* (Brno: Doplněk, 2004), 219–28; Jakub Končelík, "Dva tisíce slov: Zrod a důsledky nečekaně vlivného prohlášení," *Soudobé dějiny* 15, no. 3–4 (2008): 485–529.

27. Vaculík, "Dva tisíce slov," 256–27.

28. Havlíček, *Jaro na krku*, 74–75.

29. Alexander Dubček, "Aktualita dne," June 28, 1968, Program 68, Czech television archive online. Goldstücker, *Vzpomínky*, 155; Císař, *Paměti*, 805–11.

30. Arnošt Frydrych, "Anonymům na vědomí," Týdeník Čs. televize, 29, July 15–21, 1968; Martin Schulze Wessel, *Pražské jaro: Průlom do nového světa* (Prague: Argo, 2018), 202–7. A pasha was an Ottoman governor.

31. "Neopustíme naši cestu," *Lidová demokracie*, August 2, 1968.

32. Matthew J. Quimet, *The Rise and Fall of the Brezhnev Doctrine in Soviet Foreign Policy* (Chapel Hill: University of North Carolina Press, 2003), 31–32; Mark Mazower, *Dark Continent: Europe's Twentieth Century* (London: Penguin, 1999), 288–89; Zdeněk Mlynář, "Tváří v tvář," August 8, 1968, Czech Program 68, Czech television archive online; František Kriegel, cited in Janouch, Groman, and Štěpánek, *Na smutek není čas*, 23.

33. Havlíček, *Jaro na krku*, 153; Končelík, "Dva tisíce slov," 489; Jiří Dienstbier and Karel Lánský, "Rozhlas proti tankům," in *Srpen 1968* (Cologne: Index, 1989), 17; Jiří Boreš, "Letokruhy II," typescript.

34. Antonín Benčík, "Kauza Karel Hoffmann versus historikové aneb co se dělo v srpnu 1968 na Ústřední správě spojů," *Soudobé dějiny* 11, no. 4 (2004): 130–36.

35. Miroslav Sígl, "Srpnové události 1968 a Čs. televize," typescript; Jindřich Pecka, "Proměny Pražského jara ve světle pramenů spontánní povahy," in *Proměny Pražského jara: Sbor studií a dokumentů o nekapitulantských postojích v československé společnosti 1968–69*, ed. Jindřich Pecka and Vilém Prečan (Brno: Doplněk, 1983), 39–66; Dienstbier and Lánský, "Rozhlas proti tankům," 21–104; Josef Forbelský, *Svět se mnou, svět bez mne* (Prague: Academia, 2013).

36. Martin Štoll, *Television and Totalitarianism in Czechoslovakia: From the Democratic Republic to the Fall of Communism* (New York: Bloomsbury, 2019), 181–83; Jiří Svejkovský, *Čas marných nadějí: Roky 1968 a 1969 ve zpravodajství ČST* (Prague: Epocha, 2010), 289.

37. Vladimír Tosek, August 23, 1968, Program 68, Czech television archive online.

38. Dienstbier and Lánský, "Rozhlas proti tankům," 45–48; Jiří Dienstbier, Věněk

Šilhán, Karel Lánský, and Bohumil Šimon, "Sedm pražských dnů," in *Srpen 1968* (Cologne: Index, 1989), 21–27; Ben Lewis, *Hammer and Tickle: A History of Communism Told through Communist Jokes* (London: Weidenfeld & Nicolson, 2008), 196–97. "Kolja" is a generic male name, equivalent to "John" in English.

39. Václav Kolář and Ladislav Kejha, *Televize v srpnu 1968: Dodatek ke stejnojmennému pořadu ČT* (Prague: Czech television, 2001), available on YouTube video.

40. Kolář and Kejha, *Televize v srpnu 1968*, YouTube.

41. Martin Pulec, *Nestandardní jevy u Pohraniční stráže v posrpnovém období roku 1968* (Prague: Úřad dokumentace a vyšetřování zločinů komunismu, 2006), 9–45; Stefan Karner and Peter Ruggenthaler, "Austria and the End of the Prague Spring: Neutrality in the Crucible?" in *The Prague Spring and the Warsaw Pact Invasion of Czechoslovakia in 1968*, ed. Günter Bischof, Stefan Karner, and Peter Ruggenthaler (Boulder: Lexington Books, 2011), 419–39.

42. Vladimír Železný, interviewed by Daniela Spenser, December 16, 2013; Kolář and Kejha, *Televize v srpnu 1968*; Pulec, *Nestandardní jevy*, 12, n.16.

43. Mlynář, *Mráz přichází z Kremlu*, 313.

44. Quimet, *Rise and Fall of the Brezhnev Doctrine*, 46–48; Karen Dawisha, *The Kremlin and the Prague Spring* (Berkeley: University of California Press, 1984), 329–32; Geraint Hughes, "British Policy towards Eastern Europe and the Impact of the 'Prague Spring', 1964–1968," *Cold War History* 4, no. 2 (2004): 115–39; Muriel Blaive, "The Cold War? I Have It at Home with My Family," in *The Cold War: Historiography, Memory, Representation*, ed. Konrad H. Jarausch, Christian F. Ostermann and Andreas Erges (Berlin: De Gruyter, 2018), 197.

Chapter 11

1. Ladislav Daneš, *Můj život s můzami, televizí a tak vůbec* (Prague: Malá skála, 2005), 112–14; Jiří Kosta, *Život mezi úzkostí a nadějí* (Prague: Paseka, 2002), 132–35.

2. Ruth Tosek to Bedřich Rohan, Vienna, October 25, 1968; Miloš Forman and Jan Novák, *Turnaround: A Memoir* (New York: Villard Books, 1994), 175; Stefan Karner and Peter Ruggenthaler, "Austria and the Prague Spring: Neutrality in the Crucible?" in *The Prague Spring and the Warsaw Pact Invasion of Czechoslovakia in 1968*, ed. Gunther Bischof, Stefan Karner and Peter Ruggenthaler (United Kingdom: Lexington Books, 2011), 427–28; Vladimír Tosek, letter to Czechoslovak television, "Žádost o mimořádnou dovolenou," Vienna, Austria, November 10, 1968; Vladimír Tosek to Viktor Růžička, Vienna, Austria, November 20, 1968.

3. Kieran Williams, *The Prague Spring and Its Aftermath. Czechoslovak Politics, 1968–1970* (Cambridge, UK: Cambridge University Press, 1997), 174–76.

4. Fabio Borelli to Vladimír Tosek, Rome, Italy, December 10, 1968, p.a.

5. Vladimír Tosek, "Informace o mé návštěvě v Římě a náměty z ní vyplývající," Vienna, Austria, January 15, 1969; Vladimír Tosek to Oldřich Černík, Vienna, January 31, 1969; Arnošt Frydrych to the Toseks, Prague, Czech Republic, February 2, 1969.

6. "Záznam o jednání předsednictva Svazu českých novinářů o některých okamžitých opatření ÚV KSČ v oblasti hromadných sdělovacích prostředků," January 13,1969, typescript; Jiří Lederer, *Jan Palach: Zpráva o životě, činu a smrti českého studenta* (Prague: Novinar, 1990), 89–93; Jiří Hochman, "Words and Tanks: The Revival, the

Struggle, the Agony and Defeat (1968–1969)," in *The Prague Spring: A Mixed Legacy*, ed. Jiří Pehe (New York: Freedom House, 1988), 37–39; Jan Kavan, "From the Prague Spring to a Long Winter," in Pehe, *Prague Spring*, 109–11; Williams, *Prague Spring and Its Aftermath*, 188–90.

7. Vladimír Tosek, letter to Josef Šmídmajer, the Czechoslovak television director, Vienna, January 31, 1969. In addition to their private passports, Vladimír, Ruth, and people who traveled on business abroad were issued passports for travel on behalf of the governments or state institutions they represented.

8. Daneš, *Můj život s můzami*, 18.

9. jk, "Ve středu zájmu imperialistických rozvědek," *Zprávy*, February 1, 1969, 7; "Soviet Attack on Prague Britons," *Times* (London), February 4, 1968.

10. "Vaše otázka-naše odpověď," *Východoslovenské noviny*, orgán východoslovenského krajského výboru KSS, February 25, 1969; "Aktiv funkcionářů KSČ v Hodoníně," *Slovácko*, list OV KSČ a Rady ONV v Hodoníně, February 26, 1969.

11. For the criminalization of border crossing, see Jan Rychlík, "Překračování hranic a emigrace v Československu a východní Evropě ve 20. století," *Securitas imperii* 29 (February 2016): 10–72; Vladimír Tosek, "Kterak jsem si šel pro vlnu a vrátil se ostříhán," *Práce*, March 1, 1969, 4.

12. "Ministerstvo vnitra k případu Vl. Toska," *Svobodné Slovo*, February 26, 1969, 3; "Vl. Tosek odpovídá," *Svobodné Slovo*, February 28, 1969, 3; Vladimír Tosek, "Kterak jsem si šel pro vlnu a vrátil se ostříhán," *Práce*, March 1, 1969; Josef Váňa, "Z televizní kuchyně a zákulisí," *Zprávy*, March 15, 1969, 4.

13. Zdeněk Rajchart, "Vážený soudruhu redaktore," *Práce*, April 12, 1969, 4.

14. See also Zdeněk Rajchart, "Kdo koho ostříhal?" *Rudé právo*, April 12, 1969, 2.

15. "Závěrečné vyjádření V. Toska," typescript.

16. Josef Vávra to Vladimír Tosek, Prague, Czech Republic, April 15, 1969.

17. "Kterak jsem si šel pro vlnu a vrátil se ostříhán," *Filmové a televizní noviny*, no. 3 (April 1969): 6; "Zpráva o prohlídce zavazadel V. Toska příslušníky pohraniční stráže ministerstva vnitra," personal archive.

18. Karel Kyncl, "Vladimíra Toska poslední utkání na domácí půdě," *Listy*, no. 1 (1990): 151. Indeed, much of this book has drawn on the personal documents found in that chest.

19. Ivan Klíma, *My Crazy Century: A Memoir* (New York: Grove Press, 2010), 258.

20. Martina Miklová, "Československý exil v archivním výzkumu. Zpráva z brněnské konference," *Soudobé dějiny* 14, no. 4 (2017): 912–23; Vilém Prečan, "Poznámky ke studiu exilu a domácí antitotalitní rezistence v 70. a 80. letech," in *Češi za hranicemi na přelomu 20. a 21. století*, ed. Karel Hrubý and Stanislav Brouček (Prague: Charles University, 2000), 213–22; Nils Löffelbein, "Z 'Pražského jara' do exilu-přijímání československých uprchlíků v SRN po vpádu jednotek Varšavského paktu do ČSSR v roce 1968," in *Uprchlíci a azylanti v zemi sousedů: Československo a Německo v letech 1933 až 1989*, ed. Detlef Brandes, Edita Ivaníčková and Jiří Pešek (Prague: Česko-německá komise historiků, Masarykův ústav and Archiv AV ČR, 2019), 245–66; Rudolf Zukal, "O emigraci z Československa," *Listy*, no. 6 (December 1985): 28–32; Ota Ulč, "Ošemetnost s azylem," *Listy*, no. 6 (December 1986): 57–60; Eva Procházková, "O rozhodnutí emigrovat," *Listy*, no. 6 (December 1986): 60–61. An early version of this argument appeared as Daniela

Spenser, "Prague Spring's Demise: The Involuntary Emigration of the Journalist Vladimír Tosek," *Korpus 21* 1, no. 1 (2021): 127–42.

21. Vladimír Tosek to Láďa Daneš, Rome, July 17, 1969; on the conceptual definition of exile as different from emigration, see Kristina Andělová, Jiří Suk, and Tomáš Zahradníček, *Pro nás dějiny nekončí: Politická práce v myšlení českého levicového exilu (1968–1989)* (Prague: Argo, 2023), 14, 22–24.

22. Jan Tosek, interviewed by Daniela Spenser, Prague, November 7, 2017.

23. Ruth Tosková, letter to Daniela Spenser, Rome, September 18, 1969.

24. Myrna Goldenberg, "Memoirs of Auschwitz Survivors: The Burden of Gender," in *Women in the Holocaust*, ed. Dalia Ofer abd Lenore J. Weitzman (New Haven: Yale University Press, 1998), 328–29; Anka to Ruth, Prague, Czech Republic, December 27, 1969; Kurt to Ruth, Prague, Czech Republic, November 5, 1970; Kurt to Ruth, Prague, Czech Republic, January 14, 1971.

25. See chapter 12 in this book.

26. Jiří Pelikán, "Why I Have Disobeyed the Order to Return to Prague," *Times* (London), October 1, 1969.

27. Pelikán to Vladimír and Ruth, London, October 10, 1969.

28. Pelikán to Havlíček, London, November 12,1969, in Jiří Pelikán and Dušan Havlíček, *Psáno z Říma, psáno ze Ženevy: Korespondence 1969–1989* (Olomouc: Buran and Tichák, 2013), 13; Pelikán to Havlíček, Rome, December 5, 1969, in Pelikán and Havlíček, *Psáno z Říma, psáno ze Ženevy*, 15–16.

29. Dalimil (A. J. Liehm), "O emigraci," *Listy*, no. 6 (November 1971): 16–18; Dušan Havlíček, *Listy v exilu* (Olomouc: Burian and Tichák, 2008), 112–31; Karel Jezdinský, "Exil a domov," *Listy*, no. 4–5 (July 1971): 24–27; Tomek Prokop, "Reflexe vysílání RFE jako spojení mezi exilem a domovem," in *Politický exil z krajín strednej a východnej Európy: Motivy, stratégie, aktivity a perspektívy na Východe a Západe, 1945–1989: Zborník z medzinárodnej vedeckej konferencie, Bratislava 19.-20. novembra 2013*, ed. Peter Jašek (Bratislava: Ústav pamäti národa, 2017), 24–32.

30. Czesław Miłosz, *The Captive Mind* (New York: Vintage, 1981), vii–xiv; Otto Bauer, "O poslání emigrace," *Listy*, no. 3 (June 1973): 37–38; Havlíček, *Listy v exilu*, 112–31; Jiří Otava (Jiřina Šiklová), "Neodcházejte!" *Listy*, no. 3–4 (July 1980): 18–20; Vilém Prečan, "Právo na vlastní odpovědnost, riziko i šance," *Listy*, no. 3–4 (July 1980): 21–24; Michal Plzák and Magdalena Čechlovská, *Jiřina Šiklová, Bez ohlávky: Rozhovory* (Prague: Kalich, 2011), 156; Císař, *Paměti: Nejen o zákulisí Pražského jara*, 1011; Ludvík Vaculík, *Český snář* (Prague: Atlantis, 1990), 110, 118; Adam Michnik, *Letters from Prison and Other Essays* (Berkeley: University of California Press, 1987), 16–24; Jiří Lederer, *Touhy a iluze (vzpomínání do srpna 68)* (Toronto: Sixty-Eight Publishers, 1984), 209; Alexandr Kliment, *Nuda v Čechách* (Toronto: 68 publishers, 1978), 14; Milan Šimečka, "O odchodu do světa," *Listy* 14, no. 4 (July 1984): 34.

31. Vladimír Tosek to Erik Jančík, Reading, December 7, 1970.

32. Vladimír Tosek to Derek Viney, Reading, November 30, 1970.

33. Peter C. J. Hill, "The BBC Monitoring Service—A Short Engineering History," *2010 Second Region 8 IEEE Conference on the History of Communications* (n.d.: Madrid 2010), 1–4; Kevin D'Arcy, "Monitors for Freedom," *Sunday Telegraph* (London), September 1, 1968.

34. "BBC Monitoring Service," Caversham Park, Fact Sheet 41, 1982; Maureen Johnson, "House with an Attentive Ear on World's Radio," *Bangkok Post*, January 4, 1982, NA, FCO 26/2362; J. L. Bullard, Eastern European and Soviet department to BBC Monitoring Service, July 16, 1974, NA, FCO 26/1687.

35. Zuzana Slobodová, "Nežná revolúcia v anglickom Readingu," in *Volá Londýn: Historie českého a slovenského BBC (1939–2006)*, ed. Milan Kocourek (Prague: Otovo nakladatelstvi, 2013), 288–90; Zuzana Slobodová, interviewed by Daniela Spenser, London, May 5, 2021.

36. Ruth to Pelikán, London, August 28, 1975, FJP, box 16; Andrej A. Amalrik, *Udrží se Sovětský Svaz do roku 1984?* (Cologne: Index, 1971); Arnošt Kolman, *Zaslepená generace* (Brno: Host, 2005).

37. Ruth Tosková, letter to Daniela Spenser, January 23, 1977. See, Ruth Tosek in Brian Johnson, Flessati and Groom, writers, *The Secret War*, 1:27:18–1:28:15.

38. Tony Judt, *Postwar: A History of Europe since 1945* (London: Penguin Books, 2006), *Postwar*, 566–70.

39. Ruth Tosková to Daniela Spenser, Reading, January 23, 1977; March 19, 1977; April 19, 1977; May 9, 1977; May 20, 1977; August 28, 1977; Vladimír Tosek, "The Czechs Betrayed," *Spectator*, August 19, 1978; Pplk. Růžička, náčelník odboru dopravní služby, vyšetřovací sektor STB, Prague, Czech Republic, May 4, 1977, and October 25, 1979, ABS fond V/MV signatura V-34970.

40. Pelikán to Tosek, Rome, August 8, 1970; Pelikán to the Toseks, Rome, Italy, November 4, 1970.

41. Invoice, Škoda 1000 MB, reg. no. AM-37–97, September 30, 1970; Mjr. Komínek, "Tosek, Vladimír, čs. emigrant-předání poznatků," November 25, 1971, ABS, KR-829886 MV _1_2, f. 125; "Vyhodnocení objektovaného podsvazku, č. 2372/2 k osobě Vladimíra Toska," December 13, 1972, ABS KR-829886.

42. Paulina Bren, *The Greengrocer and His TV: The Culture of Communism after 1968 Prague Spring* (Ithaca, NY: Cornell University Press, 2010), 8, 63–84; Jan Zelenka, "Zpráva o problematice československé emigrace," *Česká televize*, no. 2 (January 1971): 4–10; Lubomír Štrougal at the meeting of ÚV KSČ in February 1971, NA, fond ÚV KSČ, 9149/1971; "Obchod s důvěrou," 1970; "Svědectví od Seiny," 1970, YouTube video, 2007; "Skandál v Římě," *Listy*, no. 3 (June 1976): 11.

43. Karel Steklý, dir., *Za volantem nepřítel*, Filmové Studio Barrandov 1974; *Listy*, no. 4 (May 1975): 47.

44. Martin Štoll, *Television and Totalitarianism in Czechoslovakia: From the Democratic Republic to the Fall of Communism* (New York: Bloomsbury, 2019), 199–200; Daniel Růžička, *Major Zeman—Propaganda nebo krimi? Zákulisí vzniku televizního seriálu* (Prague: Práh, 2005); Jan Fingerland, *Major Zeman bojuje se sionisty: Obraz Židů, sionismu a holokaustu v normalizačním seriálu* (Prague: Dvarim meatim studie pro Jiřinu Šedinovou, 2016), 239–58; David Hertl, "Televizní tvář pražského jara má svou karikaturu v Majoru Zemanovi: Kdo byl Vladimír Tosek doopravdy?" *Česká rozhlas*, December 7, 2017; Muriel Blaive, "The Greengrocer and His TV by Paulina Bren: The Culture of Communism after the 1968 Prague Spring," *American Historical Review* 117, no. 3 (June 2012): 960–61; Annemarie Sammartino, "We Are the State We Seek: Everyday Life in Czechoslovakia and East Germany, 1945–89," *Contemporary European History* 21, no. 3 (August 2012): 477–91.

45. Jarmila Cysařová, "Československá televize a politická moc," *Soudobé dějiny* 9, no. 3–4 (2002): 533–35; Zdenka Tichotová, email to Daniela Spenser, April 7, 2021.

46. Bren, *Greengrocer and His TV*, 202.

47. Tosek's association with Cyril Jonsen reappeared in another of the Ministry of the Interior's invention *Vysoká hra* (1977). See Martin Vadas, director, *Nízká vysoká hra*, Česká televise, 2014, 86:00.

48. Ruth Tosková, letter to Daniela Spenser, April 17, 1982.

Chapter 12

1. "Proč nesmíme mlčet?" *Listy*, no. 1 (January 1971): 1–2; "Socialistické hnutí čs. občanů," *Listy*, no. 1 (January 1971): 3–5; Dušan Havlíček, *Listy v exilu* (Olomouc: Burian and Tichák, 2008), 19; Francesco Caccamo, "Mezi exilem, domácí opozicí a mezinárodním veřejným míněním: Exilový časopis Listy," *Soudobé dějiny* 20, no. 3 (2013): 345–78; Pelikán to Havlíček, Rome, April 2, 1970, in Jiří Pelikán and Dušan Havlíček, *Psáno z Říma, psáno ze Ženevy: Korespondence 1969–1989* (Olomouc: Buran and Tichák, 2013), 19–20; Havlíček to Pelikán, Geneva, October 11, 1970, in Pelikán and Havlíček, *Psáno z Říma, psáno ze Ženevy*, 29–31; Kristina Andělová, Jiří Suk, and Tomás Zahradnícek, *Pro nás dejiny nekončí: Politická prace a myšlení levicového exilu (1968–1989)* (Prague: Argo, 2023). Apparently, two initial issues of *Listy* were published in 1970.

2. Petr Orság, *Mezi realitou, propagandou a mýty: Československá exilová média v západní Evropě v letech 1968–1989* (Prague: Lidové Noviny, 2016), 133–76.

3. Jiřina Šiklová, "Co pro nás doma znamenají iListy (Několik postřehů k 10. výročí)," *Listy*, no. 1 (February 1980): 7–8; Michal Plzák and Magdalena Čechlovská, eds., *Jiřina Šiklová bez ohlávky: Rozhovory* (Prague: Kalich, 2011); Vilém Prečan, ed., *Kočka, která nikdy nespí II/The Cat Who Never Sleeps II* (Prague: James H. Ottaway, Jr, 2015).

4. Vladimír Kusín to Pelikán, no place, January 29, 1973, FJP, box 16; Havlíček to Pelikán, Geneva, December 11, 1976, in Pelikán and Havlíček, *Psáno z Říma, psáno ze Ženevy*, 122–24; Pelikán to Havlíček, Rome, December 27,1976, in Pelikán and Havlíček, *Psáno z Říma, psáno ze Ženevy*, 124–27.

5. Havlíček to Pelikán, Geneva, August 1, 1976, in Pelikán and Havlíček, *Psáno z Říma, psáno ze Ženevy*, 116–19; Ludvík Vaculík, *Český snář* (Prague: Atlantis, 1990), 17.

6. Tony Judt, *Postwar: A History of Europe since 1945* (London: Penguin Books, 2006), 566–67; Jiří Pelikán, "Pražské jaro a jeho význam pro socialistickou teorii a praxi," *Listy*, no. 1 (February 1973): 33–37; Pelikán, "Nová situace—nové možnosti," *Listy*, no. 4 (August 1973): 5–9.

7. Jiří Suk, "Disent jako morální výzva a politická skutečnost (1977–1989–2000)," in *Šest kapitol o disentu* (Prague: Ústav pro Soudobé dějiny, 2017), 249–85.

8. "Zpráva o působení československé emigrace na stránkách zahraničního tisku," 1, dubna 1971—30. září 1973 a 1. října 1973—8. února 1975, Prague, Czech Republic, Český úřad pro tisk a informace, FJP, box 10.

9. Pelikán to Vladimír and Ruth Tosek, Rome, February 4, 1975, p.a.; Radovan Schovánek, "Atentát na Pelikána," *Minulost*, June 6, 2015.

10. Jiří Pelikán, *S'ils me tuent* (Paris: Grasset, 1975); Francesco Caccamo, *Jiří Pelikán a jeho cesta socialismem 20. Století* (Brno: Doplnek, 2008), 109–10, n. 24.

11. "Dubček žaluje," *Listy*, no. 3 (April 1975): 1–15; Václav Havel, "Dopis," *Listy*, no. 5 (July 1975): 32–43.

12. Pelikán to Prečan, Rome, August 20,1976, the archive of Vilém Prečan (hereafter AVP); Vilém Prečan et al., eds., "Sedm pražských dnů. 21.-27. srpen 1968. Dokumentace," Historický ústav ČSAV, September 1968, unpublished. Published under the same title in Prague: Československá Akademie Věd ed., *Sedm pražských dnů: 21.—27. srpen 1968: Dokumentace* (Prague: Academia, 1990); Milan Šimečka, "Fejeton o loučení," *Listy*, no. 6 (December 1976): 24–25; Prečan to Pelikán, Edesse, August 28, 1976; Prečan to Pelikán, Edesse, December 21, 1976, AVP; Francis D. Raška, *The Long Road to Victory: A History of Czechoslovak Exile Organizations* (Boulder, CO: East European Monographs, 2012), 135–48; Michael Žantovský, *Havel: A Life* (New York: Grove Press, 2014), 255.

13. "CHARTA 77," *Listy*, no. 1 (February 1977): 1–4.

14. Tom Stoppard, "Prague: The Story of the Chartists," *New York Review of Books*, August 4, 1977; "Charter 77—document no. 5," *Listy*, no. 2 (May 1977): 50–52.

15. Pelikán to Prečan, February 15, 1977, delivered personally by Karel Kaplan; Caccamo, *Jiří Pelikán*, 56–57. I owe this insight to the Czech historian Jiří Suk.

16. Tony Judt, "The Dilemmas of Dissidence: The Politics of Opposition in East-Central Europe," in *Eastern Europe: Continuity and Change (1987–1995)*, eds. Irena Grudzińska-Gross and Andrzej W. Tymowski (Frankfurt am Main: Peter Lang, 2014), 75–76; Gordon H. Skilling, *Charter 77 and Human Rights in Czechoslovakia* (London: George Allen & Unwin, 1981), 209–12; Jiří Suk, "Podrobná zpráva o paralelní polis. Nad korespondencí Václava Havla a Františka Janoucha," in Václav Havel, *Václav Havel, František Janouch, Korespondence 1978–2001* (Prague: Akropolis, 2007), 29; Zdenko Pavelka, *Petr Uhl, Dělal jsem, co jsem považoval za správné* (Prague: Torst, 2013), 168; Jiří Suk, "Politika jako absurdní drama. Václav Havel v letech 1975–1989," (PhD diss., Akademie věd České republiky, 2014), 12–19.

17. Alessandro Catalano, "Zdeněk Mlynář and the Search for Socialist Opposition. From an Active Politician to a Dissident to Editorial Work in Exile," *Czech Journal of Contemporary History* 3 (2015): 90–156.

18. Catalano, "Zdeněk Mlynář and the Search for Socialist Opposition," 100–102.

19. Adolf Müller to Zdeněk Mlynář, Cologne, September 14, 1978, FZM, box 4; Zdeněk Mlynář, *Mráz přichází z Kremlu* (Cologne: Index, 1979); Hejzlar to Pelikán, Stockholm, August 28, 1977, FJP, box 4; Pelikán to Havlíček, Sperlonga, August 17, 1977, in Pelikán and Havlíček, *Psáno z Říma, psáno ze Ženevy*, 147; Catalano, "Zdeněk Mlynář and the Search for Socialist Opposition," 118.

20. Jiří Pelikán, "Pražské jaro není konec, nýbrž začátek: Ani reforma, ani revoluce—nové cesty ve východní Evropě," *Listy*, extra issue (December 1978): 44–51; Zdeněk Hejzlar to Pelikán, Stockholm, Sweden, June 19, 1979, FJP, box 4.

21. Zdeněk Mlynář, "Československo po deseti letech," *Listy*, extra issue, (December 1978): 35–38; Zdeněk Hejzlar, "Reformní komunismus nepatří minulosti," *Listy*, extra issue, (December 1978): 38–40; Zdeněk Mlynář, "Kritika a úvahy o dalších možnostech skupiny Listy," March 8, 1979, FJP, box 4.

22. Zdeněk Hejzlar, "K diskusi o činnosti a možnostech v exilu," Stockholm, Sweden, April 1, 1979, FJP, box 4; Pelikán, "Poznámky k diskusi o další práci skupiny Listy," 1979, FJP, box 4.

23. "Prohlášení skupiny Listy k Polsku," *Listy*, no. 6 (December 1980): 2. In the Czech journalist Jiří Lederer, by then in exile, *Listy* found a knowledgeable reporter

and analyst of the Polish events from the beginning to the end. See also Adam Michnik, "My všichni jsme rukojmí," *Listy*, no. 2 (May 1982): 9–15; "Milý Jean," no date, no place, probably from Vladimír Mlynář Jr. and Jan Dobrovský in Prague to Pelikán, n.d. FZM, box 7.

24. "Pelikán v evropském parlamentě," *Listy*, no. 4 (September 1979): 2–4; Pelikán to Prečan, Verona-Milan, Italy, May 14, 1984, AVP.

25. Pelikán to Havlíček, Rome-Milan, May 2, 1984, in Pelikán and Havlíček, *Psáno z Říma, psáno ze Ženevy*, 255.

26. Prečan to Havel, Frankfurt, via Scheur, February 7, 1984, in *Václav Havel-Vilém Prečan:Korespondence 1983–1989*, ed. Vojtěch Čelko (Prague: Československé dokumentační středisko, 2011), 153; Havel to Prečan, Prague, February 24, 1984, via Scheur, 160, Prague, Československé dokumentační středisko, 2011; Havlíček to Pelikán, December 29, 1978, in Pelikán and Havlíček, *Psáno z Říma, psáno ze Ženevy*, 190–91; Pelikán to Havlíček, Sperlonga, July 26, 1981, 217; Havlíček to Pelikán, Plan-les-Ouates, July 13, 1981, in Pelikán and Havlíček, *Psáno z Říma, psáno ze Ženevy*, 228; Pelikán to Prečan, Verona-Milan, Italy, May 14, 1984; Prečan to Pelikán, May 21, 1984, AVP.

27. Vladimír Tosek, alias Ital, ABS, KR_829886_MV_2_2, 65.

28. Pelikán to Havlíček, Rome, January 22, 1984, in Pelikán and Havlíček, *Psáno z Říma, psáno ze Ženevy*, 246; "Vloupání do redakce Listy," *Listy*, no. 1 (February 1983): 45. I was in Rome with my mother when the burglaries happened.

29. Pelikán to Havlíček, Rome, January 22, 1984, in Pelikán and Havlíček, *Psáno z Říma, psáno ze Ženevy*, 247–48; Pelikán, "Schůze redakčního kruhu Listy," Rome, Italy, March 6, 1984, FJP, box 16.

30. Pelikán to Janouch, Rome, January 5, 1985, in František Janouch, *Korespondence: František Janouch / Jiří Pelikán* (Prague: Novela bohemica, 2015), 213; Zdeněk Mlynář, "Nový muž před starými problémy," *Listy*, no. 2 (April 1984):1–4; Pelikán to Prečan, Rome-Brussels, May 19, 1985, AVP; William Taubman, *Gorbachev: His Life and Times* (New York: W. W. Norton, 2017), 203–19.

31. Zdeněk Mlynář, "Stagnace končí," *Listy*, no. 2 (April 1985): 1–2; Zdeněk Mlynář, "Můj spolužák Michail Gorbačov," *Listy*, no. 4 (July 1985): 22–24; AZ, "Gorbačov—a co dál?" *Listy*, no. 5 (October 1985): 1–4; Jiří Pelikán and Antonio Carioti, *Jiří Pelikán—Nepohodlný exulant: Rozhovor s Antoniem Cariotem* (Prague: Novela Bohemica, 2015), 86–88.

32. W. Loth, "Moscow, Prague and Warsaw: Overcoming the Brezhnev Doctrine," *Cold War History* 1, no. 2 (2001): 103–18; Jiří Suk, "Zlom mezi 'totalitou' a 'demokracií': Československý rok 1989 v alternativách," *Soudobé dějiny* 16, no. 4 (2009): 557–601; Vilém Prečan, "Svědectví o rozpadu 'socialistického společenství': Ukázky z memoárů Michaila Gorbačova, Vadima Medveděva a Valerije Musatova," *Soudobé dějiny* 5, no. 4 (1998): 509–54; Rudolf Slánský, "Změny v Moskvě—Změny v Praze?" *Listy*, no. 5 (December 1985): 1–6; AZ, "Naděje na reformu ožila," *Listy*, no. 1 (February 1986): 24–27; Zdeněk Mlynář, "Reforma v SSSR začala," *Listy*, no. 2 (April 1986): 4–5.

33. Jan Litomiský, Libuše Šilhanová, and Josef Vohryzek, "Dopis Michailu Gorbačovovi," in *Charta 77 (1977–1989)—Od morální k demokratické revoluci*, ed. Vilém Prečan (Scheinfeld: Centre for independent literature, 1990), 324–26.

34. Taubman, *Gorbachev*, 379–81; Zdeněk Mlynář, "Gorbachev v Brežněvově objetí," *Listy*, no. 2 (April 1987):1–4; Alex Pravda, "Politika optimismu a opatrnosti: Mosk-

va a východní Evropa na konci 80. let," *Soudobé dějiny* 18, no. 1–2 (2011): 86–119; Svetlana Savranskaya, "The Logic of 1989: The Soviet Peaceful Withdrawal from Eastern Europe," in *Masterpieces of History: The Peaceful End of the Cold War in Europe, 1989*, ed. Svetlana Savranskaya, Thomas Blanton, and Vladislav Zubok (Budapest: National Security Archive Cold War Reader, 2010), 1–48; Document no. 11: Notes from CC CPSU Politburo Session. Report on Mikhail Gorbachev's Visit to Czechoslovakia, April 16, 1987, 248; Mark Kramer, "The Dialectics of Empire: Soviet Leaders and the Challenge of Civil Resistance in East-Central Europe, 1968–1991," in *Civil Resistance and Power Politics: The Experience of Non-Violent Action from Gandhi to the Present*, ed. Adam Roberts and Timothy Garton Ash (Oxford: Oxford University Press, 2009), 91–109. In his memoirs, published in 1995, Gorbachev explained why he did not admit until 1989 that the military intervention in 1968 was unfounded and wrong: "I had the impression that the Czechoslovak leadership headed by Husák was ready to embark on the road of democratization and reforms; in that case the question of the re-evaluation of the events in the year 1968 would arise by itself." Prečan, "Svědectví o rozpadu 'socialistického společenství,'" 522; Eric Hobsbawm, *Interesting Times: A Twentieth Century Life* (London: Allen Lane, 2002), 150–51.

35. Václav Havel, "Setkání s Gorbačovem," *Listy*, no. 5 (October 1987): 47–48; Žantovský, *Havel*, 269–70.

36. Jiří Pelikán, "Gorbachov, evropská levice a Pražské jaro," *Listy*, no. 4 (July 1988): 1–2.

37. Prečan to Pelikán, Scheinfeld, April 8, 1988, AVP; Havel to Prečan, Hrádeček and Prague, June 22, 1988, in Čelko, *Václav Havel-Vilém Prečan*, 579.

38. Havlíček to Pelikán, Geneva, October 22, 1987, in Pelikán and Havlíček, *Psáno z Říma, psáno ze Ženevy*, 277–80 and note 102; Zdeněk Hejzlar, Zdeněk Mlynář, Adolf Müller, and Jiří Pelikán, "Statement of the Group LISTY on the Twentieth Anniversary of the Prague Spring," *Listy*, no. 1 (February 1988): 2–3; Zdeněk Mlynář, "Prague—January 1968," *Listy*, no. 1 (February 1988): 4–6; Prečan to Havel, Scheinfeld, February 23, 1988, in Čelko, *Václav Havel-Vilém Prečan*, 564.

39. "Pohled na rok 1968 po dvaceti letech, Index-video," FJP, box 27.

40. Pelikán to Janouch, Rome, December 11, 1987, in Janouch, *Korespondence: František Janouch / Jiří Pelikán*, 227; Michael Simmons, "Burial rights," *Guardian*, December 9, 1987.

41. Havel to Prečan, Prague, April 25, 1988, in Čelko, *Václav Havel-Vilém Prečan*, 569; Havel to Prečan, June 19 and 20, 1988, in Čelko, *Václav Havel-Vilém Prečan*, 578–79; Jacques Rupnik, "Fateful Eights in Czechoslovak History," in *Střední Evropa je jako pták s očima vzadu* (Prague: Novela Bohemica, 2018), 5–31.

42. Timothy Garton Ash, "The Prague Advertisement," in *The Uses of Adversity: Essays on the Fate of Central Europe* (New York: Vintage, 1990), 229.

43. Ash, "The Prague Advertisement," 128–241; Statement by Ambassador Warren Zimmermann, Chairman of the US delegation to the Conference on Security and Cooperation in Europe's meeting, Vienna, November 15, 1988; Walter J. Jeffrey, General Secretary of the Writers' Guild of Great Britain, to Geoffrey Howe, Secretary of State for Foreign and Commonwealth Affairs, London, November 17, 1988; D. R. Todd to Camilla Blair, British embassy, "Czechoslovakia: Symposium, Czechoslovakia 88,"

Prague, Czech Republic, November 18, 1988; Camilla Blair to Lord Avebury, Eastern European Department, November 28, 1988; "Czechoslovak crackdown on dissent continues," NATO confidential, December 12, 1988; "Dissidence in Czechoslovakia," J. R. Banks to Camilla Blair, East European Section research department, London, December 14, 1988, NA, FCO 28/8377.

Chapter 13

1. Timothy Garton Ash, "Prague: Inside the Magic Lantern," in *The Magic Lantern: The Revolution of 1989 Witnessed in Warsaw, Budapest, Berlin and Prague* (New York: Random House, 1990), 78–130; Ash, "The Empire in Decay," *New York Review of Books*, September 29,1988. For a complementary view,, see Padraic Kenney, *A Carnival of Revolution: Central Europe 1989* (Princeton, NJ: Princeton University Press, 2002); Petr Pithart, *Po Devětaosmdesátém: Rozpomínání a přemítání* (Prague: Academia, 2015); Jiří Suk, *Labyrintem revoluce: Aktéři, zápletky a křižovatky jedné politické krize* (Prague: Prostor, 2020); Petr Blažek, *Happeningem proti totalitě: Společnost za veselejší současnost v roce 1989* (Prague: ÚSTR, 2022).

2. Václav Havel, "Vyložené karty," *Listy*, no. 1 (February 1989): 1–3; Komunistická strana Československa. Ústřední výbor. Zasedání, *Poslední hurá: stenografický záznam z mimořádných zasedání ÚV KSČ 24. a 26. listopadu 1989* (Prague: Cesty, 1992). It´s a stenographic record2 of the last meeting of the party.

3. Jiří Pelikán, "Nadějný rok?" *Listy*, no. 1 (February 1989): 1–4.

4. "Soud nad Václavem Havlem," and "Závěrečná řeč Václava Havla v odvolacím řízení u městského soudu v Praze," *Listy*, no. 2 (April 1989): 4 and 85; Vilém Prečan, ed., *Václav Havel, do různých stran: Eseje a články z let 1983–1989* (Prague: Lidové noviny, 1990), 375–80.

5. Rudolf Slánský, "Dubček a Havel po dvaceti letech," *Listy*, no. 4 (August 1989): 5.

6. Jiří Pelikán, "Alexander Dubček v Itálii; Projev Alexandra Dubčeka při udělování čestného doktorátu university v Bologni," *Listy*, no. 1 (February 1989): 8–12; Luciano Antonetti, "Alexander Dubček v Itálii: Symbol pražského jara po dvaceti letech," *Soudobé dějiny* 15, no. 3–4 (2008): 670–85; Michal Reiman, "Setkání s Alexandrem Dubčekem ve Vídni v listopadu 1988," *Soudobé dějiny* 10, no. 1 (2008): 36–146; Francesco Caccamo, *Jiří Pelikán a jeho cesta socialismem 20. Století* (Brno: Doplnek, 2008), 96–99; Jiří Pelikán and Antonio Carioti, *Jiří Pelikán—Nepohodlný exulant: Rozhovor s Antoniem Cariotem* (Prague: Novela Bohemica, 2015), 89–91; Slánský, "Dubček a Havel po dvaceti letech," 5.

7. Pavel Tigrid, "Zpráva o stavu střední Evropy," *Svědectví*, no. 87 (1989): 524–25.

8. Zdeněk Mlynář, "Čeho se bojí?" *Listy*, no. 4 (August 1989): 46–47; Jiří Pelikán, "Nové naděje, ale bez iluzí," *Listy*, no. 3 (August 1989): 4.

9. "Prohlášení přípravného výboru Klubu za socialistickou přestavbu OBRODA," *Listy*, no. 2 (April 1989): 20–22; Karel Kyncl, "O nové iniciativě Obroda," *Listy*, no. 2 (April 1989): 20–21; Miloš Hájek, "Proč vznikla Obroda," *Listy*, no. 4 (August 1989): 21; "Sdělení výboru klubu Obroda," *Listy*, no. 5 (October 1989): 47–48; "Teze Levé alternativy, hnutí za demokratický a samosprávný socialismus," November 26, 1989, FZM, box 5; Čestmír Císař, *Paměti: Nejen o zákulisí Pražského jara* (Prague: SinCon, 2005), 1164–166.

10. Alex Pravda, "Moscow and Eastern Europe, 1988–1989: A Policy of Optimism and Caution," in *Imposing, Maintaining, and Tearing Open the Iron Curtain: The Cold War*

and East-Central Europe, 1945–1989, ed. Mark Kramer and Vít Smetana (Lanham, MD: Lexington Books, 2014), 305–34; Svetlana Savranskaya, "The Logic of 1989: The Soviet Peaceful Withdrawal from Eastern Europe," in *Masterpieces of History: The Peaceful End of the Cold War in Europe, 1989* ed. Svetlana Savranskaya, Thomas Blanton, and Vladislav Zubok (Budapest: National Security Archive Cold War Reader, 2010); Timothy Garton Ash, "1989!," *New York Review of Books*, November 5, 2009; Petr Blažek and Jaroslav Pážout, eds., *Dominový efekt: Opoziční hnutí v zemích střední Evropy a pád komunistických režimů v roce 1989* (Prague: Ústav pro Soudobé dějiny Akademie věd ČR, 2013); Jiří Pelikán, "Velký průlom: Poláci a my," *Listy*, no. 5 (October 1989): 1, 3–6.

11. Jiří Pelikán, "Nové naděje, ale bez iluzí," *Listy*, no. 3 (August 1989): 1–4; Slánský, "Dubček a Havel po dvaceti letech," 5; T. "Jak to bylo 21. srpna 1989 v Praze," *Listy*, no. 5 (October 1989): 75–77.

12. Havel to Prečan, Hrádeček, July 19, 1989, in *Václav Havel-Vilém Prečan:Korespondence 1983–1989*, ed. Vojtech Čelko (Prague: Československé dokumentační středisko, 2011), 603.

13. Václav Havel, "Words on Words," *New York Review of Books*, January 18, 1990; Václav Havel, "Slovo o slovu," *Listy*, no. 6 (December 1989): 37–40; Havel to Gunther Christiansen, Hrádeček, July 1, 1989, in Čelko, *Václav Havel-Vilém Prečan*, 752–53; Havel to Richard von Weizsäscker, Prague, November 5, 1989, in Čelko, *Václav Havel-Vilém Prečan*, 770.

14. Jakub Doležal, "Přes ambasády ke svobodě: Drama východoněmeckého exodu v roce 1989," *Soudobé dějiny* 21, no. 1–2 (2014): 79–133; Oldřich Tůma, "9.00, Praha-Libeň, horní nádraží. Exodus východních Němců přes Prahu v září 1989," *Soudobé dějiny* 6, no. 2–3 (1999): 147–64; Oldřich Tůma, "Pad berlínské zdi," *Soudobé dějiny* 9, no. 2 (2002): 230–40; Jiří Suk, "Zlom mezi 'totalitou' a 'demokracií': Československý rok 1989 v alternativách," *Soudobé dějiny* 16, no. 4 (2009): 557–601; Michael Kocáb, *Vabank. 1989–1991: Sametová revoluce. Odchod sovětských vojsk* (Prague: Universum, 2019).

15. Jiří Suk, "Vznik občanského fóra a proměny jeho struktury (19. listopad-10. prosinec 1989)," *Soudobé dějiny* 2, no. 1 (1995): 17–41; Pelikán and Carioti, *Jiří Pelikán—nepohodlný exulant*, 91–92.

16. Jiří Pelikán, "Konečně!" *Listy*, no. 6 (December 1989): 1–2; Pelikán to Dear (Vladinir Mlynář Jr. and Jan Dobrovský), December 9, 1989, FJP, box 16; Jiří Pelikán, "Omluva Československu za rok 1968," *Listy*, no. 6 (December 1989): 10; Dalimil, "Návrat do dějin," *Listy*, no. 6 (December 1989):13–14; Jiří Suk, "Alexander Dubček—velký státník, nebo politický symbol?" *Soudobé dějiny* 9, no. 1 (2002): 92–103; Jiří Suk, *Labyrintem revoluce: Aktéři, zápletky a křižovatky jedné politické krize* (Prague: Prostor, 2020); Ivan Klíma, *My Crazy Century: A Memoir* (New York: Grove Press, 2010),, 414.

17. Alessandro Catalano, "Zdeněk Mlynář a hledání socialistické opozice: Od aktivní politiky přes disent k ediční činnosti v exilu," *Soudobé dějiny* 22, no. 3 (2013): 277–344; Daniel Kaiser, *Disident: Václav Havel 1936–1989* (Prague: Paseka, 2009), 230–31; Vilém Prečan, in *Exil a domov: Odchody a návraty* (Prague: Heinrich Böll Foundation, 1993, 34.

18. Pavel Bergmann to Mlynář, Prague, Czech Republic, December 8, 1989; Unsigned forty former members of KSČ, Roudnice, n. d.; Unsigned, retirees from Pardubice, December 9, 1969; Vera Tomanová to Mlynář, Náchod, December 11, 1989; A.

Hajská, Prague, Czech Republic, December 12, 1989; Václav Soukup to Zdeněk Mlynář, Prague, Czech Republic, December 29, 1989, FZM, box 8.

19. Michael Kocáb, *Vabank. 1989–1991: Sametová revoluce. Odchod sovětských vojsk* (Prague: Universum, 2019), 220–59; Petr Pithart, *Po Devětaosmdesátém: Rozpomínání a přemítání* (Prague: Academia, 2015), 37; Václav Havel, Dana Emingerová, and Luboš Beniak, "'Uncertain Strength': An Interview with Václav Havel," trans. Paul Wilson, *New York Review of Books*, August 15, 1991; Timothy Garton Ash, "A Century of Civil Resistance," in *Civil Resistance and Power Politics*, ed. Adam Roberts and Timothy Garton Ash (Oxford: Oxford University Press, 2009), 375.

20. Prečan to Havel, Scheinfeld, December 26, 1989, in Čelko, *Václav Havel-Vilém Prečan*, 627–28; JH, "K situaci československé historiografie," *Listy*, no. 5 (October 1989): 78–79.

21. Janouch to Havel, Stockholm, February 13, 1990; Janouch to Havel, Björknäs, June 20, 1990; Prague, July 10, 1990, in Václav Havel, *Václav Havel, František Janouch, Korespondence 1978–2001* (Prague: Akropolis, 2007), 426–29. Much of their communication is lost to the historians after 1989, because then they could use the telephone or fax.

22. Janouch to Marián Čalfa, prime minister of Czechoslovakia, Helsinki, May 31, 1992, in František Janouch, *Korespondence: František Janouch / Jiří Pelikán* (Prague: Novela bohemica, 2015), 280.

23. Janouch to Havel, Stockholm, April 5, 1991, in Janouch, *Korespondence: František Janouch / Jiří Pelikán*, 432–33; Janouch to Havel, Björknäs, April 28, 1991, in Janouch, *Korespondence: František Janouch / Jiří Pelikán*, 435–43; Janouch to Havel, Helsinki, July 20, 1992, in Janouch, *Korespondence: František Janouch / Jiří Pelikán*, 442, Janouch to Havel, Prague, March 22, 1994, in Janouch, *Korespondence: František Janouch / Jiří Pelikán*, 448–49; Havel to Janouch, Prague, Czech Republic, March 24, 1994; Janouch to Havel, Björknäs, April 5, 1994, in Janouch, *Korespondence: František Janouch / Jiří Pelikán*, 450–51.

24. Anna Grůšová and Helena Vávrová, "Po roce 1968 (pohledem dcer)," in *Vzpomínky 1945–1968*, ed. Eduard Goldstücker (Prague: G Plus G, 2005), 165–69 (Eduard Goldstücker lived from 1913 to 2000); Timothy Garton Ash, "Intellectuals and Politicians," in *History of the Present: Essays, Sketches and Dispatches from Europe in the 1990s* (London: Penguin, 2000), 150–79. I want to register their years of birth and death.

25. Ota Šik to Pelikán, n.d. 1997, FJP, box 28. Ota Šik lived from 1919 to 2004).

26. Jiří Kosta, *Život mezi úzkostí a nadějí* (Prague: Paseka, 2002) 158–59; Dušan Havlíček, *Listy v exilu* (Olomouc: Burian and Tichák, 2008), 7; Havlíček to Pelikán, Geneva, March 25, 1991, in Jiří Pelikán and Dušan Havlíček, *Psáno z Říma, psáno ze Ženevy: Korespondence 1969–1989* (Olomouc: Buran and Tichák, 2013), 285–87; Bedřich Utitz, *Kaleidoskop mého století* (Prague: Academia, 2013), 207–14. Jiří Kosta lived from 1921 to 2015; Dušan Havlíček from 1923 to 2018; Bedřich Utitz from 1920 to 2017.

27. Karel Kovanda, email to Daniela Spenser, Bánská Bystrica, Slovakia, August 15, 2021. Pavel Tigrid lived from 1917 to 2003; Ivan Medek from 1925 to 2010; Karel Schwarzenberg from 1937 to 2023; Jiří Dienstbier from 1937 to 2011. These were Havel's friends and close collaborators before and after he became the Czechoslovak president.

28. Karel Kovanda, *Já a moje peníze* (Prague: Lidové noviny, 1992).

29. Zdeněk Mlynář, *Can Gorbachev Change the Soviet Union?* trans. Ruth Tosková and Marian Sling (Boulder, CO: Westview Press, 1990); Zdeněk Mlynář, *Socialistou na*

volné noze (Prague: Prospektrum, 1992); Michail Gorbachev and Zdeněk Mlynář, *Reformátoři nebývají šťastní* (Prague: Victoria, 1995); Zdeněk Mlynář, *Proti srsti: Politické komentáře 1990–1995* (Prague: Periskop, 1996); Alessandro Catalano, "Zdeněk Mlynář and the Search for Socialist Opposition From an Active Politician to a Dissident to Editorial Work in Exile," *Czech Journal of Contemporary History* 3 (2015): 91–156; Jan Štern, "Potřebujeme Výbor na obranu nespravedlivě skandalizovaných?" *Listy*, no. 2 (1992): 47–48; Boris Buden, *Konec poskomunismu: Od společnosti bez naděje k naději bez společnosti* (Prague: Rybka, 2013); Michal Pullmann, *Konec experimentu: Přestavba a pád komunismu v Československu* (Prague: Scriptorium, 2011), 185–215.

30. Jiří Pelikán, "Kdo byl podveden," *Lidové noviny*, April 17, 1992, in Janouch, *Korespondence: František Janouch / Jiří Pelikán*, 281–83; Havlíček to Pelikán, Geneva, January 28, 1991, in Pelikán and Havlíček, *Psáno z Říma, psáno ze Ženevy*, 282; Pelikán to Havlíček, Rome, February 5, 1991, *in Pelikán and Havlíček, Psáno z Říma, psáno ze Ženevy*, 283–84. See Lubomír Blažek, Office for documentation and investigation of the StB activities to Jiří Pelikán, March 18, 1993, "Research relative to this your matter is with this terminated," in Janouch, *Korespondence: František Janouch / Jiří Pelikán*, 283–84. Archiv bezpečnostních složek became available for research in 2008. Pelikán and Carioti, *Jiří Pelikán—nepohodlný exulant*, 88–92; Caccamo, *Jiří Pelikán*, 100–110; Pelikán to Prečan, Rome, Italy, April 8, 1996, AVP; Suk, "Zlom mezi 'totalitou' a 'demokracií,'" 573–75; Ash, "Après le Déluge, Nous," in *History of the Present*, 22–47.

31. Petr Pithart, "Chladný vztah domova," *Listy* 23, no. 1 (1993): 48–52; Kohout, *To byl Můj život?*, 251.

32. Václav Havel, *Listy*, no. 1 (February 1990): 5.

33. Havlíček to Pelikán, Geneva, February 25, 1998, *in Pelikán and Havlíček, Psáno z Říma, psáno ze Ženevy*, 303; *Listy domovu 1970–1990*, no. 1 (February 1990): 1; Antonín Liehm, in *Exil a domov. Odchody a návraty*, ed. Nadace Heinricha Bölla (Prague: *Listy*, 1993), 45.

34. Zdeněk Hejzlar to Pelikán, Jävrala, Sweden, June 30, 1991, FJP, box 27.

35. Jiří Pelikán, "Jsme opět doma!" *Listy*, no. 2 (April 1990): 3–5; Jiří Pelikán, "Malá bilance," *Listy*, no. 6 (1991): 3–4; Jiří Pelikán, "Kritický rok," *Listy*, no. 1, (1991): 3–5; Jiří Pelikán, "Nepromarnit historickou šanci," *Listy*, no. 3 (1991): 3–6; Jiří Pelikán, "Volby a demokracie *Listy*, no. 2 (1992): 3–5.

36. Hobsbawm, *Interesting Times*, 151.

37. Pelikán to Petr Uhl, Rome, Italy, May 8, 1994, FJP, box 27.

38. Vladimír Kolmistr to Pelikán, December 27, 1993, FJP, box 27; Tomáš Tichák, email to Daniela Spenser, Olomouc, Czech Republic, September 15, 2021.

39. Jan Štern, "Posledni dopis," *Listy*, no. 4 (1999): 43. Štern (1924–2012), one of the pillars of that bridge.

Epilogue

Epigraph. Tony Judt, *Postwar: A History of Europe since 1945*. London: Penguin Books, 2006, 751.

1. Ruth Tosková to Ing. Josef Škoda, March 21, 1990; Ruth Tosková to the Prague Mayor, June 27, 1990, p.a.

2. Císař, *Paměti*, 1210. Ruth helped the journalist Michael Simmons from the

Guardian to gather material for his book *The Reluctant President: A Political Life of Václav Havel* (London: Methuen, 1991); Mlynář, *Can Gorbachev Change the Soviet Union?*.

3. Marta Marková, *Olga Havlová a ty druhé. Ženy ve vnitřní emigraci* (Brno: Barrister & Principal, 1996), 152–65. Ruth's portrait is full of inaccuracies. Sommerová, *Sedm světel*, 2007.

4. Ruth Tosek, "Žádost o starobní důchod," Ministerstvo národní obrany (MNO), Komise pro vydávání osvedčení podle zákona c. 255/1946 Sb., March 11, 1993, VHA, Ruth Tosková, 310614/93.

5. Tosková interviewed by Benešová.

References

Archives

Archivio storico della Camera dei deputati, Rome, fond Jiří Pelikán (1923–1999)
Czech radio archive, Prague
Czech television archive, Prague
Imperial War Museum (IWM), London
Jabotinsky Institute in Tel Aviv, Israel
Libri prohibiti, Prague
Malach Center for Visual History at Charles University, Prague
Military historical archive (Vojenský Historický Archiv [VHA]), Prague
National archive (Národní archiv), Prague
    Fond Policejní ředitelství (Police directorate)
    Fond Zdeněk Mlynář (FZM)
Personal Archive of Vilém Prečan (AVP), Prague
State Security Archive (Archiv bezpečnostních složek, ABS), Prague
United Nations Relief and Rehabilitation Administration (UNRRA) on microfilm
Wiener Library, London
USC Shoah Foundation Institute, University of Southern California
Yad Vashem, Jerusalem

Other Sources

Abrams, Bradley F. "Morality, Wisdom and Revision: The Czech Opposition of the 1970s and the Expulsion of the Sudeten Germans." *East European Politics and Society* 9, no. 2 (Spring 1995): 234–54.

Adelson, Roger. Review of *Ploughing Sand: British Rule in Palestine 1917–1948*, by Naomi Shepherd. *American Historical Review* 106, no. 4 (October 2001): 1504–5.

Albright, Madeleine. *Prague Winter: A Personal Story of Remembrance and War, 1937–1948*. New York: HarperCollins, 2012.

Amalrik, Andrej A. *Udrží se Sovětský Svaz do roku 1984?* Cologne: Index, 1971.

Andělová, Kristina, Jiří Suk, and Tomáš Zahradníček. *Pro nás dějiny nekončí: Politická práce v myšlení českého levicového exilu (1968–1989)*. Prague: Argo, 2023.

Antonetti, Luciano. "Alexander Dubček v Itálii: Symbol pražského jara po dvaceti letech." *Soudobé dějiny* 15, no. 3–4 (2008): 670–85.

Applebaum, Anne. *Iron Curtain: The Crushing of Eastern Europe 1944–1956*. London: Penguin, 2012.

Arnošt, Frydrych, "Cesta do hlubin divákovy duše." *Reportér*, no. 18 (May 1–7, 1968): 26–27.

Ash, Timothy Garton. "A Century of Civil Resistance." In Roberts and Ash, *Civil Resistance and Power Politics*, 215.

———. "Après le Déluge, Nous." In *History of the Present*, 22–47
———. "The Empire in Decay." *New York Review of Books*, September 29, 1988.
———. *History of the Present: Essays, Sketches and Dispatches from Europe in the 1990s*. London: Penguin, 2000.
———. *Homelands. A Personal History of Europe*. New Haven, CT: Yale University Press, 2023.
———. "Intellectuals and Politicians." In *History of the Present*, 150–73.
———. "The Prague Advertisement." In *The Uses of Adversity: Essays on the Fate of Central Europe*, 229. New York: Vintage, 1990.
———. "Prague: Inside the Magic Lantern." In *The Magic Lantern: The Revolution of 1989 Witnessed in Warsaw, Budapest, Berlin and Prague*, 78–130. New York: Random House, 1990.
AZ. "Gorbačov—a co dál?" *Listy*, no. 5 (October 1985): 1–4.
———. "Naděje na reformu ožila." *Listy*, no. 1 (February 1986): 24–27.
Baletka, Ladislav. *Židé v dějinách Valašského Meziříčí, Vsetín*. Valašské Meziříčí: Publikace Soka Vsetín, 2004.
Banac, Ivo, ed. *The Diary of Georgi Dimitrov 1933–1949*. New Haven, CT: Yale University Press, 2003.
Barber, Noel. *Prisoner of War: The Story of the British Prisoners Held by the Enemy*. London: George G. Harrap, 1944.
Bardgett, Suzanne, and David Cesarani, eds. *Belsen 1945: New Historical Perspectives*. London: Vallentine Mitchell, 2006.
Bárta, Milan. "Cenzura československého filmu a televize v letech 1953–1968." *Securitas Imperii* 10 (2003): 5–57.
———. "My jsme rozhodnutí zneškodnit každého, nikoho se nebojíme." *Paměť a dějiny* 4 (2012): 9–22.
Bartková, Truda. "Očima vzpomínek, 1943-prosincový transport." *Terezínské listy*, no. 21 (1993): 102–5.
———. "Očima vzpomínek. Osvobození v Bergen-Belsenu a návrat domu." *Terezínské listy*, no. 23 (1995): 101–12.
Bauer, Otto. "O poslání emigrace." *Listy*, no. 3 (June 1973): 37–38.
Bauer, Yehuda. "Death Marches." *Modern Judaism*, no. 3 (1983): 1–21.
Beaumont, Joan. "Prisoner of War in the Second World War." *Journal of Contemporary History* 42, no. 3 (July 2007): 535–44.
Běhal, Rostislav. "Rozhlas po nástupu totality 1949–1958." *Od mikrofonu k posluchačům*. Prague: Český rozhlas, 2017.
Bell, Susan Groag. *Between Worlds: In Czechoslovakia, England, and America*. New York: Dutton, 1991.
Benčík, Antonín. "Kauza Karel Hoffmann versus historikové aneb co se dělo v srpnu 1968 na Ústřední správě spojů." *Soudobé dějiny* 11, no. 4 (2004): 130–36.
Beneš, Edvard. "Z Moskvy—po podpisu sovětsko-československé smlouvy (21. prosince 1943)." In *Šest let exilu a druhé světové války: Řeči, projevy a dokumenty z r. 1938–1945*, 212–22. Prague: Orbis, 1946.
Benn, Rita, Julie Goldstein Ellis, Joy Wolfe Ensor and Ruth Wade, eds. *The Ones Who Remember: Second Generation Voices of the Holocaust*. Westport, CT: City Point Press, 2022.

Blaive, Muriel. "The Cold War? I Have It at Home with My Family." In *The Cold War: Historiography, Memory, Representation*, edited by Konrad H. Jarausch, Christian F. Ostermann, and Andreas Erges, 194–214. Berlin: De Gruyter, 2018.

———. "The Greengrocer and His TV by Paulina Bren: The Culture of Communism after the 1968 Prague Spring." *American Historical Review* 117, no. 3 (June 2012): 960–61.

Blatman, Daniel. "The Death Marches January–May 1945: Who Was Responsible for What?" *Yad Vashem Studies* 28 (2000): 155–201.

Blažek, Petr. *Happeningem proti totalitě: Společnost za veselejší současnost v roce 1989*. Prague: ÚSTR, 2022.

Blažek, Petr, and Jaroslav Pážout, eds. *Dominový efekt: Opoziční hnutí v zemích střední Evropy a pád komunistických režimů v roce 1989*. Prague: Ústav pro Soudobé dějiny Akademie věd ČR, 2013.

Blažek, Petr, and Pavel Žáček. "Czechoslovakia." In *A Handbook of the Communist Security Apparatus in East Central Europe, 1944–1989*, edited by Krzysztof Persak and Łukasz Kamiński, 85–161. Warsaw: Institute of National Remembrance, 2005.

Blodig, Vojtěch. "Poslední dny války, první měsíce míru: Terezín v roce osvobození." *Terezínské listy*, no. 23, (1995): 7–23.

Blodig, Vojtěch, ed. "Z deniku Evy Roubíčkové." *Terezínské listy*, no. 20 (1992): 67–97.

Bondy, Ruth. *"Elder of the Jews": Jakob Edelstein of the Theresiendstadz*. New York: Grove Press, 1981.

———. "Women in Theresienstadt and the Family Camp in Birkenau." In Ofer and Weitzman, *Women in the Holocaust*, 310–26.

Bondyová, Ruth. "Humor jako zbraň." In Kárný and Kárná, *Terezínské studie a dokumenty*, 228–43.

Borowski, Tadeusz. *This Way for the Gas, Ladies and Gentlemen*. New York: Penguin, 1976.

Bortlová, Hana. *Československo a Kuba v letech 1959–1962*. Prague: Charles University, 2011.

Bouverie, Tim. *Appeasing Hitler: Chamberlain, Churchill and the Road to War*. London: Penguin Random House, 2019.

Brade, Laura E. "Networks of Escape: Jewish Flight from the Bohemian Lands, 1938–1941." PhD diss., University of North Carolina, 2017.

Brade, Laura E., and Rose Holmes. "Troublesome Sainthood: Nicholas Winton and the Contested History of Child Rescue in Prague, 1938–1940." *History & Memory* 29, no. 1 (Spring/Summer 2017): 3–40.

Bren, Paulina. *The Greengrocer and His TV: The Culture of Communism after 1968 Prague Spring*. Ithaca, NY: Cornell University Press, 2010.

Brenner, Hannelore, writer. *The Girls of Room 28: Friendship, Hope, and Survival in Theresienstadt*. Published by Audiogo, September 15, 2009, 11 CDs.

Březinová, Kateřina. "Spanish Political Emigration in Czechoslovakia, 1948–1958: Cold War Transregional Mobilities." Unpublished paper.

Brinson, Charmian, and Marian Malet, eds. *Exile in and from Czechoslovakia during the 1930s and 1940s: The Yearbook of the Research Centre for German and Austrian Exile Studies*. Vol. 11. New York: Rodopi, 2009.

Browning, Christopher R. "Giving in to Hitler." *New York Review of Books*, September 26, 2019.

Bryant, Chad. "All the Germans Must Go." In *Prague in Black: Nazi Rule and Czech Nationalism*, 208–52. Cambridge, MA: Harvard University Press, 2009.

Buden, Boris. *Konec poskomunismu: Od společnosti bez naděje k naději bez společnosti*. Prague: Rybka, 2013.

Burešová, Jana. "The Czech Refugee Trust Fund in Britain 1939–1940." In *Yearbook of the Research for German and Austrian Exile*, vol. 2, 133–46. Amsterdam: Rodopi B.V., 2009.

———. *The Dynamics of Forced Female Migration from Czechoslovakia to Britain 1938–1950*. Oxford: Peter Lang, 2019.

Burgerová, Lenka, and Radek Spála. *Židé v Teplicích—600 let historie*. Teplice: Jan Zykmund, 2014.

Buruma, Ian. "The Hell of Victory." *New York Review of Books*, November 24, 2011.

———. *Their Promised Land? My Grandparents in Love and War*. New York: Penguin, 2006.

Buser, Verena. "In Detention: Memories of Jewish Refugees Interned in Atlit near Haifa." In *British Internment and the Internment of Britons: Second World War Camps, History and Heritage*, edited by Gilly Carr and Rachel Pistol, 189–206. London: Bloomsbury, 2023.

Caccamo, Francesco. "Mezi exilem, domácí opozicí a mezinárodním veřejným míněním: Exilový časopis Listy." *Soudobé dějiny* 20, no. 3 (2013): 345–78.

———. *Jiří Pelikán a jeho cesta socialismem 20. Století*. Brno: Doplněk, 2008.

Čapková, Kateřina. "Between Expulsion and Rescue: The Transports for German-Speaking Jews of Czechoslovakia in 1946." *Holocaust and Genocide Studies* 32, no. 1 (Spring 2018): 66–92.

———. *Češi, Němci, Židé? Národní identita Židů v Čechách, 1918–1938*. Prague-Litomyšl: Paseka, 2005.

Caquet, P. E. *The Bell of Treason: The 1938 Munich Agreement in Czechoslovakia*. London: Profile Books, 2018.

Catalano, Alessandro. "Zdeněk Mlynář a hledání socialistické opozice. Od aktivní politiky přes disent k ediční činnosti v exilu." *Soudobé dějiny* 22, no. 3 (2013): 277–344.

———. "Zdeněk Mlynář and the Search for Socialist Opposition. From an Active Politician to a Dissident to Editorial Work in Exile." *Czech Journal of Contemporary History* 3 (2015): 90–156.

Čejka, Eduard. *Československý odboj na Západě (1939–1945)*. Prague: Mladá fronta, 1997.

Celinscak, Mark. "At War's End: Allied Force at Bergen-Belsen." PhD diss., York University, 2012.

Čelko, Vojtěch, ed. *Václav Havel-Vilém Prečan: Korespondence 1983–1989*. Prague: Československé dokumentační středisko, 2011.

Černý, Bohumil. "Emigrace židů z Českých zemí v letech 1938–1941." In Kárný and Kárná, *Terezínské studie a dokumenty*, 61–68.

Československá Akademie Věd, ed. *Sedm pražských dnů: 21.–27. srpen 1968: Dokumentace*. Prague: Academia, 1990.

Chadwick, William. *The Rescue of the Prague Refugees 1938–1939*. Leicester: Matador, 2010.

"CHARTA 77." *Listy*, no. 1 (February 1977): 1–4.

"Charter 77—document no. 5." *Listy*, no. 2 (May 1977): 50–52.

Císař, Čestmír. *Paměti: Nejen o zákulisí Pražského jara*. Prague: SinCon, 2005.

Clayton, Aileen. *The Enemy Is Listening*. New York: Ballantine, 1980.

Cohen, Judy. *Song of the Silent Bell. My Parents' Memoir: Their Separate Roads to Survival during the Holocaust Era*. Bloomington, IN: Universe, 2016.

Cysařová, Jarmila. *Česká televizní publicistika: Svědectví šedesátých let*. Prague: Edice České televize 66, 1993.

———. "Československá televize a politická moc." *Soudobé dějiny* 9, no. 3–4 (2002): 533–35.

———. *Televize a moc, 1953–1967*. Prague: Ústav pro Soudobé dějiny, 1996, 62–72.

D'Arcy, Kevin. "Monitors for Freedom." *Sunday Telegraph* (London), September 1, 1968.

Dalimil. "Návrat do dějin." *Listy*, no. 6 (December 1989):13–14.

———. "O emigraci." *Listy*, no. 6 (November 1971): 16–18.

Daneš, Ladislav. *Můj život s můzami, televizí a tak vůbec*. Prague: Malá skála, 2005.

Darvas, Miriam. *Farewell to Prague*. Isle of Man, UK: MP Publishing, 2015.

Davies, Norman. *Europe: A History*. New York: Harper, 1998.

Davis, Gerald H. "Prisoners of War in Twentieth-Century War Economies." *Journal of Contemporary History* 12, no. 4 (October 1977): 623–34.

Dawisha, Karen. *The Kremlin and the Prague Spring*. Berkeley: University of California Press, 1984.

Deák, István. "Could Stalin Have Been Stopped?" *New York Review of Books*, March 21, 2013.

Demetz, Peter. *Prague in Black and Gold*. New York: Hill and Wang, 1997.

Dickins, Tom. "The Political Slogan in Communist Czechoslovakia (1948–89)." *Central Europe* 15, no. 1–2 (2017): 58–87.

Dienstbier, Jiří, and Karel Lánský. "Rozhlas proti tankům." In *Srpen 1968*, 5–104. Cologne: Index, 1989.

Dimitrov, Georgi. "19 July 1941." In Banac, *Diary of Georgi Dimitrov*, 289.

Dirkin, Guy. *Missing the Boat: War Stories of Thomas Alan Dirkin*. No publication data, 2018.

Doležal, Jakub. "Přes ambasády ke svobodě. Drama východoněmeckého exodu v roce 1989." *Soudobé dějiny* 21, no. 1–2 (2014): 79–133.

Drtina, Prokop. *Československo můj osud*. Toronto: 68 Publishers, 1982.

"Dubček žaluje." *Listy*, no. 3 (April 1975): 1–15.

Dworjetski, Mark. "Adjustment of Detainees to Camps and Ghetto Life and Their Subsequent Readjustment to Normal Life." *Yad Vashem Studies* (1963): 193–219.

Edelstein, Jeffrey. "Piecing Together a Puzzle with Newly Received Digital Collections: Paris and Prague Materials Provide Answers to a 70-Year-Old Mystery." Personal communication to Daniela Spenser.

Epstein, Franci Rabinek. *Franci's War: A Woman's Story of Survival*. New York: Penguin, 2020.

Escott, Beryl E. *The WAAF: A History of the Women's Auxiliary Air Force in the Second World War*. London: Shire, 2003.

Fantlová, Zdenka. *Klid je síla řek' tatínek*. Prague: Primus, 1996.

Farré, Sébastian. "The ICRC and the Detainees in Nazi Concentration Camps

(1942–1945)." *International Review of the Red Cross* 94, no. 888 (Winter 2012): 1394–97.

Fast, Vera K. *Children's Exodus: A History of the Kindertransport*. London: I. B. Tauris, 2011.

Feinberg, Melissa. *Curtain of Lies: The Battle over Truth in Stalinist Eastern Europe*. Oxford: Oxford University Press, 2017.

———. "Fantastic Truths, Compelling Lies: Radio Free Europe and the Response to the Slánský Trial in Czechoslovakia." *Contemporary European History*, no. 1 (February 2013): 107–25.

Feingold, Eduardo D., and Juan Buchas. *The Kalamata Diary: Greece, War, and Emigration*. Lanham, MD: Rowman and Littlefield, 2010.

Ferguson, Niall. *The War of the World: Twentieth-Century Conflict and the Descent of the West*. New York: Penguin, 2007.

Fingerland, Jan. *Major Zeman bojuje se sionisty: Obraz Židů, sionismu a holokaustu v normalizačním seriálu*. Prague: Dvarim meatim studie pro Jiřinu Šedinovou, 2016.

Forbelský, Josef. *Svět se mnou, svět bez mne*. Prague: Academia, 2013.

Forman, Miloš, and Jan Novák. *Turnaround: A Memoir*. New York: Villard Books, 1994.

Friedländer, Saul. *When Memory Comes*. New York: Other Press, 1978.

Fromings, Hedy. Interviewed by Ian Willoughby. Prague Czech radio, part 1, October 24, 2006. Audio, 7:46.

Frommer, Benjamin. "Retribution as Legitimation: The Uses of Political Justice in Postwar Czechoslovakia." *Contemporary European History* 13, no. 4 (2004): 477–92.

Fry, Helen. *The M Room: Secret Listeners Who Bugged the Nazis*. London: Marranos Press, 2012.

Frydrych, Arnošt. "Anonymům na vědomí." *Týdeník Čs. televize* 29 (July 1968): 15–21.

Geiss, Robin. "Name, Rank, Date of Birth, Serial Number and the Right to Remain Silent." *International Review of the Red Cross* 87, no. 860 (December 2005): 721–35.

Gelber, Yoav. "Palestinian POWs in German Captivity." *Yad Vashem Studies* 16 (1981): 89–137.

Gide, André. *Le traité du Narcisse*. Paris: Mercure de France, 1899.

Gilbert, Adrian. *POW: Allied Prisoners in Europe, 1939–45*. London: John Murray, 2006.

Gilbert, Martin. "British Government Policy towards Jewish Refugees." *Yad Vashem Studies* 13 (1979): 127–67.

Gissing, Vera. *Pearls of Childhood: The Poignant True Wartime Story of a Young Girl Growing Up in an Adopted Land*. London: Robson Books, 1994.

Gleizer, Daniela. "La política mexicana frente a la recepción de refugiados judíos (1934–1942)." In *México, país refugio: La experiencia de los exilios en el siglo XX*, edited by Pablo Yankelevich, 119–40. CDMX: Plaza y Valdés, Conaculta, INAH, 2002.

Goldenberg, Myrna. "Memoirs of Auschwitz Survivors: The Burden of Gender." In Ofer and Weitzman, *Women in the Holocaust*, 328–29.

Goldstücker, Eduard. *Vzpomínky 1913–1945 and 1945–1968*. Prague: G Plus G, 2005.

Gorbachev, Michail, and Zdeněk Mlynář. *Reformátoři nebývají šťastní*. Prague: Victoria, 1995.

Graham, Simon. "Internationalising the Intelligence History of the Prague Spring." *Cold War History* 20, no. 3 (2020): 293–310.

Gruenbaum, Michael, and Todd Hasak-Lowy. *Somewhere There Is a Sun: A Memoir of the Holocaust.* New York: Aladdin, 2015.

Gruner, Wolf. "Jewish Forced Labor as a Basic Element of Nazi Persecution: Germany, Austria, and the Occupied Polish Territories (1938–1945)." In *Forced and Slave Labor in Nazi-Dominated Europe: Symposium Presentations,* 35–48. Washington, DC: United States Holocaust Memorial Museum, 2004.

Gruner, Wolf, and Jörg Osterloh, eds. *The Greater German Reich and the Jews: Nazi Persecution Politics in the Annexed Territories 1935–1945.* New York: Berghahn Books, 2015.

Grůšová, Anna, and Helena Vávrová. "Po roce 1968 (pohledem dcer)." In *Vzpomínky 1945–1968,* in Eduard Goldstücker, 165–69. Prague: G Plus G, 2005.

Gutterman, Bella. *A Narrow Bridge to Life: Jewish Forced Labor and Survival in the Gross-Rosen Camp System, 1940–1945.* New York : Berghahn, 2008.

Haag, John. "Knights of the Spirit': The Kameradschaftsbund." *Journal of Contemporary History* 8, no. 3 (July 1973): 133–53.

Hájek, Miloš. "Proč vznikla Obroda." *Listy,* no. 4 (August 1989): 21.

Hájková, Anna. "Between Love and Coercion: Queer Desire, Sexual Barter and the Holocaust." *German History* 39, no. 1 (2021): 112–33.

———. *The Last Ghetto: An Everyday History of Theresienstadt.* Oxford: Oxford University Press, 2020.

———. "Řekla jsem si, že se prostě musím nějak přizpůsobit: Mladé ženy v ghettu Terezín." *Soudobé dějiny* 18, no. 4 (2011): 603–26.

Halkin, Hillel. *Jabotinsky: A Life.* New Haven, CT: Yale University Press, 2014.

Hames, Peter. *Czech and Slovak Cinema: Theme and Tradition.* Edinburgh: University Press, 2009.

Hammel, Andrea. "'Why Is Your Czech So Bad?' Czech Child Refugees, Language and Identity." In Brinson and Malet, *Exile in and from Czechoslovakia,* 215–28.

Hargrave, Michael John. *Bergen-Belsen 1945: A Medical Student's Journal.* London: Imperial College Press, 2014.

Harris, Mark Jonathan, and Deborah Oppenheimer. *Into the Arms of Strangers: Stories of the Kindetransport.* London: Bloomsbury, 2017.

Hartman, John J., and Jacek Krochmal. *I Remember Every Day . . . The Fates of the Jews of Przemyśl during World War II.* Przemyśl: Towarzystwo Przyjaciøł Nauk, 2002.

Hastings, Max. *The Secret War: Spies, Ciphers, and Guerrillas 1939–1945.* New York: HarperCollins, 2016.

Hauner, Milan. "Beginnings of the Czechoslovak Government in Exile 1939–1941." In Brinson and Malet, *Exile in and from Czechoslovakia,* 108–18.

Havel, Václav. "Dopis." *Listy,* no. 5 (July 1975): 32–43.

———. *Listy,* no. 1 (February 1990): 5.

———. "Setkání s Gorbačovem." *Listy,* no. 5 (October 1987): 47–48.

———. "Slovo o slovu." *Listy,* no. 6 (December 1989): 37–40.

———. "Vyložené karty." *Listy,* no. 1 (February 1989): 1–3.

———. "Words on Words." *New York Review of Books,* January 18, 1990.

Havel, Václav, Dana Emingerová, and Luboš Beniak. "'Uncertain Strength': An Interview with Václav Havel." Translated by Paul Wilson. *New York Review of Books,* August 15, 1991.

Havlíček, Dušan. *Jaro na krku: Zážitky ze zákulisí sekretariátu ÚV KSČ od června do prosince 1968*. Prague: Ústav pro Soudobé dějiny, 1998.

———. *Listy v exilu*. Olomouc: Burian and Tichák, 2008.

Hayes, Peter. "Forced and Slave Labor: The State of the Field." In *Forced and Slave Labor in Nazi-Dominated Europe: Symposium Presentations*, 1–9. Washington, DC: United States Holocaust Memorial Museum, 2004.

Hejzlar, Zdeněk. "Reformní komunismus nepatří minulosti." *Listy*, extra issue (December 1978): 38–40.

Hejzlar, Zdeněk, Zdeněk Mlynář, Adolf Müller, and Jiří Pelikán. "Statement of the Group LISTY on the Twentieth Anniversary of the Prague Spring." *Listy*, no. 1 (February 1988): 2–3.

Hertl, David. "Televizní tvář pražského jara má svou karikaturu v Majoru Zemanovi: Kdo byl Vladimír Tosek doopravdy?" *Česká rozhlas*, December 7, 2017.

Higham, Robin. *Diary of a Disaster: British Aid to Greece 1940–1941*. Lexington: University Press of Kentucky, 1986.

Hill, Peter C. J. "The BBC Monitoring Service—A Short Engineering History." *2010 Second Region 8 IEEE Conference on the History of Communications*, Madrid, 2010, 1–4.

Hoare, Michael R. "In the Beginning: A Memoir of Boyhood and an Extraordinary Family." Unpublished undated manuscript.

Hobsbawm, Eric. *Interesting Times: A Twentieth Century Life*. London: Allen Lane, 2002.

Hochman, Jiří. "Words and Tanks: The Revival, the Struggle, the Agony and Defeat (1968–1969)." In Pehe, *Prague Spring*, 27–40.

Hochschild, Adam. *Spain in Our Hearts: Americans in the Spanish Civil War, 1936–1939*. Boston: Houghton Mifflin Harcourt, 2016.

Holden, Wendy. *Born Survivors: Three Young Mothers and Their Extraordinary Story of Courage, Defiance, and Hope*. New York: Harper, 2015.

Hoppe, Jiří. *Pražské jaro v médiích: Výběr z dobové publicistiky*. Brno: Doplněk, 2004.

Höss, Rudolf. *Death Dealer: The Memoirs of the SS Kommandant at Auschwitz*. Edited by Steven Paskuly. New York: Da Capo Press, 1996.

Hughes, Geraint. "British Policy towards Eastern Europe and the Impact of the 'Prague Spring', 1964–1968." *Cold War History* 4, no. 2 (2004):115–39.

Jabotinsky, Eri. *The Sakarya Expedition: A Story of Extra-Legal Immigration to Palestine*. Johannesburg: Newzo, 1945.

Janouch, František. *Korespondence: František Janouch / Jiří Pelikán*. Prague: Novela bohemica, 2015.

Janouch, František, Martin Groman, and Daniel Štěpánek, eds. *Na smutek není čas: Korespondence mezi Františkem a Rivou Krieglovými a Františkem Janouchem a Adou Kolmanovou (1974–1979)*. Prague: Nadace Charty 77, 2009.

Jay, John. *Facing Fearful Odds: My Father's Story of Captivity, Escape and Resistance 1940–1945*. Barnsley, UK: Pen and Sword, 2014.

Ješutová, Eva. "Budovatelský rozhlas, 1945–1948." *Od mikrofonu k posluchačům*. Prague: Český rozhlas, 2003.

Jezdinský, Karel. "Exil a domov." *Listy*, no. 4–5 (July 1971): 24–27.

JH. "K situaci československé historiografie." *Listy*, no. 5 (October 1989): 78–79.

jk. "Ve středu zájmu imperialistických rozvědek." *Zprávy*, February 1, 1969.

Johnson, Brian Dominic Flessati, and John Groom, writers. *The Secret War*. BBC and Imperial War Museum, January 5–February 9, 1977.

Johnston, Rosamund. "Red Tape and Hot Media: Radio, Politics and Socialist Celebrity in Czechoslovakia, 1945–1969." PhD diss., New York University, 2019.

Jones, Kevin. "From the Horse's Mouth: Luftwaffe POWs as Sources for Air Ministry Intelligence during the Battle of Britain." *Intelligence and National Security* 15, no. 4 (2008): 60–80.

Judt, Tony. "The Dilemmas of Dissidence: The Politics of Opposition in East-Central Europe." In *Eastern Europe: Continuity and Change (1987–1995)*, edited by Irena Grudzińska-Gross and Andrzej W. Tymowski, 75–76. Frankfurt am Main: Peter Lang, 2014.

———. *Postwar: A History of Europe since 1945*. London: Penguin Books, 2006.

Judt, Tony, and Timothy Snyder. *Thinking the Twentieth Century*. New York: Penguin, 2012.

Kadlec, Josef. *Svatá Země v Československém odboji*. Prague: Orientální ústav, 1947.

Kaiser, Daniel. *Disident: Václav Havel 1936–1989*. Prague: Paseka, 2009.

Kaplan, Karel. *Poválečné Československo: Československo, 1945–1948, národy a hranice*. Munich: Národni Politika, 1985.

———. *The Short March: The Communist Takeover in Czechoslovakia 1945–1948*. New York: St. Martin's Press, 1981.

Kaplan, Karel, and Dušan Tomášek. "Zpráva ministra vnitra R. Baráka politickému sekretariátu ÚV KSČ o činnosti Hlavní správy tiskového dohledu." In *O cenzuře v Československu v letech 1945–1956*, 153–58. Prague: Ústav pro Soudobé dějiny, 1994.

Kaplan, Karel, and Pavel Paleček. *Komunistický režim a politické procesy v Československu*. Prague: Barrister & Principal, 2001.

Kaplan, Petr. "The Sudeten Germans and the Twilight of the First Republic." *Czech Journal of Contemporary History* 1, no. 1 (2013): 149–54.

Karas, Joža. *Music in Terezín 1941–1945*. New York: Beaufort Books, 1985.

Karner, Stefan, and Peter Ruggenthaler. "Austria and the End of the Prague Spring: Neutrality in the Crucible?" In *The Prague Spring and the Warsaw Pact Invasion of Czechoslovakia in 1968*, edited by Günter Bischof, Stefan Karner, and Peter Ruggenthaler, 419–39. Boulder, CO: Lexington Books, 2011.

Kárný, Miroslav. "Výsledky a úkoly Terezínské historiografie." In *Terezín v konečném řešení židovské otázky*, edited by Miroslav Kárný and Vojtěch Blodig, 23–33. Prague: Logos, 1992.

Kárný, Miroslav, and Margita Kárná, eds. *Terezínské studie a dokumenty*. Prague: Academia, 1997.

Kavan, Jan. "From the Prague Spring to a Long Winter." In Pehe, *Prague Spring*, 103–30.

Kavan, Rosemary. *Freedom at a Price: An Englishwoman's Life in Czechoslovakia*. London: Verso, 1985.

Kemp, Paul. "The British Army and the Liberation of Bergen-Belsen, April 1945." In *Belsen in History and Memory*, edited by Jo Reilly, David Cesarani, Tony Kushner, and Colin Richmond, 134–48. London: Frank Cass, 1997.

Kenney, Padraic. *A Carnival of Revolution: Central Europe 1989*. Princeton: Princeton University Press, 2002.

Kershaw, Ian. "Calamity in the East." In *The End: The Defiance and Destruction of Hitler's Germany, 1944–1945*, 167–206. New York: Penguin, 2011.

Kilián, Jan. *Teplice: Historie, kultura, lidé*. Prague: Lidové noviny, 2015.

Klapálek, Karel. *Ozvěny bojů*. Prague: Naše vojsko, 1987 [orig. 1968].

Klíma, Ivan. *My Crazy Century: A Memoir*. New York: Grove Press, 2010.

Kliment, Alexandr. *Nuda v Čechách*. Toronto: 68 publishers, 1978.

Knapík, Jiří. *Děti, mládež a socialismus v Československu v 50. a 60. Letech*. Opava: Slezská universita, 2014.

Knapík, Jiří, and Martin Franc. *Průvodce kultůrním děním a životním stylem v Českých zemích 1948–1967*. Prague: Academia, 2011.

Kocáb, Michael. *Vabank. 1989–1991: Sametová revoluce. Odchod sovětských vojsk*. Prague: Universum, 2019.

Kochavi, Arieh J. *Britain and the United States and Their POWs in Nazi Germany*. Chapel Hill: University of North Carolina Press, 2005.

———. *Confronting Captivity: Britain and the United States and their POWs in Nazi Germany*. Chapel Hill: University of North Carolina Press, 2005.

———. "The Struggle against Jewish Immigration to Palestine." *Middle Eastern Studies* 34, no. 3 (July 1998): 146–67.

Kohout, Pavel. *To byl můj život?* Prague: Odeon, 2018.

Kolář, Václav, and Ladislav Kejha. *Televize v srpnu 1968: Dodatek ke stejnojmennému pořadu ČT*. Prague: Česká televize, 2001.

Kolman, Arnošt. *Zaslepená generace*. Brno: Host, 2005.

Komunistická strana Československa. Ústřední výbor. Zasedání, *Poslední hurá: Stenografický záznam z mimořádných zasedání ÚV KSČ 24. a 26. listopadu 1989*. Prague: Cesty, 1992.

Končelík, Jakub. "Dva tisíce slov: Zrod a důsledky nečekaně vlivného prohlášení." *Soudobé dějiny* 15, no. 3–4 (2008): 485–529.

Konečný, Zdeněk, and František Mainuš. *British Prisoners-of-War in Czechoslovakia, and Silesian Territory during the Second World War* (Brno: Sborník prací filozofické fakulty Brněnské univerzity, 1966).

Kopecký, R. *Československý odboj v Polsku v r. 1939*. Rotterdam: Modrá revue, 1958.

Kosta, Jiří. "Pochod smrti-Osvobození-návrat. Gliwice-Blechheimmer-Medzilaborce-Praha." *Terezínské listy a dokumenty* (2005): 15–24.

———. *Život mezi úzkostí a nadějí*. Prague: Paseka, 2002.

Kotek, Joël. *Students and the Cold War*. New York: St. Martin's Press, 1996.

Koudelka, František. *Státní bezpečnost 1954–1968*. Prague: Ústav pro Soudobé dějiny, 1993.

Kovályová, Heda, and Erazim Kohák. *Na vlastní kůži: Dialog přes barikádu*. Toronto: 68 Publishers, 1973.

Kovanda, Karel. *Já a moje peníze*. Prague: Lidové noviny, 1992.

Kramer, Mark. "The Dialectics of Empire: Soviet Leaders and the Challenge of Civil Resistance in East-Central Europe, 1968–1991." In Roberts and Ash, *Civil Resistance and Power Politics*, 91–109.

Kraus, Dita. *Yo, Dita Kraus: La bibliotecaria de Auschwitz*. Barcelona: Roca Editorial, 2021.

Kraus, Ota, and Erich Kulka. *Továrna na smrt*. Prague: Naše vojsko, 1964.

Krejčová, Helena, and Anna Hyndráková. "Postoj Čechů k Židům: Z politického zpravodajství okupační správy a protektorátního tisku v letech 1939–1941." *Soudobé dějiny* 2, no. 44 (1995): 578–605.

Křen, Jan. *Dvě století střední Evropy*. Prague: Argo, 2005.

"Kritický rok," *Listy*, no. 1, (1991): 3–5.

Kudrna, Ladislav. "Projevy antisemitismu v Československých pozemních a leteckých jednotkách za druhé světové války." *Terezínské listy*, no. 36 (2008): 59–88.

Kulka, Erich. *Židé v Československém vojsku na západě*. Prague: Naše vojsko, 1992.

Kyncl, Karel. "O nové iniciativě Obroda." *Listy*, no. 2 (April 1989): 20–21.

———. "Vladimíra Toska poslední utkání na domácí půdě." *Listy*, no. 1 (1990): 151.

Langbein, Hermann. *People in Auschwitz*. Toronto: Fitzhenry and Whiteside, 2005.

Láníček, Jan. *Arnošt Fischer and the Jewish Politics of Early 20th Century Europe*. London: Bloomsbury, 2017.

———. "The Postwar Czech-Jewish Leadership and the Issue of Jewish emigration from Czechoslovakia." In *Postwar Jewish Displacement and Rebirth, 1945–1967*, edited by Françoise Ouzan and Manfred Gerstenfeld, 76–96. Leiden: Brill, 2014.

———. "The Powerlessness of Czechoslovak Jews during the Second World War." *East European Jewish Affairs* 44, no. 1 (2014): 21–50.

Larres, Klaus. "Churchill's 'Iron Curtain' Speech in Context: The Attempt to Achieve a 'Good Understanding on All Points' with Stalin's Soviet Union." *International History Review* 40, no. 1 (2018): 86–107.

Lasker-Wallfish, Anita. *Inherit the Truth 1939–1945: The Documented Experiences of a Survivor of Auschwitz and Belsen*. London: Giles de la Mare Publishers, 1996.

Laštovička, Bohuslav. *V Londýně za války: Zápasy o novou ČSR 1939–1945*. Prague: Svoboda, 1978.

Lederer, Jiří. *Jan Palach: Zpráva o životě, činu a smrti českého studenta*. Prague: Novinar, 1990.

———. *Touhy a iluze (vzpomínání do srpna 68)*. Toronto: Sixty-Eight Publishers, 1984.

Lederer, Zdeněk. *Ghetto Theresienstadt*. London: Edward Goldston, 1953.

Lees, Ted. "Life as a Prisoner of War." StalagVIIB/344 Lamsdorf Prisoners of War. Accessed April 8, 2020.

Levi, Primo. *The Drowned and the Saved*. London: Abacus, 1989.

———. *Survival in Auschwitz*. New York: Collier, 1993.

Lewis, Ben. *Hammer and Tickle: A History of Communism Told through Communist Jokes*. London: Weidenfeld & Nicolson, 2008.

Liehm, Antonín. In *Exil a domov: Odchody a návraty*. Prague: Heinrich Böll Foundation and Listy, 1993.

Litomiský, Jan, Libuše Šilhanová, and Josef Vohryzek. "Dopis Michailu Gorbačovovi." In *Charta 77 (1977–1989)—Od morální k demokratické revoluci*, edited by Vilém Prečan, 324–26. Scheinfeld: Centre for independent literature, 1990.

Loebl, Eugene. *Sentenced and Tried: The Stalinist Purges in Czechoslovakia*. London: Elek, 1969.

Löffelbein, Nils. "Z 'Pražského jara' do exilu-přijímání československých uprchlíků v SRN po vpádu jednotek Varšavského paktu do ČSSR v roce 1968." In *Uprchlíci a azylanti v zemi soused: Československo a Německo v letech 1933 až 1989*, edited by Detlef Brandes, Edita Ivaníčková and Jiří Pešek, 245–66. Prague: Česko-německá komise historiků, Masarykův ústav and Archiv AV ČR, 2019.

London, Louise. *Whitehall and the Jews 1933–1948: British Immigration Policy and the Holocaust*. New York: Cambridge University Press, 2003.

Longden, Sean. *Hitler's British Slaves: Allied POWs in Germany 1939–1945*. London: Constable and Robinson, 2005.

Longerich, Peter. *Goebbels: A Biography*. New York: Random House, 2015.

Loth, W. "Moscow, Prague and Warsaw: Overcoming the Brezhnev Doctrine." *Cold War History* 1, no. 2 (2001): 103–18.

Luke, Doreen. *My Road to Bletchley Park: The Memories of WAAF*. London: M. & M. Baldwin, 2003.

Lukeš, Igor. *Rudolf Slánský: His Trials and Trial*. Cold War International History Project, Woodrow Wilson International Center for Scholars, working paper no. 50.

Margalit, Avishai. "The Spell of Jabotinsky." *New York Review of Books*, November 6, 2014.

Marková, Marta. *Olga Havlová a ty druhé: Ženy ve vnitřní emigraci*. Brno: Barrister & Principal, 1996.

Martinec, Jan. *Bastard*. Prague: Klub čtenářů, 1991.

Mazower, Mark. *Dark Continent: Europe's Twentieth Century*. London: Penguin, 1999.

———. *What You Did Not Tell: A Russian Past and the Journey Home*. London: Allen Lane, 2017.

McKay, Sinclair. *The Secret Life of Bletchley Park: The WWII Codebreaking Centre and the Men and Women Who Worked There*. London: Aurum, 2010.

———. *The Secret Listeners: How the Y Service Intercepted German Codes for Bletchley Park*. London: Aurum, 2012.

Michnik, Adam. *Letters from Prison and Other Essays*. Berkeley: University of California Press, 1987.

———. "My všichni jsme rukojmí." *Listy*, no. 2 (May 1982): 9–15.

Miklová, Martina. "Československý exil v archivním výzkumu: Zpráva z brněnské konference." *Soudobé dějiny* 14, no. 4 (2017): 912–23.

Miłosz, Czesław. *The Captive Mind*. New York: Vintage, 1981.

Milotová, Jaroslava. "Ústředna pro židovské vystěhovalectví v Praze: Geneze a činnost na počátku roku 1940." In Kárný and Kárná, *Terezínské studie a dokumenty*, 10–29.

Ministerstvo spravedlnosti. *Proces s vedením protistátního spikleneckého centra v čele s Rudolfem Slánským*. Prague: Orbis, 1953.

"Ministerstvo vnitra k případu Vl. Toska." *Svobodné Slovo*, February 26, 1969.

Mlynář, Zdeněk. *Can Gorbachev Change the Soviet Union?* Translated by Ruth Tosková and Marian Sling. Boulder: Westview Press, 1990.

———. "Čeho se bojí?" *Listy*, no. 4 (August 1989): 46–47.

———. "Československo po deseti letech." *Listy*, extra issue, (December 1978): 35–38.

———. *Československý pokus o reformu 1968: Analýza jeho teorie a praxe*. Cologne: Index-Listy, 1975.

———. "Gorbachev v Brežněvově objetí." *Listy*, no. 2 (April 1987):1–4.

———. *Mráz přichází z Kremlu*. Cologne: Index, 1981.

———. "Můj spolužák Michail Gorbačov." *Listy*, no. 4 (July 1985): 22–24.

———. "Nová situace—nové možnosti." *Listy*, no. 4 (August 1973): 5–9.

———. "Nový muž před starými problémy." *Listy*, no. 2 (April 1984):1–4.

———. "Prague—January 1968." *Listy*, no. 1 (February 1988): 4–6.

———. "Pražské jaro a jeho význam pro socialistickou teorii a praxi." *Listy*, no. 1 (February 1973): 33–37.

———. *Proti srsti. Politické komentáře 1990–1995*. Prague: Periskop, 1996.

———. "Reforma v SSSR začala." *Listy*, no. 2 (April 1986): 4–5.

———. *Socialistou na volné noze*. Prague: Prospektrum, 1992.

———. "Stagnace končí." *Listy*, no. 2 (April 1985): 1–2.

Mornštajnová, Alena. *Hana*. Brno: Host, 2017.

Morris, Heather. *The Tattooist of Auschwitz*. London: Zaffre, 2018.

Müller, Melissa, and Reinhard Piechocki. *Alice's Piano: The Life of Alice Herz-Sommer*. New York: St. Martin's Press, 2012.

Murášková, Galina P. "Mocenská vertikála a nálady v československé společnosti v padesátých letech 20. století. Pohled sovětských diplomatů v Praze." *Soudobé dějiny* 20, no. 4 (2013): 605–27.

Naor, Mordechai. *Haapala: Clandestine Immigration 1931–1948*. Israel: Ministry of Defence and IDF Museum, 1987.

Němeček, Jan. "Československý londýnský exil a židovská otázka." In *Terezín Studies and Documents*, edited by Jaroslava Milotová and Eva Lorencová, 324–40. Prague: Terezín Iniatitive Institute, Academia, and Sefer, 2002.

Neumann, Ariana. *When Time Stopped: A Memoir of My Father's War and What Remains*. New York: Scribner, 2020.

O'Neill, Betty. *The Other Side of Absence: Discovering My Father's Secrets*. Edgecliff, Australia: Impact Press, 2020.

Ofer, Dalia. *Escaping the Holocaust: Illegal Immigration to the Land of Israel, 1939–1944*. Oxford: Oxford University Press, 1990.

———. "The Rescue of European Jewry and Illegal Immigration to Palestine in 1940. Prospects and Reality: Berthold Storfer and the Mossad le' Aliyah Bet." *Modern Judaism* 4, no. 2 (May 1984): 159–81.

Ofer, Dalia, and Lenore J. Weitzman, eds. *Women in the Holocaust*. New Haven, CT: Yale University Press, 1998.

Orság, Petr. *Mezi realitou, propagandou a mýty: Československá exilová média v západní Evropě v letech 1968–1989*. Prague: Lidové Noviny, 2016.

Osterloh, Jörg. "Sudetenland." In Gruner and Osterloh, *Greater German Reich and the Jews*, 72–74.

Ostermann, Christian. "'This Is Not a Politburo, but a Madhouse.' The Post-Stalin Succession Struggle, Soviet Deuthschlandpolitk and the SED: New Evidence from Russian, German, and Hungarian Archives." *Cold War International History Project Bulletin* 10 (March 1998): 61–72.

Otava, Jiří. "Neodcházejte!" *Listy*, no. 3–4 (July 1980): 18–20.

Papagos, General Alexander. *The Battle of Greece 1940–1941*. Athens: J. M. Scazikis "Alpha," 1949.

Parrish, Scott C. "New Evidence on the Soviet Rejection of the Marshall Plan, 1947." *Cold War International History Project*, working notebook 9 (March 1994).

Pavelka, Zdenko. *Petr Uhl, Dělal jsem, co jsem považoval za správné*. Prague: Torst, 2013.

Pecka, Jindřich. "Proměny Pražského jara ve světle pramenů spontánní povahy." In *Proměny Pražského jara: Sbor studií a dokumentů o nekapitulantských postojích v československé společnosti 1968–69*, edited by Jindřich Pecka and Vilém Prečan, 39–66. Brno: Doplněk.

Pehe, Jiří, ed. *The Prague Spring: A Mixed Legacy*. New York: Freedom House, 1988.

Pelikán, Jiří. "Alexander Dubček v Itálii; Projev Alexandra Dubčeka při udělování čestného doktorátu university v Bologni." *Listy*, no. 1 (February 1989): 8–12.

———. "Gorbachov, evropská levice a Pražské jaro." *Listy*, no. 4 (July 1988): 1–2.

———. "Jsme opět doma!" *Listy*, no. 2 (April 1990): 3–5.

———. "Konečně!" *Listy*, no. 6 (December 1989): 1–2.

———. "Malá bilance." *Listy*, no. 6 (1991): 3–4.

———. "Nadějný rok?" *Listy*, no. 1 (February 1989): 1–4.

———. "Nepromarnit historickou šanci." *Listy*, no. 3 (1991): 3–6.

———. "Nové naděje, ale bez iluzí." *Listy*, no. 3 (August 1989): 4.

———. "Pražské jaro není konec, nýbrž začátek: Ani reforma, ani revoluce—nové cesty ve východní Evropě." *Listy*, extra issue (December 1978): 44–51.

———. *S'ils me tuent*. Paris: Grasset, 1975.

———. "Volby, aneb demokracie jako možnost alternativy." *Listy*, no. 2 (1992): 3–5.

———. "Why I Have Disobeyed the Order to Return to Prague." *Times* (London), October 1, 1969.

Pelikán, Jiří, and Antonio Carioti. *Jiří Pelikán—nepohodlný exulant: Rozhovor s Antoniem Cariotem*. Prague: Novela Bohemica, 2015.

Pelikán, Jiří, and Dušan Havlíček. *Psáno z Říma, psáno ze Ženevy: Korespondence 1969–1989*. Olomouc: Buran and Tichák, 2013.

"Pelikán v evropském parlamentě." *Listy*, no. 4 (September 1979): 2–4.

Penkower, Monty Noam. *Palestine to Israel: Mandate to State, 1945–1948*. New York: Touro University Press, 2019.

Perl, William. *The Four-Front War: From the Holocaust to the Promised Land*. New York: Crown, 1979.

Pešta, Mikuláš. "Journalists as Communism's Fellow Travellers? A New Look at the International Organization of Journalists." *Soudobé dějiny* 28, no. 3 (2021): 787–90.

Pidgeon, Geoffrey. *The Secret Wireless War: The Story of MI6 Communications 1939–1945*. Richmond, UK: Arundel Books, 2008.

Pithart, Petr. "Chladný vztah domova." *Listy* 23, no. 1 (1993): 48–52.

———. *Po Devětaosmdesátém: Rozpomínání a přemítání*. Prague: Academia, 2015.

Plzák, Michal, and Magdalena Čechlovská, eds. *Jiřina Šiklová bez ohlávky: Rozhovory*. Prague: Kalich, 2011.

Poellath, Moritz. "Agents, Fascists and Provocateurs: Disinformation as an Instrument to Delegitimize Uprisings in Eastern Europe (1953, 1956, 1968) and Its Impact on the Politics of Memory." *Journal of Intelligence History* 22, no. 2 (2021): 1–23.

Pravda, Alex. "Moscow and Eastern Europe, 1988–1989: A Policy of Optimism and Caution." In *Imposing, Maintaining, and Tearing Open the Iron Curtain: The Cold War and East-Central Europe, 1945–1989*, edited by Mark Kramer and Vít Smetana, 305–34. Lanham, MD: Lexington Books, 2014.

———. "Politika optimismu a opatrnosti: Moskva a východní Evropa na konci 80. let." *Soudobé dějiny* 18, no. 1–2 (2011): 86–119.

Prečan, Vilém. In *Exil a domov: Odchody a návraty*, 34. Prague: Heinrich Böll Foundation, 1993.

———. "Poznámky ke studiu vztahu mexi exilu a domácí antitotalitní rezistence v 70. a 80. letech." In *Češi za hranicemi na přelomu 20. a 21. století*, edited by Karel Hrubý and Stanislav Brouček, 213–22. Prague: Charles University, 2000.

———. "Právo na vlastní odpovědnost, riziko i šance." *Listy*, no. 3–4 (July 1980): 21–24.

———. "Svědectví o rozpadu 'socialistického společenství': Ukázky z memoárů Michaila Gorbačova, Vadima Medveděva a Valerije Musatova." *Soudobé dějiny* 5, no. 4 (1998): 509–54.

Prečan, Vilém, ed. *Kočka, která nikdy nespí II/The Cat Who Never Sleeps II*. Prague: James H. Ottaway, Jr, 2015.

———. *Václav Havel, do různých stran: Eseje a články z let 1983–1989*. Prague: Lidové noviny, 1990.

Procházková, Eva. "O rozhodnutí emigrovat." *Listy*, no. 6 (December 1986): 60–61.

"Proč nesmíme mlčet?" *Listy*, no. 1 (January 1971): 1–2.

"Prohlášení přípravného výboru Klubu za socialistickou přestavbu OBRODA." *Listy*, no. 2 (April 1989): 20–22.

"Prohlášení skupiny Listy k Polsku." *Listy*, no. 6 (December 1980): Francine. *Anne Frank: The Book, the Life and the Afterlife*. New York: HarperCollins, 2009.

Prose, Francine. *Anne Frank: The Book, the Life and the Afterlife*. New York: HarperCollins, 2009.

Pulec, Martin. *Nestandardní jevy u Pohraniční stráže v posrpnovém období roku 1968*. Prague: Úřad dokumentace a vyšetřování zločinů komunismu, 2006.

Pullmann, Michal. *Konec experiment: Přestavba a pád komunismu v Československu*. Prague: Scriptorium, 2011.

Quimet, Matthew J. *The Rise and Fall of the Brezhnev Doctrine in Soviet Foreign Policy*. Chapel Hill: University of North Carolina Press, 2003.

Rajchart, Zdeněk. "Kdo koho ostříhal?" *Rudé právo*, April 12, 1969.

———. "Vážený soudruhu redaktore." *Práce*, April 12, 1969.

Raška, Francis D. *The Long Road to Victory: A History of Czechoslovak Exile Organizations*. Boulder, CO: East European Monographs, 2012.

Redakce. "Vloupání do redakce Listy." *Listy*, no. 1 (February 1983): 45.

Reilly, Joanne. *Belsen: The Liberation of a Concentration Camp*. London: Routledge, 1998.

Reiman, Michal. "Setkání s Alexandrem Dubčekem ve Vídni v listopadu 1988." *Soudobé dějiny* 10, no. 1 (2008): 36–146.

Reynolds, David. *From the World War to Cold War: Churchill, Roosevelt, and the International History of the 1940s*. Oxford: Oxford University Press, 2006.

Roberts, Adam, and Timothy Garton Ash, eds. *Civil Resistance and Power Politics: The Experience of Non-Violent Action from Gandhi to the Present*. Oxford: Oxford University Press, 2009.

Roberts, Geoffrey. *Stalin's Wars: From World War to Cold War, 1939–1953*. New Haven, CT: Yale University Press, 2006.

Rosenberg, Göran. *A Brief Stop on the Road from Auschwitz*. New York: Other Press, 2002.

Rothkirchen, Livia. *The Jews of Bohemia and Moravia Facing the Holocaust.* Lincoln: University of Nebraska Press, 2005.

Rupnik, Jacques. "Fateful Eights in Czechoslovak History." In *Střední Evropa je jako pták s očima vzadu,* 5–31. Prague: Novela Bohemica, 2018.

Růžička, Daniel. *Major Zeman—Propaganda nebo krimi? Zákulisí vzniku televizního seriálu.* Prague: Práh, 2005.

Růžička, Jiří. "Poststalinismus jako (ne)stalinský projekt modernity? Možnost koncepčního uchopení intelektuálních `reformních' diskursů v období 1956 -1968." *Soudobé dějiny* 25, no. 1 -2 (2018): 208–28.

Ružičková, Zuzana, and Wendy Holden. *One Hundred Miracles: A Memoir of Music and Survival.* London: Bloomsbury, 2019.

Rychlík, Jan. "Překračování hranic a emigrace v Československu a východní Evropě ve 20. století." *Securitas imperii* 29 (February 2016): 10–72.

Salivarová-Škvorecká, Zdena. *Osočen: Pravdivé příběhy lidí z "Cibulkova seznamu".* Brno: Host, 2000.

Sammartino, Annemarie. "We Are the State We Seek: Everyday Life in Czechoslovakia and East Germany, 1945–1989." *Contemporary European History* 21, special issue 3 (2012): 477–91.

Savranskaya, Svetlana. "The Logic of 1989: The Soviet Peaceful Withdrawal from Eastern Europe." In Savranskaya, Blanton, and Zubok, *Masterpieces of History,* 1–48.

Savranskaya, Svetlana, Thomas Blanton, and Vladislav Zubok. *Masterpieces of History: The Peaceful End of the Cold War in Europe, 1989* (Budapest: National Security Archive Cold War Reader, 2010).

Schormová, Františka. "Stalinův černý apoštol: Afroamerický zpěvák Paul Robeson v Československu." *Soudobé dějiny* 28, no. 1 (2021): 183–213.

Schovánek, Radovan. "Atentát na Pelikána." *Minulost,* June 6, 2015.

Schulze Wessel, Martin. *Pražské jaro: Průlom do nového světa.* Prague: Argo, 2018.

Schwarz, Géraldine. *Those Who Forget: My Family's Story in Nazi Europe—A Memoir, a History, a Warning.* New York: Scribner, 2020.

"Sdělení výboru klubu Obroda." *Listy,* no. 5 (October 1989): 47–48.

Sedlíčková, Magdalena. "Antisemitismus v československé zahraniční armádě." Master's thesis, Charles University, Prague, 2012.

Semmel, David R. *11th of Av.* North Charleston, SC: CreateSpace, 2010.

Sharon, Assaf. "This Obstinate Little Man." *New York Review of Books,* November 4, 2021.

Shephard, Ben. *After Daybreak: The Liberation of Bergen-Belsen, 1945.* New York: Schocken Books, 2005.

———. *The Long Road Home: The Aftermath of the Second World War.* New York: Anchor Books, 2012.

Shepherd, Naomi. *Ploughing Sand: British Rule in Palestine 1917–1948.* New Brunswick, NJ: Rutgers University Press, 1999.

Shore, Marci. "Engineering in the Age of Innocence: A Genealogy of Discourse inside the Czechoslovak Writers' Union, 1949–1967." *East European Politics and Societies* 12, no. 3 (1998): 397–441.

Šiklová, Jiřina. "Co pro nás doma znamenají Listy (Několik postřehů k 10. výročí)." *Listy,* no. 1 (February 1980): 7–8.

Šimečka, Milan. "Fejeton o loučení." *Listy*, no. 6 (December 1976): 24–25.

———. "O odchodu do světa." *Listy* 14, no. 4 (July 1984): 34.

Simmons, Michael. "Burial Rights." *Guardian*, December 9, 1987.

———. *The Reluctant President. A Political Life of Václav Havel.* London: Methuen, 1991.

Skilling, Gordon H. *Charter 77 and Human Rights in Czechoslovakia.* London: George Allen & Unwin, 1981.

———. *Listy z Prahy.* Toronto: Sixty-Eight Publishers, 1988.

Sladký, Hanuš H. "Epizody ze života přeživšího." In *Terezínské studie a dokumenty*, edited by Miroslav Kárný, Margita Kárná, and Eva Lorencová, 96–97. Prague: Academia, 1998.

Slánský, Rudolf. "Dubček a Havel po dvaceti letech." *Listy*, no. 4 (August 1989): 5.

———. "Změny v Moskvě—změny v Praze?" *Listy*, no. 5 (December 1985): 1–6.

Šlingová, Marian. *Truth Will Prevail.* London: Merlin Press, 1968.

Slobodová, Zuzana. "Nežná revolúcia v anglickom Readingu." In *Volá Londýn: Historie českého a slovenského BBC (1939–2006)*, edited by Milan Kocourek, 288–90. Prague: Otovo nakladatelstvi, 2013.

———. "Ruth Tosek Obituary." *Guardian*, October 6, 2013.

Šmejkalová, Jiřina. "Command Celebrities: The Rise and Fall of Hanzelka and Zikmund." *Central Europe* 13, no. 1–2 (2015): 72–86.

Smetana, Vít. "Pod křídla Sovětů: Mohlo se Československo vyhnout 'sklouznutí' za železnou oponu?" *Soudobé dějiny* 15, no. 2 (2008): 276–302.

Sniegon, Tomas. *Vanished History: The Holocaust in Czech and Slovak Historical Culture.* New York: Berghahn, 2014.

"Socialistické hnutí čs. Občanů." *Listy*, no. 1 (January 1971): 3–5.

Sommerová, Olga, dir. *Sedm světel.* Czech television, 2007.

"Soud nad Václavem Havlem." *Listy*, no. 2 (April 1989): 4.

"Soviet Attack on Prague Britons." *Times* (London) February 4, 1968.

Soyfer, Valery N. *Lysenko and the Tragedy of Soviet Science.* New Brunswick, NJ: Rutgers University Press, 1994.

Spenser, Daniela. *In Combat: The Life of Lombardo Toledano.* Leiden: Brill, 2020.

———. "Prague Spring's Demise: The Involuntary Emigration of the Journalist Vladimír Tosek." *Korpus 21* 1, no. 1 (2021): 127–42.

Srba, Bořivoj. *Můzy v exilu: Kulturní a umělecké, aktivity čs. exulantů v Londýně v předvečer a v průběhu druhé světové války, 1939–1945.* Brno: Masarykova universita, 2003.

Stegurová, Karolina. *I ženy chtěly bojovat: Československé ženy v britských armádních pomocných sborech ATS a WAAF za druhé světové války.* Prague: Academia, 2021.

Steinbacher, Sybille. "East Upper Silesia." In Gruner and Osterloh, *Greater German Reich and the Jews*, 72–74.

Steklý, Karel, dir. *Za volantem nepřítel.* Filmové Studio Barrandov 1974.

Štern, Jan. "Posledni dopis." *Listy*, no. 4 (1999): 43.

———. "Potřebujeme Výbor na obranu nespravedlivě skandalizovaných?" *Listy*, no. 2 (1992): 47–48.

Štoll, Martin. *Television and Totalitarianism in Czechoslovakia: From the Democratic Republic to the Fall of Communism.* New York: Bloomsbury, 2019.

Stone, Tessa. "Creating a (Gendered?) Military Identity: The Women's Auxiliary Air

Force in Great Britain in the Second World War." *Women's History Review* 8, no. 4 (1999): 605–24.

Stoppard, Tom. "Prague: The Story of the Chartists." *New York Review of Books*, August 4, 1977.

Suk, Jiří. "Alexander Dubček—velký státník, nebo politický symbol?" *Soudobé dějiny* 9, no. 1 (2002): 92–103.

———. "Disent jako morální výzva a politická skutečnost (1977–1989–2000)." In *Šest kapitol o disentu*, 249–85. Prague: Ústav pro Soudobé dějiny, 2017.

———. "Je v pražském jaru 1968 alternativa k dnešnímu kapitalismu? Politická úvaha nad historickou interpretací." *Soudobé dějiny* 17, no. 3 (2010): 461–67.

———. *Labyrintem revoluce. Aktéři, zápletky a křižovatky jedné politické krize*. Prague: Prostor, 2020.

———. "Podrobná zpráva o paralelní polis. Nad korespondencí Václava Havla a Františka Janoucha." In Václav Havel, *Václav Havel, František Janouch, Korespondence 1978–2001*. Prague: Akropolis, 2007.

———. "Politika jako absurdní drama. Václav Havel v letech 1975–1989." PhD diss., Akademie věd České republiky, 2014.

———. *Veřejné záchodky ze zlata: Konflikt mezi komunistickým utopismem a ekonomickou racionalitou v předsrpnovém Československu*. Prague: Prostor, 2016.

———. "Vznik občanského fóra a proměny jeho struktury (19. listopad-10. prosinec 1989)." *Soudobé dějiny* 2, no. 1 (1995): 17–41.

———. "Zlom mezi 'totalitou' a 'demokracií': Československý rok 1989 v alternativách." *Soudobé dějiny* 16, no. 4 (2009): 557–601.

Summerfield, Penny. *Reconstructing Women's Wartime Lives*. Manchester: Manchester University Press, 1998.

Svejkovský, Jiří. *Čas marných nadějí: Roky 1968 a 1969 ve zpravodajství ČST*. Prague: Epocha, 2010.

Svobodová, Jana. *Prague*. Prague: Ústav pro Soudobé dějiny, 1994.

T. "Jak to bylo 21. srpna 1989 v Praze." *Listy*, no. 5 (October 1989): 75–77.

Tarsi, Anita. "Práce v pasti: Ústředna práce v prvním roce existence ghetta Terezín." In *Terezínské studie a dokumenty*, edited by Miroslav Kárný and Eva Lorencová, 127–40. Prague: Academia, 2000.

Taubman, William. *Gorbachev: His Life and Times*. New York: W. W. Norton, 2017.

Taylor, Dalma Darnley. "Intelligence" WAAF's in 'Y' Service." *BBC WW2 People's War*. Last modified March 14, 2004.

Tigrid, Pavel. "Zpráva o stavu střední Evropy." *Svědectví*, no. 87 (1989): 524–25.

Tomanová, Eva, dir. *Syn nepřítele státu*. Czech television, 2022.

Tomek, Prokop. *Pavel Tigrid. Volá Londýn: Ze zákulisí československého vysílání z Londýna*. Prague: ÚSTR, 2017.

———. "Reflexe vysílání RFE jako spojení mezi exilem a domovem." In *Politický exil z krajín strednej a východnej Európy: Motivy, stratégie, aktivity a perspektívy na Východe a Západe, 1945-1989: Zborník z medzinárodnej vedeckej konferencie, Bratislava 19–20*. November 2013, edited by Peter Jašek, 24–32. Bratislava: Ústav pamäti národa, 2017.

———. "Svazek StB jako historický pramen." Soudobé dějiny 12, no. 2 (2002): 208–14.

Tosek, Ruth. Interviewed by Olga Sommerová, 2007.

Tosek, Vladimír. "The Czechs Betrayed." *Spectator* (London) August 19, 1978.

———. "Kterak jsem si šel pro vlnu a vrátil se ostříhán." *Práce* (Prague) March 1, 1969.

———. "Mezi námi." *Reportér* (Prague) no. 14, Prague (April 1968): 3–10.

Tůma, Oldřich. "9.00, Praha-Libeň, horní nádraží. Exodus východních Němců přes Prahu v září 1989." *Soudobé dějiny* 6, no. 2–3 (1999): 147–64.

———. "Pad berlínské zdi." *Soudobé dějiny* 9, no. 2 (2002): 230–40.

Tyas, Stephen. "Allied Intelligence Agencies and the Holocaust Information Acquired from German Prisoners of War." *Holocaust and Genocide Studies* 22, no. 1 (Spring 2008): 1–24.

Ulč, Ota. "Ošemetnost s azylem." *Listy*, no. 6, (December 1986): 57–60.

Urban, Susanne. "'Unknown Dead.' Unsettling Finds from the Archive of the International Tracing Service." *Yad Vashem Studies* 40, no. 1 (2012): 197–216.

Urqhhart, Brian. *A Life in Peace and War*. New York: Harper & Row, 1987.

Utitz, Bedřich. *Kaleidoskop mého století*. Prague: Academia, 2013.

Vaculík, Ludvík. *Český snář*. Prague: Atlantis, 1990.

———. "Dva tisíce slov." In *Jaro 1968: Čítanka pro děti a mládež*. Cologne: 150000 and Index, 1988.

Vadas, Martin, dir. *Nízká vysoká hra*. Česká televize, 2014.

Váleční zajatci v Muně. "Deník vojína Irvinga Georga Becka: Váleční zajatci v Muně." Youtube video, accessed April 10, 2020.

Váňa, Josef. "Z televizní kuchyně a zákulisí." *Zprávy*, March 15, 1969.

Vance, Jonathan F. "The Politics of Camp Life: The Bargaining Process of Two German Prison Camps." *War & Society* 10, no. 1 (1992): 109–26.

Velecká, Hana. "Britská pomoc uprchlíkům z Československa od okupace do vypuknutí války v roce 1939." *Soudobé dějiny* 8, no. 4 (2002): 659–91.

"Vl. Tosek odpovídá." *Svobodné Slovo*, February 28, 1969.

"Vloupání do redakce Listy." *Listy*, no. 1 (February 1983): 45.

Vourkoutiotis, Vasilis. "What the Angels Saw: Red Cross and Protecting Power Visits to Anglo-American POWs, 1939–1945." *Journal of Contemporary History* 40, no. 4 (October 2005): 689–706.

Vrbová, Gerta. *Betrayed Generation: Shattered Hopes and Disillusion in Post-War Czechoslovakia*. Cambridge, UK: Zuza Books, 2010.

Warriner, Doreen."Winter in Prague." *Slavonic and East European Review* 62, no. 2 (April 1984): 209–40.

Waterman, Peter. *From Coldwar Communism to the Global Emancipatory Movement*. Helsinki: Into Kustannus, 2014.

Wehle, Kurt. "Očima vzpomínek. Tam někde musí být židovská obec." *Terezínské listy*, no. 22 (1994): 109–21.

Wendehorst, Stephan E. C. *British Jewry, Zionism, and the Jewish State, 1936–1956*. Oxford: Oxford University Press, 2012.

White, Joseph Robert. "'Even in Auschwitz . . . Humanity Could Prevail': British POWs and Jewish Concentration Camp Inmates at IG Auschwitz, 1943–1945." *Holocaust and Genocide Studies* 15, no. 2 (Fall 2001): 266–95.

Williams, Dick. "The First Day in the Camp." In Bardgett and Cesarini, *Belsen 1945*, 27–30.

Williams, Kieran. *The Prague Spring and Its Aftermath: Czechoslovak Politics, 1968–1970*. Cambridge, UK: Cambridge University Press, 1997.

Willingham, Matthew. *Perilous Commitments: Britain's Involvement in Greece and Crete 1940–41*. Staplehurst, UK: Spellmount, 2005.

Wolf, Michaela, ed. *Interpreting in Nazi Concentration Camps*. New York: Bloomsbury, 2016.

Yahil, Leni. "Select British Documents on the Illegal Immigration to Palestine (1939–1940)." *Yad Vashem Studies* (1974): 241–76.

Zahra, Tara. *The Great Departure: Mass Migration from Eastern Europe and the Making of the Free World*. New York: W. W. Norton, 2017.

Žantovský, Michael. *Havel: A Life*. New York: Grove Press, 2014.

"Závěrečná řeč Václava Havla v odvolacím řízení u městského soudu v Praze." *Listy*, no. 2 (April 1989): 85.

Zelenka, Jan. "Zpráva o problematice československé emigrace." *Česká televize*, no. 2 (January 1971): 4–10.

Zukal, Rudolf. "O emigraci z Československa." *Listy*, no. 6 (December 1985): 28–32.

Zweig, Stefan. *The World of Yesterday*. Lincoln: University of Nebraska Press, 2013.

Index

Page numbers in italics refer to figures